How Could She Do That?

Books by Edith deRham

How Could She Do That? A Study of the Female Criminal
The Love Fraud

How Could She Do That?

A Study of the Female Criminal

by

Edith deRham

 Clarkson N. Potter, Inc./Publisher NEW YORK

Distributed by Crown Publishers, Inc.

© 1969, by Edith deRham
Library of Congress Catalog Card Number: 68–26886
Printed in the United States of America
Published simultaneously in Canada by
General Publishing Company Limited
Designed by *Dorothy Detelj*

Acknowledgments

ALTHOUGH the facts and events which are described in the following stories are based on actual criminal histories, the names of many of the characters who appear in them have been changed, together with geography and other forms of identification, in order not to violate the privacy or anonymity which the subjects may presently enjoy.

Under normal circumstances, I would also be obliged to extend my gratitude to the many prison authorities, lawyers, social agencies, and police officers who cooperated with me to such a great extent. It is probable, however, that they would choose to maintain an anonymity which is both prudent and considerate.

Once again, too, I must express my appreciation of the facilities made available by the New York Society Library, which provides what is undoubtedly the most sympathetic atmosphere for work in the city of New York.

E. DeR.

Contents

Introduction   1

Bajour   23

A Family Affair   57

La Libératrice   79

Millie   111

Flora   163

How Goes the Life?   211

For Love and Money   261

Conclusion   313

Suggested Further Reading   339

How Could She Do That?

Introduction

Where women are concerned, crime and the legal process which attempts to deal with it take on a special character; an intensified atmosphere of tolerance develops, along with a curious willingness to "understand," to excuse. Although prosecutors are not necessarily reluctant to prosecute, juries are less willing to convict, and the public less quick to condemn.

For the world is still charmed by the notion that Woman is soft, nonviolent, pacific by nature, and a repository for most of the more admirable human qualities. She is the Mother. If she does wrong, she has probably been led astray by the dominant, more innately violent male, and as all the world knows, she will do anything for love.

The history of the legal process as it affects the ordinary criminal is the story of an ever-increasing compassion—an effort to analyze, understand, restore, and, above all, to prevent rather than to condemn and to punish. Many people, both professionals and laymen, feel that trend has gone entirely too far, and that what with the restrictions imposed upon the various

1

agents of law enforcement, the tolerated abuse of constitutional guarantees, and the soft-hearted sociologists, the common crook is enjoying an unwarranted prosperity. Certainly the female lawbreaker has been the particular beneficiary of the new liberalism, for the "feminine mystique" operates in her favor, as does the modern tendency to view the criminal as a mutable sociopath, rather than as an instrument through which the Devil is busily at work.

The stories which follow have not been written from a technical, sociological point of view, because in so many ways, this approach is irrelevant to the subject. What interests the sociologist, and what is essential to his being able to form conclusions, is discovering what it is that makes people the same; what interests the reporter is what makes them different. For it is the fact that they are different, which makes any problem difficult to "solve."

Talking at length with various sorts of professional people who have been constantly involved with lawbreakers, one cannot fail to come away with the impression that there are few respectable generalizations to be made in this area. Like women, Negroes, or Americans, the individuals within the group reflect more differences, apart from the single aspect of physical features or nationality, than points in common. As one California litigator put it: "You'll search in vain for a pattern, something which links them all together, because there is no pattern, except that they seem to lack that internal 'governor' or brake which stops the rest of us at the crucial moment."

Naturally, certain social conditions—principally poverty and the absence of disciplined parental and academic training which creates ethical inhibitions in people—are conducive to crime. Nevertheless, while it is true that the poor and underprivileged elements of society account for the majority of everyday crimes, it is also true that, within their own cultural group, the lawbreakers constitute a very minor percentage of the whole. In New York City, for example, it has been estimated that only a little over 10 percent of Negroes and Puerto Ricans become involved in serious crime, whereas the remaining majority miraculously manage to stay out of it. This figure is probably low, being based solely on the number of apprehended lawbreakers, but even if it were closer to 20 percent, it would still be low, considering the circumstances. Unfortunately we are made so fearfully aware of this group's activities by the press and the sociologists that we forget about the others.

Criminality knows no single social class, although a middle-class thief will steal in a different manner from a lower-class thief, and he will be differently regarded by society: A college girl who shoplifts is presumed to be a kleptomaniac because she can afford not to steal, while a Negro prostitute who does the same is more apt to be characterized simply as a thief. The so-called criminal type, however, exists at all levels and may appear in the form of a corporation executive, window washer, or baby-sitter.

In their efforts to solve the problems of crime, those who must deal with criminals in one way or another seek the qualities which these people may have in common so that they may know what it is they must attack and destroy. Among criminal women, analysts may look for a connection between menstruation and criminal behavior, whereas others will seek other physical, though not necessarily sexual, differentiations to explain the aberration of antisocial behavior. In so doing, it would seem that they easily dissipate their energies. Otto Pollak, in his study on the criminality of women, states that menopause, menstruation, and pregnancy are much overrated as causative factors. Within the age group committing most crimes, the law of averages implies that many women will be in one or another of these circumstances while committing crimes. The connection is arbitrary in any case, since menstruation, to take but one, slows the mental and physical processes to such an extent that a woman in this condition is simply much more apt to be vague and careless and therefore more easily caught.

Sheldon and Eleanor Glueck of Boston seem to have spent the better part of a lifetime trying to discover whether chronic lawbreakers have any physiological features in common which are directly related to their bad behavior. Criminality, they say, is a combination of economic and biological factors. In response to this revelation one might ask if, indeed, most human behavior is not so oriented. And as to the practical purpose of their quest, one cannot help wondering what good it would do to discover that all potential murderers had, say, enlarged ear-lobes or abnormal chromosomes. Our system of justice strictly prohibits the detention of anyone who has not actually—provably—broken the law, at which point any consideration as to the size of earlobes or construction of chromosomes is academic, especially so far as the victim is concerned. We cannot lock people up because of what we believe they *might* do any more than we can prevent people from breeding because they might produce undesirable human specimens. It would appear, therefore, that certain "causes" are inalterable, and that certain problems will, as a result, always be with us. But we are a problem-solving nation, and are not sympathetic to the notion of inevitability.

However, the Gluecks did, in a study of five hundred delinquent women back in 1934, hit on something which has become a disturbingly common and recurring theme. Noting that a large proportion of their delinquent girls came from "abnormally large" families, they suggest that "the more the underprivileged and underendowed breed, the more hopeless it is for community organizations to try to help them." Twenty years later, in 1965, the chief of Federal prisons asserted in a *Herald Tribune* interview that "constructive family planning could help stop crime that resulted when parents are unable to provide adequate material benefits and guidance for their children, because they have failed to put limitations on their offspring."

More recently, the cry of Negro militants that whites are trying to destroy blacks through birth control brought the following response from columnists Evans and Novak in Washington: "This recalls the self-deception of French Canadians, who felt they could take over Canada from the English by outbreeding them, when, in fact, their higher birth rate only deepened their poverty." In a similar vein, James Q. Wilson asks, in a recent article: "Why are there more serious and violent crimes every year? Simply because there are more young people every year, and because young people have always had a higher crime rate than adults. Because the size of the young group is increasing twice as fast as that of the older age group, and . . . what appears to be a crime explosion may, in fact, be a population explosion. . . . For the present, the only sure way we know of fighting crime is birth control."

So far as the distinctions between male and female criminality are concerned, the principal difference is not in the crimes they commit but in the manner in which they commit them and in the nature of their victims.

Women commit all the crimes which men commit—that

is, crimes against the person, against property, and against the state. Of the crimes against the person, they commit murder and assault along with the worst of men, but they do not rape—principally because it is a physical impossibility. Of the crimes against property, they steal nearly as much but do not destroy as much. As for the last category, there are women spies as well as men and female political activists as well as male seditionists. "It is thus," Pollak explains, "not so much the interest which women violate, or the degree to which they do so, as the victim they choose, the person with whom they cooperate, the opportunities of which they avail themselves, and the part they play in the actual perpetration of certain offenses, which seem to express the sex specificity of female crime."

Women possess, as most criminologists, policemen, prison authorities, and husbands would agree, an inordinate talent for concealment and deception which both characterizes the feminine style and makes the female lawbreaker harder to catch. The reasons for this are primarily cultural, having to do with the prescribed social role wherein women are required to be subordinate to men and acquire the things they want indirectly through the beneficence of their male protectors. Like all groups of people who have been arbitrarily placed in an inferior position to some other group, women habitually try to compensate by deceit and dissimulation, much in the same fashion as the Negro did in the old South.

In addition to the cultural aspect, there are also physical phenomena which affect the tendency and ability of women to manipulate rather than to challenge directly. The fact that some women are able to participate in the sex act without particularly wanting to and may even pretend to enjoy it, causes them to be fundamentally more oriented to the whole idea of pretense and deception than are men, who cannot pretend what they cannot demonstrate.

Lacking the physical strength possessed by men, the criminal woman avoids situations which will expose her to physical violence or where sheer force is necessary to accomplish her task; rarely do women crack safes, rob banks, mug people in the street, or generally engage in any act of overt aggression against total strangers, who might regard their appearance with suspicion or fear. However, they may easily plan such activities, and encourage and lead others to expedite them. As in the noncriminal world, culture makes the man the actor and the woman the instigator or accomplice; she may participate equally in the enjoyment of the spoils, but she lets someone else do the actual job.

It has been suggested by certain criminologists that the "masculinization" of female crime has been more apparent in the Middle and Far West, where social conditions have favored the assumption of male pursuits by women in and out of crime. This is related, presumably, to the move westward in the 1800's, when the rigors and dangers of life on the frontier made it impossible for men to protect women from the harsher chores and realities, as they might have done in the genteel environment of the more civilized East.

Certainly in the crime-ridden thirties the Midwest produced scores of devotedly evil women bent on playing a leading role in the life of crime. In 1931, Margaret Sherman was arrested when a .38-caliber pistol was found on her person by a wary member of Chicago's vice squad. She admitted that she had lured better than a hundred men to her room by promising them sex, and had instead robbed them at gunpoint of everything but their gold teeth. Though only twenty-seven years old, she weighed two hundred pounds, which makes it difficult to imagine the sort of men who would be attracted by her proposition.

In the same year, Mrs. Gladys Carlson, the widow of Carl Carlson, the bank robber, was executed for the murder of two policemen. She had assisted her husband in at least two robberies, and had never been reluctant to use her gun, especially on policemen.

In 1932, Helen Lyons, a twenty-one-year-old mob-mother, made the mistake of recruiting two policemen for her gang, thereby depriving her loyal followers of their leader.

Another young girl, this one a nineteen-year-old mother, confessed to being the leader of a group of holdup specialists who robbed according to her plans and instructions while she remained safely behind with the baby. A victim of the Depression, she had fallen into this way of life to escape poverty when her unemployed husband deserted her during her pregnancy.

One of the most illustrious criminals of this period was Buda Godman, a renowned extortionist who was ultimately seized for a $350,000 job she had masterminded sixteen years earlier. She was for many years acknowledged as one of Chicago's shrewdest female crooks, serving as the leader of the then-famous Tyson Hotel blackmailing ring.

Possessing an exceptionally beautiful face as well as an intelligent mind, she had no difficulty in attracting male colleagues. Following her first arrest in 1916, she jumped bail and fled to Cuba, turning up years later in New York as the wife of a wealthy New York businessman living in a chic 55th Street apartment. But her new identity had not caused her to put aside her larcenous ways, for in 1932 she was caught trying to market some jewels which she and five of her current associates were accused of having stolen from a lady on Park Avenue. Her husband hadn't the remotest idea of what his wife had been up to, either at that time or in the past.

The Victorian era produced its share of murderous women, particularly in Europe, many of whom managed characteristically to evade the law. Madeleine Smith, the daughter of a good solid Scottish architect, was accused of giving arsenic to her hopelessly unsuitable lover, Pierre Emile L'Angelier—not because he was false to her but because she had tired of the relationship and he was threatening to show her father the letters she had written. This, in the Glasgow of 1855, would have been disastrous. The evidence against her was strong, but there were gaps in it, and the peculiarly Scottish verdict of "Not Proven" may be interpreted as the jury's way of saying, "Probably she did it, but anyhow he deserved it."

Arsenic, in the form of flypaper, was also said to have been administered by the twenty-six-year-old Florence Maybrick, daughter of an Alabama banker, to her fifty-year-old English husband, when he died in 1889. The case is a fascinating one: Certainly Florence bought an extraordinary amount of flypaper just before her husband's death, and certainly she was seen soaking the papers in water. But, then, arsenic was at that time much in use as a cosmetic, and perhaps she really did intend it for that purpose. And then again, Maybrick was in the habit of taking both arsenic and strychnine in small doses as a tonic and an aphrodisiac. After his death, a great deal of arsenic was found in the house in bottles, glasses, rags, and even in a dressing gown. At Florence Maybrick's trial, the medical experts were so totally at odds about the cause of death that an acquittal was confidently expected. The blunders of fact made by Mr. Justice Stephen in his summing up, however, may have contributed to the verdict of "Guilty." Her sentence was commuted to one of life imprisonment and in 1904 she was released. Like Madeleine Smith, she settled in the United States.

The ravishingly pretty Adelaide Bartlett was tried at the Old Bailey in 1886 on the charge of poisoning her husband with chloroform. There were many suspicious circumstances, not the least being her friendship with a young Wesleyan minister named George Dyson who had bought chloroform for her a few days earlier, but again the essential problem was a medical one. How had the chloroform been administered? Nobody would have drunk it voluntarily because of the burning sensation it induced. Could she have given it to him while he was unconscious? Even the prosecution's expert admitted that this would have been a difficult operation, and Edward Clarke, counsel for the defense, pointed out that there was no sign of chloroform in the windpipe.

Adelaide Bartlett was triumphantly acquitted. Whether she also went to the United States is not certain; her later career is unknown. Here, then, evidently, was a poisoner who got away with it. The caustic comment of Sir James Paget, consulting surgeon at St. Bartholomew's Hospital, shows what medical men thought of the verdict: "Now that it is all over, she should tell us, in the interests of science, how she did it."

The type of victim generally chosen by the female offender is not distinguished necessarily by who or what he is, but by his or her relationship to the oppressor. Among criminal women there is a tendency to choose relatively willing victims, people who cooperate with them, either consciously or unconsciously, thereby facilitating the criminal's efforts.

Whether the victim of the female criminal is a member of the family, an acquaintance or lover, the owner of a store from which a woman may steal, or the client of a thieving prostitute, a woman's victim is almost invariably a person who trusts her or is accustomed to her presence. And this fact is essential to the successful concealment of her crime.

For those to whom it is natural to prepare food, care for the young and the sick, spend hours wandering about in shops handling merchandise, and minister to the sexual needs of men who must pay for sex, passive victims are not difficult to find. The husband, child, or father-in-law, who lies ill in bed, hardly suspects that the hand that lovingly feeds him may have seasoned the food or medicine with a pinch of strychnine. The manager of a department store from which an unmasked shoplifter may have been stealing hundreds of dollars worth of goods yearly may decide that, rather than court the trouble and unpleasant publicity of litigation, he will allow the thief to pay for the stolen goods and let the matter pass.

A 1966 newspaper squib announced that, according to a recent study, 60 percent of shoppers are not averse to stealing. Another survey showed that shoplifting among college students, including men, had reached an all-time high. The author made the point that many petty thieves escape detection, because even when suspects are caught, store managers are reluctant to take action lest they be charged with false arrest. It is estimated that only 12 percent of shoplifters are prosecuted.

Similarly, the prostitute-addict could not possibly enjoy even current standards of success were it not for the willingness of policemen to be paid for protection, even though addiction and theft are corollaries to her prostitution. The man who has been robbed by a prostitute will rarely report the crime, so anxious is he that no one should discover with whom he has been passing the time.

The general apathy and corruption of society is, in fact, a major and very necessary ingredient to the success of any criminal venture, and the victim himself often cooperates with the aggressor without being aware that he is doing so. Those who watch passively from apartment windows while girls are attacked and killed are contributors. So are those "respectable" people who accept gratuities from the mob, thereby eliminating certain obstacles in the path of criminal enterprise. People who foolishly venture alone into unpopulated and unpatrolled areas late at night assist the nocturnal mugger to achieve his aims, as does the miniskirted, tight-sweatered siren who walks her dog in secluded places and winds up in the hospital, the victim of rape. The simple carelessness of forgetting to lock the door can cost a person his life.

A young burglar explained in a recent interview with John Bowers in *Harper's Magazine* that he preferred to have a key when he went into a place, and described how, a few days earlier, a man had sold him the key to a model's apartment and told him the hours she would be out. The man had been living with her at some earlier time and hadn't returned the key. "Man," he said, "you'd be surprised at the larceny in people's hearts. I got a habit. I got an excuse." Other people, he confided, had paid him to burglarize their apartments and then split the insurance money with him.

The "masculine" quality of female crime in the West

and Midwest during America's earlier history has begun to char acterize the style of many delinquent girls in other parts of the country. "Emancipation" and the achieving of equal status with men is doubtless having its effect on the evolution of women as criminals as well as in other areas. That female crime is habitu ally passive no longer stands up as a safe generalization.

In April, 1965, the New York *Herald Tribune* reported that a pair of girls, with identically tinted red hair, black leather jackets, boots, and revolvers, had broken into a home in—of all places—Snug Harbor, New Jersey, and robbed a family of three hundred dollars. On the same day, a gun-toting female drug addict held up a cab driver in New York City, threatening to kill him if he failed to give her all the money he had.

In June of the same year, *Harper's Magazine* carried a story about two Negro girls, sisters, who stole over a million dollars in jewels on New York's Upper East Side, posing as domestics and entering unlocked servants' doors while the maid was downstairs doing the wash or running errands. At the height of their crime wave, twenty-five detectives were stationed for surveillance at strategic blocks along Park Avenue.

In July, a twenty-eight-year-old forger, who had sawed her way out of a Connecticut jail, burst through the door of a motel in Idaho, and fired wildly at local police and detectives with a gilded .30-caliber M-1 carbine. The gun had been specially altered for use as a handgun with a pistol grip, and with it, the girl managed to wound several of her potential captors seriously. Inside her room, the police later found a loaded .38-caliber snub-nosed revolver, a .22-caliber rifle, a .44-caliber magnum semiautomatic rifle, a tear-gas gun, and large quantities of am munition.

In September, 1965, a group of Argentine nationalists were arrested in the Falkland Islands with their beautiful blonde female leader, and temporarily incarcerated in the annex of a Roman Catholic church. The group had hijacked an airliner a few days earlier in an attempted "invasion" of the Falkland Islands, and were subsequently charged with piracy. Even in South America women are becoming equal, at least in breaking the law.

In 1967, the summer issue of *Esquire*, long famous for its photos of beautiful "birds," displayed glossy pictures of three female jailbirds under the following caption: "With the 19th

Amendment, women have achieved full equality with men; now they are able to participate fully in all great American enterprises —crime, for instance." One of these cuties had been convicted of armed robbery, another of burglary, and the third of assault, the latter two being chronic drug users.

Meanwhile, the newspapers have been kept busy report- ing the activities of the more "typical" female offenders: MUR- DER OVER SIP OF WINE: BRONX GIRL, 16, STABS BOY, 18; BILK WOMAN OF $900; 8TH SUFFOLK VICTIM; NAB WOMAN IN THEFT OF FIRM'S FUNDS; MOTHER FREED HERE IN SLAYING OF BOY, 4, DESPITE CONFESSION; HELD IN DOPE CASE—MOTHER OF FOUR. The fecund dope peddler had, in addition, run over the two policemen who arrested her in her car, thereby complicating her situation by adding charges of assault, driving while intoxicated, and driving without lights or driver's license.

This woman, a thirty-four-year-old resident of the Bed- ford-Stuyvesant section of Brooklyn, apparently saw no irony in the fact that, while she strictly admonished her own children against the use of drugs, much of the junk she peddled for a net profit of around $100,000 annually, found its way into the hands of their classmates.

On March 18, 1966, a *New York Times* headline an- nounced: MILLIONAIRE WHO WED EX-CON NURSE DIES. Beneath the headline, there appeared a story about the demise of Mr. A. O. Birch of Grand Prairie, Texas, who, a few months earlier at the age of ninety-five, had married a fifty-nine-year-old giantess called Mrs. Pearl Choate.

One would think that Mrs. Choate, who stood over six feet tall and weighed 205 pounds, would have possessed a limited appeal for members of the opposite sex, but such was not the case. At the time she married Mr. Birch in October, 1966, Pearl had already had six husbands. It was Pearl's tastes in men that were limited—limited to the extent that they had to be over ninety and very rich. A strict adherence to these specifica- tions had resulted in all six husbands dying shortly after marrying Pearl, including one whom Pearl shot four times during a dis- agreement. The state of Texas took a narrow, unimaginative view and, refusing to interpret the action in terms of self-defense, sent Pearl away for twelve years.

Upon release, Pearl went to Houston, where she ap- parently indulged a burgeoning taste for grand larceny and got

herself locked up again for a while. This time, when her stretch
was up, she decided that there had to be easier and safer ways
to make a buck than stealing out in the open, so she turned to
nursing, specializing in antique millionaires with dead or moribund wives. Pearl found, as have so many others in business, that
it pays to specialize, for somehow she always managed to wind
up in considerably better financial condition after her husbands'
deaths than before.

Pearl does not take kindly to cynical speculations as to
why her creaking spouses never seemed to last more then a few
months after tying the knot with her. As she told New York
columnist Jimmy Breslin: "They keep bringing up my six other
husbands. What's that got to do with today's love? . . . They
were all about Mr. Birch's age when I married them. So what?
I done the decent thing. You never heard of Pearl Choate not
marrying a man. Pearl Choate don't shack up." Heaven forbid.

Be that as it may, women like Pearl find themselves in
an ideal position to engage in foul play for monetary gain, with
maximum opportunities for concealment and minimum risk of
discovery. Many a man has suffered a premature death at the
hands of his professional companion or nurse, with no crime
being subsequently proved or even detected. In training for their
profession, nurses (and to a lesser degree companions) learn a
great deal about drugs, poisons, and the functioning of the
human body, which frequently comes in handy when their
thoughts turn to extortion or murder. They may well learn how
to make a death look as though it results from natural causes or
an accident.

It may hardly be imagined how many "heart attacks,"
"strokes," "food poisonings," and other deadly and apparently
spontaneous catastrophes have been visited upon people by non-
professional "nurses," to whom the necessary technical knowledge is available at any medical library. The famous "Lonely
Hearts Murder" featured a housewife called Mrs. Wagner who
killed eleven husbands for money. In any case, the key to success
is the cultivation of trust and facility of concealment.

Sex—and its use, exploitation, or neurotic manifestation
—is so frequently involved in the criminality of women that it
deserves some special consideration. On the simplest level, it is
used as a lure or diversion to set up a robbery or blackmail attempt. The prostitute uses it to earn money, but also depends
on it, as previously suggested, as a deterrent to betrayal.

Men who are under the influence of sexual stimulation make ideal victims, for they are passive, distracted, vulnerable, and unwary—in short, cooperative. Furthermore the promise of sex has lured any number of men into criminal acts, not only those acts that satisfy their own sexual lust, but those that satisfy the greed of the female instigator. Sex is to the female offender what physical strength and skill are to the male; if combined with intellect, sex may afford the female criminal considerable power as well as an assured anonymity.

There is impressive evidence that chronic shoplifting, particularly among women who can afford to buy, is sexually motivated. With many female thieves, the compulsion to steal is a form of sexual sublimation and may be minimized by psychiatric treatment of the sexual problem which causes it.

The constant exposure to sex-oriented advertising, moreover, with its relentless exhortations to own things which promise to make the consumer more alluring, has been found to contribute to feminine larceny. Women, exploited as the principal consumers, are the prime target of advertisers who habitually urge them to "get" something "today"—to the extent that some who cannot afford to buy end up stealing what they have been made to want.

The most obvious areas in which sex is basic to criminal behavior are, of course, abortion and prostitution. Through some curious and arbitrary moral quirk, both parties involved in abortion—he who performs the service and she who seeks it—are considered equally culpable, whereas with prostitution only she who performs the service is legally reprehensible. It is quite unreasonable, however, that either of these acts should be considered criminal.

In both cases a contract is entered into, generally by two consenting adults, to engage in an action which is highly personal in its consequences and which directly involves no other living person. So far as disease is concerned, furthermore, the highest rate of V.D. currently exists among high school students, not prostitutes. In neither prostitution nor abortion is any form of coercion whatsoever employed. The problem, then, lies in the assumptions which underlie the definition of the term "criminal."

There appeared in the summer, 1965, issue of *The American Scholar* a symposium on morality in which one of the participants explained that mutual consideration was a factor in the successful evolution of any animal species. Ethics are there-fore derived from the pragmatic necessity of "getting along" with other individuals; without rules—that is, considerate laws —animal society simply does not survive. In conclusion, the writer stated that "crime" was simply that kind of action which is most *offensive* to members of a social group.

It is in the concept of offensiveness that the trouble lies. Many of our laws still reflect parochial habits of thought related to atavistic religious beliefs which, apart from having been formed at a time in history when the world bore no re-semblance whatsoever to the urban cosmopolis of today, are rarely shared by more than a fraction of the population that they affect. Logically, what is "most offensive" to members of any social group is that which is directly harmful to them. It would therefore be considerably more correct to describe criminal be-havior in terms of what harms people rather than in terms of what merely offends them.

People who smoke cigars in elevators, wear pink plastic hair curlers in public, fail to use a deodorant when they need it, or become drunk and disorderly at social gatherings all mani-fest behavior which is offensive, but we are not yet prepared to clap them in jail. Implicit in the concept of "harm" is the idea of coercion—the fact that he who is offended is brought unwillingly to the point where real harm may befall him. If a young girl is forced into prostitution against her will and under false pretenses, as still frequently happens, then he who is re-sponsible for her entrapment should be punished to the fullest extent of the law. The girl herself, coerced or not, may hardly be held responsible for "corrupting" her eager clients.

Both the abortionist and the prostitute perform a service —that is to say, they would not exist were it not for the demand for their talents. While the presence among us of people who peddle sex and terminate unborn lives offends, disgusts, and even saddens us, their actions are primarily offensive to those *not involved*, whose feelings, whether they are aware of it or not, have been conditioned by what are fundamentally religious precepts. Are these not, in the end, highly personal matters, best dealt with by the private conscience of the individuals involved?

The bitterness of the prostitute toward a hypocritical so-ciety—which creates the need for her existence on the one hand, then denigrates and persecutes her on the other—is well known, but what of the abortionist? Most significant is the fact that the abortionist, whether male or female, considers that he or she is performing an invaluable public service and an admirable one, considering the deep appreciation of his clients and the considerable risk to himself. Speaking of female abortionists, the criminologist Katherine Sullivan in her book, *Women in Prison*, reports that they are mostly very pleasant, competent women, seldom young and mostly foreign born or with foreign backgrounds. Generally they are of average or high intelligence. Miss Sullivan goes on to assure us that, within her own experience, she never knew of one who was an alcoholic or a drug user, that they always seemed to own their own homes, have large families, and were adored by their children.

On the basis of certain studies of the populations of women's prisons, prostitutes have been generally categorized as lazy, vain, man-hating, self-denigrating, and starved for love, admiration, or even respect. Although it is undeniable that some of these qualities are found in all prostitutes, it is doubtful whether the generalization would stand up if applied to the total prostitute population, even assuming that could be known, counted, and evaluated.

What is certain, is that prostitution remains the easiest way for any woman to acquire money, and whereas the young boy reacting to the circumstances created by poverty and neglect in an overcrowded environment will go out and steal, the young girl in similar circumstances will turn automatically to prostitution. There are many classes of prostitutes, ranging from the socialite who allows her select men-friends to pay her rent and buy her clothes to the lower-class streetwalker who solicits strangers in public. The high-class prostitute does not generally consort with strangers, and therefore does not get mixed up with the vice squad or detectives. Her crime is easily concealed and difficult to prove. So she rarely goes to jail. The others, less fortunate, become familiar figures in Women's Court and spend a good portion of their lives in the "revolving door" between prison and the world outside.

The seven stories which follow were chosen as much because the relationship of the woman to the crime is somehow typical, as because of the commonness of the crime itself. In several of the stories, all details of identification have been changed, but the salient facts relating to the inducement of the crime and the commission of the crime are accurately reported. Valda Adams the gypsy and Ellen Riley are both thieves, but they steal in different ways and for different reasons, the one functioning as a thorough professional, while the other had simply been at it a long time, which is not quite the same thing. Valda is not a sociopath, for she does not violate any accepted code of behavior within her own social group; it is, in fact, the historic, accepted function of gypsy women to support their families through stealing. Valda's criminality is a conditioned manifestation of an esoteric culture. Ellen, on the other hand, with her entire family, represents a definite perversion of the accepted forms of behavior within the community in which she lives, and her personality reflects this.

Annette Le Duc committed a crime against the state and would commit others in her political fervor, should the opportunity arise. What is curious about this girl is not her passionate involvement in a political movement, resulting in the breaking of Federal laws but her unusually compelling drives for power and personal glory—unusual, that is, for a woman. Apart from people like Clare Boothe Luce or Indira Gandhi, who function more or less normally as public servants, without the characteristic neuroticisms, Eva Peron is the only such figure in modern times who is truly representative of the genre.

For there is, in these people—the Perons and the Le Ducs—the desire for a kind of power that is peculiarly feminine: charismatic, personal, manipulative. They are fascinated by their own effect on people and, confident of their charm, walk brazenly where men and angels fear to tread. Possessing the invincible combination of sex *cum* intellect, their appeal is emotional rather than rational, and their methods spontaneous rather than pragmatic. Self-consciously aware of the superiority of their minds, they tend to imagine that they perceive the objective realities of the situation they control, failing to see that they are themselves ultimately enthralled by their own image, and robbed of rationality.

Annette is, in a way, more "criminal" than any of the others, for she deliberately rejected all the values which spawned and sustained her, and perverted them one by one, utterly indifferent to who or how many would be hurt. She remains unchastened and unrepentant, sufficient only unto herself and still causing trouble.

Although most urban streetwalkers are local products,

springing like weeds from the streets of the slums, many prostitutes may still trace their roots to the country, which they leave, as did Margaret O'Brien, to find excitement and money in the Big City. Maggie was unusual in that she was in the "big time," well protected and in charge of her own operation. But the basis on which she ran her "house" vividly illustrates the eternal link between prostitution and drugs, which still obtains today. The houses of pleasure may have disappeared from our midst, but girls are held just as harshly in bondage by their need for drugs and are forced to continue in The Life in order to support their ever-increasing drug habit.

It is, therefore, within the framework of its inevitable connection with drugs that prostitution falls legitimately into the area of criminal behavior. Prostitutes who become thieves and pushers fall clearly into another category—a category which includes people who are dangerous to others and whose aggressive behavior threatens the well-being of other people.

There are many crimes which are inspired by the need for drugs, and among women the most common one, apart from prostitution, is forgery. Next to assault, forgery seems to account for more of the population in women's prisons than any other single crime. In her wartime book, *Women in Crime*, Florence Monahan, for twenty years the superintendent of various women's prisons, takes the liberty of generalizing about forgers: "Forgers have exaggerated egos, pleasant personalities, and delusions of grandeur. They always lie about their origins, and generally want things without working for them. They think the world owes them a living."

Basically there are two kinds of forgers: embezzlers—that is, people who steal from the company they work for, either by juggling the books or by doctoring company checks—and people who sign other people's names to checks and credit cards. While many of these people need the money for drugs, some of them are simply, as Mrs. Monahan suggests, acquisitive beyond their capacity and desire to earn. The bum-check passer may be generally included in this category also, though she does not forge.

The woman mentioned earlier in a headline had been accused of stealing $80,000 from petty cash over a period of less than one year from a firm cutely called We're Associates, Inc., where she worked as bookkeeper.

Sometime during the winter of 1967, the New York City

police apprehended a woman who had been passing bad checks in all the smarter boutiques along Park, Fifth, and Madison Avenues. Her success was based on the deceiving aspect of her appearance, which placed her securely among the privileged ladies of leisure who inhabit the Upper East Side.

Mrs. Van Sythe, as the lady called herself, would appear, beautifully coiffed, gloved, and hatted, wearing a mink coat, and equipped with a batch of personalized checks. Her voice was cultivated and her manner refined, and on first meeting, no one had the slightest reason to doubt her authenticity. After selecting several items of clothing, Mrs. Van Sythe would ask if she might write a check for her purchases, and as a rule, she would be permitted to do so. By the time the check bounced, Mrs. Van Sythe had sold the clothes to a fence who gave her a pretty good price, because the stuff was expensive and new. On other occasions she would steal a credit card or two, and sign its owner's name on department store sales slips. The money she received was applied toward a growing supply of heroin, which was necessary to keep Mrs. Van Sythe out of the doldrums.

Forgers and check-passers like Mrs. Van Sythe generally represent a better-educated class of people than prostitutes, and they are usually immensely clever in concealing their iniquities. A "clean" crime involving the employment of considerable skill and shrewdness, forgery has always been popular with the high-class crook and will probably remain so. This is especially true of women, who are generally looked upon with less suspicion by the society on which they prey than are men.

The world is always stunned by the spectacle of women who kill. For, while an implicit violence is accepted as an integral and even necessary part of an historically flamboyant "creative" male psyche, it is a quality abhorred in women as antithetical to the ideal of maternal gentleness and passive feminine grace, and therefore is believed not to exist. One is apt to hear a good deal of loose talk: "Let's not kid ourselves—women are worse than men. . . . When you get down to it, they're more sadistic. . . ."And so on. Actually this is nonsense; women as a whole cannot be measured against men as a group in this or any other area.

Individuals will tend to display more or less of any human quality than their peers in either sex. An unsympathetic environment combined with a deleterious collection of genes and chromosomes will produce individuals, male and female, who are sadistic, violent, weak, or generally evil. Sometimes they are simply mentally ill, and often pushed beyond the limits of their already scant capacity for self-restraint.

Although love and money figure prominently in the motivation of both men and women who commit violent acts, the love/hate syndrome is certainly most often responsible for the homicidal behavior of women. They kill the people who are closest to them—husbands, children, lovers, the people, in fact, who should have the least cause to fear them.

In the past, the two most frequent crimes against the person committed by women were acid-throwing (motivated generally by a desire for vengeance) and infanticide. The acid craze has subsided to a great extent, but women are still doing more than their share of baby killing. In recent years the corpses of unwanted infants have been discovered in incinerators, rivers, and trash barrels, the 1965 toll in New York City alone having been eleven sons and thirteen daughters.

Not all attacks upon children result in their death, of course, and each year the hospitals report an increasing number of victims of what has come to be known as the battered-child syndrome. These are cases in which children with bruises, burns, or broken bones are brought to the hospital by distraught mothers who, having dissipated their wrath, become terrified and alarmed by the results of their brutality, and rush to the hospital fortified with stories of how the child fell downstairs or set fire to a box of matches. The hospital personnel, now well acquainted with the pattern, know full well that it is probably the mother or father who has inflicted the damage in an uncontrollable rage, but since the general absence of witnesses makes it difficult to prove, there is nothing they can do but patch the child up. Thus, the mother too often escapes prosecution.

Of the seven women whose stories appear in subsequent pages, three are involved in murder. The nature of the crime, however, is far less important in these cases than the manner in which the women became involved in it.

Millicent Adams was mentally ill at the time she shot her lover, and so far as this study is concerned, she represents the general category of psychopathically motivated offenders. Her case is also significant in that it demonstrates the immense flexibility of which the law is capable when the defendant has a respectable social background, and when there is money available to prepare a thoughtful and thorough defense.

Flora Black was actually guilty only of assault, the death of her paramour having occurred as the incidental result of her spontaneous attack on him. Under different circumstances, Flora would have been charged with manslaughter. However, Flora's chances, as an impoverished, relatively rootless Negro, were comparatively slim, particularly since she committed her crime in a part of the country not generally known for its tolerance toward its black citizens. When a black woman causes the death of a white man in the South, her prospects are not promising even if she can hire the shrewdest criminal lawyer on earth. Flora was not given the opportunity to hire anybody, so the question of her not being able to afford it is academic.

These two very similar stories have been placed in deliberate juxtaposition to each other for the purpose of dramatizing the fact that there is an arbitrary quality about the law, which rightfully causes us to be exceedingly uneasy. This is not to imply in any way that Millicent Adams "got away" with anything; the disposition of this case was imaginative, constructive, and entirely fair to all concerned, including the public. On the contrary, the point really is to demonstrate, by contrast, how strikingly unfair was the treatment of Flora Black, even though she was ultimately saved by a stroke of unaccustomed good fortune.

No one will ever be able to establish with absolute certainty the extent to which Carole Tregoff functioned as a Lady Macbeth or was simply led by Dr. Finch, but her role as loving accomplice is almost a classic in the annals of feminine crime. The women who become involved in criminal activity as the helpmates of male criminals are legion, and their stories are generally sad. In crime, as in ordinary life, the woman most frequently serves as a subordinate to the man, but unlike the bourgeois man, the male criminal is not always around to help and protect his mate when danger threatens her. More often than not, when the law reaches out for them both, she is punished equally or even finds herself "taking the rap" for him.

It is not especially significant that Carole Tregoff was involved in a murder; as an accomplice she could have as easily assisted in a bank robbery, a blackmail attempt, or a kidnapping (where women are invaluable because of their understanding of how to care for children). What is important is that it rarely occurs to this sort of woman to engage in a criminal action on her own; she must be inspired to do so by someone else, and her emotional involvement must be so great as to corrupt thoroughly all reason as well as the instinct for self-preservation. Carole's story reflects just such a problem. So attractive were the prospects opened to her by Dr. Finch that all good sense, all restraining impulses, fled in the wake of his promises.

Reaching back in search of classic examples of feminine crime, into areas of history or drama far removed from us now by time, one is reminded of Medea, Lady Macbeth, Charlotte Corday, and even Lizzie Borden. However, it is doubtful that, if we apply modern standards and definitions to them, that any of these familiar figures could be characterized as criminals.

Although their behavior is archetypal, Medea and Lady Macbeth were produced by cultures in which violence was so prevalent and so habitual that no one would have thought to consider the overall social implications of such behavior. In the absence of organized law enforcement, the definition or criminality becomes a highly subjective thing. Charlotte Corday was certainly no criminal. Criminality is as much a question of motive and intent as the results of harmful actions, and this woman, a beautiful lady of generally high moral principles, believed that, in committing the single crime of her life, she was performing a patriotic duty. Her intent was to rid France of the pestilence of republicanism, embodied in Marat, and with no prospects of personal gain.

Nor was Lizzie Borden a criminal. Like others, she was no professional, coolly repeating the same crime in the advancement of private aims. Lizzie was a desperately sick girl who was eventually institutionalized for the protection of herself as well as society.

It is apparent, then, that outside the realm of professional, organized crime, it is difficult to define or depict true criminality. Those who apply their energies to the search for the "criminal" mind, especially insofar as women are concerned, do so most probably in vain. There are ways in which we are all criminals, and other ways in which none of us are, and one enters a hall of mirrors in efforts to define the essential elements.

Chapter I

Bajour

IT was well over thirty years ago that Thomas Dewey, then a crusading district attorney in the La Guardia days, discovered that most of the professional criminal activity in New York City was directed by a Sicilian called Lucky Luciano. Ever since that major dramatic revelation of the genesis and social configuration of organized crime in the United States, the Mafia, or Cosa Nostra, has been steadily subjected to the glare of publicity—so much so that people are relatively unaware of the existence of another less conspicuous nuisance, the gypsies.

Just as many people for years characterized the Mafia as a figment of the imagination of law-enforcement officials, so today most people are oblivious to the activities of peripatetic bands of gypsies who live in exclusive but enduring little communities in more than half the states.

Unlike the Mafia, gypsies do not involve themselves in organized supercrime—"the rackets." Moreover, they do not kill either one another or the ordinary "gajo" (a nongypsy), nor do they commit their crimes in an atmosphere of overt violence.

23

Therefore, they do not pose the same caliber of threat to the public and are not the subjects of so much concern as the Mafia. Essentially, they restrict their activities to what has been their principal occupation for centuries—outright theft.

Both groups are excellent examples of the kind of society in which crime is a cultural phenomenon rather than an individual dereliction. But while most Sicilians are not gangsters, the same cannot be said of the true gypsies, the words "crook" and "gypsy" being synonymous. The term "gyp," in fact, is derived from the word "gypsy."

Gypsies are a bona fide nomadic ethnic group which came originally from northern India more than a thousand years ago, slowly drifting across Central Europe and Russia, thence to the United States in the late 1800's. Contrary to popular opinion, the term "gypsy" does not merely refer to any category of swarthy people with a predilection for bright colors, violin-playing, and frequent shifts of residence. They are a distinct social group with particular racial and cultural associations. Although unusually large numbers of gypsies appear to have settled in Central Europe, not all the olive-skinned fiddlers from that part of the world, dressed in blazing satin blouses and asymmetrical ear baubles, are gypsies; many are merely ordinary Rumanian or Hungarian transplants, trying to make an honest living by exploiting the gypsy myth. In the old days no self-respecting male gypsy would dream of making an honest living.

Among gypsies, women do all the "work"—that is to say, they steal one way or another, employing methods ranging from simple pocket-picking to an advanced confidence game known as the boujeau, bajour (bag, trick), or "gypsy blessing." The men, meanwhile, pass the time watching TV, playing checkers or dominoes (at which they cheat), drinking tea strong enough to shrink the stomach of a goat, and belaboring their women, who never seem to work hard enough for them. They prey on the old and the sick, the disturbed and the unhappy—people who fear something or who are generally going through a bad period in their lives. Menopausal women and neurotics are favorite targets, and people who will pay a lot of money to have their problems lifted from their shoulders by means of a "gypsy blessing."

Few gypsies are ever convicted of their crimes, so successful are they in shielding each other and hiding in various gypsy communities throughout the country. In court, they easily confuse witnesses who may already be psychologically disabled by chagrin, age, and terror. They are themselves dreadful witnesses, as perjury means nothing to them, and *in extremis* they will demonstrate an almost total failure to understand the English language. At such times, they communicate in some Central European tongue, or in Romany, the universal but moribund gypsy language spoken only among themselves.

As might be expected, gypsy children are brought up rather differently from others. They are taught to steal from early childhood onward, and are not permitted to go to school, lest they be influenced by damaging bourgeois ethics concerned with honesty and consideration for other people. Besides, as one of the gypsy "kings" once put it to a member of the New York City police, "School is all right for you gaje. You've been going for hundreds of years, and you're used to it, but gypsies aren't, and it puts a strain on their minds which is liable to lead to epileptic fits." On the subject of work: "Once, that damned Roosevelt said all people on relief had to work on state projects. One of my boys went to work on a road gang, and after swinging that damned shovel for half an hour, he turned purple in the face and had to be taken to the hospital in a taxi." On stealing: "To a gypsy, there ain't but two kinds of merchandise—the lost kind and the unlost kind—and anything that ain't nailed down is lost. Anyhow, if people don't nail things down or hide them, they couldn't want to keep them very bad." The net result of this philosophy is that not one gypsy in ten knows how to read or write, although they are adept enough at basic arithmetic, and they almost invariably supplement their pilfered earnings with public welfare payments, the intricate rules of which they know backward. They live in perpetual flight from the law, and not by means of colorful, painted wagons, but in Cadillacs—if possible.

Gypsies are great believers in early marriage, and mothers buy brides for their fourteen- or fifteen-year-old sons for prices ranging from three hundred to five thousand dollars, depending on the status of the girl's tribe, and the essential qualities of the girl herself.* The latter is determined not only by her looks and

---

* Gypsies are divided into various complicated tribal units, all of which are somehow interrelated, but which sustain various hostilities and snobberies just the same. The identity of each tribe is basically determined by what part of

the prestige of her family within the tribe, but by her capabilities as a thief. Generally the boy and his mother are invited to observe the girl in action; a sucker well fleeced is proof that she is worthy and that she will be able to support the boy in a style to which he has every intention of becoming accustomed. The mothers then meet, and the deal is formalized after the customary bargaining ritual has been observed.

Should any moral justification for this way of life be

Europe it came from originally; the Machwaya, for example, come from the Machva, a region in west Serbia, whereas the Kalderash (coppersmiths) are Russians and Serbians. Many of these call themselves Argentinas, Greeks, or Mexicans, depending on which parts of the world they went after they left Russia or Serbia. In addition, there are, within the tribes, subgroups called "vitsas" which are very important and among which there are tremendous rivalries and dark suspicions. As in all human society, some groups seem to be infinitely more successful and affluent than others, a situation which breeds the usual envy and resentment. If a woman from one vitsa pulls off a big bajour, the news travels fast, and a man from a second group is apt to appear and demand a cut under the threat of turning police informer. Gypsies will inform on each other over this sort of thing, over a woman, or just because of some ancient insult; were it not for this tendency, it is doubtful that the police would ever be able to nab a single gypsy. Within the Mafia, an informer is the worst sort of scum, and the Mafioso who "sings" does not generally live long enough to savor the results of his treachery. Gypsies, however, are not given to extreme violence, although they enjoy cutting each other up from time to time, and informing is simply a normal part of the basic fabric of cheating and deception of which their lives are made.

The gypsy tribes are themselves subdivisions of two basic gypsy breeds—the nomadic, coppersmith gypsies, to which both the Machwaya and the Kalderash belong, and the Boyasch, which are less numerous. The Boyasch are Serbo-Rumanian gypsies, and usually speak Rumanian or Anvatski, a Serbo-Croatian tongue; Romany, a derivative of Sanskrit, is dying out among them. They tend to be small, dark, cleaner, and neater than the nomads, and the women are giving up gypsy dress, although older ones still wear gold-coin necklaces. The two groups do not get along at all. The Boyasch don't travel as much as the nomads, and they tend to work more, mostly as mechanics and in factories, making tents, awnings, and hammocks. When young, the girls stay at home; later they go out more to "work." Unlike the nomads, they don't wait for their victims to come to them in their fortune-telling establishments, but go out in search of them, often selling something door-to-door, such as a "resurrection" plant.

Gypsy girls do not prostitute, for gypsies generally view sex with fear and suspicion. They are, in fact, very superstitious about the various parts of the body, using different linen on the reproductive areas than on the rest—that is, if they wash at all. They will often pretend to be prostitutes and use seductive ploys to attract male victims, but sex is never the end result—only robbery.

found necessary, the gypsy invariably falls back on the legend of the Silver Spike, an outrageous tale on which every gypsy child is nurtured: Among the faithful who followed Christ along the tortured route to Golgotha was a gypsy who observed that one of the Roman soldiers carried four silver spikes; two of these were to be used to nail Jesus' hands to the cross, one was intended for the feet, and an extra-long one was to be driven into his heart—or his head, depending upon what sort of mood overtakes the teller. The gypsy, wanting to save Jesus, set about stealing the spikes and was discovered after having only got hold of the largest one. The centurion in charge of the spikes then set upon the gypsy and beat him bloody in an effort to retrieve the stolen nail, but the gypsy bravely refused to tell him where he had hidden it. Thus Jesus was crucified with only three nails, and before he died, he spoke to the gypsy from the cross, saying that from that time forward the gypsies could roam the world stealing whatever they needed to sustain themselves. And that is just what they have been doing ever since.

Two things particularly hurt the gypsies in the early twentieth century. One was the Depression, and the other was the appearance of the automobile. Before the Depression, the gypsies, who then traveled in huge wagons serving as home and workshop combined, were excellent metalworkers. They could fix absolutely anything and would go from one community to another offering to do jobs that ordinary metalworkers would refuse to take on. During the economic crisis of the 1930's, however, the regulars fought one another for any work they could get, and the gypsies found that there was nothing left for them. To make matters worse, the construction of highways made travel by horse and wagon completely impractical, and although they loved the new cars (gypsies are superb mechanics, if they can be persuaded to work), the average gypsy could not afford to buy gas. They could always keep their half-starved horses moving when times were hard, but they found that automobiles stubbornly refused to run without fuel. Consequently, they would often have to hole up in tenements and play the relief game for all it was worth, always devising new and ingenious methods of evading work, landlords, and officials, such as truant officers and census takers.

Another setback occurred when Roosevelt ordered everybody to turn in their gold in exchange for silver or paper. Gypsy women, who for centuries had served as ambulatory banks, wearing solid-gold necklaces and bracelets and going about with hundreds of dollars worth of gold sewn into the hems of their many skirts, soon discovered that they could swap the American coins for Mexican ones of nearly the same value, the fifty-peso coin being the most popular. Many were still in evidence as late as 1955, at which time these coins fetched about sixty dollars each in New York.

Present times seem to be very good for gypsies, for there has evolved a whole new wonderland of things for people to become deeply disturbed about: The Bomb, creeping Socialism, LSD, cancer, as well as the old reliable problems of sex and old age. Since at least 90 percent of gypsy business derives from the various forms of professional doom-mongering, times of trouble are best, and people in trouble make the easiest victims.

For many years, following the untimely death of her husband, Mrs. Kurt Mayer was a person in trouble. Although Mrs. Mayer became a widow at the relatively early age of forty-seven, her husband at least had left her in comfortable financial circumstances. She now lived alone in their apartment on Manhattan's West Side, and passed her time shopping, working in a desultory way on projects pertaining to Jewish philanthropy, and involving herself rather more than might be considered desirable in the affairs of her son and daughter-in-law. Their baby daughter was the object of Mrs. Mayer's particular affection and concern, and hardly a day passed that she did not call to find out whether she could take the baby out in her carriage, baby-sit, or just come over to see her. Since Mrs. Mayer's only other child lived in another part of the country, she endeavored to mitigate the loneliness which engulfed her by concentrating her maternal instincts exclusively on this younger son's family.

Like many mothers, Mrs. Mayer had always exercised certain proprietary rights over the lives of her children, even after they were grown. But as her life had been principally taken up with the needs and demands of Mr. Mayer, the point had not yet been reached where her attentions and intrusions were burdensome. Suddenly, within the space of two days, during which time Mr. Mayer had succumbed to a heart attack, Mrs. Mayer found herself without companionship, without her husband's love, and without that welcome demand upon her in-

dustry to which she had grown accustomed. Profoundly frustrated, she compensated for the loss of these things as best she
could.

Always a superstitious person, leery of ladders, black
cats, and the number thirteen, Mrs. Mayer now took to reading
her horoscope daily in the evening paper, hoping that it would
aid her in plumbing the depths of her empty and uncertain
future.

She realized also that she was beginning to experience the
disturbing and much advertised effects of early menopause, but
she had read at the hairdresser's that this should not necessarily
change things for the worse. To add to her anxiety, her beloved
grandchild had lately developed an unsightly rash on her neck,
which caused the baby much discomfort; consequently, everyone's nerves were frayed. The child wailed constantly and produced in her mother and grandmother that unique quality of un-
rest born of the combination of irritation of the senses and impotent compassion.

One afternoon in August, 1956, Mrs. Mayer, together with
her friend Esther, strolled up Madison Avenue, having completed an unrewarding shopping expedition in midtown. It was
one of those steaming, sooty, summer days in late summer from
which all New Yorkers with sufficient income endeavor to flee.
The buses were crowded, and the two women had decided to
walk a while to avoid the ultimate necessity of close body contact with other overheated people till the last possible moment.

After walking several blocks, Esther began to feel a bit
wheezy, and suggested that they stop for a glass of iced tea. As they
looked about for a soda fountain or luncheonette, Mrs. Mayer's
eye was caught by a curious sign in the window of a ground-floor
store front on Madison Avenue in the 70's. It read: MADAME
LILLIAN—TEAROOM—COME IN AND RELAX. Stacked all around
the sign in haphazard display were various tatty paperbound
books on astrology, the art of palmistry, and the secrets of
dream interpretation, such as *Old Gypsy Nan's Fortune Teller
and Dream Book.**

This was a typical gypsy "ofisa," or office—typical in

---

* Fortune telling, that is, "predicting," is illegal in New York, and when gypsies
are brought into court having been charged with it, they curse, scream, and
swear to God they weren't telling fortunes, but only selling people a book, and
explaining how to use it.

every way except that they are not often found in this part of town, but are more frequently discovered in seedy second-floor-front joints on side streets in the theatre district. An ofisa can be rigged up in an hour, and later on, if the gypsy pulls off a bajour and has to get out of town in a hurry, she and her family can dismantle it in much less time than that, and be across the state line within the hour.

Mrs. Mayer, who found herself oddly attracted to the place, suggested that they go in. After all, they did advertise tea.

"You must be crazy," Esther commented. "There'll probably be roaches all over the place and dirty cups."

"I'd sort of like to get my fortune told," Mrs. Mayer admitted.

"Well, all right. Why not?"

They entered and found that the booths and "rooms" were constructed primarily of heavy fabrics hung from wires. The walls were decorated with huge charts depicting giant human palms, phrenological heads, crescents, and zodiacs. Camp chairs were strewn around with the tables holding thick candles. The women sat down gratefully, and presently a slim, dark young woman emerged from the rear maze and smiled upon them benevolently. She wore a loose, gathered blouse and flowered shawl over the many brightly colored skirts which swirled about her legs, and a scarf held her long, straight, inky hair more or less in place.

This was a Machvanka—that is, one of the women of the Machwaya tribe, who are rarely found in any other but gypsy attire, except when trying to elude the police or confuse a victim. The ladies found her perfectly sweet, and ordered iced tea. The gypsy, prepared to steal everything but their corsets and back teeth, smiled graciously and suggested hot tea instead. In hot weather, she explained, it is actually better to drink hot liquids. The ladies accepted this, not realizing that gypsies have no ice-making facilities anyhow. They also wondered what a gypsy tea-room was doing in this part of town, but the Machwaya are a rich successful tribe, and they have been known to pay up to six hundred dollars per month for a good location, although that would be unusual.

The tea arrived and tasted good, if a bit strong; both women were feeling decidedly better, and Mrs. Mayer asked the young gypsy if she could tell her fortune. The large black eyes sparkled, and the gypsy asked them to wait a moment while she went to look for her aunt, who would come and help her. The two women were ushered into separate booths, and while Esther had her palm read by the young gypsy who called herself Dorothy, Mrs. Mayer awaited the arrival of a woman with whom she would be involved for many years to come. She also amused herself by playing with Dorothy's four-year-old daughter Fatima, whose eyes and dimpled alabaster smile made a lasting impression on the lonely widow—an impression which she would later be called upon to recapture in less sympathetic circumstances.

One skill in which gypsies become very proficient over the years is spotting a likely victim. Dorothy, in the booth adjoining Mrs. Mayer's, was already discovering that Esther was much too sensible and generally well-balanced a character to fall for the bajour or any other con-game. She read the lady's palm, collected a few dollars, and dismissed her as quickly as possible.

Policemen who work the Pickpocket and Confidence Squad and who have interrogated hundreds of "suckers," have observed that they have much in common: Most of them are unhappily married, or have never been married, or are divorced or widowed; most are deeply depressed for reasons they cannot logically explain. They tend to be worried about their health; most are half convinced that they have cancer. They have a passion for talking about themselves to anyone who will listen, and although they may be capable of shrewdness in certain areas, they are fundamentally and profoundly unsophisticated.

Many criminologists and prosecutors alike speak of the complicity of the victim as being a recurrent factor in certain kinds of crimes. That is not to say that people consciously aid the criminal in the realization of his plans to harm them, but that frequently there may be an unconscious desire on the part of a victim to be victimized in some way, and, sooner or later, that desire bears fruit. The police describe this species of female as the kind who, if she goes out at night to walk a dog, will unerringly head for some vacant lot or some dark corner of the park; if she has to be out late and go home alone, she will take a shortcut through areas in the city that the ordinary person wouldn't go through at that hour fully armed; or if she is sitting in a bar and it gets late and some stranger on the next stool offers to see her home, she goes right along. Just as there is this type who the police figure get raped, robbed, mugged, or murdered because she is in some measure looking for it, there is also the type who solicits the "help" of gypsies.

Superstitious themselves to the point of childishness, gypsies are well acquainted with the fears and foolish notions which lurk in the minds of middle-aged women. By the time they have reached middle age themselves, they need only to spend a few minutes with a woman—observing the expression in her eyes, the set of her mouth, and the wrinkles and hollows of her face—and to know exactly what the chances are of her being receptive to the gypsy blessing.

The gypsy who walked into Mrs. Mayer's booth that summer day was between forty-five and fifty, five feet one inch tall, weighing 190 pounds, with the jet black hair and eyes common to her kind, and a soft, mellifluous voice, smooth as silk. Dressed in typical gypsy attire, she was ablaze with color and expensive gold jewelry. This was Valda Adams, alias Mary or Lillian Adams—or Johnson, or Morgan—one of the shrewdest, most successful Machvanka "dukkerers" (fortune tellers) in the business, and the second she clapped eyes on Mrs. Mayer, she knew she had a live one.

"Well, hello, dear," she cooed. "My name is Lillian. What a pretty dress you have on—so becoming. I understand you'd like me to tell you about your future."

"Oh, yes. Yes, I would," Mrs. Mayer replied, thinking how charming and sympathetic the woman appeared. Lillian lighted the thick candle which rested on the table between them, and the light from the flame glittered in her eyes and rebounded in tiny sunbursts from the golden coins of her necklace. She took Mrs. Mayer's hand in hers, stroking the palm soothingly, smoothing it out, and Mrs. Mayer began to talk—about herself, her problems, the baby. Lillian, who appeared to be concentrating on the lines in Mrs. Mayer's hand, was listening intently, wondering how much this rich widow was worth. If there was a pause in Mrs. Mayer's narrative, Lillian raised her warm, dark gaze, smiled, and asked her a question or two, encouraging her to talk some more. Soon she had the whole picture: another lonely widow who never really appreciated her husband till he was gone and who believed that there wasn't a single soul left in the world who cared a damn what happened to her. They all had somebody; she was alone. Probably there was something the matter with her. This, thought Lillian, was a sucker sent from heaven.

"I've seen a lot of this in your hand, dear," she said softly, "but there's so much—so very much. I think you'd better come back to me alone—maybe tomorrow, when there's more time. And better not tell anyone. All right? Your friend is waiting now." Gently, Lillian led Mrs. Mayer from the booth into the outer section of the ofisa, where Esther waited impatiently.

"What on earth took you so long? Your future couldn't have been that much more exciting than mine."

"I think it's fascinating, don't you?" Mrs. Mayer asked.

"I think it's a lot of garbage," Esther summarized, and they spoke no further of it.

The following day Mrs. Mayer returned to the ofisa alone. Lillian was there to greet her with the same soothing phrases and earnest concern. Having commented that Mrs. Mayer was looking a bit more tired and paler than she had on the previous day, she ushered her into one of the rear booths. Again the heavy candle was lighted, and Lillian gazed into Mrs. Mayer's right palm, stroking and massaging the hand all the while for the maximum relaxing effect, a tactic which was highly successful in the present case.

"Have you noticed any unusual pains lately, dear? Had any unusually bad dreams?" Lillian inquired anxiously. Mrs. Mayer thought she had, but she couldn't describe them very clearly. Lillian studied the left palm intently, then the right one again, comparing the lines. After several minutes she looked up and said, "I don't want to frighten you, dear, but I see something bad in your hand—very bad."

"What is it?" the widow pleaded. "Please tell me. I knew there was something."

"I felt it the moment I held your hand yesterday. The spirits must have sent you to me."

"Tell me what you saw. What did you see in my hand?"

"I can't tell you today," Lillian replied. "It's too soon, and there's something we have to look into first. I think I can help you, but you must do everything I tell you, and don't breathe anything about it to a living soul, not even a rabbi. If you do, you'll break my power so far as you're concerned, and there won't be a thing I can do for you. Which would be too bad, because the spirits who sent you here meant for me to help you. I'm your only hope."

By this time Mrs. Mayer was thoroughly terrified and said she would do anything the gypsy asked. Lillian took both of

Mrs. Mayer's hands in hers, in the manner of a mother impart-
ing some vital point of ethics to a somewhat dubious but anxious
child.

"I want you to go home now, and on your way home,
buy a fresh white egg, and tonight you're to get out the three
warmest blankets you have and put them on your bed. (The
temperature at the time had been regularly hitting the 90's.)
Then get undressed and get under the blankets and lie on your
back. Then I want you to take the egg and hold it on your
navel with both hands clasped over it, and lie there that way
till the egg feels warm, real warm. Then wrap it in one of your
husband's handkerchiefs, place these in your shoe under the
bed before going to sleep, and tomorrow morning I want you to
bring them to me."

The widow's mind raced as she struggled to commit each
detail of these instructions to memory. Lillian, meanwhile, continued the familiar litany, uttered dozens of times before, in the
usual urgent spellbinding tones.

"I don't want you to pay me anything now or ever; in
cases like yours we work in close connection with the spirits, and
we don't take money. And, remember, if you tell a living soul,
my power is broken."

Earnest and conscientious as a teen-aged initiate entering
some exclusive organization, Mrs. Mayer did exactly as she had
been told. The next morning, bright and early, she went back
into the ofisa with the egg all wrapped up in one of her late
husband's handkerchiefs. As soon as she got into the booth, she
tried to give the egg to Lillian.

"Just a minute," said the gypsy. "I need a fresh candle
for this." Mrs. Mayer thought she could feel the heat bursting
from the egg, burning a mark into her hand.

While Lillian was in the back of the ofisa fetching a new
candle, she slipped a tiny object between two fingers of her left
hand. She then returned to the booth, placed the candle in its
holder, and lighted it. She took the egg from Mrs. Mayer, un-
wrapped it, handed the handkerchief back to her, and asked
her to spread it on the table. For a moment she looked intently
into Mrs. Mayer's eyes. She broke the egg into the handkerchief,
and as she did so, let the object in her fingers slip neatly into
the mess. When she removed her hands, a hairy devil's head,
carved in ivory, was revealed lying in the yoke—a hideous little

gargoyle about an inch and a quarter long, its horns turned down over the brow, the eyes shut, cheeks sunken. It regarded them malevolently, its lips twisted in an awful, humorless grin. Mrs. Mayer emitted a tiny gasp and began to weep, softly but copiously.

According to a large, uptown pawnbroker, who is an expert on peculiar jewelry and bibelots, this type of ivory miniature was quite popular in Germany during the late nineteenth century. They turn up now and then in antique stores, curio shops, and pawnbrokers' establishments, where the gypsies pick them up for a song. Lillian had glued some of her own hair to this one, just to make it more grotesque. The last time she had used it, she had conned an old Irish hotel maid out of nearly eight thousand dollars. The woman had been cleaning up after other people in cheap side-street hotels for better than forty years, and these had been her life savings.

"Don't cry, dear," she implored. "No need to cry. Lillian can help you. It's just as I thought, you see. You have evil within you that has to come out. That's probably what was giving the baby her rash. But don't worry—we'll do something about it."

Mrs. Mayer quieted down a bit under the calming influence of Lillian's gentle voice, and the gypsy asked her for a dollar bill, which Mrs. Mayer hastily produced, along with some Kleenex for her nose. Lillian tore the bill in half, placed it in the handkerchief after folding the pieces up as small as possible, mumbled an incantation over it, and said that if it once again became whole, it would mean that a miracle had been done and God would help them. Mrs. Mayer was instructed to pin the whole thing to the inside of her dress next to her breast.

"You have money in the bank, don't you, dear?" the gypsy inquired, casually and somewhat rhetorically. Mrs. Mayer raised her eyes.

"Yes, I do."

"Well, tomorrow you'd better bring me all your bankbooks and whatever else there is, and we'll see about this. The curse might be on the money, you see, dear. The evil may be there—in that money."

"But how could that be?"

"Well, dear, that money may have been stolen before your husband got it, or it may have passed through the hands of

Antichrist, or maybe a man killed himself making it. There are a hundred different ways that money can get to be dirty, and we've got to find out if it is."

When Mrs. Mayer returned the next day with her bankbooks and stock certificates, Lillian was waiting with an intact dollar bill concealed in the folds of her skirt in a white handkerchief. The widow unpinned the mess inside her blouse with trembling hands and gave it to the gypsy, who quickly switched the two handkerchiefs while Mrs. Mayer rearranged her clothes. Then she carefully spread the white square out on the table, and there was the dollar bill, whole again. Lillian looked up at Mrs. Mayer, beaming, her velvet eyes filled with joy and satisfaction.

"God is on our side now, dear," she breathed. "A miracle will take place. Did you bring the things I asked you for?" Mrs. Mayer, now very excited and feeling encouraged and optimistic for the first time, tore open the catch of her handbag and snatched out the various documents. Lillian handled them gingerly and none too eagerly, for they too could be slightly contaminated. A quick glance through the various papers revealed what the gypsy had so fervently hoped: Harriet Mayer was loaded. She placed her hands over the papers piled on the table and closed her eyes, lifting her chin slightly out of the glow of the candle. The light played over her hands, which began to tremble. Suddenly, she opened her eyes, withdrawing her hands hurriedly from the pile, as though it were in flames. Rubbing her fingers, she said to the startled woman sitting across from her, "The whole trouble is in that filthy, stinking money lying there in the bank. It has to be cleansed, and that's all there is to it."

"How are we going to do that?" the widow inquired.

"Well, dear, I'm going to tell you exactly how much money to draw out of each one of those accounts, and when you've got it all together, you bring it back to me. And for God's sake, do it as fast as possible before that filthy money does any more harm."

It took Mrs. Mayer nearly two weeks of harried transacting to complete the gypsy's instructions, but when she was finished, she had a total of $118,273 in cash all set to go to Lillian in a Macy's shopping bag. Then she waited to hear from the gypsy.

In mid-October, Mrs. Mayer was told to go to a new lo-

cation further north on Madison Avenue, as Lillian did not wish
to carry with them the evil with which the old place was now
infested. Mrs. Mayer was delighted to see Lillian again and, eager
to get on with the purifying process, thrust the shopping bag,
stuffed with bills of large denomination, toward the apparently
horrified gypsy.

"Oh, no. God, no!" she gasped, throwing her hands in
the air. "I don't want to touch that money." She led Mrs. Mayer
to a booth in the back of the ofisa, which was set up with a
complicated little candlelit shrine of ambiguous religious orienta-
tion. The place reeked of cheap incense, which caused Mrs.
Mayer to feel rather nauseated.

"Now you put the money up there," Lillian ordered, indicating the altar, "and swear to God that it is evil." This done,
she further instructed Mrs. Mayer to put the money in a vault
overnight and return the next day with it wrapped in a brown
paper bag. She was also to bring with her a live chicken and a
flowerpot filled with earth.

"Do you think you could possibly supply the chicken,
Lillian?" the widow asked. "I wouldn't have the faintest idea
where to lay my hands on a live chicken in New York City, to
tell you the truth."

"Certainly, dear. I'll be glad to do that for you. I should
have thought of it myself." It was a small enough investment,
considering the total haul.

The money passed a quiet night in the Mayers' safe and
was brought back to Lillian the next day in a paper bag, along
with the required pot of earth. Once more the gypsy ushered
Mrs. Mayer into the room with the shrine, and told her to sit
on the floor. The gypsy then departed, reappearing within a
moment or two with a cackling emaciated chicken in her grasp.
When both women were seated on the floor, Lillian mumbled a
brief and incomprehensible prayer and thrust the chicken's head
into the paper bag. After a few minutes, the animal died, primarily because Lillian's left hand inside the bag was clamped
around its scrawny throat with a grip of steel. The gypsy raised
her head and gave Mrs. Mayer a penetrating, compassionate look,
pregnant with meaning. "You see, dear, the evil that is in this
money entered the poor chicken and killed it. I'll bury it out
back in the earth you brought in the flowerpot." Actually, she
would have it for supper.

Lillian could see that the incident had profoundly affected her victim, and took advantage of the psychological momentum she had built up. Without waiting for Mrs. Mayer's verbal reaction, she made her final pitch: "We have to get rid of that money, dear, right away. It must be destroyed immediately before it's too late."

"How?"

"By fire, and right now."

The two most common conclusions to a successful bajour are the "sew-up" and the "burn-up." If the gypsy is not secure in the power she holds over the woman and feels she'd better work fast, she does a sew-up. This involves placing the money in an envelope made of white cloth, folding the whole thing over once, if it is not too bulky, and sewing it up on the three open sides to form a snug little bag. From this derives the term "bujeau," or "bajour" (little bag of money), a derivative of a Serbian word, "bozur," (anything beautiful). And there is nothing more beautiful to a gypsy than a bagful of tax-free cash for which she has not been required to strain herself too much.

At the conclusion of the sew-up, the gypsy gets down on her knees with her victim beside her and tells the woman to hold her left hand, close her eyes, and pray in her own way while she goes through the gypsy rigamarole with the spirits. In the meantime, an empty slit pocket in the right side of her skirt is ready to receive the money bag, while a second one, containing several similar bags of varying sizes and thicknesses—all filled with crackly bond-paper "money"—provides an appropriate substitute. This accomplished, the gypsy springs up with a cry of joy and proceeds to pin the bag to the inside of the woman's slip. She instructs the woman to wear the slip to bed and to sleep with the bag under her pillow for eight days, and on midnight of the eighth day, the money will be clean, and the curse will have left her. If, however, the woman opens the money bag one minute sooner or tells anyone about it, the money will be turned to plain white paper, and the curse will jump back on her. Whether she peeks or not, of course, the unfortunate lady finds that she not only has been left with a neat stack of blank, white, money-sized paper, but a very dirty undergarment.

Lillian, realizing that she had Mrs. Mayer completely transfixed, had decided to do a burn-up; this is more trouble, but it makes a deeper impression on the victim and in the long run is safer. It is difficult to get a conviction on a burn-up, as there is no evidence of the switch, and the woman will often be too chagrined or too terrified to testify anyway. In many cases the victim doesn't go near the police until some relative finds out what has happened and forces her to do so.

Mrs. Mayer reacted with some alarm to Lillian's announcement, but at the thought of being soon rid of her troubles, allowed herself to be swept into the dramatic climax of her gypsy's blessing. Now, for the first time, Lillian summoned her niece Dorothy, and the lovely girl who had greeted Mrs. Mayer and her friend on that first day appeared with a gleaming new metal garbage can.

"Now give the money to Dorothy, dear, and she'll put it in the can. I'm going to pray."

Mrs. Mayer, whose eyes up till now had remained fixed on the bag of money, was absorbed with Lillian, who had apparently gone into a kind of trance. This is a gypsy's finest hour, and she uses herself unsparingly in the final histrionics.

Lillian had begun to keen, whimper, and moan, grinding her teeth in a fearful manner. She beat her head on the floor, and tore at her blouse till it was in shreds and blood had sprung to the surface of her neck and breast. Blood collected under her grimy nails as she clawed at her face, rolling her eyes to the heavens, shuddering and gurgling. One moment she was on her hands and knees, quivering like an animal poised for its own death, the next minute she was thrashing about on the floor in the dust, chanting and jabbering all the while.

Presently Lillian was worn out, and she stopped as abruptly as she had begun, lying face down on the floor, gasping like a fish. When she got up, she was dirty and covered with sweat; her blouse hung down in rags, her eyes were wild, and her face scratched and bloody. It had unquestionably been one of her better performances, during which Dorothy had quietly absconded with the money-bag and left a bag full of paper in the bottom of the can where the original had been placed earlier.

"Now, dear," Lillian began, pulling herself together as best she could, "the spirits have drawn the curse off you, but it's time to burn up this evil money. Light a match and drop it on the bag." Dorothy had already poured on the kerosene. "This part you've got to do yourself." Totally mesmerized and moving as though in shock, Mrs. Mayer lighted the proffered match, and dropped it on what was presumably $118,273 of her own money. At once the flames leaped high, and in minutes the "money" was reduced to a filmy ash. Lillian stirred it with a stick to make sure the last of it was gone. "Let me see. Can I see?" cried the widow.

"No, dear," Lillian replied. "You've been through enough. You know the smoke is contaminated. Now you wouldn't want to inhale it and let the evil crawl right back inside of you."

"No, no. All right. I must keep the evil away now—from now on."

Lillian quickly placed the dazed woman's handbag firmly in her grip and, speaking gently to her, led her tenderly to the door.

"Go home now, dear, and sleep. I'll call you tomorrow, and I know you'll be feeling better—much better." She smiled and waved cozily, as Mrs. Mayer made her way to the sidewalk and hailed a cab.

The moment the taxi disappeared around the corner, the gypsies were galvanized into action, and in less than half an hour they were packed up and away, leaving no trace.

Lillian did call Mrs. Mayer the next day, though from where, God only knows. She advised the widow to take a nice vacation somewhere in the mountains and forget about the whole business for about two weeks. After this, she was sure Mrs. Mayer would be in top form once more and that all the evil would have departed from her. Mrs. Mayer, still numb from her experience, took the gypsy's advice.

Following a pleasant stay in the Catskills, Mrs. Mayer returned and was subsequently contacted by telephone on many different occasions by her friend Lillian who was anxious to continue their friendship, just in case she should feel in need of more cash. This went on for close to a year, during which time it never occurred to Mrs. Mayer that the gypsy was not really her friend.

In July, 1957, Lillian felt the need developing. She promptly telephoned her unwitting benefactress, who agreed to meet her in the park at 72nd Street and Central Park West. Mrs. Mayer was, as usual, happy to see the gypsy, for she still regarded her as one who had redeemed her from an unpalpable evil and brought about the spiritual catharsis which she so avidly sought.

She was not to bask in the warmth of gratitude for long, however, for as she sat there in the sun with her friend, chatting and thinking benevolent thoughts, she heard the gypsy say that she hadn't been resting too easy of late, because it had been mystically revealed to her that the amount of money she had originally required of Mrs. Mayer was wrong; she needed ten thousand dollars more to make it right.

For the first time, a shaft of doubt pierced the widow's conscious mind, and the September air grew suddenly chill. As she turned to ponder the gypsy's words, she noticed that the sun had indeed taken temporary refuge behind a massive thunderhead. Come to think of it, she did not feel that much better, though the baby's rash was gone and hadn't returned.

"Lillian, I'll get the money for you, but you're not to burn it."

"But I must destroy it with the rest. Otherwise it cannot be cleansed."

"I won't give it to you unless you promise me you won't destroy it. There must be another way. You can just keep it for me—pray over it or something. I haven't been resting too easy either, thinking about that hundred and eight thousand dollars just burning up like that." The gypsy was cornered.

"All right. I don't know if it will help, but I won't destroy the money. I'll think of something. You must rid yourself of this, Harriet, or the whole thing will have been for nothing, and things will be bad for you again."

They parted in an atmosphere of mutual gloom and foreboding, having arranged to meet a few days later at the Park Plaza Hotel, at which time Mrs. Mayer was to bring the additional ten thousand dollars. As she climbed into a cab, she saw Lillian get into a white convertible which had swung around the corner as they walked off in different directions.

Having obtained the cash through the sale of negotiable bonds, Mrs. Mayer appeared at the hotel on the appointed day. This time, she felt a deep depression and a nagging reluctance which had never before characterized her meetings with Lillian. Formerly, she had anticipated even the most casual telephone conversation with eagerness, and had been left afterward with a residual peace of mind which lasted for days. Today it was disturbingly different. Lillian was smooth as ever when she opened the door, but she perceived at once that the widow was in a disturbed state of mind. Once more, Mrs. Mayer exhorted the gypsy not to burn the money or otherwise destroy it; at first, in fact, she did not admit she had it with her. This time, the gypsy put up no resistance whatever to the idea of preserving the cash —a circumstance the widow thought rather odd, considering her passionate words in the park.

But after listening awhile to Lillian's familiar intonations, Mrs. Mayer fell once again under the gypsy's charismatic spell, and, as in a nightmare—with hundreds of silent and subconscious restraining voices urging her not to do it—she opened her handbag, took out the money, and placed it on a table before her. The gypsy made no move toward the bundle, sensing that the situation called for more of the soothing formulas with which she had always calmed Mrs. Mayer before and, above all, the utmost delicacy of touch. She said she would take the money with her to the mountains, where the air is pure, and pray over it and cleanse it of the evil which had been poisoning Mrs. Mayer's life and inhibiting her total recovery from the depression which still lingered on. Perhaps some day in the near future the demons would be completely exorcised, and the money could be returned.

Temporarily placated by these offerings of hope, Mrs. Mayer departed. The moment she was gone, the gypsy departed as well, by means of a rear exit, and Mrs. Mayer did not see or hear from her again for a very long time.

For the next two years, Mrs. Mayer was tormented as she had never been before—not only by the frustration and loneliness which had formerly plagued her, but by the additional specters of doubt and humiliation which grew like tumors within her as the tiny kernel of suspicion born in Central Park matured into the full and unbearable realization that she had behaved like the original fool. From time to time, she would still hear from Lillian—calling collect, as a rule, from some unidentified resting place—and the spell would be temporarily revived. But finally, late in July, 1959, the desire to end the intolerable suspense—to know for certain and to confide in someone who would not mock her too cruelly—drove Mrs. Mayer to the police.

Quite naturally, she went first to her local precinct, fully prepared to unburden herself. At first mention of the word "gypsy," however, the young policeman cut her off in midconfession, and headed her downtown, with instructions to take her story to the Pickpocket and Confidence Squad, know within the profession as the Gypsy Squad.

There she met Sergeant James Forman, and from him she learned about gypsies. She was supplied with masses of police photographs, and after many hours she was able to identify positively Valda, or Mary Adams, No. 313937, as being the same person as Lillian and the person responsible for her loss. Records of the Bureau of Criminal Investigation showed that at this moment Valda Adams was in full flight.

Sergeant Forman knew a lot about gypsies, and as he spoke, the widow's eyes, stinging from lack of sleep, grew more troubled, and the shadows and lines around them seemed to deepen until at last, flushed with shame, indignation, and chagrin, she lowered her head onto trembling hands. Still, now that her worst suspicions had been confirmed, Mrs. Mayer felt somehow relieved, and she determined to devote her remaining energy to assisting the police in their search for the errant swindler.

In the meantime, hoping to forestall Mrs. Mayer's inevitable contact with the police, Valda continued to call, inquiring about the widow's health. Each time, she carefully avoided supplying any details as to her whereabouts or future plans; it was apparent, however, that she did not remain in any one spot for very long. These calls were the only link between Mrs. Mayer and her predator, and she awaited them in almost insupportable suspense. The last call she received came from Los Angeles on September 8, 1959. After months of frustrated attempts to establish personal contact with the gypsy once more, Mrs. Mayer's flagging hopes were now revived, for this time Valda Adams stated that she was planning to come to Washington, D.C., for a few days and that she wanted the widow to come down and see her there. She was on her way, she said, to Birmingham, Alabama, and would not be traveling north.

But the gypsy never showed up in Washington, and the only action possible for the New York police was to alert their counterparts in every state in which gypsies were known to have formed communities or had operations that Valda Adams, wife of George "Blackie" Adams, was wanted in New York for grand larceny. The police, notified of the above facts, filed and distributed "wanted" cards, and sent out alarms to twenty-eight cities in the United States, plus Mexico City, with instructions to be on the lookout for the Adamses.

It was at this point that the gypsy began to lose ground, although it would be many years before the net cast by the police held her in its meshes. But policemen are very patient, and a month or so after the alarm went out, something happened to speed up the gathering-in process.

One day, in an obscure California suburb, a rather simple-minded young police officer, momentarily inspired by the general alert, decided that he knew where to find the Adamses, for he had heard that a gypsy enclave existed right on the outskirts of town. So off he went, accompanied by two other officers, in search of the wanted pair. What he found, instead, was a handful of relatively unprosperous and decidedly uncooperative gypsies, all called Williams, who claimed they had never heard of the Adamses. There followed a good deal of rough talk and some shoving about, but the policemen went back to their headquarters with empty handcuffs.

The gypsy grapevine, certainly one of the most effective operations of its kind in existence, took care of the rest, and within two or three days, Blackie and Valda Adams far away in Birmingham, Alabama, got word that Valda was wanted in New York. (For once Valda had told Mrs. Mayer the truth—she *had* gone to Alabama.) The idea that an interstate alarm was out for them did not sit at all well with the pair, and after the usual panoply of shrieking fits, accusations, vilifications, and tantrums had been displayed, Blackie decided to suspend his tea-drinking and TV viewing long enough to pay a visit to the FBI.

He had hatched what he considered a brilliant scheme, but which was, in fact, a serious blunder. The plan was as follows: He would go to the FBI in Birmingham, pretending that he thought it was he who was wanted, and turn himself in; in the process he would try to find out in what capacity and for which of her myriad swindles Valda was wanted.

The FBI in Birmingham had received the alert on the Adamses from New York, and when Blackie sauntered in, the inspector who greeted him knew at once with whom he was dealing. Fortunately, this officer was a good deal more circum-

spect than the policeman in California, and feigned total ig-
norance of the matter. He told Blackie that not only was he not
wanted, but if his wife was wanted, it was news to him. This was
a rather crucial ploy, for had the FBI jumped at the bait, Blackie
and Valda would have been out of the state by morning and
once again on the run. Instead, Blackie strode out of the inspector's office bloated with self-righteous pride in his own cunning and upon returning home, announced to Valda that there
was nothing to worry about; it had all been a mistake—a vile
rumor, started, undoubtedly, by one of his enemies. Then, in a
fit of smug confidence, Blackie did something even more foolish.

On December 13, 1959, the day after the visit to the
FBI, Sergeant Forman in New York received a long-distance
midnight call at his home. It was Blackie. (To this day Forman
has no idea how the gypsy obtained his home telephone number, or how he knew whom to call.) Blackie was triumphant
and, in a stream of crowing obscenity, abuse, and vilification,
let Forman know what he thought of the policeman's shabby
efforts to scare or trick Valda into what he was sure was a bribe
attempt. As he warmed to his task, he accused the entire Police
Department of New York City of sustaining a perpetual effort
to shake down the Machwaya gypsies, and on it went until, his
polemic exhausted, he hung up.

Despite the lateness of the hour and the insults, Sergeant Forman had been delighted by all this, for while Blackie
roared, the detective had managed to have the call traced, and
by the following day, he knew that the number belonged to a
gypsy couple, listed as Mr. and Mrs. Louis Adamo, living on
Melody Lane, Birmingham, Alabama.

Now that they had a legitimate lead on the Adamses,
the New York police flung themselves with renewed vigor into
the task of having Valda arrested and extradited from the state
of Alabama. This, however, proved to be mysteriously difficult.

The first indication of the protracted resistance which
they were to encounter came when they put in a request to the
Alabama police to arrest Valda. The day after Blackie's call,
they had obtained an open indictment which had been forwarded to the authorities in Birmingham. The answer they received was, "Do you really want her?" Thoroughly puzzled and
more than a little annoyed, New York responded, "What is this,
Twenty Questions? Of course, we want her." On December 29,

a general-sessions warrant was forwarded to the sheriff of Jefferson City, Alabama; but even so, Valda was not arrested until January 15, 1960. Bail was set at five hundred dollars, a ludicrously low sum which the gypsy had no trouble raising, but she refused to waive the rendition proceedings, so a hearing was scheduled before the Governor on February 18. At this time a rendition warrant was signed by the Governor.

Between January, 1960, and January, 1961, Valda Adams was free on $300,000 bail in Birmingham, the bail having been raised when rendition proceedings were instituted, while Valda indulged in various devious legal maneuvers. In April she entered into habeas corpus proceedings which failed, and she was ordered to be extradited. In May, a transcript of the record was filed with the Court of Appeals in Montgomery, and in June, the Assistant Attorney General of Alabama made a motion to strike the record and dismiss the appeal, but, curiously, no action was taken. In December, the appeal was dismissed by the Court of Appeals. At the end of the same month, Valda's legal counsel appealed for certiorari to the Supreme Court of Alabama and was again denied.

Several times during the course of this year, Sergeant Forman and other members of his squad made trips to Alabama to try to ascertain what was holding up the proceedings in the case and who was assisting the gypsy in the avoidance of the inevitable. The stunned New York police found themselves alternately accused of endeavoring to shake down the Adamses and of using their pursuit of them as an excuse to stir up trouble and discontent among Birmingham's "niggers." It was held that "northern justice being what it is," the gypsy would never get a fair trial in the state of New York. Somebody, thought the New York police, must be kidding down here.

It soon became patently clear how Valda was using her money, of which there was obviously plenty. Normally Alabamans rated gypsies as "niggers" along with the blacks; hence the efforts to keep this one in Alabama seemed unnatural—unless it was somehow convenient to certain local officials.

Having exhausted all possible methods of procrastination as well as a good portion of her treasure, Valda was given fifteen days to surrender to the authorities. This she failed to do, and on January 11, a writ of arrest was issued by the Attorney General's office, and a three-state alarm went out—in Mississippi, Georgia, and Tennessee—in case she tried to jump bail.

On January 24, an apparently gratuitous appeal was made to the Governor by one of his legal advisers, to revoke his rendition warrant—a thing heretofore unheard of in such cases —and on January 25, the Governor granted the appeal, giving no notice to the office of the Attorney General. On January 27 the Assistant District Attorney in New York was apprised by the Associated Press of this development. He verified this fact by contacting the Assistant Attorney General in Alabama by phone, and was advised at the time that the Governor was to give no reason for his action. Referred to another of the Governor's legal advisers, the prosecutor was still left unsatisfied. On January 30, official notification was received of the Governor's action with no further explanation, and the New York authorities were informed that their papers would be returned in the future. Thus, after a full year's work, the New York police found themselves right back where they were in December, 1959, and again they prepared themselves for a period of anxious waiting.

Around March, 1961, the Adamses heard that Blackie's father, whom the couple had set up comfortably in Stockton, California, after Valda's New York coup, had died. Sergeant Forman in New York was similarly notified by a gypsy informant, and it was expected that Valda would show up in Stockton for the usual "pohamana," or feast of the dead, which was sure to be staged for her father-in-law according to gypsy custom. The San Diego police were alerted in case the pair attempted crossing the border into Mexico, as it was indicated they might. (This information had been supplied by an Alabama lawyer, evidently not on Valda's payroll, to Mrs. Mayer's lawyer in New York.)

The funeral was scheduled for March 26, and on March 18, New York received notice from San Diego that the Adamses had already been in Stockton from March 10 to 13, when they had left California for an unknown destination. But it seems that they soon returned, because, again on March 18, Lieutenant Bailey in New York received a call from a Sergeant Rumsey of the San Diego police, who said that he has just spoken personally to Blackie Adams on the telephone. Blackie, once more in a confident frame of mind, told Rumsey that he was now able to produce papers indicating that he was no longer wanted for any crime; he even invited the sergeant to his home. At Sergeant Forman's insistence, it was agreed that Rumsey should go there the following Sunday and arrest Valda. However, when he later reported to Forman, he said the Adamses were gone when he arrived. The departure certainly seemed odd in view of Blackie's expansive invitation, but these are mysteries never to be penetrated.

Although the police at this point could easily have been faced with another very long period of waiting, they had a bit of unexpected luck: On April 17, 1961, this message from Miami was received in New York: "Volga Adams, alias Mary Adamo, in custody here. Subject refuses to waive extradition. Arraignment Friday, April 21, 1961. [Signed] Michael Fox, Chief of Police." This information as to the Adamses whereabouts had been rather mysteriously acquired by a special agent of the FBI through a paid informant—probably another gypsy who had a private score to settle with the Adamses—and, having forwarded warrants and photos, New York instructed a Detective Green of the Miami Beach police force to arrest Valda.

Extradition papers were prepared at once and sent with the other information to a judge in Dade County, with a request for $100,000 bail. Valda, instead, was held on five hundred dollars bail, which she paid. Infuriated by this, Forman called the judge before whom the gypsy had been arraigned, and was surprised to discover that the man had a rather special interest in extradition cases: For years New York had been endeavoring to have *him* extradited to answer charges of being involved in a black-market-baby business operation in the East. This judge is no longer on the Florida bench.

On the same day that this latest communication was sent, Sergeant Forman signed certificates of the bench warrant, which were to be forwarded to Governor Rockefeller for his signature. During this time, Valda, who was happily living at Collins Avenue in Miami Beach with Blackie, made no attempt to leave the state; she was confident that there were yet many more legal maneuvers available to her and was curiously ignorant of the fact that, in the state of Florida, bail is denied once rendition proceedings are in effect.

Thus it was in a carefree mood that Valda appeared at an identification hearing in Tallahassee on April 21. She again refused to waive extradition proceedings and thus, in accordance with the Uniform Extradition Act, was to be held in jail upon receipt of the signed warrants from the Governor of New York. There was some delay, but finally the warrants were signed and received at the Governor's office, and a hearing was set for May 9, to establish the right of New York State to extradite Valda from Florida. Pending the outcome of the hearing, Valda was free on bail, and Sergeant Forman, knowing his subject, requested that a deputy be assigned to follow Valda after she left the Governor's hearing, so that she would not flee with Blackie to another state such as Alabama. The hearing was held as 2:30 P.M. before an aide of Governor Ferris Bryant, at which both Mrs. Mayer and Sergeant Forman testified.

Afraid that Valda and Blackie might give their deputy the slip, Sergeant Forman had first taken the precaution of running down to the parking lot with the Assistant District Attorney and pulling the hot wire out of the distributor of the gypsy's new black Cadillac—a move which proved to be justly motivated. Indeed, before the hearing, Valda had been seen rushing around the building trying to find the Governor's aide to persuade him to see things her way. She failed to do this, however, and at the close of the hearing, the Florida warrant was issued. Forman then dashed up the back stairs of the court building and found the Governor himself, who signed the warrant then and there. It was then sent directly to the sheriff's office, and a deputy sheriff was dispatched to bring Valda in. But she could not be found. The assembled pursuers descended at once to the parking lot, where, sure enough, they found Valda and Blackie bent over the hood of the Cadillac, cursing as they had never cursed before—at one another, the cops, and the world.

Valda was arrested and immediately arraigned before a judge from the Circuit Court of Leon County who ordered Valda held on no bail, pending a hearing on a writ of habeas corpus scheduled for May 12 at 9:00 A.M.

Up to now, things had gone as smoothly as could be expected, notwithstanding the time involved in getting through the normal legal procedures and red tape. But new complications arose as Valda and her attorney from Tallahassee assayed additional legal maneuvers, which were to delay further her ultimate rendition to New York. The decision to go through habeas corpus proceedings, as in Alabama, was the first step in the delay. Having begun by requesting an adjournment of the May 12 hearing till 4:00 P.M. that day, at which time the court was to hear testimony from Sergeant Forman and Mrs. Mayer, Valda's lawyer then requested a further extension until June 26. He stated that at this time he expected to have depositions from people in New York which would impeach the credibility of the witnesses testifying on behalf of New York State. The extension was granted, although Valda remained in jail, and once again the New York authorities and Mrs. Mayer flew back to New York empty handed.

This was on May 13, 1961. Valda remained in jail in Tallahassee for nearly nine months awaiting the outcome of her various appeals, but finally her spirit began to crack. Since she was not free on bail and was losing her appeals one after the other, she decided to give up and return to New York and start the whole thing over again on a new footing. Thus on November 6, 1961, Sergeant Forman again flew to Tallahassee to claim his prisoner. This time he got her.

Valda's trial generated an inordinate amount of interest. The press covered the proceedings thoroughly, and various elements of a curious public jammed the courtroom at Centre Street each day. It took a full week to form a jury, and the trial —one of the longest of its kind on record—lasted for seven weeks. It was a long, hard piece of work for the Assistant District Attorney who prosecuted the case; Valda still had plenty of fight in her, and she brought some bizarre elements into her defense.

On the opening day of the trial, the antagonists and their witnesses milled about in the hall outside the courtroom, flashing suspicious glances at one another. Valda turned to her counsel, her black eyes narrowing.

"Which is he?"

"Which is who?"

"The bum who's going to prosecute me."

"Over there. The guy with red hair."

"Get me one of those red hairs."

"What the hell for?"

"I'll put a curse on his damned head."

Amused, the lawyer strode over to the corner, where the prosecutor stood chatting with his colleagues. They knew each other, and the greeting was friendly.

"Hey, Bert, my client wishes to have one of your crimson locks, so she can throw a curse on you." His tough freckled face breaking into a grin, the prosecutor replied, "Well now, she may just win her case, but I'll be damned if I'm going to help her any." He walked briskly into the courtroom, chuckling. These gypsies were too much.

From the beginning, the defense leaned heavily on the aspect of ethnic prejudice to capture the sympathies of the jury. The twelve people ultimately chosen for the job represented a good cross-section of the population of New York City; it included many whose own national groups had not always been made to feel especially welcome on American soil, so counsel could assume that he was on firm ground in choosing this line.

Even during the voir-dire proceedings, the defense counsel had repeatedly let fall comments to the effect that the world hated gypsies and that the police especially hated gypsies. This was illustrated, he said, by the fact that the Pickpocket and Confidence Squad was known as the Gypsy Squad. The issue, he reminded the jury, was whether Mrs. *Adams* stole $118,273 from Mrs. Mayer, not whether a *gypsy* stole $118,273 from the lady. So determined was counsel, in fact, to minimize his client's ethnic association that he never referred to her by her gypsy name; "Mary," he held, was her true name—an alias bespeaking all that was innocent and benign—even though she was known to her friends and the police as Valda, and to Mrs. Mayer as Lillian. This tactic did not always work, for when two of the state's witnesses testified that they saw Valda at one of the locations on Madison Avenue and were able to pick her out of a seething crowd in the hall of the Criminal Courts building, the defense was obliged to respond that "all gypsies look alike."

The defense's second contention was that the whole thing had been a deliberate plot against her—a frameup engineered by James Forman of the Police Department, and Nick and George Adams, chiefs of the Machwayas, who had it in for Blackie. This, however, did not seem to make a great deal of sense, since the prosecution did not even try to implicate Blackie in the crime; besides, neither of them had seen Nick Adams since 1958.

Whereas the Mafiosi are pledged to vows of silence about one another's activities on pain of death, evidently no such loyalty binds the gypsies. One after the other the "co-conspirators" of Big George and Nick Adams took the stand against Valda and Blackie. A gypsy called Teenie Bimbo testified that he had heard that Blackie had made a big "score," and that Forman and Bailey of the squad each got $25,000. Valda, who maintained an apartment on Second Avenue, responded to this by screaming, "If I made a hundred-and-eighteen-thousand-dollar score, would I still be living at Fifteen Ninety-seven Second Avenue? Here I am. I haven't fled. Here I am!" This, after six years of pursuit by the police of twenty-three states. So vitriolic was Valda in her denunciation of Forman, her captor, that the prosecutor had continually to intervene with objections to the "outrageous vilification and slander of police officers of the city." She said, among other things, that she had been paying Forman a hundred dollars per month to avoid arrest, in addition to the payment of fines for fortune telling, which, up to this point, did not even total a hundred dollars. She accused him of virtually everything from adultery to bribery, as did Blackie when he took the stand, and the party got very rough indeed. All these charges were denied by Forman, his vindication being reflected in the plea that was formally entered in the case. Asked if he had ever been convicted of larceny, Blackie stood up in the stand, his face purple, and shouted, "I fought Bailey [head of the Gypsy Squad], and I'll fight you, any time, anywhere, so come on up here, and I'll fight you!"

There was testimony to the effect that signs reading MADAME LILLIAN—FORTUNES were seen in store-front windows in other towns where Valda was known to have lived, but she insisted that Lillian was a common name among gypsies. Efforts on the part of the prosecution to link Blackie's acquisition of a new Cadillac to the swindle elicited only a contemptuous snort from the raffish gypsy: He had always driven Cadillacs! But Mrs. Mayer first saw the car subsequent to the burn-up, when Blackie had collected Valda in it after the fateful meeting in Central Park. The same car had been observed near one of the store fronts with a trailer attached. Blackie grew suddenly inarticulate when the moment came to explain the source of the funds by which he paid for such conveniences. And finally, although it was established that a conviction was not needed to allow a tax deduction on her loss, the defense insisted that Mrs. Mayer—a scrupulous and conscientious tax payer for twenty years—had lost the money through some indefensible act of foolishness, and was simply trying to pave the way for a large reduction on her taxes.

The defense's trump card, however, was neither a trick of argumentation nor another perjuring gypsy, but a witness of a different stamp entirely. This witness was Hanna Sulner.

Hanna Sulner was the daughter and devoted pupil of Julius Fishof, a renowned European graphologist of the early twentieth century. (As one of the leading examiners of questioned documents in Europe, Fishof was asked to testify in the Dreyfus case, finding Dreyfus innocent against the opinion of the prosecution's man, Bertyens.) As a paid witness and handwriting expert, her role in this trial was to create doubts as to the authenticity of certain letters written by the gypsy to Mrs. Mayer. For Valda had used letters as well as the telephone to hold Mrs. Mayer in her thrall, and once she gave her a gold brooch with a card enclosed, bearing a sympathetic, if illiterate, message. All, claimed the defense, had been forged by Mrs. Mayer, or someone in her employ. In spite of the fact that there were some fifty-eight letters involved, which would make Mrs. Mayer one of the most prolific, if not the most adept, forgers of all time, Mrs. Sulner testified that there were several elements in the hand which precluded any possibility of its belonging to an untutored, semiliterate such as Mary Adams.

The prosecution, however, had been doing some homework, and had discovered that there might well be good reason to doubt Mrs. Sulner's integrity as a witness. She testified that she had studied criminology in Budapest and in Germany, and, having passed the tests, receiving her LL.D. and Ph.D. simultaneously, was sent to the Hungarian courts as an apprentice; she could not, however, recall the date on which any university degree had been bestowed upon her. She stated that she worked for the Minister of Justice in Budapest as a court and police expert between 1937 and 1944, but said later that she didn't have that job till 1945. As a graphologist, she had given reports to the Vatican, the American Bar Association, and the U.S. Labor Department, and had been retained by the governments of many countries; but she was not a member of any association of documentary experts. She had escaped from Hungary in 1949 after the Communist takeover and came to the United States in 1950.

Taking the stand as a defendant's witness, Mrs. Sulner read her answers from a paper until the prosecution made objection and required her to answer spontaneously. Things seemed to progress less smoothly then. Some of the cross-examination follows:

> Q. Is it not true that you worked for the Nazis previous to 1944?
> A. No.
> Q. As an interpreter for the Minister of Justice, did you not forge the document incriminating Cardinal Mindzenty?
> A. I was given a handwriting report to the Vatican—to Cardinal Spellman. I was brought to this country by the U.S. government. I was called to testify for the U.N. We escaped during the Mindzenty trial because they tried to force us to testify. We did not testify, my late husband and I. And my late husband, due to his refusal and our escape, was killed by the Communists in France. So don't try to disguise at a trial—to impress the jury— because you underestimate their intelligence.
> Q. In an affidavit, Mrs. Sulner, to the State Department and in a statement to Cardinal Spellman as it appears in his autobiog- raphy—
> A. I never heard of it. And I never wrote anything.
> Q. I will bring it down to you tomorrow, madam, including your affidavit. And I am asking you, madam, did you state, to the State Department of the United States of America—
> A. I never did.
> Q. That your husband, Lazlo Sulner, forged for two years—for two years!—the papers attributed to Cardinal Mindzenty, which in- carcerated him in prison in Hungary?
> A. This is the most ridiculous thing that you can bring up in court. Not one word is true.

The court, while admonishing the witness about being unresponsive and answering questions before they were com- pleted, cautioned the jury about collateral issues: If the witness answers in the negative, the line of questioning must be dropped and the implications of the question ignored.

The prosecution then produced a copy of the article written by Lazlo Sulner and printed in the New York *Herald Tribune* on July 6, 1950, describing his work for the Commu- nists, and their role in the Mindzenty affair. Hanna's explana- tion of the article was that her husband lied; he needed money, so he wrote the article to make a sensation. Unfortunately, he could not testify, for Lazlo Sulner was dead.

In the final tally, the question of Valda's many places of residence and business was the keystone in the edifice of incrimination which the prosecution had built around her. She said that at the time of the swindle, she wasn't even in New York but in Atlanta; the state held that she was. Apart from the two witnesses who had their fortunes told at the first Madison Avenue ofisa and recognized Valda in the court hallway, a mailman was produced who had seen her at the second location used later. Furthermore, they all remembered seeing Fatima, Valda's charming and unforgettable little niece. The mailman was also able to pick Valda out in the courtroom, in spite of the fact that she wore conventional clothes for the occasion, covered her head with a pale scarf, and arrived with an entourage of four friends, all dressed in traditional gypsy "working" clothes. (To avoid identification in Alabama, Valda had lost twenty-five pounds between the time she was released on $300,000 bail and her trial four months later.)

When it was shown that Blackie had signed the leases for both Madison Avenue store fronts, the defense asserted that, since he was one of the few gypsies who could write, he served as the renting agent for all the gypsies in his area; a gypsy called Duda Adams then got up and said it was she, not Valda, who originally told Mrs. Mayer's fortune—this, despite the fact that Mrs. Mayer had seen the gypsy at very close quarters at least ten times.

But it was Blackie, who once again upset the apple cart. A couple of gypsies called Lee had testified that Blackie and Valda had been at their home in Atlanta on October 19, when Mrs. Mayer's cash was supposed to have been burned up. Then, under a crisp cross-examination, centered on how he had paid for the $65,000 house he maintained there, Blackie mentioned the Bowery Savings Bank in downtown New York. Upon investigation it was found that a large cash deposit had been made by the Adamses at the Bowery at the time they were supposed to have been in Atlanta. Every time Blackie opened his mouth, things looked worse for his wife.

However, so convincingly, had Valda, alias Mary Adams, played the role of the innocent victim of prejudice and conspiracy, that at the end of many hours of deliberation, the jury failed to reach a verdict. A date was set for a second trial, and Valda went back to the Women's House of Detention.

By this time, the gypsy was utterly played out. Disgusted with prison, tired of conniving, and fresh out of tactical legal ploys, she hadn't the stamina to go through another trial. She pleaded guilty.

Valda was sentenced to two years, but since she had cumulatively served at least that in the various jails which had held her periodically during her six-year evasion of justice, she was freed. All concerned were stunned at the lightness of the sentence; after years of pursuit and months of litigation, Valda and Blackie drove off into the sunset in their Cadillac.

Chapter II

A Family Affair

On February 22, 1931, in the bustling mill town of Lawrence, Massachusetts, Mrs. Gerald Riley gave birth to her eleventh child, a little girl whom she named Ellen. She was glad because it was the same day that George Washington was born, and he did all right for himself.

Ellen was a thin, listless child whose efficiency in undertaking almost any task seemed to be seriously impaired by the extreme fragility of both her mind and her constitution. Pathologically nervous, she had an I.Q. of 77, a rating which classified her clinically as "dull normal." Her entire being seemed anemic; gazing out from lifeless, pale-gray eyes, she would frequently toss her head with a spastic, birdlike motion in an effort to rid her pallid brow of an unwelcome hank of colorless hair. Pallid, pale. That was Ellen Riley.

Ellen, who never grew taller than five feet, had no playmates other than her own brothers and sisters. With that many children running around the place, you didn't really need anybody else to play with, and anyway, her father didn't like his kids to bring friends home from school. If they did, he would only bombard them with insulting remarks and make them wish they'd never come. Ellen soon began to realize that the community at large did not think any more highly of her family than her father did of outsiders, a situation which she was not to understand fully until much later in her life. She and her brothers were referred to only in the most contemptuous and derogatory terms, and many of the older of "those Riley children" were known to the courts and social agencies before they were in their teens. Ellen wondered sometimes what "shanty Irish" meant and why people thought she was Irish for she had been born right there in Lawrence. She didn't even have red hair.

Mrs. Riley was certainly never one to indulge in affectionate demonstrations toward her children. Neither was Mr. Riley, who ran a bar and preferred the companionship of his customers. But Ellen did think it was a little bit peculiar that neither her father nor her mother seemed terribly upset when an older brother, Billy, was run over by a truck. They didn't even miss him for two days, but when he was found by some of the others and brought home by the police, Ellen cried for a long time.

Apart from Richard, the oldest, she had loved little Billy the best. Standing next to her at the funeral and looking down at the cheap casket, Richard said, "I think I'll probably end up the same way."

Richard was retarded, and Ellen couldn't help thinking now about all the times that her father and mother had yelled at him so frightfully and called him dreadful names in front of the others. One of the girls told her that when he was small, Ma had thrown Richard right out the second-floor window once, because he wouldn't stop crying. Other times she would tie a string around his penis and pull him around like that to make him stop wetting his bed.

Ellen answered: "Well, I guess we all will sooner or later."

Years later, Richard, who had just been released from prison after serving a short term for petty larceny, drowned himself in a creek in another town.

None of the Riley children was very good in school, nor were they popular there with either the children or the teachers.

So, despite the efforts of truant officers and the local priest, they attended as little as possible. The elder Rileys did not seem to mind this too much, for it left the children free to run errands for them.

Every few days, some of the children would be gathered together and driven into the center of town by one parent or the other in a moribund family jalopy. Each one had a list, compiled jointly by the parents, of things he or she was to steal from the store at which he would be deposited. Anyone who failed, received a beating upon his return home; success, on the other hand, brought smiles to Mother's lips and even elicted an occasional kiss or rare word of kindness and praise. It was worth keeping Ma happy, for the children yearned for affection, and the warmth she emanated in times of triumph over the world of commerce was lovely, and very sorely missed on other occasions.

Ma Riley—for that is what they called her, after Ma Barker, of Chicago—was clearly not an ordinary woman. A professional and very accomplished thief, she instructed all her children in the refinements of shoplifting from the time they were old enough to know what they were doing and understand that they must never be caught. This was another reason little Ellen had no need of playmates; all her spare time was taken up with stealing for her mother. For all practical purposes, Ma Riley had no conscience, no capacity to love, and a firm belief that she had an absolute right to whatever she wanted, whether she was able to pay for it or not; she resented having to pay for anything and, in fact, never did pay for anything which she was physically able to carry. Now that she had the children, she no longer needed to "work" much herself. The law was easier on kids anyhow.

By Ellen's own account, this attitude was not inspired by need, which is the natural consequence of extreme poverty. Riley's bar had made them enough money to buy the nine-room frame-and-shingle house in which they lived, and all the furnishings, none of which was secondhand. They ate off decent plates, and all the bathrooms worked. They had plenty to eat, because the children stole from the grocery stores at least three times a week and came home with enough stuff to feed a small army. And it wasn't as though Ma wanted the money to spend on other things; her clothes were nothing to write home about, and she drank only when she got mad about the way things were going or when Pa did something she didn't like. She just didn't like to pay.

Although she had never set foot in church in her life, as far as Ellen knew, Ma was not beyond lifting her eyes to the heavens and calling upon the Almighty to observe and pity her miserable condition, having to live with "Gerry the gorilla" and all these ungrateful stupid brats. Should the children fail to do her bidding, they would be treated to lengthy recitations from the Bible—or a facsimile thereof—and vivid, mind-shattering prophesies as to the fate that awaited them in the blazing regions of the underworld if they did not behave themselves. What was Right was what Ma wanted; Wrong was whatever irritated, disappointed, or otherwise displeased her.

It wasn't until Ellen was first caught stealing in a grocery store that she realized that other people had somewhat different ideas as to what was right and what was wrong. She knew that to get caught was wrong, but it evidently came as a considerable shock when she was given to understand that taking things was wrong too. On this particular occasion, Ma Riley was called at home and told to come right down to the grocery store to answer for this gangly twelve-year-old who had been caught trying to leave the store without paying for a big bagful of food. When Ma arrived, she found her youngest daughter—eyes filled with terror, dirty face streaked with tears—standing, or hanging, between a massive Irish cop and the corpulent, menacing figure of the owner of the store, who held her tightly by the arm. Ellen, still more apprehensive of the consequences of her failure than of those of her capture, derived some comfort from the authoritative figure of her mother bearing down upon them, armed to the teeth with righteous indignation.

The jolt came with the onrush of words that followed. With jaws agape and ears unable to accept what they were hearing, Ellen stood on melting legs while her mother explained the situation.

"Oh, Officer—Mr. Gambetti—I'm so terribly sorry! If you knew what my life is, trying to get some morals into these kids—I have eleven you know—well, I try, God knows, I try with every ounce of strength in me, but some of them are just—well, bad I guess, especially this one. You know, don't be too hard on her, because—well, I think she's not really right in the

head, you know what I mean? She probably didn't even know
what she was doing. She's only twelve, and I've got my hands
full, believe me!" And, turning on Ellen, eyes like flint: "How
on earth could you ever do a thing like this? Why, that's stealing! What am I going to do with you?" Then she struck the
astonished little girl across the face with her open palm, for the
benefit of Officer Murphy and Mr. Gambetti, who were not
particularly impressed. From that moment on, Ellen ceased to
feel that she had a mother.

"Look, Mrs. Riley," the cop said wearily, "you can count
yourself lucky. Mr. Gambetti here's got his stuff back, and he
don't want no trouble. Now take the kid home, and, remember,
next time she might learn better at the reformatory." And as
Ellen was dragged to the jalopy, she heard Mr. Gambetti shouting in the background, "Rileys! I know you. I'm looking out
when you come around. You no-good trash!"

The only good that came of this incident was that Ma
Riley was fearful of using Ellen again, at least in the near future.
She was so disgusted with the child anyway that she let her just
sit by herself in the yard or wander alone in the swamps and
factory yards, hoping, Ellen felt sure, that she would get run
over like little Billy.

When she reached the age of thirteen, Ellen quit going
to school entirely. She was seriously anemic and was eventually
given a permit so that she could legitimately remain absent from
school "due to illness."

One day, in her fifteenth year, while wandering about
alone in her desultory manner, she found herself in the midst of
a housing development and became interested in a group of men
who were hammering and sawing on the framework of a new
house. Construction. That was her Uncle Frank's business, she
thought, and wondered if he were there. Stumbling over the
large clods of unseeded earth, she moved closer to the structure.
One of the men working on the roof noticed her standing there
watching them with her mouth open. He thought to himself that
she was not really very good-looking, but that she would certainly look better, if she closed her mouth. Not a bad figure, if
you don't mind them a bit skinny.

"Are you looking for somebody?" Ellen, shading her eyes
against the sun, lifted her pale gaze to the roof. The man who
had spoken to her had crisp black hair and a dark face. His T-

shirt was dirty and stained with sweat, but Ellen saw that he was well built and reasonably young, no more than twenty-five or so.

"Oh, well, I thought maybe my uncle was here," she replied vaguely.

"What's his name?"

"Riley."

"Nobody called Riley here. Did he tell you he was working here?"

"No."

"Well then, how come you thought he was here?"

"He's in the construction business."

The man threw his head back and laughed. It occurred to Ellen that she had never seen a really good set of teeth before, including her own. Maybe they just looked better because the man had such dark skin.

"There are a lot of other jobs around that people are working on, you know," he concluded.

"Yeah. I guess that's right." Ellen laughed and lowered her head. Feeling silly and somewhat humiliated, she went away. The man waved to her.

The next day, she went back to the house, and the next, and the one after that. She liked watching the men at work and talking to the young man with the nice teeth. It gave her something to do and somewhere to go. One day he told her to come later in the day when they were about to finish work, because the boss didn't like people hanging around talking to the boys while they were on the job. She did.

His name was João Souza. Ellen laughed because the name sounded funny. Juan, or Johnny as he was now known, explained that his parents were from Brazil in South America, which was why he had a name like that. He liked making Ellen laugh; she seemed to think everything he said was amusing, and it lighted up her face a bit. Ellen did not actually think everything Johnny said was all that funny; she was simply basking in the unaccustomed warmth and kindness of this simple man, and soaking it up, storing it away, against the day when it might be removed from her.

Soon they were seeing a lot of each other, and Ellen liked him so much that she let him make love to her whenever he wanted to. She didn't mind it so much either. Johnny told her that he was married and had quite a lot of children but that he was unhappy with his wife and wanted to leave her. She had always been a good, moral woman, as far as he knew—clean, good housekeeper, and good mother. But while he was in the Army during the Korean war he heard that she had been fooling around, and after that he was a changed man. Ellen thought she had better not tell him about her mother, and stealing and all, until later. If he felt that way about his wife, what would he think about somebody who had been stealing for the last five years of her life?

This went on for nearly four years, during which time Ellen was again doing a great deal of shoplifting at her mother's insistence, but also, she had to admit, picking up a few pretty things now and again for herself in order to please Johnny. One evening, casually, innocently, with no ulterior motives, he asked Ellen where she got so many nice things, and much to his astonishment, the floodgates were opened, and he heard the whole sordid story. Ellen, sure that this would bring about the end of this comforting, consuming relationship upon which she had grown so dependent, wailed like some Celtic widow keening over the grave of her dead infant as the horrified young man tried to soothe and calm her.

"What a way to bring up little kids," he ventured. "I never heard of anything like that in my life. Now you just quiet down there, and everything'll be all right. Don't you worry about it now."

As the realization slowly penetrated Ellen's inadequate mind that her lover was not going to beat her up and throw her back to the wolves, she put an end to her howling and managed a feeble smile of relief through the sobs.

That year Johnny left his wife, and Ellen moved in with him, elated at the prospect of leaving the rabbit warren of turmoil and depravity which had been her home for eighteen years. If she stole now, it was for herself not for Ma Riley, although Johnny tried his best to persuade her to stop. She knew it was wrong, and that she should do everything in her power to get over it, but she could not restrain herself; after all, they were poor, much more so than her own family. She would frequently make "New Year's resolutions" to the effect that her stealing days were over, but she had only to enter the seductive confines of a store, and the familiar, powerful compulsion to steal would possess her. Sometimes, to test herself, she would leave the indispensable appurtenances of her trade at home—the oversized shopping bags and the "booster bloomers," * the use of which her mother had so carefully taught her—and go into a shop relatively unencumbered and with money in her pocket to pay. But it was no good. She was not able to steal as much, but she stole nevertheless, concealing the stuff in her handbag, pockets, and beneath her clothes. Johnny was patient during these lapses, and employed kindness and reason where violence had failed, but sometimes he would chastise Ellen severely, though more out of fear than anger. One day she had to get caught; the law of averages was decidedly against her.

Ellen and Johnny were good to each other, and happy, in spite of all their difficulties, and she bore him five illegitimate children. She still saw her mother, although they no longer went on "sprees" together; her older sister Mary was now the favorite companion in crime, and they ridiculed Ellen for having gone moral on them—a cruel joke, considering her marital status.

The blackest cloud on their horizon was the Commonwealth of Massachusetts, which pursued Johnny like the Furies because he was not sending enough money to his wife and her five children by him, and which prosecuted them both relentlessly for "lewd and lascivious cohabitation." Ellen was first arrested on this charge four years after she began living with Johnny, and once she was arrested for using the telephone for obscene purposes—the basis of which was a rather overly explicit but loving long-distance telephone call to Johnny when she was away in Fitchburg, visiting friends. During this period she was also arrested for larceny on four occasions in various towns but was paroled each time, two of the thefts having been assessed at under a hundred dollars and therefore constituting the lesser charge of petty larceny.

At this point, two aspects of this case might be considered in order to render more realistically the true coloration of this girl's life. One is the obvious puritanism of the local laws in regard to sex misdemeanors—not to mention the attitudes of some of the locals who had dealings with Ellen and Johnny—and

* A shoplifter is known among her peers as a booster, and booster bloomers, voluminous pants held up by suspenders, are frequently worn underneath ordinary clothes, serving as a storage spot for stolen goods until the thief is safely home.

the other is the extent to which the community in general "complies" with Ellen's criminal intentions.

One must concede certain points at the outset: It was entirely irresponsible of Johnny to abandon his wife and five children and become delinquent in the payments for their support, whatever the reasons. Ellen should not have stolen, nor should she have moved in with Johnny and begun producing children with him, despite the fact that he was trying to get a divorce so that he might marry her. In short, these were not "nice" people in the middle-class sense, and their behavior was in many ways thoroughly offensive.

Still, these two people did evidently love each other quite genuinely in their own way and had lived together faithfully for nearly nine years—a phenomenon which, for people who had been harshly treated by a life that gave them nothing to start with, is rare enough. The state was particularly hard on them as to the matter of their children, and at the instigation of the local priest, the case was referred to a charitable institution, with a view to having them removed from the Souza home and placed in an orphanage. There was no question that these children were loved by their parents and that they were provided with a relatively stable home, but to the unyielding Puritan mind it is better to subject five small children to the emotional poverty of institutional life than to leave them in the care of people who had neglected to avail themselves of the marriage ritual.

In fact, it was Father Murphy's judgment that, as the Riley children had all clearly been the products of "lust and not love," sex being, in his view, thoroughly incompatible with love —they could none of them be expected ever to become decent parents. The elder Rileys had had little feeling for their brood— a fact disputed by no one—therefore, he reasoned, Ellen probably had none for hers. It was further observed by Ellen's parole officer that the baby-sitters with whom the children were left when Johnny and Ellen occasionally went out, had bleached hair and were frequently found in the company of a man—both clear indications of their moral corruption. During Ellen's first stay in prison, it was decided that "inasmuch as Souza is on probation for nonsupport of his legitimate children, the probation officer could not permit him to associate with our Subject by coming here [jail] to visit her."

Ma Riley, as might have been expected, was no help whatsoever. When visited by the parole officer in charge of Ellen, Ma went to endless lengths to justify her own attitudes, citing the children's "religious upbringing" and her many trials and tribulations. Life was hard. Here was Ellen doing all these terrible things, she knew not why, and one of her other daughters, Florence, was living with a nigger and having one little black bastard after another, bringing shame upon them all. The police often remarked in regard to Florence, who was frequently arrested for drunkenness, that "she wouldn't have a chance in this town anyway, so long as she's known to be one of the Riley children."

Thus Ellen had several things working against her at all times: the profound weaknesses in her own character; the ruthless spirit of New England puritanism, the pious primness of an Irish-Catholic priest, and the prevailing local prejudice against "those Riley kids," which had dogged her over the years. Through it all, Ellen and Johnny stuck together, and heaven only knows how.

The mystifying aspect of Ellen's case lies in the fact that while the community at large was always ready to send her to the stocks because she lived with a married man, it was often perfectly willing to overlook the fact that she was an incorrigible thief.

One of the many things which Ma Riley taught her children was to carry enough money to pay for what they stole, for the store would rather have the money, should they catch you stealing, than report you to the police. This was often demonstrated to Ellen as a child when she and her mother were caught loading up by the store detective. Her mother always smiled till she thought her cheeks would crack, and said that she always meant to pay, and as soon as the store manager saw the money, he forgot about the police. Sometimes the police would already be there, but Ma never worried; even if she didn't have enough money, the store owner was satisfied most of the time just to have the stuff back, for—as he would explain to the cop—going into court was time consuming and produced bad publicity for the store.

When Ellen started on her own, she was already so infamous that every store detective in town knew her on sight. She

often went to work in other towns, and several times was arrested on these trips, but she was always paroled. When she was
finally sent to a reformatory in 1955, it was after over fifteen
years of stealing. Clearly, in a society sincerely concerned with
the prohibition of wrongdoing, every store owner would prosecute every thief every time, and let the judge decide whether
the individual merited forgiveness or special consideration.

The judges know that each time a person evades taxes—
regardless of the apparent injustices of the tax system—and each
time someone offers a "tip" to a police officer for overlooking
some minor infraction, or foolishly carries a package across an
international border for somebody else, or supports a black
market in order to get the goods he wants, or closes an eye to
some illegal operation because it brings income into the community, he provides the necessary underpinnings for criminal
activity. Those who are complacent or stupid enough to allow
children to wander around among strangers unsupervised, who
leave their jewels and money on top of dressers in hotel rooms
as well as at home, who walk in empty parks or on unlighted
streets late at night, who send money through the mails for
products they have not seen, who are careless about how they
carry their credit cards, who fail to lock their doors—are all guilty
of contributory negligence. Unfortunately, people are not so
much indignant about crime because it is harmful to the ethical
structure of society as they are infuriated when it harms them
personally. Perhaps the judges should spend some time admonishing the "victims," and never mind about Ellen Riley's sexual
idiosyncrasies.

There were several periods, when on parole, during which
Ellen made a tremendous effort to straighten out, primarily for
Johnny and the children. Her parole reports were frequently
very encouraging, and showed that she was establishing a good
rapport with the parole officer and listening to what she said.
Her intent, however, was stronger than her will, and soon she
was at it again. She landed this time in a women's reformatory.
She was disgusted with herself for having failed everybody, and
infuriated when, for reasons cited earlier, the authorities would
not allow Johnny to see her. She missed him and the children,
and worried terribly about them, even though she knew that
good friends were looking in on them and helping in every way

they could. Poor, besotted Florence came to see her a couple of times, and Jimmy, her favorite remaining brother, but apart from this, her family helped her not at all.

During her first months in prison, Ellen was defiant, uncooperative, and thoroughly miserable. Paroled that same year, she was able to get a job, with the help of the prison authorities, in a factory and at a decent salary—a job which she managed to stick to for almost two years. She left only when Johnny's long-awaited divorce was finally granted, and they were able to get married, which was, for Ellen and Johnny, truly the happiest day in their dismal lives. Thus, as befits a bride with five children, Ellen stopped working and became a matron.

In the next two years, Ellen had two more children, and the family budget was squeezed beyond its limits, in spite of the fact that Johnny worked steadily, weather permitting, and brought home decent pay. Ellen did not wish to be tempted to start stealing again, so she arranged to have friends help look after the children, and Johnny's eldest daughter, who had come to live with them, agreed to take charge of the brood while Ellen went back to work. This time she found a job in a large textile factory at a salary of sixty-five dollars per week, which contributed enormously to the welfare of the family. Her employers, moreover, found her performance, ability, and conduct very good, and it looked as though the Souzas' fortunes were at last directed on an upward course.

But it was not long before Ellen discovered that she was pregnant an eighth time, and as she approached her seventh month, she was again forced to leave her job, this time in an exceedingly depressed state of mind. She felt beaten and victimized by powerful forces over which she apparently had no control and which were clearly malicious insofar as she was concerned. Curiously enough—and what is so frequently the case with people of this type—Ellen to this day is unable to see the connection between the constant arrival of babies and the generally depressed configurations of her life; she loves her children, and it would never have occurred to her that there was such a thing as too many or that having children involved a rather broad social responsibility. This kind of reasoning or basic understanding is simply not within the scope of an Ellen or a Johnny, even without the religious barriers to an artificially limited family.

This time Johnny's son went out to work, as he was now

old enough, but Ellen remained sullen, nervous, and broken in
spirit. She just didn't see how anything was ever going to come
right "with their luck," and no matter how hard she tried,
nothing went any better. Everything and everyone was against
her.

While in this bitter and dangerous mood, Ellen received
a visit from her sister Mary. Ellen had never liked Mary, whom
she had always considered "as wicked as Ma," and wondered
why, after all this time, she was bothering to come and see her
—like a buzzard come to pick at the corpse, Ellen thought rue-
fully. Sensing that Mary's appearance would probably bode no
good for her, Ellen was inhospitable and testy. Choosing to
ignore her sister's hostility, Mary cheerfully came to the point.

"Hey, listen, El, there's a monster sale on at Lomar's,
an' you know how it is with all them dames tearin' around in
there, nobody knows what the hell is goin' on. Ma an' me were
goin' to go there an' have a real spree, but now she's sick. . . ."

"What happened, did somebody finally slip her some
arsenic, or what?" Ellen interrupted.

"Ha, ha. That's a good one, I must say, but listen, why
don't you come on down with me an' pick up a few things for
the kids? What the hell, you could use it from the looks of
things. I mean, let's face it, it ain't goin' to do nobody no harm
around here to get a few new rags. Then we can pick up some
stuff for you at the A & P, you know—nice things, like a pie
an' stuff."

Much as Mary revolted her, Ellen couldn't help thinking
how nice it would be to see little Amy in a clean dress and the
babies in some cute nightgowns without spitup all over them;
she might even be able to grab something for herself, so that
Johnny wouldn't look at her like the creature from the black
lagoon, or something.

"I don't want to steal anymore," she said unconvincingly.

"Oh, for crissake, you been stealin' all yer goddam life.
Now you really need stuff an' you won't steal? You know, you
never was much on brains, kiddo, but I think yer gettin' worse."

"Why don't you drop dead?"

Mary could see she was getting nowhere on this tack, so
she forced a kind of smile onto her pinched, unpleasant face and
said in soothing tones: "Listen, El, do it for the kids. You know,
Ma an' me, we're always talkin' an' sayin' how good you been,

tryin' to straighten out an' all that, but face it, kiddo, them kids needs things, an' so do you. It's not right to hold out on 'em now, even for good reasons." It made sense, and Ellen fell for it; she agreed to go.

It was October, and the dawn brought one of those clear brilliant quiet days for which New England is known. You could hear a bell ringing in a church tower five miles away, and the dying leaves rioted in kaleidoscopic color. A cerulean sky without a trace of cloud arched over the whole, as young dogs and children leaped, shrieking, in and out of piles of fallen leaves carefully raked by their owners. Nevertheless, Ellen was overcome with an unaccustomed foreboding, her whole body embued with a reluctance which weighed on her and slowed her movements as she dressed that morning and went through the ritual feeding process. Johnny was puzzled, for although Ellen had been dull and unresponsive for several months, he sensed something new in her demeanor today.

"What's with you, El?"

"Nothin'. What should be with me?"

"I dunno. Just thought there might be somethin'. Who was that came to the house yesterday? Jimmy said somethin' about somebody. . . ."

"Oh, that was just Mary. . . ."

"What's she want?"

"I dunno."

"Well, why'd she come then?"

"Jesus! Will you eat your damn breakfast and stop goin' at me!"

"I'm not goin' at you, El. . . ."

"Well just eat your breakfast. Nothin's happenin'."

"Okay, El."

At ten o'clock Mary showed up in Ma's new car. She honked the horn, and Ellen went to the door, the weight of apprehension increasing on her chest. She turned away to the interior of the house again, not sure for what reason, and, noticing the quizzical expression on the face of her friend Sylvia Fagan, gave her a few additional and quite unnecessary instructions about the children's lunch. Then she went out and got into the car.

"Hi, El," Mary piped. "Gee, ain't this fun to be goin' out again? Just like old times, hey, El?"

"Yeah, just like old times."

As they approached the center of town, Ellen all at once did feel some of the old excitement coming back into her veins. After all, things couldn't really get much worse, and besides, didn't they all deserve it? She'd get something for Johnny too. He'd be so pleased, maybe he'd forget she stole it. He'd get upset, if he knew. . . .

They were sitting now in the big parking lot provided by the store for its customers, discussing their modus operandi. In agreement, they got out of the car and walked toward the store; Ellen went in the door nearest the parking lot, while Mary went around and entered from the street side. Once inside, surrounded by all the pretty, useful things, the apprehension left her, and a joyful anticipation came flooding in. She had forgotten how long it had been since any of them had had anything new, and how fresh new merchandise looked and smelled.

Each sister had a large shopping bag on her arm, and entering at opposite ends of the store, they began drifting round the various counters, picking things up, peering at price tags, pawing over the merchandise along with the other women, all keen to find a rare bargain or two. Every so often an odd piece would be popped into the shopping bag while the hunt went on. Somewhere along the way, Ellen and Mary each got hold of a plastic container with a lid on it; one had a diaper pail; the other, a covered trash barrel. They had agreed to leave after twenty minutes, and as the time approached, each one shifted what she had taken from the shopping bag into the barrel, with the exception of one or two items. They then headed for separate checkout counters. Ma always said, to divert suspicion, always pay for a couple of things. Ellen bought the diaper pail, one little girl's dress and a pair of boy's overalls; Mary bought the trash barrel and two men's shirts, which would go to Pa, along with some other stuff inside the barrel. Nobody thought to look inside the barrels.

Once outside the store, a person cannot be stopped and searched unless the arresting officer has a warrant or has actually seen the goods being stolen and taken, concealed, from the store; otherwise the officer risks a charge of false arrest. Mary spotted the store detective near the checkout counters, and as soon as she was outside the store, she headed straight for the parking lot, where she was to wait for Ellen. Ellen, however, had not

seen the man standing near the far counter observing her movements, or she would not have stopped just outside the door to
stuff her shopping bag hurriedly into the diaper pail before head-
ing for the car. The man watched her through the glass doors,
and as Ellen lifted the lid, he caught a glimpse of the other
things—for which she had not paid—inside the pail. This barrel
caper was turning into a real favorite with the boosters, he
thought, lifting the phone, which would summon a policeman
who patrolled the block in front of the store.

Halfway between the store and the car they stopped her.

"Let's see what you got in that pail there, lady."

"What d'you mean? Listen, I got to get home to my
kids. I got seven kids an' . . ."

"Lady, you didn't pay for the stuff in that pail. Detective Lannon here saw you."

Ellen was completely panicked, just as in the old days
when she was caught and Ma would come down and paste her
in the mouth and tell the cops she didn't know anything about
it. It was as though all the wind had been knocked out of her;
she could hardly get her breath.

"Where's your car, lady?"

"Right there," Ellen replied, pointing, hardly able to
get the words out. By God, Mary had got her into this mess, and
if she was going to be run in, so was Mary. She knew it was
no good denying that the stuff was stolen, because there were
only three items on her sales check instead of fourteen, and the
dick had seen her anyway. Mary was smoking and looking at
her watch, her back to the scene in which Ellen was now involved. Her barrel had been deposited on the floor by the back
seat of the car. As she heard the door open, she heaved a great
sigh of relief, then tightened when she saw the blue uniform.

"Hey, El, I thought—Jesus! What's goin' on here? For
crissake, El, what've you done? What are these guys doin' here?"

The officer had by this time observed the trash barrel on
the floor in back of Mary's seat, and noticed part of a suede coat
sticking out from under the lid.

"How much did all that stuff cost you, missus?"

"What stuff? I don't know what the hell you're talkin'
about. You got a warrant? You ain't got no right to go bustin'
around in my car without a warrant. I don't know what she's
done, but I ain't done nothin', an' I'm gettin' outa here." With

that Mary started the engine. Ellen had remained silent during all this, staring at the ground in her listless way, resigned to the inevitable treachery.

"Just a minute, lady. You ain't goin' no place. Hey, ain't you one of them Rileys?"

"Yeah, an' so's she. So what?"

"So you just wait here with the detective, and I'll be back."

Detective Lannon eyed them balefully and leaned against the car parked next to them, pulling on a cigarette. Ellen sat in the front seat of the car, mute, gazing at nothing, while Mary told the detective what she thought of the Police Department and the world in general. The detective looked at her from time to time, his expression filled with disgust, as though he were observing the last twitchings of a disemboweled frog in a laboratory.

Within fifteen minutes the police officer returned with a warrant. The barrel was opened, and Mary, who could not explain away the contents, said that she had thrown her check in the gutter as soon as she left the store. She never saw any point in keeping checks anyway. The local police were contacted and responded immediately. One of them suggested that if Mary was innocent, she surely would not mind coming down to the station with them while they questioned her sister. Ellen was transported there under arrest.

At the police station it was discovered that both women had a long record of arrests for boosting, although Ellen had a longer record than Mary, who had been more successful in evading the law all her life. Ma, the worst of them all, had never spent a day in jail, a circumstance which Ellen now viewed with increasing bitterness as she thought of poor Johnny and all those miserable kids.

Ellen and Mary shared the services of an attorney well versed in the saga of the Riley family, and he did his best for them. Several days after the arrest, both women were arraigned before a Judge Potter, who was also no stranger to the dreary history of the Rileys, and indicted. Both pleaded guilty. Bond was set at two hundred dollars apiece, and then a very curious thing happened. Mary, as expected, admitted to the finding of guilty and was fined a mere twenty-five dollars. But Ellen, overcome with rage, frustration, and panic over the future of her

family, suddenly decided to change her plea to not guilty, over
the objections and protestations of her lawyer.

"What the hell do you think you're doing?" he raged.
"You haven't got a chance in the world of beating this rap."

"It wasn't my fault! Mary made me do it, and Ma before
her. It isn't my fault."

"Are you out of your mind? That doesn't cut any ice in
court. You took the stuff with your own hands and were caught
with it. Now how do you think you're going to get away with
that? For God's sake, Ellen, be sensible like your sister. Take the
fine, and be done with it."

"Where am I goin' to get the money? He'll fine me
more."

"We'll get the money," the lawyer said, moving his head
from side to side in an attitude of despair and frustration. "That
isn't the point. Don't you see that if you stand trial, a lot of
things are going to be brought out about you which are going
to sound terrible to a jury? You're crazy!"

"Don't say that to me!" Ellen snapped, her normally
dull gaze blazing for a moment. "I'm pleading innocent because
I *am* innocent." And, dropping her voice to a whisper, she
amended: "I should be innocent."

The trial, of course, was a disaster. Unable to bring herself to say any of the dreadful things about her family that were
burning in her mind and consuming her thoughts, she sat, answering the questions mechanically in a barely audible voice, as
the state demolished her "case." She was found guilty and sentenced to prison for an indefinite period. She appealed, but the
sentence was sustained.

It was made clear to Ellen that the purpose of the indefinite sentence was to leave open the possibility of early parole
—a condition which depended largely on her behavior and attitude while in prison. She said she would certainly try. Once
again, Johnny and his eldest girl, with the help of kind and sympathetic friends, took over the job of mothering Ellen's brood.
A few of the younger children unfortunately had to be sent to
live with friends or foster parents until Ellen came back home
again. Johnny said that if he ever got his hands on Mary, he'd
hang her eyeballs from the chandeliers. Four-year-old Jamie
said, "What's a chandeliers?"

During the early part of her prison term, Ellen allowed

herself to wallow in despair and self-pity. She was profoundly disgusted with herself for having "let everybody down" again, and was, more than ever, the victim of a crippling sense of inferiority. Unstable, tearful, and defensive, she was always quick to tattle on other prisoners and interfere in other people's affairs. Although highly critical, she was utterly incapable of admitting to faults in herself and would easily resort to tears to gain the sympathy of any critic, regardless of how well meaning.

It was suggested to Ellen that she pay a visit to the prison psychiatrist, and although at first she scoffed at the idea, she agreed to go just to break the monotonous routine of prison life and have something to laugh about with some of the other women.

This, however, turned out to be one of the most successful human contacts Ellen was ever to have. By a stroke of luck, this doctor appeared to Ellen as everything that a figure of authority should be. He was knowledgeable without making her feel inferior and ignorant, understanding without pitying her, and able to criticize her without harshness. She came to look forward to their talks each week almost as much as Johnny's visits, which were frequent.

The doctor explained to Johnny that Ellen's bitterness about being brought up the way she had been was related to her apparent inability to stop stealing—that the stealing reflected her feelings, whether real, anticipated, or imagined, of deprivation. He admitted that at first he had a very hard time with Ellen and hadn't been able to elicit anything from her but the utmost contempt. But gradually, as she came to trust him—a thing which life had taught her never to do—they began to make progress, and now she was doing very well. Much of her ability to improve and the motivation for so doing, the doctor pointed out, could be attributed to Johnny's loyalty and love, not to mention his rather extraordinary patience. Johnny was embarrassed and lowered his head to stare at the worker's cap, which he turned nervously over and over again in his hands.

"Well," he said, "you know, she's not so bad, really, and in a funny kind of way, she's—well, she's—made me happy too. I hope she can come home soon."

After nearly a year, during which Johnny came faithfully every Saturday to see his wife, bringing one or the other of the children, Ellen began to take much more responsibility onto herself and to blame others less for all her troubles. She would not see Mary if she came to pay a visit at the prison, for she felt that Mary only came to laugh at her and to gloat over her stupidity at having let herself get put in jail. There were other people she wouldn't see either, but for different reasons. She was ashamed, for example, about the Fagans, for they had always been understanding and reliable friends to her and Johnny, and she had disappointed them all terribly. It was Sylvia Fagan who babysat for her the day she and Mary went off together, and who subsequently wrote her the following note in prison, one lonely, dark, February day:

> DEAR EL:
> Just a few lines to let your [sic] know we all thinking of you and missing u very much. Ted and I are very sorry to know about what happened and all. When we found out, it was as if we lost a part of our family.
> I know you and I were never really very close, but you know that we have always thought of your [sic] as someone near to us. I know we never showed it, but how do you tell someone how you feel about them. And that includes Johnny and all your kids.
> Well, everything here is just about the same. Ted went down to see Johnny, and he looks lost and sad. We want to come to see your [sic] and your Johnny said he would let us know when.
> I am looking forward to seeing you, as I do miss your hollering. Ho, ho! All kidding aside, I hope to see you soon.
> Well, El, I have to close now, so take things in stride because time does pass no matter how slow.
> May God keep you and protect you,
>
> Your Friends Always,
>
> TED AND SYLVIA

So chagrined was Ellen about what these people must have thought of her that she refused even to read any correspondence from them. She has never read this letter, fearing, perhaps, that it too would mock her.

After fifteen months had elapsed, it was decided that Ellen had responded so well to psychiatric help, and her emotional stability seemed so greatly improved, that she should be paroled. It was hoped that, being an intensely susceptible, dependent type, she would be able to establish a close working relationship with her parole officer, who would see to it that she stayed on "the straight and narrow." On Christmas Eve, her entire family having been reunited, Ellen went home.

A few days before she left she explained in an interview how she felt now about her family. Neither her mother nor her father had bothered to come to visit her at any time during her stay in prison. The outcast Florence had come, and her brother Jimmy, and that was about it. Mary was just like Ma, she maintained, and she had heard that Mary was already teaching her twelve-year-old daughter to boost. Ellen still feels that people probably talk about her a lot and say awful things, but she thinks that she has good children, thanks to Johnny and the older kids, who have helped a lot, and she wouldn't want them to turn out the same as she and her brothers and sisters for anything in the world. The annoying thing, she muses, is that she never meant anyone any harm; there was something so impersonal about stealing from a store. She would never steal from an actual person, especially somebody she had met and liked.

Ellen realizes that the big difference between her and her mother is that she loves her children, whereas her mother had no feeling for her offspring whatsoever. Still, she cannot "hate" Ma, although she knows that she is "wicked," a word Ellen uses a great deal in speaking of Ma Riley and some of the other "bad ones" in her family. She has often told the police about her mother, but they say that there is nothing they can do about her until she is actually caught; and "that," says Ellen, "will be a cold day in hell." Asked whether she would testify against her mother in court, should the opportunity ever present itself, Ellen looked up and, smiling her wan, humorless smile, said, "You know something? After everything she did to me and all of us, I still couldn't do it. It's not her fault there's no love in her. And after all . . . she *is* my mother, you know?"

Chapter III

La Libératrice

THE morning of May 16, 1963, was clear and sunny in Quebec, and the mailman, feeling chipper at the arrival of spring, whistled a jaunty French tune as he approached the mailbox at the corner of St. Catherine and Hallowell streets, in the fashionable Westmount section of Montreal. Upon opening the box, he was startled by the sight of a bundle of identical, symmetrical sticks tied together with cord, a cheap pocket watch attached to the bundle, lying on top of a pile of letters. He stared at it for a few moments; then, turning abruptly, he ran into the nearest house and requested permission to use the telephone.

In a matter of minutes, a group of police and firemen had arrived, bringing with them Sergeant Major Leslie Walters, a demolitions expert serving in the Royal Canadian Engineers. Ropes were looped gingerly over the mailbox and pulled, from a considerable distance, until the box tipped over. The bomb, consisting of several sticks of dynamite wrapped in cord, rolled out of the box onto the sidewalk. It lay there, threatening, the face of the timing device casting shafts of deflected sunlight upon all who watched silently as Sergeant Major Walters, a rugged, stocky man of forty-two, wearing a stethoscope, walked toward it, picked it up, and with one huge hand, threw it into an empty field nearby. "All right," he said. "Where's the next one?"

The police took him to another mailbox on the corner of Claremont Avenue and Sherbrooke Street. At this stop, to save time, Walters simply reached into the chute at the bottom of the box, felt the bomb, and dismantled it by touch; the first one had taught him how it was built, and the stethoscope had told him it was still alive. Once disarmed, this one was thrown into the back seat of the police car.

As they moved on to the corner of Lansdowne and Westmount Avenues, Walters said, almost abstractedly, "You know, these things contain three pounds of dynamite. We're all getting too close." So when they arrived at the corner, all but Walters moved back between fifty and seventy-five feet from the mailbox.

By this time, word had got around in the immediate neighborhood that something rather exciting was going on in Westmount, and the curious citizenry began to gather. Minor bombings had been occurring for ten weeks or so, but people were intrigued rather than fearful, for thus far the only consequence had been a certain amount of property damage. The Separatist movement was, after all, a bit of a joke.

A woman paused, urged by her two fascinated children, before entering her house on Westmount Avenue—not ten feet from where the demolitions group was standing. With caught breath, they watched as the stolid little man with the stethoscope around his neck, who showed signs now of apprehension, reached into the mailbox.

The next thing of which the woman was aware was a large piece of metal flying over the heads of her children, grazing her own shoulder, and falling with a clatter to the pavement behind them. The children looked up at their mother, round-eyed. Without looking back, she hustled them into the house, then ran to an upstairs window and pulled aside a film of curtain.

The smoke was drifting gently away with the warm spring breeze, and she saw the man lying in masses of blood next to the place where the mailbox used to be. The others, who had turned away, wrapping their arms about their heads for protection from the blast, were just lowering their hands slowly, and turning toward the corner. In seconds they had rushed to the side of their friend. "Walt" Walters had been virtually torn apart by the bomb as it exploded in his hands, but he had somehow failed to die. Chunks of the mailbox had flown in all directions, and Walters lay there crumpled, his hands still inside what was left of it.

At lunch the children asked, "Was the man hurt, Mummy?"

"Yes, he was," the mother replied. "Come on now, eat your soup."

"Aren't you going to eat with us?"

"No, darling, I'm not hungry just now."

The bomb which dismembered Sergeant Major Walters was the sixth one to explode in Westmount between three o'clock and ten o'clock that morning, and it was not the last.

In January of the next year, 1964, there were a series of armed robberies, attributable again to the Separatists and their desperate need to raise money for their revolution. The most serious of these was the armed looting of the Fusiliers Mont Royal Armory, from which guns and rifles were stolen to supply the revolutionaries. Since the Separatist movement was divided, as with most revolutions, into subgroups characterized by varying degrees of militancy, no one knew exactly who was to blame. The FLQ (Front de Libération Québecois) had admittedly been behind the mailbox plot and the robbery of the FMRA, but later, when another armory in Shawinigan was ransacked, it appeared that the ALQ (Armée de Libération de Québec), a group even more dedicated to the principle of terrorism than the FLQ, was responsible.

In September there was a third wave of terrorism led by a young Hungarian-born malcontent who had been a paratrooper in the French army. He was shot in the thigh while trying, with four others, to hold up the International Firearms Company. Up to this point, Walters was still the only serious victim of the terrorists, but in the skirmish which ensued on this occasion the vice-president of the company was shot to death, as was a policeman. It is believed that—ironically—the police officer was killed by bullets fired by a fellow policeman and intended for the thieves. Some twelve suspects were rounded up as a result of this

incident, some of whom were students at the University of
Montreal, and many of whom carried cards identifying them as
members of the RIN (Rassemblement pour l'Indépendance
Nationale), yet another revolutionary group devoted to "national independence."

By March of the same year, seven young acolytes of the
ALQ had been caught trying to hoist a flag bearing their mark
on the post office in St. Lambert at midnight. All were between
eighteen and twenty-three years old; none was armed, and none
was an active terrorist, but there had been many suspects belonging to various Separatist groups or parties who were held in St.
Lambert in connection with the FMRA robbery, and they were
not spared interrogation in this regard. Apropos of their tendency
to smear mailboxes with the initials ALQ, they were described
by the locals as *barbouilleurs barbouillés* ("dirty-faced daubers"),
and dismissed as adolescent amateurs. Later, another bunch was
picked up for possession of explosives.

In the meantime, Leslie Walters continued to cling to
life, although the doctors had told his wife and children that the
odds against his surviving were staggering. But evidently Walters
was tougher than anybody suspected, and money to help him
poured in to a special fund established immediately after the
accident. By June, 1963, this had grown to the sum of $23,964.

Those members of the FLQ who had been ferreted out
of hiding and jailed as a result of the mailbox tragedy told the
press that they were very sorry about Walters. The bombs were
supposed to go off between three and four o'clock in the morning, they said, when nobody would be anywhere near them.
They had not intended to kill anyone, only to cause the apathetic
rich people of Westmount to wake up to the fact that the
French Canadians (many of whom lived on Westmount)
wanted to be "free."

Very few people are allowed to see Walters, who is still
in the hospital, but one who has seen him described the once-
vigorous officer, with more indignation than pity, as "a vege-
table."

One Québecoise, known to thousands of local TV fans
as a competent and charming interviewer whose shows were
always exceptionally stimulating, read of these events with more
than a conventional interest. Her name was Annette Le Duc.
She was twenty-seven years old, blonde, dimpled, shrewd, and

very attractive to men. Although she was disturbed about the tragic maiming of Walters, she, unlike most of her audience, applauded rather than censured the activities of these idealistic young people. A passionate believer in separatism, she had a compelling aspiration to emerge prominently as one of their number and to be among those to lead Quebec out of its historic "enslavement" to British Canada.

Born of bourgeois parents, Annette, her sister Claire, and brother Jacques were all subjected to an upbringing which was relentlessly "respectable" and appropriate to a middle-class French Catholic family. Every morning the three children, meticulously starched and bowed, were sent off to school in their prim uniforms, including thick black stockings and heavy shoes for the girls.

Annette hated it from the beginning. Whenever she could get away from the nuns and her nervous, stiff-backed mother, she ran into the woods to watch the animals, pick flowers, and draw in huge gulps of clear, fern-scented air in a daily effort to purge herself of the pall of asceticism and the stifling odor of incense and disinfectant. She cherished comfort, privacy, and things that were pretty, divesting herself gratefully each evening of the habiliments of the convent in favor of her warm, flannel nightgown and robe. Once, having slipped a pair of new patent-leather party shoes into her schoolbag and taken them to school to show her young friends, she was severely reprimanded by the sisters, who told her that it was sinful to wear shiny shoes because boys would be able to see the reflection of her thighs in them.

At the evening meal Annette generally sat between her parents, the other two children facing her from the other side of the table, beseeching her with their eyes not to introduce some disturbing subject which would anger their father and embarrass their mother. The mother, a fragile, nervous, flowerlike creature, would sit at her end of the table, darting apprehensive glances at the various members of the family, while the father, a stern European patriarch, sat glaring at them all as though sitting in judgment. No one spoke unless Papa chose to speak to them—except Annette.

The day of the shoe episode Annette began to inquire why people should not look at her legs, but was quickly silenced by her mother. It did not seem to matter how often she was told that children should not speak at table unless bidden to do so, for she could not bear to sit silently with scrub-nailed hands in her lap while her parents spoke diffidently of this and that or nothing at all.

Annette's adolescence was characterized, as might be expected, by an increasing conflict between the stiff parochial values of her family and her free and spontaneous nature. Ultimately her feelings of simple disorientation developed into an outright hostility toward her father and mother and the bourgeois "establishment" of which they were representatives. The only member of the family with whom she continued to get along throughout this difficult period was her sister. Claire was never to be as dynamic as Annette, who dominated her easily, and she remained a shy reticent little person—a conformist who emerged a much more logical product of the convent than her maverick sibling.

Following her welcome release from school, Annette briefly attended the University of Montreal, where, among the restless and idealistic students, she first became aware of the Separatist movement. Almost at once, she became captivated by the principles which inspired the movement and by the passion which fired its adherents. Longing to become part of this dramatic force which was sweeping Canada, she joined the RIN, which was formed some time later, and began to attend meetings regularly.

Essentially, however, her conscious personal ambitions lay in the general realm of the theatre. She telephoned the offices of CFTM-TV one day, stating her hopes and qualifications, and asked for a job. Much to her surprise, she was immediately hired as a makeup girl, and was soon promoted to script assistant. At the time of this promotion, Annette indicated that she would like to be a producer some day, but her employers thought she had more talent for announcing; and eventually she was put on the air.

By now it was the summer of 1961, and a reporter from the Montreal *Star*, who had become intrigued with this French Canadian girl and her burgeoning career, went to CFTM-TV to interview her. She explained how, for several months while she was trying to learn as much as she could about all aspects of the business, she had functioned in three separate capacities, often working sixty to seventy hours per week.

She appeared confused, however, as to what her precise aims were. She wanted to be an actress, she wanted to travel—to "see everything"—and, like any other French Canadian, she wanted to go to France. She was taking singing lessons and had been accepted as a pupil of the National Theatre School in Montreal. She wanted to do some singing, but, more than anything, she wanted to be an overseas reporter. "I am not good yet," she conceded, "but I intend to be."

By 1963 this ambitious girl had fulfilled at least part of her dream, for the network had given her a fifteen-minute show of her own, as a result of which her name and face were becoming known throughout Canada. The program was an intimate sort of show in which Annette interviewed assorted Canadians prominent in the areas of politics, industry, and the arts, and in her capacity as interrogator, she had many opportunities to insinuate certain of her own views as well. This phase of her career was highly successful, and Annette and her program became very popular, once she decided to give it her full attention.

Annette's romantic ego was constructed along Olympian lines. Her enthusiastic participation in any project or movement was invariably accompanied by a powerful psychological drive to achieve a certain sovereignty over her colleagues. Hearing her speak about the Separatist movement in Canada—which she would gladly do, endlessly and with the slightest encouragement—one felt very much in the presence of a latter-day Jeanne d'Arc, a role she clearly fancied.

Prior to establishing herself as a permanent fixture on the interview program, Annette decided to take a six-months' leave of absence in 1963. During this period she worked in what she has described somewhat vaguely as "the artistic field," and she traveled, primarily in France, returning to Montreal in time for Christmas of the same year.

While in Paris, Annette met an Algerian military officer to whom she had been given an introduction by one of her friends in the RIN. The man was an officer of relatively high rank and position in the Ben-Bella régime, and the two discovered instantly that they had a great deal in common; many French Canadian insurgents had come to Algeria to be trained in the use of explosives and firearms, as well as in methods of raising money for their needs, and Annette found that there was a lot to be learned from the Arabs who had so recently won

their freedom from France. She evidently found the officer himself fascinating, as well as what he had to say, for she became his
mistress almost immediately.

Completely enthralled by the rather glamorous situation
in which she found herself, Annette was persuaded to go with
her officer to Algeria, where they lived together in a kind of
common-law arrangement for several months. She was his
"woman," and when he was not attending to political business,
they sat around in cafés on the clear warm evenings, smoking,
drinking, eating the savory North African food, and talking
about socialism.

During her stay in Algeria, Annette was introduced to a
number of French-speaking African diplomats, some of whom
were delegates to the United Nations, and found them an easy
mark for her practiced charm, and the novelty of her blondeness.
She hoped ultimately to influence the thinking of many of
them.

Eventually Annette's "husband" became annoyed with
the spectacle of Annette preening herself before his colleagues,
and after a brief but violent explosion, the "marriage" was dissolved.

When Annette was later relating the Algerian portion of
her saga to American authorities, she enlarged upon the story
considerably, so that her paramour became Ben-Bella himself,
with whom she claimed to have "adopted" several children. She
delighted in telling her interrogators how many times a night
her lover had required her ministrations, and how tiring it all
was. "But shit," she would say in her own colorful idiom, flashing her profane, dimpled smile, "who wants to sleep anyway?"

What added considerably to the general confusion at the
time of Annette's first contact with the United States Attorney's
office in New York, was that the Ben-Bella story was first repeated as having involved Ben-*Gurion*; this caused a considerable stir, but was soon clarified.

Upon her return from Algeria, Annette went immediately
back to her job at CTFM in Montreal and started running the
interview program in earnest. In the meantime, she shared an
apartment with her sister Claire who did not take a very great
interest in Separatist activities but continued to stand in awe of
her big sister.

One evening in the fall of 1964, while visiting a friend,

Annette met a young woman named Thérèse Laval who was a psychology instructor at the Ecole Normale Jacques Cartier. They fell to gossiping and discovered that they shared many common interests, not the least of which was a mutual preference for Negro men. Subsequently, Thérèse introduced her new friend to some of the black students she knew in Montreal, including one from New York whose name was Dick Collins and who was said to be deeply involved in the American civil-rights movement. Annette was fascinated by him. He and Thérèse had been to Cuba earlier in 1964 with a group of other American "students" in defiance of a State Department ban, and he seemed to know a lot of very important people there.

Annette's employers at the television station had only the barest inkling of her rather unorthodox nighttime activities, but noted that she frequently came to work disheveled and extremely tired. So long as she turned up, however, they did not make it their business to pry into her affairs. Finally, it was Annette herself who decided to leave her job and devote more time to the movement. For too long she had functioned on the periphery as a mere hanger-on; it was time she became more active and made herself known.

Shortly after leaving CFTM, she and Claude Giroux, a thirty-year old typewriter repairman with a wooden leg, started a news journal to inform the revolution. It was called *Parti Pris*, and soon folded for lack of funds. Out of its ashes, however, rose still another revolutionary group—La Mobilisation pour la Libération de Québec, of which Giroux and Annette were cochieftains, and whose aims essentially prescribed less theorizing and more action.

As it happened, there was at that time a goodly amount of thinking along those lines going on in New York, and resolutions being made there were similar in tone to those articulated by Annette.

One day early in December, a young Negro named Charles Stone went to visit his friend Dick Collins at the latter's apartment in the Bronx. Collins had just returned from a highly controversial trip to Cuba, and Stone was eager to hear about it.

Greeting Collins in a loud voice, he said, "Hey, man. I hear you took a trip to sunny Cuba." He made a sweeping, expansive gesture with one arm, taking notice of the many huge posters depicting Castro and Guevara on the various walls of the cluttered, dirty room.

"Yeah. I got to know Ché. He's the greatest, baby. Wants us to help him get some books up from Philly and ship 'em down there to Cuba. They got troubles, man. They got to know about heating and plumbing, and—hey, say hello to Henry and Asa."

Stone was now introduced to Asa Aberrian and Henry Bowden, and thus they identified themselves to one another, testing each other as they did so for false reactions. Aberrian, very black, with heavy, balanced features, wore thick, black-rimmed glasses and a white turtleneck sweater. A former student at the Howard University School of Engineering in Washington, he now worked for SNCC.

Bowden, whose heavy-jowled face was rendered even more so by a large, black moustache, was evidently employed as a judo instructor at the Henry Street Settlement and was an avid supporter of the Fair Play for Cuba Committee. Stone said he worked for CORE, but did not feel the group was doing enough to dramatize the Negro cause. "I mean, look at these murders and bombings down South, man! We oughta get down to business and do what *men* are supposed to do in these situations—get after whitey!"

"Yeah," Bowden mused. "I wouldn't mind startin' with some of them Yid store owners up in Harlem, man. Yes, sir." Aberrian, who up to now had been pensive, turned to Stone, speaking softly, poetically: "Baby, we got a plan that gets down to business—it sure as hell does." And, shifting his gaze out the window onto the grimy tenement walls, he said, "When I was a kid, we lived way downtown, man, and I used to be able to see that bitch from my window . . ."

"What bitch is that?" Stone ventured.

"Why, the Statue of—you should pardon the expression —Liberty, man! Yeah, I used to see her standing there, the symbol of equality and fraternity, and—well, I thought to myself, isn't that just great?" They all laughed.

"So what are you gonna do?" Stone inquired facetiously. "Blow her up or something?"

"That's right. We're going to blow the bitch up, and how!" Aberrian was elated now as he looked into the astonished face of Charlie Stone.

"Say, that's a pretty cool idea, man," he said, regaining his composure. "You just might waste a few ofeys while you're at it too, you know?"

"Yeah, well, a few of those fancy-pants bastard Marine guards might just have to be sacrificed to the cause. 'Charlie' won't miss 'em all that much."

"When you planning to make this scene, man?" Stone asked, turning now to Collins, who was their leader.

"Sometime before March," Collins replied solemnly. "I'll let you know."

Around the end of the third week in January, Charlie Stone received a call from Collins. Dick said he was going away for a few days, and he wanted to know if Charlie would look after his cat. He also wanted Charlie to start making arrangements about renting a car and getting supplies together for a trip to Canada, which he wanted to take within the next couple of weeks, and said he would explain to Charlie later.

When next they met, Aberrian and Bowden were also present once more as Dick outlined the plan.

"Now, Charlie and I are going up to Canada next week an' get in touch with my chick, Thérèse, and she's goin' to fix us up with the people who can help us get the stuff we need to do this job."

"Who the hell is Thérèse, man?" Aberrian interrupted. "I don't dig names. Who's this Thérèse?"

"Thérèse is my girl up in Canada. She's been working with these types who been puttin' bombs in people's mailboxes, man, and she's real straight. You don't have to worry about her."

"I just want to know who the hell this babe Thérèse is," Aberrian continued. "I want to know who everybody is, because my ass is involved."

"How do we get back over the border at Rouses Point with the stuff sittin' there in the car, man?" Stone ventured, to which Collins sanguinely replied, "Man, that's no problem. If anybody bothers us, we can waste them cats right there on the scene."

"Listen," Bowden put in, "why stop at the Statue of Liberty? Let's blast the goddam Liberty Bell as well. We shouldn't have any problem about tamping. The fucking thing's cracked anyway." This remark produced a burst of laughter from the others, and, inspired, Bowden went on to suggest that they include the Washington Monument.

"As long as you're going all the way to Canada, you might as well get a whole bunch of stuff, baby, and we can really give The Man something to think about. I got a friend in Washington who'd just love to make this scene. Look, Charlie and Dick are going up to Canada to get the word on these explosives. Why don't Asa and Dick take care of the Statue of Liberty, and me 'n Charlie'll take care of the Liberty Bell, and Doug and my buddy Bob Maynard can blast the Washington Monument? I used to live in Philadelphia for quite a while, and I know the town pretty good. If anybody tries to stop us, I'll just waste him with my karate."

Thus it was settled, and on January 29, Dick Collins and Charlie Stone took off for Canada with $112 and $57 in their respective pockets. Crossing over the Jacques Cartier Bridge, they entered Montreal. Inquiring as to how to get to 5566 Rue de Cell, they were instructed to take St. Catherine's to Autremont, and then a right on de Cell. The house was not hard to find, and before long they were knocking on the door of flat number seven.

Thérèse Laval seemed surprised but pleased to see Charlie Stone, to whom she was now introduced by Collins. As they entered, Collins said, "Listen, baby, I want you to let Charlie stay here for a couple of days. Where can he sleep?"

"Right here," Thérèse replied gaily, indicating an inflatable mattress. "Why don't you get some sleep now? I have some errands to do. I just want to put on some slacks." Charlie thanked her, making some comment about the large photo of Castro in her bedroom. "Oh, yes," she said. "Dick and I got that when we went down to Cuba." Then, freshly reminded of those halcyon days, she put some Cuban music on the phonograph, saying as she left, "Listen, don't worry about the price of the stuff. I'll make up the difference if you don't have enough money to buy what you need." And closing the door behind her, she left Charlie and Dick to sleep off the effects of their long journey.

On the morning of January 30, 1965, Thérèse Laval paid a visit to her friend Annette at the latter's apartment. She knocked gently on the door of number eighteen and was presently greeted by Claire. Annette was still in bed. Looking up from her pillow, she gazed wearily at her visitor.

"*Bonjour.* What can I do for you at this ungodly hour?"

"Well, it's eleven o'clock. Listen, my American friends are in town."

"And?"

"And they want to get in touch with the organization."

"What for?" At this point Thérèse handed her sleepy friend a piece of paper, on which was scrawled: "10 blasting caps; 30 lbs. explosives; 30 feet of primer cord."

"Well, I can't talk to them today."

"All right. Come to my apartment tomorrow evening around six o'clock. They'll all be there."

It was a well-rested, radiant Miss Le Duc who walked into Thérèse's apartment the following evening, albeit nearly an hour late. She greeted Dick Collins cheerfully, kissing him on the cheek, and was introduced to Charlie Stone, to whom her first reaction was how much blacker he was than Dick.

"How are you, Dick? I see you cut your beard."

"Yeah, well, I only had it when I was down there in Cuba, but I had to get rid of it, because it was itching me."

"They told me you had dinner with Ché Guevara in New York."

"Yeah, that's right," Collins replied proudly. "I had dinner with Ché, and spoke with him at some length. He's the one who gave me the idea for this job, the one I want to talk to you about."

"I think he's handsome," Annette bubbled, "and I think you're so lucky to have seen him. . . ." Thérèse said that she did not think Guevara was very good-looking, and they went on to other topics. They discussed books which Guevara had written, and agreed generally that the Cubans had conducted their revolution extremely well. At last, this conversation exhausted, Annette was ready to get down to business and, turning to Collins, said, "Thérèse said you wanted to get in touch with our organization."

"Yes."

"Well, you don't want to get mixed up with the *Parti Pris* people or the Rassemblement pour l'Indépendance Nationale. The one is only interested in writing down ideas and theories, and the other one is so busy trying to please everybody and moving gradually by legal maneuvering that they are getting absolutely nowhere. My group is getting trained for whatever might come. I assume you want to be involved with activists and not just a bunch of talkers. What do you want anyway, I mean specifically?"

"If you'll shut up for a minute," Collins said good naturedly, "I'll tell you. We need explosives—you know, plastic."

"Why do you come up here to get it? I mean, we get ours from the black market in New York."

The Americans looked at each other, chagrined. "Well, if we'd known that, we wouldn't have made the trip." At this they all laughed sheepishly, not knowing what should follow.

"Do you know how expensive *plastique* is?" Annette asked and, not waiting for the answer, added, "Anyway, our organization has none available at the moment."

"We'll take dynamite—it's cheaper, I guess."

"Yes." She paused, examining her fingernails. "You know, if you could find us a couple of apartments in New York, this would be more useful to us than money. You see, we need someplace to go with men, but sometimes we have no place to take them. Two places would be enough. I've been doing a lot of work in New York myself, and I've been very busy. To tell the truth, guys, I've been prostituting myself quite a bit down there, mostly around the U.N."

"Oh, yeah," Collins said finally. "Well, I think we could work something out. That's one way to raise money, isn't it?" Everyone laughed.

"The best there is," Annette replied, her eyes twinkling.

"Hey, we could use some broads like her in our organization, right, Charlie?"

"How much dynamite will you need?" Annette broke in.

Collins and Stone put their heads together a moment or two, and finally said, "We have three big jobs. We thought ten pounds of plastic apiece would do it. We'll take the equivalent in TNT."

"What kind of blasting cap do you want?"

"Three-day delay."

"I never heard of a cap with three days delay. I've heard of two hours, four hours, and six hours. Any others you have to make yourself with clocks and watches, and that's extremely dangerous. I don't like those. Don't like them at all. One of our boys already ruined one of his hands in training, while making one of those damn things."

Annette thought for a moment, as much for dramatic

effect as for reflection. "Look, I go to New York quite often, and always by the fifteenth of the month. I'll be there on February fifteenth, and I'll bring you an answer then."

"We need it sooner than that, and not an answer either —the stuff!"

"Well, I can't tell you for sure now that you can have it." And then, with combined reluctance and irritation, she added, "I don't make the final decisions."

Collins looked annoyed, and Annette, determined not to lose the upper hand, asked, rather condescendingly, "Just how serious is your organization?"

"We are very serious, I can assure you." Annette looked doubtful, superior. "And we intend to do this job right."

"Well, just what is the job?"

"We can't tell you, but, baby, there is going to be a loud noise that will be heard around the world."

"Just how," Annette insisted, "do you maintain your relation with the other groups, and how do you know you're not infiltrated by the police?"

"Oh!" Collins exclaimed, tossing his head to one side as though such a thing were virtually impossible. "I'd like to see one of those bastards get close to us. That'll be the day, eh, Charlie? Hell, we've all known each other since we were kids."

"Yeah, man," Stone replied through a curl of smoke.

"Does this dynamite—this use of dynamite—does it involve the killing of anybody?"

"No," Stone said. "But I don't think it would matter very much if we killed any white American. Because if you think about the way they treat our colored people in the South, you would have no kind of pity for any white American. . . . If Dick showed you the picture of the dead man—the dead old colored man on a slab, all tortured and dead—you could have no pity for white Americans." His eyes blazed, and his voice became hoarse as he raised it to the climax. Collins merely nodded his head and said, "Yeah. That's right, man."

"I'm sorry," Annette ventured, "that you should dislike the American that much, because if you didn't tell me you were a Negro, I couldn't tell. To me you look just like an Italian or Spaniard or an Arab, but you don't look Negro."

Indeed, Collins' photographs revealed a light-skinned man, with a Graciano nose and a fine mouth supported by a massive jaw. Thick, curly hair encroached on a narrow brow, where one eyebrow perched higher than the other, giving the face a rather quizzical expression.

Stone, who had up to now been leaning listlessly against the window smoking, came forward, gesticulating with his cigarette.

"You know, that's a very big insult. How would you feel if I told you you look like an English Canadian?"

"Well, I understand your point of view," Annette replied, unconvinced, "but that's a little bit different, isn't it?"

Not wishing to intensify this argument, Collins asked Annette what her organization was called.

"Names are not important," she said, shrugging. "It is simply a very secret organization, which nobody knows anything about."

At this point, Thérèse, who, thus far had been listening disinterestedly from the kitchen where she was brewing some coffee, burst in, saying, "You could just call it Le Maquis, and they could call theirs Le Maquis Noir!" Delighted with this contribution, she was put down immediately by Annette, who gave her a withering look and asked if the coffee was ready. The conversation then turned to the prospects of getting caught and arrested.

"We work in fours," Collins explained, "and if one gets caught, the others must try to free him. Those goddamn white bastard cops have ways to make us talk. . . . I wouldn't mind killing every damn cop around if I was arrested, even if there were a dozen of 'em." The room by now was filled with smoke from Annette's strong Gravena cigarettes, and the talk drifted to violence and terrorism, bombs and money.

A lengthy discussion on the construction of various types of bombs—during which coffee was produced, and Annette explained how to make the fuse of a Molotov cocktail burn longer by soaking it in sugar—was followed by a dissertation by Collins on the ways and means to hold up trucks late at night. He described one method, which involved the placing of nail-studded boards in the road and lying in wait further on, at a place calculated to be the spot where the driver would be obliged to stop and do something about his damaged tires. Annette asked that this be explained to her in detail, for she thought that her group ought to consider trying to rob armored cars; she had heard something about this in Algeria.

However, she did not enjoy being in the position of being taught something by someone from an inferior, amateurish outfit, not to mention a cause which had nothing whatever to do with her. Taking the lead once more, she stated rather maternally that organizations should not throw themselves into activity until they had the money to back it up, an assertion which provoked a lively talk about the possibility of attracting foreign aid to their various revolutions. Red China was mentioned by one of the Negroes as a likely candidate for this honor, but Annette was determined to hold the floor and stick to the areas in which she was particularly indoctrinated.

"The best way to do this," she began, "is through an embassy in the United States whose government is friendly with both sides, such as Algeria. I can easily provide you with an introduction to the people in the Algerian embassy, where I have —many friends," she concluded suggestively. "If you have people from your own organization in the government, who are important enough," she added, "you can get aid through political blackmail. You can also get false passports and find people who can forge the IBM plates used to issue government checks. And, of course, sexual blackmail of diplomats is still one of the best ways of getting money, as we were saying. In fact I've been thinking about setting up a ring of girls to do nothing else. We'd do anything to get the money we need. That's why we *must* have those apartments. We could form a liaison between our two groups so that we could use each others' apartments for hideouts. We can get you false Canadian passports if the FBI gets too close to you."

"Yeah, okay. We'll get you a pad," Collins said, a trifle weary of the lecture. "Here's my address in New York," he concluded, scribbling on a piece of paper, "and the key to my pad. Now why don't you take Charlie out for a little tour of Montreal and some food. Thérèse only has enough here for the two of us. And anyhow, four's a crowd, know what I mean?"

Piqued that it was not she but Collins who put an end to the meeting, Annette rose abruptly, stuffed the address and key into her handbag, and indicated to Charlie that he should come with her. They put on their coats, said good-bye, and departed, leaving Collins alone with Thérèse.

Days later, after Collins and Stone had returned to New York, Annette explained the situation to Giroux, who agreed to let her have some dynamite. She was told that it had been stolen off a construction site and that she would have to fetch it from a small farmhouse up in the Laurentians.

Following Giroux's instructions, she and two others drove up one bitterly cold Sunday to collect the contraband and found that, as they had been informed, the stuff was kept on a high shelf in the loft of an ancient barn. Annette instructed the two young men who had accompanied her to go up and get it, but, glancing sheepishly at each other, they demurred, saying the shelf was too high and it was too dangerous. Disgusted, Annette went up herself, climbing the crude wooden ladder into the loft and fetching it down with aplomb, then handed it to her nervous cronies.

Each stick had written on its side: FORCITE 45%, BENOIT, QUÉBEC: EXPLOSIVE. The boys did not realize that the stuff was quite harmless until detonated; neither in fact knew as much about explosives as Annette did.

It was boldness that had attracted Giroux to her in the first place—the fact that she seemed afraid of nothing, including prosecution. As for Annette, now she felt that she was at last truly engaged, committed to an action. There had been enough theorizing, talking, and dreaming.

The dynamite arrived in Montreal packed in a box, which was soggy, evidently from having sat out in the snow at some stage. Having slipped the blasting caps into her purse, Annette decided to stay the night at Thérèse's apartment and to put the explosive into a dry box before the sticks themselves were damaged. Besides, it would be awkward and dangerous to have to tell Claire what she was doing—the youngest Le Duc was disapproving enough as it was. At Thérèse's, she found an old carton from a paint company. Wrapping the individual sticks carefully in newspaper, Annette placed them inside the box, then covered them with two layers of books in order to deceive the customs inspectors, should that prove necessary.

That was February 14. The next morning, as the first timid shafts of sunlight crept over the ice and snow of a freezing Quebec, Annette sprang out of bed and immediately called two other young acolytes recently acquired by the Giroux-Le Duc team, and told them to get over to the apartment as soon as possible to help her carry the explosives and her luggage to the car, parked just outside. This done, the three set out for New York.

They were all slightly nervous as they approached the border, and the car, which had been ringing with raucous French songs and gay argument about revolution, suddenly became still as it rolled up to the customs gate. Annette applied her most winning smile, which froze as the thought suddenly came to her that it would have been better to wrap the dynamite in an English-language newspaper instead of obsolete sheets of *La Presse.*

Her fears, however, did not materialize. Informing the customs inspector that they were students on their way to visit friends in the States, they declared nothing and were waved on, the box remaining unobserved and unchecked in the rear. The inspector touched his cap to the dimpled blonde driver, and thus he remained for several moments, grinning in the frosty white morning and watching the car disappear down the highway in clouds of frozen exhaust.

It was snowing gently and after midnight by the time the trio arrived in New York. Annette drove directly to the Riverdale section of the Bronx, near the Hudson River, stopping in front of an ultramodern, high-rise brick apartment building, complete with automatic temperature control and sunless, soot-filled "terraces." From these terraces the lucky middle-income inhabitants could gaze out upon a vast empty lot filled with beer cans, moribund cinder-blocks, and various other waste products of human life.

The lot was surrounded by a high wire fence, parts of which had been torn away by vandals and the natural erosions of time, and it was through one of these gaps that Annette and her two companions—one clutching a flashlight—carried their burden. Spotting a small shrub which had managed to grow up against the fence, they dug a hole underneath it and placed the box inside, covering it with dirt, leaves, and refuse. Annette then dismissed the two others, instructing them to get away from there and find a place to sleep. She then got into the car and drove to Colonial House, a hotel on 112th Street, and called Charlie Stone.

Waiting nervously for Stone to arrive, Annette sat in the hotel lobby, chain-smoking and wondering whether the three sets of footprints in the snow would lead anybody to the box before Charlie and the others could get there. When Stone finally arrived, Annette jumped up eagerly to greet him.

"Charlie . . ."

"So how did everything go?"

"Fine, fine. But listen, I think I was followed down here. I shook them before going to the lot, but they may get onto me again. It's that damn Thérèse who put them on my tail. She and her group were demonstrating in front of the U.S. Embassy, and they probably traced me through her. You'd better get over there and get that stuff. . . ."

"All right now, calm down. Tell me where it is, and Dick and I will go on over and get it."

"Come into the hallway." Leading Charlie by the arm, Annette pulled him into a dark passage at the foot of the back stairs. He produced a piece of paper and a pencil, indicating that Annette should draw him a diagram pinpointing the whereabouts of the dynamite. Annette was outraged.

"Are you crazy?" she hissed in her most powerful stage whisper. "We don't do those things on a piece of paper, to be read by anyone who finds it!" And, eyeing him like the mother of a precocious but bumbling child, she proceeded to outline the directions on the wall with one leather-gloved finger, indicating the apartment building, the lot, the fence, the bush.

"Now, have you got that in your head?"

"Yeah, I guess so."

"All right then, I'm going, so at least if the tail picks me up again, you'll be free."

"Hey, you're all heart, you know that?" Stone chuckled.

"Don't be so funny. And if anything goes wrong, call Mr. Pariso at the Excelsior Hotel. Good-bye, and good luck." And so she departed, making the final gesture of tearing up all papers in her possession bearing names and addresses of people involved with Charlie and his group, and tossing the pieces in a trash can on her way out. Annette did not, however, go to the Excelsior Hotel.

Stone left the hotel as soon as Annette had gone and ran around the corner, where Dick Collins was waiting in a 1965 Impala. Stone got into the driver's seat, and as they made their way toward the empty lot, he said, "I'll stay in the car and keep an eye out for whitey. You go in and get the stuff."

"Okay," Collins replied. When they arrived, Stone pulled right up alongside the fence, scanning its length for the clump of bushes. "There it is!" he said at last, and Collins threw open his door and made for a break in the fence. It was still snowing, and Stone could see Collins' dim figure through the silent flakes, first clawing the ground and then lifting something heavy out from under the shrubs. His back arching under the weight of the box, Collins half ran, half walked back to the hole in the fence and stumbled through it, nearly letting the box slip to the ground. Then, as he approached, Stone leaned over and opened the door on the passenger side, and Collins, his wavy black hair sprinkled with snow, heaved the box onto the front seat and threw himself in after it, breathing hard after his exertion. "Okay, man," he said. "Let's get out of here."

But as Stone put the car in gear, a voice broke the cold stillness, yelling, "Hold it! And get out of the car with your hands behind your head."

Collins, breathing in sharply through his teeth, snapped his head around, his eyes wide and blinking. Seeing the revolving red light, he got out, his hands raised. Stone was already out and had fallen across the hood of the car, with his arms outstretched, as a policeman searched him for weapons. While another one patted Collins from head to toe, two detectives stood staring at the box in the front seat which said MOORE PAINTS, and which was soggy from being snowed upon.

With Stone and Collins in handcuffs, they then went off to collect Aberrian and Bowden at Collins' apartment, dispatching another pair of detectives to Manhattan for Annette, who had, of course, been followed. She was found at a smart East Side apartment building, preparing to spend the night with a distinguished delegate from French Africa. Arresting Annette turned out to be somewhat more complicated than had been anticipated, since the police had first to work their way through two enormous black guards, who stood outside the door, evidently to guard His Excellency's person with their lives.

Certain formalities having been got through, Annette was finally dragged from the apartment, protesting volubly and cursing in French. As the detectives led her to the police car, Annette's mind raced as she tried to imagine what had gone wrong and how she was to extricate herself from the situation. Arriving at the police station, she found Collins, Aberrian, and Bowden sitting together, handcuffed, heads bowed in dejection. But she was surprised not to see Charlie Stone. As she was being booked, Stone came in, hands in the pockets of a new topcoat, and without so much as a glance at Annette, greeted one of the detectives who brought her in. "Well," he said, "I guess that's the lot."

"Yeah. Nice going, Charlie. Great job. See ya."

And smiling back, his hand describing a mock salute, Detective Charles Stone sauntered off toward a waiting patrol car, whistling a tune he had learned in Quebec.

Annette jerked her head around and, staring into the stunned countenance of Dick Collins, snarled, "Known each other since you were kids, eh? You black idiot!"

On February 16, 1965, the Montreal *Star* carried the following headline: CITY WOMAN HELD IN U.S. BOMB PLOT, and went on to explain that "A white woman from Montreal in local TV and Separatist circles and three American Negro men, described by police as pro-Castro and pro-Chinese Communists, were arrested today." The four were identified as Richard S. Collins, 28, Henry F. Bowden, 32, Asa Aberrian, 22, and Annette Le Duc, 28, and their explosive intentions defined.

On the morning of February 17, various American newspapers bore photographs of policemen wearing hoods, face masks, and special protective asbestos suits as they seized the rather insignificant cache of dynamite. The Royal Canadian Mounted Police were praised by the American authorities for having alerted the FBI to the fact that Annette had left Montreal in a station wagon, with dynamite, early in the morning of February 15, and everybody was very happy that the plot had been foiled by the commendable and daring efforts of Detective Stone.

That same day, at 1:00 P.M., carrying search warrants issued on the basis of information supplied by Detective Stone, Detective First Grade Patrick Kelly and seven other detectives went to Richard Collins' apartment in the Bronx. Kelly had been a cop for seventeen years, a detective for fifteen in the Safe, Loft, and Burglary Squad, and he knew what he was doing. In less than an hour, they had found everything they were looking for: maps, boxes, nails, Pepsi-Cola bottles, rolls of cotton twine, a funnel, a three-gallon plastic container, a Clorox container, a handwritten note, saying, "Annette: call me at this number (YU 2-4550) any time you arrive here. Dick!"

They also found several postcards, showing various views

of the Statue of Liberty. One, a view from the crown, gave all the statue's dimensions:

> Rt. arm, 42″ (two persons in torch); bet. eyes, 2′6″; mouth, 3′; 40 persons in head; tablet length, 23′7″, width, 13′7″; height, 305′; nose, 4′6″; weight, 450,000 lbs.

Everything was carefully initialed and sent down to police headquarters; this was the evidence that would substantiate the testimony of Charles Stone.

It was reported that Annette was being held on $100,000 bail (which is to say no bail at all, since she could hardly come up with anything approaching that sum) and that she had protested her detention to the U.S. Commissioner on the basis of the fact that she was an "honorable person" and had to make a living. The Commissioner, however, unmoved by the pleas of this now-humble working girl, sent her to the Women's House of Detention in Greenwich Village to await trial.

The ignominious failure of Annette Le Duc was a great disappointment to the French Canadians, to whom she represented a kind of shining hope. It galled them that she had come to grief the way she had—caught in a stupid and second-rate plot, among people who had nothing to do with their cause.

Annette's arrest, furthermore, inspired a good deal of police activity in Montreal as well as New York, during which eight people, including Annette's benign little sister, were rounded up by a raiding party in a St. Denis Street boarding-house. Claire was very hostile and eager to protect her sister. There were five men and three women in all, described as "friends or close associates" of Annette. All were released after being questioned except one man, who was charged with the illegal possession of a revolver and who was suspected of being an associate of the leaders of a movement known as Les Chevaliers de l'Indépendance. The police apparently had their hands full trying to keep the players and their associations straight, considering the plethora of movements, cadres, sects, maquis, and *rassemblements* involved in the game of revolution. Many perfectly innocent students found themselves unhappily involved with the police simply because they knew somebody who was somewhat less innocent.

The Montreal police discovered without too much trouble that Annette belonged to the RIN, whose president, Pierre Bourgault, admitted that she had been a member for quite a long time. Bourgault remembered Annette as a girl who was irresistibly attracted to causes, and the Separatist cause in particular. This observation was made in response to a comment by the police that her three Negro companions belonged to a ten-member, para-military terrorist group calling themselves the Black Liberation Front.

"She was very interested in Quebec's independence, but I never heard her discuss civil rights in the United States," Bourgault said. "Actually, she usually did only stenographic work for us. Occasionally she talked at the meetings—not often, but when she did, she was very effective. Maybe all this is in her temperament. She was always ready to attract attention in some particularly dramatic way, and her enthusiasm caught on very quickly—especially with the men. Annette is a very attractive girl, the men were always around her. As a matter of fact, we had all been looking for her for the past few months because she hadn't been around. At least now," he added, laughing, "we know where she is. As far as we're concerned, she is still a member of the organization and will continue to be, so long as these charges remain unproved."

On February 27, the Montreal *Star* announced that three more Separatists had been arrested and would be arraigned in Montreal in criminal court the following Monday. Then, early in March, they arrested Thérèse Laval in connection with the American conspiracy, and simultaneously the district judge in New York, before whom Annette and the three Negroes had pleaded not guilty to the charge of conspiracy, signed a warrant for her arrest. This turned out to be a mere formality, since Thérèse would be obliged to stand trial in Canada before extradition proceedings could be initiated in an effort to get her out of Canada to be tried in New York. Meanwhile she was being held without bail on charges of conspiracy and illegal possession of explosives, it having been definitely established by now that the dynamite which Annette took to New York from Thérèse's apartment had been stolen from a Montreal subway construction site. The Chief of Police acknowledged that they were still seeking the "mastermind" of the smuggling plot in Quebec.

On March 10, it was reported that Thérèse Laval had refused to testify at her preliminary hearing, afraid that anything she said in Canada might subsequently be used against her in the United States. The three terrorists arrested in late February were also formally charged, along with Thérèse, and their identities revealed. One was a post-office employee, another an office clerk, and the third a crippled TV repair man called Claude Giroux.

Up to this point, Annette had been enduring her incarceration in the Women's House of Detention with considerable gusto, throwing herself with customary flair into the general and prevailing spirit of complaint which seems to characterize such institutions, and each day either the bugs, the food, the matrons, or the bed linen became the unfortunate objects of her energetic polemical assaults. Having observed that the vast majority of the inmates were black, she would doubtless have greatly enjoyed building some sort of damaging case against the prison authorities, relating conditions in the prison to the apparent indifference with which white Americans generally treat their Negro compatriots. Mindful of the fact, however, that many of the "screws" were Negroes themselves, this rare opportunity remained largely unexploited.

But in spite of her expansiveness, Annette was anything but optimistic. The very idea that she should be locked up seemed outrageous to her, and, deeply worried as to what she would suffer at the hands of the United States courts, she frequently and tearfully confessed her fears to her lawyer, her favorite social worker, or her fellow inmates. They found her ready, as always, to discuss any and all questions with whoever was available to listen.

So ebullient and stimulating was all this chatter that her audience ceased to be disturbed by the fact that through it all ran a steadfast current of pseudo-Marxist dogma, which conditioned even the most casual observation. It was obvious, however, that she had been taken in by those aspects of Marxism which were merely propagandistic; it was apparent that, while the girl had a good head, she was still primarily governed by her emotions and her excessively romantic nature.

Annette's lawyer, Paul Steinor, found her an easy client, charming and intelligent and, unlike many of his brighter clients, willing to place herself completely in his hands. It was Steinor's view that Annette talked a lot of rubbish in which she did not really believe; one only had to listen to her speak about her coconspirators to realize that she was fundamentally a snob.

It was generally agreed among those who had got to know Annette that she did not give a damn about the Negroes or their cause, that she thought they were stupid, and saw them chiefly as a means of acquiring the apartments; that, in fact, she found blacks more easy to manipulate than whites and was always ready to use them when necessary. Annette was quite adept at using people of any color, at any time, in achieving her own ends.

Steinor enjoyed talking with Annette and often complained of the "Gestapolike" procedures in the prison, with a guard sitting three feet away from them as they conferred and insisting on censoring all writing that passed between them. This, said Mr. Steinor, inhibited his preparation of Annette's case, as did the unreasonably arbitrary visiting hours of the prison, which he found exceedingly inconvenient to a busy trial lawyer.

The darkest day by far, however, was that day in March when Annette read in the morning newspaper that Giroux had been arrested. Happily, this was also the day of the week on which popular social workers generally appeared at the prison to counsel the women on personal matters. There was one worker in particular to whom Annette had become quite attached, for she was not only *sympathetique*, but also spoke French, and Annette felt that the confidences imparted to this woman were, therefore, more private.

When her confidante arrived, Annette told her immediately about Giroux, exclaiming, "My God, if he talks, we're all cooked!" At first it sounded to her mentor as though Annette had been somehow romantically involved with the man. But it soon became apparent, as the outpourings increased in intensity, that the involvement was strictly of a political nature, and that young Mr. Giroux was feared as well as admired among his following. Perhaps the Canadian authorities had unwittingly found their "mastermind."

Having unburdened herself of the more acute anxieties and been assured (somewhat arbitrarily) that Giroux's arrest would not jeopardize her position in the United States, Annette was at least partially soothed. Still, it became increasingly evident to her that should she succeed in extricating herself from the mess in New York, she must avoid returning to Canada, a condition which disturbed and saddened her considerably.

The United States Attorney was, in the meantime, preparing his case against Annette's three unfortunate fellow conspirators, who were to be tried late in May. It was obvious by now that, inasmuch as Thérèse Laval was unavailable as a witness, and the defense would undoubtedly try to show that the indiscretions of the three Negroes were the result of Detective Stone's policy of entrapment, Annette Le Duc would have to be persuaded to testify against them.

Early in April the suggestion was made to her through Steinor, and she replied, predictably, "Why the hell should I? I'm no Judas." These, she maintained, had been her friends, and she believed in their cause, even if she did not necessarily endorse their methods of pursuing it. (She evidently believed that the end justifies the means, but not to the extent of blowing people up in the Statue of Liberty.) What, furthermore, would her collaborators in Canada think of her were she to turn on these people, whom she had aided and abetted, and who had trusted her? The answer at this stage was definitely "No," and Annette settled down again to waiting it out in the House of Detention.

In mid-April, however, Annette was once more in distress, for one damp misty day, Claude Giroux, using his belt for an unorthodox purpose, hanged himself in his prison cell in Quebec, and the news hit all the morning papers in North America. Annette's reaction to the suicide was characteristically ambivalent as she fluctuated among manifestations of grief, anger, and fear—the latter evoked by the fact that she did not know how much Giroux had told the police before he died. No one knew why he took his life: Was he afraid that he would speak sooner or later? Could he simply not face up to the long prison term? Or was it shame that drove him to it? But in spite of her grief, it appeared to some people that Annette was relieved, less nervous and less apprehensive than previously.

Word got around the U.S. Attorney's office that Annette was less than enchanted with life at the Women's House of Detention and that, what with one thing and another, she might be more receptive to the idea of cooperating than she had been earlier. Another approach was made, again through Steinor, who had been negotiating steadily with the United States authorities, and this time Annette agreed to have a talk with the two assistant United States attorneys who would be prosecuting the government's case against the three Negroes.

As might be expected, they were charmed by her—smiling and carefully coiffed as she was—and responded not only to the allure which she possessed as a woman, but to her cunning and ready intelligence, which showed itself in her ability to grasp instantly the procedural points and legal technicalities which were explained to her. She evidently found them equally charming and persuasive, for in a matter of hours, Annette—who ostensibly viewed the United States as a social and political dungheap, redolent of every gross injustice and unmitigated evil by which capitalistic systems are known—had agreed to turn state's evidence and testify against her erstwhile friends and fellow revolutionaries. While being persuaded, she took great delight in teasing the shyest and most reserved of the young lawyers, admiring his tie, his cufflinks, and telling him how sexy she thought he was. Those who were not entirely charmed were at least amused, for it looked as though everyone was well on the way to getting what he or she wanted.

Thus it was that on May 13, 1965, Annette pleaded guilty to the charge of transporting dynamite illegally, understanding that she could receive a maximum sentence of five years in prison and a fine of ten thousand dollars; it was expected that the pending conspiracy charge would be dropped, inasmuch as there seemed to be insufficient evidence that Annette was informed as to what use the explosives were to be put.

On May 14, the day that the young postal clerk, arrested in Canada with Giroux, was convicted of stealing the dynamite from a construction site, Annette threw herself on the mercy of the court, saying she was very sorry for what she had done. Two weeks later, she appeared as a witness for the government against Richard Collins, Asa Aberrian, and Henry Bowden.

Annette's performance in court was nothing short of masterful. Though revealing more than was really necessary to answer the questions under direct examination, her handling of the cross-examination was characteristically skillful. Utilizing all her charm, shrewdness, and alleged unfamiliarity with the English language, she was winsomely unhelpful to the defense.

Q. Has the United States Attorney made you any promises as to a more lenient sentence resulting from your testimony against Mr. Collins, Mr. Aberrian, and Mr. Bowden?

A. No sir.

Q. And therefore you have no reason to expect that, because you are testifying as a government witness, you may be treated more leniently, do you?

A. Well do you want me to say "no" or "yes" to your question? You put it in a way that it looks like if I say "no" it means "yes," and if I say "yes" it means "no." [This answer was capped by an adorable smile.]

COURT. He wants to know, do you have any expectation . . .?

A. Well, there were never no conversation of that sort between me and the U.S. Attorney. . . .

Q. Do you have any hopes or expectations that, because of your testimony here yesterday and today, you may be given a more merciful or lenient sentence?

A. Well, the day I pleaded guilty, I have thrown myself on the mercy of the court.

Q. That is correct. Good luck.

Immediately following this exchange, the court was recessed for lunch, during which time the judge arranged to have some blasting that was going on in a nearby excavation stopped, for the noise tended to drown out the witnesses' answers, especially those of Annette, who spoke on this occasion in the most dulcet tones imaginable. The judge had continually to remind her to speak up so that her answers could be heard by the court stenographer.

After lunch Annette was asked whether she was married or had ever been, to which she replied in the negative.

Q. Do you know the maximum sentence you face on the charges made against you?

A. Five years and/or a ten thousand dollar fine. Yes, sir. . . .

Q. . . . Is it your expectation that, by [your] becoming a witness for the government of the United States, they will intervene in your behalf and encourage and ask or request the government of Canada not to press charges against you?

A. Yes sir, your honor . . . well, this is a feeling, and I thought that in court we deal with facts, and as a fact, I don't know anything of the sort.

Q. Did the filthy, unwholesome, and horrendous conditions of the

Women's House of Detention in any way bear upon your decision to become a government witness?
A. Oh, no, sir. It's not *that* bad.

Although it was known that Annette faced charges of
sedition if returned to Canada, in addition to that of illegally
procuring explosives, the defense counsel indicated through
his examination that it was Charles Stone's participation in the
plot that was inflammatory, that the proposed acts of violence
had been inspired by him, and that his methods of obtaining
information during his association with the conspirators may
have been somewhat unorthodox:

Q. Did you [Stone] invite Miss Le Duc to spend the night of
January thirty-first with you in Montreal?
A. No, I did not.
Q. Did you kiss her?
A. To the best of my recollection I did not kiss her.
Q. Are you sure you did not kiss her?
A. To the best of my knowledge.

In a final attempt to discredit Annette as a witness, the
defense, noting that on April 5 her lawyer had moved that she
undergo a psychiatric examination, put Dick Collins on the
stand, and he proceeded to give testimony designed to reveal
that Annette was mentally incompetent. The prosecution, in a
somewhat weary rebuttal, pointed out that nothing had been
done about this examination, that there was therefore no report
available, and that, in any case, the psychiatrist had only been
introduced to serve as an intermediary between Annette and her
legal counsel.

On May 28, the Montreal *Star* reported that the efforts
of the United States Attorney General to extradite Thérèse
Laval had failed; thus she would not only be spared testifying
against the Negroes, but she would never face charges in the
United States. The following day, in New York, Annette again
denied having made any kind of deal with the United States
government or having received any promise of preferential treatment in return for her cooperation with them. Then, this being
the last day of the trial, she was remanded to the Women's
House of Detention to await sentencing three weeks later.

When the day arrived, the courtroom seemed to be imbued with the aura of *opèra comique*—that is, in view of the fact that it was Annette Le Duc about whom people were speaking. On June 17, 1965, a judge sentenced Annette to five years in prison in Alderson, West Virginia; however, she was to be returned to court in three months' time for her case to be reviewed; then he would alternatively place her on probation, make her sentence permanent, or modify it. The judge disclosed that, in making his decision, he was influenced by the fact that he found Miss Le Duc to be thoroughly repentent and a truthful and cooperative witness.

The chief prosecutor, an attractive young man of about thirty-five and one of the assistant United States attorneys explained to the court that Annette came from a good family and that her father had had an excellent record of service during World War II. The judge nodded, as though he understood exactly in what manner this was relevant to the girl's criminal action, while the young attorney went on to stress the improbability of Annette's knowledge of the details of the plot; after all, one of the targets was to have been the Statue of Liberty, a gift to the United States from France, and she was a French Canadian. With grave countenance the judge continued to nod, either ignorant of or choosing to ignore the fact that, if there is one bunch the French Canadians despise more than the English Canadians, it is the continental French.

However, it was Mr. Steinor who fixed the desired image of his client by stating that Annette was not only fully repentent but was obviously a very attractive young lady who looked forward to the day when she could marry and become a housewife and mother. Whereupon, still standing demurely before the judge—hands folded, hair freshly dyed and dressed for the final courtroom performance—Annette smiled sweetly and said how glad she was that she had been able to be such a help to government, and was led away by two solicitous court officers.

The next day, June 18, Collins, Aberrian, and Bowden got ten years, pending parole.

Annette was packed off to Alderson Federal Prison in West Virginia, where things weren't so bad either; word reached New York by way of the grapevine that, by applying her ubiquitous and unfailing charm to the powers that be, she managed to get a more comfortable bed for her cell, a desk, and—what is truly marvelous—a private telephone. She remained at Alderson for three months, and on September 20 she stood once more before the judge in New York, who, thanking her again for her cooperation, modified her sentence to five years' parole and banishment from the United States forever. The American government, it would seem, was not terribly concerned about what she had done or what she might do in the future—so long as she did it somewhere other than in the United States.

Annette was not returned to her own country, where she faced serious charges; she was deported to Paris, where, when last heard from, she held a job as personal secretary to an internationally famous actor whose wife was believed to be a French Canadian.

The story of Annette Le Duc is a lesson, if nothing else, in how to land on one's feet without worrying about the expense to others. As a result of her activities in Quebec and the United States, Annette irrevocably alienated both her brother and her father (who lost his job as a result of her activities), sent three men with whom she had plotted equally to jail for several years (they did not have to serve the full term), and caused Thérèse Laval, in whose apartment she had kept the dynamite, to face trial in Montreal for a conspiracy in which she took no active part. (Thérèse was finally acquitted on December 16, 1966, having spent almost a year in detention.)

Annette's mother, now estranged from her husband, lives alone in a luxurious, modern, wall-to-wall-carpeted apartment from which she rarely emerges. In happier days, before Annette began behaving so peculiarly, she did go out a bit, for her elder daughter would come sometimes on Sundays to chat with her and take her for walks. Annette had been fond of her mother, without having understood her for an instant.

There are those who feel that we have not heard the last of this liberator. Precisely how Annette managed to disarm so many people and manipulate circumstances to her own advantage will never be fully revealed, but such are the secrets of those who traffic in deception in or out of crime.

Chapter IV

Millie

LATE one chill night in early October, 1962, a man and a woman lay together on a narrow bed in a Philadelphia townhouse and listened to the radio. The man, a brilliant young graduate student in the school of engineering and applied physics at the University of Pennsylvania, was stretched out with his face to the wall, dozing. The girl, a postdebutante with silky blonde hair hanging below her shoulders and framing a round and unsmiling face, reclined in the attitude of a twentieth-century odalisque, propped up on one elbow, and stared down the barrel of a .22-caliber revolver. By the small hours of the next morning, the young man would be dead, and the girl would find herself sitting in the kitchen, gazing remotely at the revolver as it lay on the table before her, one bullet spent. The man was Axel Schmidt, twenty-six years old, of German parentage; the girl, his current mistress, was Millicent Adams of Chestnut Hill.

In spite of the privileges which normally accrue to being a well-born resident of America's golden East Coast, Millie's life was not a happy one. Millie's mother had been unsatisfied with her marriage to Timothy Adams almost from the outset, and as a result, Mrs. Adams had been unable to feel any but the most minimal affection for the two children, Millicent and Timothy, Jr., which she bore him. Millie and Tim both recall that they seldom saw their parents together, and when they did, it was to be witness to harsh words and, frequently, violent acts. Little Tim, a rather frail child, clung to his sister, older by three years, for sustenance and warmth, their mother hardly being able to bring herself to kiss them good night after tucking them into bed in the evening.

In the late forties, when Millie and Tim were seven and four respectively, the Adamses were divorced, and some years later, both remarried. Mrs. Adams' new husband, whose name was George McLeland, was nearly six years younger than his restless patrician bride, who, with her heart-shaped face, bangs, and dark brows, looked almost as young as Millie, and he found it hard in some ways to cope with the situation. He did seem genuinely fond of the children, though his compassion for them was somehow impotent. Ultimately the McLelands produced three children of their own, two boys and a little girl, whom Millie mothered and fussed over as if they were her own.

All her young life Millie had displayed an easy affection for little children and animals which was not manifest in her relations with her peers or with older people, among whom she was equally shy. Disturbed by the fact that her teeth were badly discolored, she seldom smiled, but maintained a solemn, some would even say sullen, expression most of the time. Sensitive and introverted, Millie spent hours reading poetry, writing a little, and playing with her half-brothers and -sisters—as though dreading the day that she would herself be an adult and have to live within a framework of reality, where doubtless too much would be expected of her. For Millie, material objects were invested with a magnified importance, and she was frequently seen wandering around in the streets, both day and night, browsing and window shopping, clutching some trinket or cherished artifact. "It was a way she had," people said. "She always carried something with her—some bit of art. Perhaps it was like a teddy bear to a child."

After her mother and McLeland were married, Millie attended a series of good private schools, the last of which was a fashionable institution on Philadelphia's Main Line. Always shy, she seldom talked to anyone other than her few close friends, keeping almost entirely to herself. She giggled a lot, probably to hide her nervousness when confronted by other people, and was often the object of mild ridicule, because she was forever reading novels or poetry or listening to classical music. While at school she also developed a passion for ballet and took to wearing ballet slippers, indoors and out on all occasions even after a heavy snowstorm. She never went to dances, nor was she ever seen out with a boy, and when she made her debut in Philadelphia in 1958, after graduating from boarding school, she certainly had little in common with the other pretty debs whose thoughts revolved almost entirely around boys, clothes, and parties.

Millie had not been the least interested in making her debut, but her mother and her maternal grandmother, Mrs. Alice Copley, had insisted that she should for her own sake and, to a certain extent, for theirs. Ever concerned about Millie's apparent indifference to young men and to the social scene which was popping all around her, they had hoped that by sending her to some of the better parties of the season, they would be laying the foundation for a new social life in which the girl would somehow become interested. Millie only suffered through it all and continued to be generally disinterested in her life as a debutante and in the immature young men who were a part of it. They had nothing to say to her, nor she to them.

When all the social agony was ended, Millie went abroad as a guest of the parents of her good friend Mary Purvis. Mary had been her best chum at school, and the two girls, like so many others, made the tour of the usual museums, palaces, cathedrals, and spas.

Upon returning, Millie discovered that her father had remarried for a second time, had a child by this latest marriage, and was living in California. Although she had rarely had anything to do with him as a child, and even less after the divorce, this current news elicited a curious wave of nostalgia and longing to see her handsome father again and perhaps to reestablish some sort of contact with him. She decided to postpone college for a year and go to California to see him, meet his new wife, and view the baby.

This turned out to be a tragically disappointing pilgrimage. When she arrived on the Coast, she discovered that her father was unemployed and that his wife was going to work every day in an effort to support the family. Millie and her new stepmother got along rather well, however, and her father seemed glad enough to see her. The baby was adorable, and it looked, on the face of it, as though she had finally found a nesting place.

In the beginning of her visit, Millie had enjoyed sitting up at night with her father and talking to him about her dreams and plans. She told him of her developing love of ballet and about her desire to study dancing herself, thinking that a devotion to this taxing art might win her father's esteem. She had rather counted on his helping her financially in this area, but it soon became evident that he was barely managing with his own small family and that he was hardly in a position to do anything for her. Indeed, he had never done much for her.

Millie had not been in California long when her father decided that this would be a good time to go to New York and hunt for a job; and thus it was that Millie, full of optimism and having pinned all her fragile hopes on this reunion, was left to serve as a baby-sitter in her father's unfamiliar home while her stepmother left her each morning to go out and earn sixty-five dollars a week.

This was the beginning of a very bad period for Millie, whose psychological constitution, never strong, began now to deteriorate critically. Bitter, resentful of her father's "deserting" her—for the second time in her life—she was persuaded by her grandmother, who was also in California at the time, to leave as soon as possible and not attempt to see him again. Hopelessly caught up in his own immediate problems, Adams had no way of knowing, and little capacity for sensing, that his daughter's spirit was in a perilous condition, and he did not see any particular significance in her precipitous departure which followed his return from the East. The experience had, however, left a lasting and dangerous wound.

Autumn had nearly ended, and Millie, who had always found this to be a wistful, sad time of year, with everything around her dying or dead, could not face going back to the ménage in Philadelphia to watch the dying leaves collecting in her mother's unkempt garden. She decided to stay in New York for a while with a friend from school who had an apartment of her own and an extra bed in it for Millie. Inasmuch as ballet school

was now out of the question, her grandmother being unenthusiastic, she resolved to enroll in secretarial school and learn how to
type so that she would be able, at least, to get some kind of job.
Her grandmother had always been very generous, but she clearly
did not intend to support Millie indefinitely. With the help of
her roommate, she found a good stenographic school and settled
into her new routine.

At the school, Millie met a girl called Hanya, whose
parents were Yugoslav, and who seemed to have many of the
same problems and related feelings that Millie did. The two fed
on each other's misery and sense of melancholy isolation from
other happier people, and formed a morbid, almost pathological,
bond. Hanya spoke constantly of a certain Dr. Beyer, a psychiatrist who had been treating her for some time, and it was not
long before Millie found herself making weekly appointments
with him as well. She was getting some financial help from her
mother and a more substantial amount from Grandmother
Copley, who little knew that, although most of it was applied to
Millie's secretarial training, some was now finding its way into
the coffers of Dr. Beyer.

By the time Christmas came along, Millie was very much
looking forward to going home; she had missed the little ones
and bustled about New York in the frantic preholiday weeks
looking for presents for them and the rest of the family. It was
with considerable cheer that she greeted them all again, and,
happily, they all appeared to be very glad to see her. She had not
seen the family for several months, although her brother Tim
had frequently come to spend the weekend with her in New
York. The little McLelands, who raved over their carefully
chosen presents, were beside themselves with joy at having their
favorite adult back among them, and all things considered, it
was a happy Christmas for Millie.

Millie spent that summer at her grandmother's house in
Bay Head, New Jersey, reading, sailing, playing endlessly with
the children and seeing no one except her brother Tim. Her
mother simply could not understand why Millie had no beaux;
she was nice looking and had a good-enough figure. There were
any number of suitable young men around, not only in Philadelphia but there in Bay Head; and yet none of them seemed to
interest Millie. She had reached the age when most girls are
obsessed with boys and social life, but she remained totally in-

different to them, a circumstance which her mother found utterly baffling.

Thus the summer passed, and Millie sank ever deeper into the profound recesses of her dark inner world; loneliness was a comfort, solitude a friend, the love of three children her only fragile connection to the real world.

In the autumn of 1959, Millie had concluded that most of the jobs for which she might be eligible around Philadelphia would be insupportably dull, so she enrolled at Bryn Mawr. Her mother and stepfather, knowing neither how to regard her nor what to do with her, were greatly relieved, for they found Millie and her problems rather trying.

At college, Millie became increasingly despondent, and she began to make long weekend trips into New York to see Dr. Beyer. At one stage she tried to transfer her enrollment to Barnard College in New York so as to be nearer the doctor, but when the college authorities discovered that she had been under psychiatric care and planned to continue, they refused her admission.

One night, at Bryn Mawr, alone and brooding about her deteriorating personal appearance, the lost world of ballet, her father's indifference and treachery, and the empty rootless future which apparently lay ahead of her, she slashed her wrists with a razor. The attempt to die failed, as the cuts had not been sufficiently deep. Ashamed of her motives and her failure, she told no one about the incident then.

Christmas vacation brought her back home to the inevitable burden of holiday parties arranged by her female relatives, which she endured with her accustomed reticence. One night, however, she had an exceptionally good time, for she met a young man—the first ever who really interested her, and who appeared to like her as well. His name was Axel Schmidt.

Axel had beautiful European manners, and these, combined with his intelligent good looks and reserved confidence, attracted Millie at once: He seemed to fulfill a kind of poetic ideal she sustained as to the way men ought to be—an ideal derived in part from her favorite poems and novels, the sanguine, safe stories she often read to the children at bedtime, and partly from her own cherished fantasies. Courtliness presents a kind of barrier to the harsher realities and may disguise a multitude of sins and insensibilities. Axel's manner spoke to

Millie of strength and security, saying, "Here is a noncombatant; I am the shield."

Intrigued by the bizarre quality projected by this fey creature, Axel was equally drawn to Millie and paid her a great deal of attention during the course of the evening. This, among other things, rendered bearable an evening which might otherwise have passed into the limbo of unmemorable occasions to which Millie normally relegated such events as parties, and permitted her for once to regard the assembled guests with a relatively benevolent eye. If Axel found her attractive, then it was quite possible, she supposed, that others might do so as well. She was happy, moreover, that she was not disappointing her mother and grandmother by hating it all as usual.

In spite of the success of this one evening, the highlight of which was having met Axel, nothing very much developed as a result of the initial contact with Axel. The holidays came to an end, and Millie went back to college. Axel, in the meantime, reported to a colleague that he had met a girl who was a real screwball and that, although he had been rather intrigued by her, he would never want to become involved with anybody who had so many problems as she seemed to have. It could present real difficulties.

The inevitable rolling back of winter brought midyear exams to students all over America, and, subsequently, the welcome release of spring vacation.

On one of her first nights home, Millie was invited to a charity function at the Philadelphia Art Museum, which she attended only because it had to do with art. Entering the main hall, she was delighted to see the politely smiling face of Axel Schmidt gazing solemnly at her from a corner near the bar. Having passed the winter among the dark phantoms of her brooding mind, she had hardly thought of Axel, but now, much to her surprise, she found herself overjoyed at the prospect of talking again with this intelligent young man and perhaps getting to know him better. The evening went well, and they spoke of many things—books, music, and their respective academic experiences. The only thing that inhibited complete candor was the shameful suicide attempt, which, seemed futile—even silly —but nevertheless hovered menacingly at the brink of their dialogue.

From that time on, Millie and Axel were inseparable.

They saw each other constantly throughout the vacation, Axel having evidently overcome his original wariness of this strange, distracted girl, and it was with considerable regret that they parted in April to return to their studies. Mr. and Mrs. Mc-Leland, who had despaired of ever seeing Millie happy with any human being other than her brother Tim, were pleased that at last she was behaving "normally," and they were comforted by the thought that perhaps all their worry over her had been gratuitous. They found Axel charming, polite, and trustworthy, but, what was infinitely more important, he was making Millie happy—a thing which they had failed to do. In a sense, too, it relieved them of a certain responsibility.

In June, 1960, when the school year was finished, Millie began living with Axel in his tiny apartment on Spruce Street, near the university campus; at least she was always there when he wanted her around, which was most of the time. On the few occasions when he returned from the day's business and found that Millie was not waiting for him, he became angry and reprimanded her severely on her return. This made Millie miserable, for even though Axel insisted that she spend all her time with him, he had never expressed any love for her. Often she spent whole days sitting in the apartment, musing over the notion that no one could love her, thus dwelling on, even luxuriating in her misery. For Millie, happiness fled when sex emerged as an important factor in life.

The McLelands, who paid little or no attention to Millie's comings and goings at home, were unaware of the transformation which had occurred, and encouraged the pair to spend weekends at the house in Bay Head, as this was where Millie had always been especially happy. Axel, too, seemed to love the vast expanses of sand and waving sea grass among the dunes, the haze of the day's heat, the primordial smell of the ocean and all its life, which permeated the heavy mists of evening, and the gray weathered ramble of a house which had embraced the summer doings of several generations.

Once, during one of these sun-filled weekends, the McLelands sat on the porch of the house and watched Axel and Millie as they walked toward them along the beach at the end of a blistering, bright day. They had been sailing, which Millie adored, and collecting samples of the myriad shells found along the beach, trying to identify the various types of gulls and other birds which abounded. The tide had gone out, and they had to moor the boat quite far from shore and walk in across the sandbar. Strolling with the hot blaze of a waning sun behind them, they had been transformed into two dark, elusive shapes linked only by a frail handclasp. Millie was laughing and tossing her blonde hair from side to side, as a child would in playing a game. Suddenly they stopped and dropped their hands. Axel waved his arms in a gesture of exasperation, and Millie's shoulders sagged. She said something brief, and they once again joined hands and continued slowly back in silence. Mrs. McLeland often wondered what passed between them that evening.

Millie dissipated almost two years of her life in this manner, her days taken up with devising entertainments for her beloved half-siblings and serving as Axel's willing companion and mistress. Occasionally she would take a job—spasmodically, diffidently, just for some extra money—but ultimately she would become overwhelmed with boredom, at which point she would simply resign without regret or sense of failure.

In spite of Axel's presence in her life, Millie's habitual and intense preoccupation with objects and possessions continued to grow, and she steadily increased her collection of books, papers, pictures, bits of jewelry, furniture, and objets d'art, all of which seemed to hold some special meaning for her. Tim was increasingly puzzled by it, for he remembered the days before Axel, when they had been among the "night people," drifting about the town in the small hours from coffee house to pub, searching for the insalubrious warmth of fellow displaced persons and never finding it, even then, Millie always embracing some small treasure. Now that she had Axel, a person of her own, why was she still enslaved by things?

One day, early in 1961, Millie told Tim that she thought she would move out of their mother's house because she wasn't wanted there. George McLeland had tried to be kind to his stepchildren—not an easy task at best—but had not the maturity, depth of perception, or strength of will to create any true rapport with either of them. And as for their mother, they could not bring themselves to feel anything whatever for her, except a growing distaste for her physical touch. Millie began speaking about anything handled by her mother as being permeated by "fallout" and subject, therefore, either to sterilization or destruction.

It was finally arranged that Millie should go to live with her grandmother, Mrs. Copley, who owned a lovely house on Chestnut Hill Avenue, not far from Mrs. McLeland's. There Millie found a welcome haven of solitude in her own tiny private apartment right on the ground floor. From her bedroom window, she could look out on flowers and blooming shrubs from which she would pluck fresh bouquets each day for her cluttered little rooms in spring and summer. She thought vaguely about hanging a bird feeder outside the window but never got around to it.

Eventually she sought the help of a local psychiatrist who worked at the University of Pennsylvania hospital, and began going to see him twice a week. When she had a job, she managed to pay him out of what she was able to earn, but often, finding herself jobless and without funds, she had to borrow the money from Tim. These visits went on for several weeks, after which the doctor, with whom she had established a sound rapport, ultimately decided that Millie was in need of an intensive psychoanalysis; this introduced a time factor, which his own busy schedule could not absorb, and he was obliged to turn her over to a colleague at the university. To Millie, it simply constituted another rejection.

Paul Riesman, of the psychiatric institute at the University of Pennsylvania, turned out to be a somewhat less sympathetic figure than his predecessor. Millie sought compassion and commiseration, but Riesman took a more clinical, hard-headed tack with her, hoping to shake her out of the morass of self-pity in which she allowed herself to wallow. This did not improve their relations or make Riesman's task easier, and may even have caused Millie to exaggerate the failings of those around her and those aspects of her life which she most resented.

As Riesman himself was later to testify: "Her relationship with me, despite all my therapeutic efforts, remained superficial and tenuous, and never achieved any depth. Occasionally she would show signs of a beginning attachment, but this immediately frightened her, and she withdrew into her narcissistic preoccupation with suffering. She expected that, once again, she would have a major rejection—which had happened to her, in her opinion, with every person with whom she had developed a relationship all her life."

Millie's version, when solicited, was slightly different.

She detested Riesman, and thought he was a "cold fish," and claimed that as the reason why she ultimately left him. The very fact that the girl had remained with a doctor she considered unsympathetic through seventy-seven sessions is indicative of her masochistic tendencies.

What would constitute a true evaluation of these circumstances and the nature of the people who formed them is difficult to know for certain, for as Millie projected herself toward the inevitable act of destruction and despair, events and characters, motives and meanings were invested with a troublesome ambiguity. By October, 1962, Millie had reached a point where her grip on reality, outside of her small and tormented life with Axel, had been all but lost.

She had learned that Axel was planning a long vacation —without her—and that he had accepted a new job far from Philadelphia. The mechanics of departure were in motion, and Millie, in a miasma of emotional agony and confusion, had been helping him. He had told her some time ago, on November 21 of the previous year—she remembered the day— that he would never marry her, and her delicate world had begun to crumble again. She had not minded so much, as long as there had been no question of his leaving Philadelphia, but now it was different. If only she had succeeded in dying that frostbound night at Bryn Mawr, she would have been spared all this pain.

One day early in October, Axel suggested that they spend the afternoon driving and walking in rural Germantown outside Philadelphia. Autumn had not yet arrived in all its gaudy splendor, but there was a crispness in the wood- and smoke-scented air warning of the harsh winter to come, and the newly invigorated citizens appeared willing to do anything to get out in it. As the lovers tramped through the yellow, first-fallen leaves, Axel thought that Millie appeared quieter, more contemplative, than usual, but as he was not in the habit of taking particular notice of her nuances of feeling, he made no comment, enjoying his walk and his private thoughts. They made a long tour of the famous battle monuments where brave men fought and fell during the Revolution, paying special visits to the quaint and picturesque graveyards which contained so many rebel bones. Axel commented on the extraordinary sweet scent of the woods all around them and the reflections in the opaque waters beneath

the rustic bridges connecting one area of the cemetery to another. This was the first time Millie had heard Axel articulate
any response he had to his surroundings or demonstrate any
aesthetic sensitivity, and it moved her nearly to tears.

Having covered the desired territory, they bought grapes
and some cider at a roadside stand to bring back with them to
the city, Millie remaining quiet and generally unenthusiastic. At
last, walking back to the car, she broke the silence which hung
about her like a shroud.

Little is known about the actual conversation which then
took place between them, apart from general content; we may
imagine, however, that the dialogue ran along the following
lines:

"Axel?"

"Yes. What is it?"

"Do you think you will ever want to have children?"

"I suppose so—sometime. Why do you ask now? I've
told you, Millie, that I am not going to marry you. In fact I told
you I don't want to get married until I'm much older—maybe
forty, even—and have plenty of money, after reaching a certain
position in my profession. A man can't do his best work with a
wife around his neck—responsibilities, worries. I don't want to
be just another good engineer. I want to be a great one."

"I'm sure you will be, Axel."

"And how do you know, anyway?" he said, laughing
without mirth.

"Where are you really going on your vacation?"

"I told you. I'm going to Zurich to see my parents. And
then to California, where I've been offered this fantastic job."

"Then why have we been sending so much of your stuff
to Rio?"

"We've hardly sent anything anyplace. Most of it is still
sitting here in that warehouse with all your junk."

"But it's going to Brazil eventually."

"Look, what is this, the third degree? My parents live in
São Paolo a lot of the time, which you know very well. So why
on earth shouldn't it go to Brazil? I don't need all that stuff in
California. Besides, I don't like people prying into my affairs, so
why don't you just drop the subject and walk along with me
quietly?"

"Axel, I've found out something." She had stopped

walking now and was standing stock still facing him, her long hair blowing gently in the wind, the penetrating blue eyes filled with pain. "I know you're going to get married in Rio—to a Brazilian girl. Isn't that right?"

"Yes, that's right," he replied, calm as the day. "I think I told you that some time ago, come to think of it. You just forgot, I'm afraid. It won't be for quite a long time, anyway."

"No, Axel. I think I would have remembered. You've always said you planned to wait till you were forty to get married. I saw a letter—you know, when we were moving all your things out of your apartment—but I couldn't believe it was true."

"Why shouldn't it be true, Millie? I never told you that I was going to marry *you* in any case, so what difference does it make? You agreed to stay with me while I was here, knowing just what the situation was. Isn't that right?"

"Yes, that's right. But—well, I don't know if I can accept this."

"Listen, Millie," Axel said, taking her hands. "This girl is the daughter of very good friends of my mother and father. I've known her since I was a child. She comes from a very good family and has a great deal of money. She is very independent. It has been planned for a long time. Besides, if you wouldn't read my mail, you wouldn't be troubled by these things."

"Do you love her?"

"Love!" He shrugged. "You are so full of romantic notions, Millie. I am European. Marriage to us is a contract between two people who respect each other and who are suited, both socially and temperamentally. Who on earth speaks of love after the first year? I will probably have a mistress by then. You Americans are so filled with love," he scoffed. "It is undoubtedly why you divorce so much."

"Yes, Axel. You're probably right. But I do love you," she said quietly and without drama.

"I know," Axel replied not unkindly. "And I have been very happy with you—honestly."

What Axel was never to learn was that Millie had spent part of the previous day with the doctor, who had confirmed the fact that she was pregnant. She had already, in desperation, told the wife of a cousin of Axel's whom they had visited in New York the previous weekend, but she clearly felt that she could not risk telling Axel himself.

There were other facts of which Axel was innocent. In March of that year, a combination of too much hostility and too few funds had forced Millie to terminate her sessions with Dr. Riesman. Having seen her seventy-seven times since she first came to him in September of 1961, he felt that little had been accomplished; his conclusion, in fact, was that Millie did not really want to get better, and that she had not been responding either to him as a person or as a doctor. She spoke often of suicide, but Riesman had not yet made up his mind whether she was actually apt to expedite this threat, or whether this constituted the familiar cry for help, attention, and sympathy.

In May, Millie applied for a gun permit, which she was promptly refused, but by June, she had succeeded in procuring a weapon.

Mary Purvis had got married, and Millie had been in the wedding, which took place early in June. The reception, a large, hot affair, staged at the Purvis' Main Line establishment, was a grueling business for Millie, who hated crowds and social effort. Immediately after the reception line broke up, she fled to the cool, dark recesses of the second floor and searched for an empty room in which to lie down for a moment and take off her shoes.

As she lay there, her head reeling in the semidarkness, she realized that she must have stumbled into the bedroom of Mary's older brother, who had been in Korea, for she found herself surrounded by the relics of extensive travel and the mementos of war. The young man no longer lived in his family's house, but as he was still unmarried, he had left behind many of his youthful possessions in the room where he grew up. The place was infused with the mingled aromas of shoe polish, after-shave lotion, leather, and must. It also smelled of gun oil.

Millie opened her eyes. On the far wall, opposite the bed where she lay, stood a glass-faced cabinet containing rifles and shotguns, and on an adjoining peg hung a belt and two holsters which held a pair of .22-caliber Smith & Wesson revolvers. Millie sat up in bed, staring intently at the curved, cross-hatched butts thrusting out from their stern leather cases. Jumping suddenly from the bed, a renewed quickness in her frame, she crossed the room swiftly and lifted one of the guns from the belt. She was surprised at its weight. No wonder it was difficult to achieve accuracy with a revolver, she thought, as she held the weapon straight out in front of her, her hand wavering uncertainly at the end of the plump, white arm. Hearing steps in the hall, she hurriedly replaced the gun and returned to the party.

In the car going back to the city the next day, Millie thought a great deal about the gun, and resting her head against the window, she dozed, dreaming of some alien land full of beauty, where she was a different person—serene and free of anxiety.

Two weeks later, Millie paid a visit to the Purvis household. Mary and her husband were off on their wedding trip, and her parents had moved up to their summer place in New England, leaving only the housekeeper in residence.

Millie had no trouble persuading the maid that she had lost a brooch at the time of the wedding and, insisting that she knew just where she must have dropped it, went up to look for it herself. On leaving, she proclaimed success in her hunt—and walked out with the revolver in her handbag.

The last months of the summer were passed in a jumbled, semiconscious world of self-hatred, pain, and fantasy. Axel was leaving. He was leaving *her*. Was this true? Or was it simply a recurring nightmare that she had when Axel would turn his back to her in bed and instantly sink into a heavy sleep, untroubled by conscience or the awareness of love? He would brush his teeth, make love to her—if one could call it that, for he rarely spoke, nor were his actions betrayed by affection—and go to sleep, only sometimes remembering to say good night.

Millie had helped him move his things from the familiar bachelor flat, selecting some things for storage and others for shipment to Brazil. He was really going, then, or he wouldn't be moving all this stuff. . . . Didn't he realize that, apart from the children, he was her entire world? How could he simply deprive another person of her world, her life? How was she to live then?

Anyway, she had the gun. If the pain got worse, she could use the gun and end it. Who would miss her, except the children, for a little while, and maybe Tim? It was, after all, quite absurd to think that a strong, worthwhile person such as Axel would want to stay with a homely, helpless, untalented weakling; it was perfectly logical, on the other hand, that inasmuch as she did not merit anybody's love, she did not get it. Axel was, above everything, intelligent, and clearly gave her only what she deserved.

Rio must be a beautiful place. Axel had told her so many times about it and São Paolo, where his parents had a beautiful house. If only they could go there together and just be alone, away from Mother, Grandmother, and all the prying friends who knew how dumb and silly she was, and who probably wouldn't be at all surprised that Axel was not going to marry her. But the girl was there, in Rio. . . . Still, it would be nice just to have a ticket, in case she needed to get out, to escape. . . . Rio de Janeiro—River of January. It must have been discovered in January. She could change her name, and perhaps, with a new name, construct a new self—a self which would be lost in anonymity.

During this difficult period, Millie virtually never went out without the revolver and a plane ticket on her person. These were her two most palpable avenues of escape—an escape held in reserve—in case she should be forced to flee from her misery and the dreary shell of her lackluster self. She could leave any time. Meanwhile, she bathed—often several times a day—to purge herself of the "fallout" which emanated now even from her grandmother and bound her insupportably to her family and present life.

The logistics involving Millie's fantasies of escape and self-eradication ultimately became utterly bewildering. Having borrowed a thousand dollars from her brother, presumably for continued psychiatric care, she bought at different times tickets to Rome, Rotterdam, and Rio, arranging simultaneously to have large batches of furniture and personal belongings shipped to these places for storage prior to her arrival. Having made and cancelled any number of reservations for transcontinental flights, during the course of the summer, Millie also opened negotiations with several major moving companies who were to be in charge of getting her increasing mass of personal treasures from Philadelphia to sundry warehouses in New York, Europe, and South America. At one point she had 850 pounds of stuff stored somewhere in New York and another 1,183 pounds in Rotterdam. (It would be interesting to know just what made Rotterdam appear in her tormented mind as a sympathetic haven of retreat, the place being notoriously cold, damp, and dull; perhaps it seemed especially remote, and this was sufficient to make it attractive.)

In the third week of September, having totally vacated his own apartment, Axel moved in with Millie, and since her grandmother usually stayed in Bay Head right up until October, they had the house more or less to themselves. Each night they slept together on Millie's narrow studio bed, although at times Axel would crowd her out, forcing her to drag off a blanket in the middle of the night to the nearest couch.

Around September 21, Millie went with Axel to New York, where they spent the weekend with Axel's cousin and his wife. Millie got along well with them and invited them to Philadelphia for the following weekend; it was during that first visit in New York that Millie confided to the wife that she thought she might be pregnant.

By this time, Millie had missed her period by at least two weeks, and she thought seriously again about the gun. Only a week or so earlier, she had written to her friend Hanya, who was in Munich, saying, "It is the end of the summer, and the end. Good-bye." She had made a will leaving everything to Hanya, and she wanted her friend to know this.

Late in September, she picked up a St. Bernard at the local dog pound, took it back to an unoccupied servant's room, and shot it through the head. Not wishing to suffer pain when she died, Millie had chosen an animal of her approximate size, in order to make sure that the gun would definitely kill it—and therefore, subsequently, herself. Having demonstrated this to her satisfaction, she slipped the carcass distractedly beneath the unused cot and forgot about it.

It was three days later that Axel and Millie had their tour of Germantown, returning after dark to Millie's little room. They ate their fruit, cheese, and bread in silence, and drank the cider they had bought on the way home. Millie sat, chewing, and staring at a shoe she had kicked off, as it lay, listing slightly to port, on the blue of her worn and rumpled cotton rug. It looked like a boat, she mused, making its way across a deep swelling sea—to Rio.

She looked at Axel. His dark hair had grown somewhat too long—the way she liked it—and fell becomingly over one eye. His square well-proportioned and full-lipped face had caught the final rays of summer sun and was healthily ruddy, his glasses having left a narrow white line across the temple and nose. Millie wanted to touch him, pour out the affection which rose in her at times like this, and tell him about the baby. But he would be too angry. She could not. He had told her many times that if she failed to take the necessary precautions and became pregnant, the burden would be entirely upon her—he would take no responsibility in the matter, either toward her or any child that resulted from her carelessness. He had been very frank, very honest. Now he was leaving.

As she thought about these things, Millie's chest seemed to constrict, as though a wide belt had been tightened around her ribs, causing her intense pain. Her head swam, and she reached for a worn bit of pre-Colombian sculpture which always stood by her bed and, clutching it to her chest, tried to soothe the turmoil there. She looked at the little statue and rubbed its head, wishing that the comfort she had often derived from looking at its calm face would spread over her now. But the pain grew worse, and tears began to roll down her silent cheeks, dampening the hair which framed them, and, almost imperceptibly she rocked back and forth in her chair.

Axel finally noticed that something was wrong with her. He had finished eating and turned, looking for a napkin.

"Now, Millie, why are you crying? Didn't we just have a nice day together? You're not used to walking that much, and I'm sure you're just tired. Get undressed and get into bed. We'll listen to the opera on the radio. It's *Don Giovanni* tonight, I think. Would you like that?" Axel could be kind, and he was gentle with her now. It always rather surprised him that this curious girl could become so utterly absorbed in her own emotions, with no apparent restraint or discipline. The milieu in which he had grown up had taught him, in any case, that it was simply crude to overtly mistreat women; they were weak and dependent creatures, and responded best when treated more like large children than adults. This one was more vulnerable, more childlike than most, it seemed, and full of strange currents.

He turned on the radio, found the station, and smiled patronizingly at Millie.

"There. It's just starting the first act."

"You're going away," she mumbled miserably, almost unable to form the words.

"What? I can't hear you," he replied, leaning over her

chair. The face Millie turned up to him was streaked, puffy, and tragic. Axel thought that she really looked unbelievably ugly at this moment, but women always did when in tears.

"You're leaving me," she cried. "And I'm so unhappy."

"It's going to be all right. You'll be all right," Axel soothed. "You'll miss me for a while—and I'll miss you too." He added cheerfully, with sudden inspiration, "But then we'll get settled in our new lives, and everything will be fine. You'll see. Now get into bed and listen to the music with me." Putting his arm around her, he led her to the bathroom, where she mechanically prepared for bed, moving like a zombie.

When she came out, Axel was already in bed, lying on his side, face to the wall. Millie regarded him dispassionately for a moment, then went to her worn bureau, covered with photographs of Axel and opened the bottom drawer. Amidst the awful jumble of tatty sweaters and frayed underwear lay the revolver. There were no mirrors in the room, other than in the bathroom, and no photographs of her and Axel together; she did not wish to see herself these days in any medium. Holding the gun behind her, she slipped into bed next to Axel, and thrust the gun under the pillow.

She lay for several minutes, staring at the ceiling, as the sound of Axel's deep, even breathing mingled with the strains of the Don's melodic enticement of Zerlina:

> *"La ci darem la mano,*
> *La mi dirai di si.*
> *Vedi non e lontano,*
> *Partiam ben mio da qui.*
>
> *Vorei, e non vorei,*
> *Mi trema un poco il cor.*
> *Felice e ver sarei,*
> *Ma puo burlarmian cor."*

Poor girl, Millie thought. She's just like me. When she begins to love this man, he will leave her and go off with someone else. Perhaps it's inevitable that he should be destroyed in the final act.

Millie pulled the gun out from under the pillow, and as Axel dozed, she gazed intently down its long barrel, alternately pointing it at her temple and the smooth spot between her eyes.

It was loaded and ready to go, thanks to an accommodating friend, who had bought the bullets for Millie.

"Andiam, andiam mio bene,
Aristorar le pene,
D'un inocente amor."

Suddenly, or so it seemed, Axel stirred, and Millie, who had actually been toying with the revolver for nearly two hours, hurriedly pushed it back under the pillow. Turning toward him, she said, "You haven't been listening."

"Oh, yes, I have," Axel responded, stretching. "I know every line of this opera by heart. I hear it in my sleep. The Elvira is perfectly dreadful in this recording. I wonder who it is?"

"I don't know. I didn't hear."

"Ah, to be Don Juan and make love to any girl who takes one's fancy . . . I think I'm rather like him actually. I'm going to sleep now. If you want to hear the end, it won't bother me." And then he rolled back to the wall and dropped off to sleep.

Millie struggled to contain her rocketing emotions. Staring at her lover's back, she mouthed the words, "I love you," wondering whether a feeling that was strong enough could really penetrate to another person's consciousness, as some believed. Taking the revolver once more from its nest, she pointed it again at her head. Then she held it so that the muzzle was no further than an inch from the shadowed nape of Axel's neck. Quickly, she turned it back to her own temple, then placed it under her heart, then back to the temple.

Millie had now entered into what is sometimes technically termed a fugue state.

Explosions full of vibrating color were occurring behind her eyes: roman candles, bursting with visions of Rio amidst green-spiked palms, a blue sea filled with boats, a rowdy banquet at which a man, Don Juan—or was it Axel?—was confronted with the prophetic apparition forewarning his own destruction, and she, a different Millie, or perhaps not Millie at all, presided over his demise. She waved the gun from side to side as she was caught up in each fantasy, forgetting for the moment why she had it there and losing awareness of the purpose to which such an implement is generally put. The present was lost to her, drowned in a flood of imagining. The radio announced that it was midnight.

Some time later, Millie found herself sitting in the kitchen in front of a cold cup of tea. The gun was on the table too, next to the teacup. Taking no particular notice of it, she went back into the bedroom and called Tim on the telephone. He was surprised to hear from her so late at night, as she rarely called him after ten or eleven o'clock. But he was pleased that she had rung, and noticed that her voice seemed brighter and her attitude less despairing than it had for several weeks. They launched almost immediately into a discussion about a book by a renowned theologian they had both been reading, and spoke for nearly forty-five minutes before hanging up. Millie was by now thoroughly used up, exhausted, but calmly so. Leaving the room, she drifted upstairs to the living room and went to sleep on the couch.

What had apparently been thoroughly eclipsed in her mind, along with the pain, the constricting weight on her chest, and the stampeding fantasies, was the fact that Axel lay dead on her cot, with dark blood slowly congealing around a hole in the back of his head. The cover which Millie wearily pulled up around her chin upstairs consisted only of a blanket for at some point during the chaos, Millie had covered Axel's body with the sheet.

Millie woke later that morning feeling somehow refreshed. The milkman came as usual around 8:30, walked into the kitchen, and placed the milk in the icebox, as was his custom. Hearing the refrigerator door slam, Millie called out from behind the bedroom door, "Thank you!" Responding as always to the cheery, sing-song of Millie's daily acknowledgment of his efforts, he touched his cap, though no one was there to see, and replied, "Welcome, ma'am." They had never, in fact, actually seen each other.

Having showered, Millie then proceeded to make arrangements to spend the day with the children; they had already begun to plan what they would do for Halloween, and Millie was helping them. That evening Millie brought Amanda, the eldest of the three, back to her grandmother's house, as she often did, to spend the night. The child loved these occasional visits, for they constituted a series of small adventures for her— sleeping away from the other children for a change, in the tiny maid's room on the second floor—and it meant that she would get read to by Millie, which she never did at home.

That was Wednesday, and since Mrs. Copley was due back on Friday, Thursday would have to be a day of reckoning for Millie. She could not go on indefinitely, unconscious of the body which continued to lie in her room; she could not pretend that what had happened had not happened. Thursday morning she confronted the fact while sipping tea and eating toast in the kitchen: She had shot and killed Axel, why or how she could not remember, but the gun was there on the table, fully loaded but for one spent cartridge. All that was left of him now was the growing thing in her womb, a mass of memories, and a motley collection of furniture and personal belongings stored cozily in a warehouse in downtown Philadelphia.

Why—when it was she herself and not he whom she had intended to extinguish—she had emerged from her trance to find him dead was more than she could now explain to herself; she would certainly have difficulty explaining it to anyone else. At least now he would not be able to commit the act of leaving her or of taking another woman into his life. And she possessed his child. What, though, would become of her without him to tell her which way to go and what to do? She had to leave everything behind—Axel, the family, that room—to forget and start again.

Millie spent the early part of the morning hunting for clothes and locating a padlock for her bedroom door. No one must touch Axel. She telephoned various warehouses and moving companies, advising each one as to the disposition of her possessions, and made a reservation on Varig Airlines on their evening flight to Rio. She already had the ticket; they would validate it when she got to the airport. She then put on a singularly inappropriate pale-blue satin dress, a beige sweater, black suede shoes, and her favorite necklace of gold beads, which was always around her throat, regardless of what else she wore. She twisted her hair into an unsightly bun, dug some sunglasses out of a sandy beach bag, and, throwing some toilet articles into a shoebag, departed for Philadelphia International Airport to catch the shuttle to New York. In her handbag she carried a few dollars, some personal checks, a lipstick, and an open ticket to Rio. Seven other items of baggage had been sent out to the airport first thing in the morning, to be held until her departure.

Arriving in New York around noon, Millie decided that she needed some clothes, and embarked upon one of the most surrealistic and frantic shopping sprees within contemporary recollection. In just over two hours she visited three major department stores and several smaller shops, including a small Chinese retailer from whom she bought several dresses in various colorful brocades. In each case she paid by check and deliberately chose things at least two sizes too small, explaining to the salespeople that she was shopping for a friend. She also dropped in at Tiffany's where she ordered a diamond bracelet, modest but sufficiently expensive to cause the store to take some precautions. Informing Millie that the bracelet would have to be cleaned and thoroughly scrutinized before it would be released, they asked her to come back later in the afternoon to collect it. This would give them time to check on her identity and credit. She never returned.

By this time Millie had begun to think about getting herself out to Idlewild Airport, in order to check in with her flight and leave final instructions with the people in Air Cargo as to the handling of the masses of luggage which had been sent to them from Philadelphia. These instructions were rather unclear, apart from the definite statement that an exact address in Rio would be received later to which the things were to be sent. Having seen to all these details, Millie boarded the plane, in which she ate and slept a bit, arriving in Rio at 6:40 A.M. on Friday.

That day Mrs. Copley returned from the Cape and, entering her house, noticed that the door leading to Millie's quarters was padlocked. She was not particularly surprised, as her granddaughter quite frequently did odd and unexpected things, but this observation was underscored by the fact that there was a strange and decidedly unpleasant odor coming from that part of the hall. Then she found a note from Millie on the hall table, with directions pertaining to the children's Halloween party along with suggestions as to which among Millie's remaining possessions should be distributed among them. Mrs. Copley called her daughter immediately and told her that she was afraid that Millie had committed suicide.

The next person to be summoned was Thomas Welch, the family's lawyer and friend for many years. As soon as he arrived, they set about trying to force the padlock, but their efforts were unsuccessful. Explaining the situation as obliquely as possible to the handyman, they finally procured a ladder, which Welch placed outside in the garden next to Millie's bedroom window. The sun was out and streaming into the little room, as Welch, jittering on his unaccustomed perch, squinted through the glass.

"Can you see anything?" Mrs. Copley inquired anxiously.

"Yes, but I don't know what it is. There's something on the bed—looks like it's under a sheet." Mrs. Copley covered her mouth. "Oh, my God," she said, "it's Millie."

"Now hold on a minute." Welch had turned to look down at her. "How do you know it's Millie?"

"Well, I don't *know* it's she, but you know, Tom, she spoke so often of doing away with herself. She was an unhappy girl." Welch looked back into the room, his fears rising slowly.

"But if she killed herself, how could she then cover herself with a sheet? We'd better get Arthur over here."

Dr. Arthur Pearson had been looking after the family's health almost as long as Welch had been attending to their legal affairs, and he lost no time in responding to Mrs. Copley's call.

After uttering a few reassuring words on arrival, the doctor, with the help of Welch and the janitor, removed the screen from the window and, finding it unlocked, climbed in. By now Mrs. McLeland had arrived and stood in the garden with her mother, weeping and looking nervously up at the men as they prepared to enter the room.

In spite of their many years as professional witnesses to life's harsher, seamier spectacles, neither Welch nor Pearson was quite prepared for what they encountered that October day in the home of one of their old friends.

It was Indian summer now, and a warm, sluggish sun still fought to keep the nip out of the air which would announce the arrival of autumn. The windows in Millie's room had remained shut for three days, and with the sun pouring in from the garden each day, the heat had built up inside. Axel's body had begun to decompose, and the stench that filled the nostrils of the two men as they entered this room—the bedroom of a girl they had known since she was a child—was stunning. Both men quickly wrapped handkerchiefs around their faces and tried to breathe through the mouth. Pearson walked without hesitating to the place where the body lay, and uncovered it. It was not an attractive sight, bloated and discolored as it was, but at least it was not Millie. The women were shouting from the garden: "Tom! Who is it? What's happened?" Rushing to the window, Welch removed the mask from his face, and answered, "It's not Millie. It's her young man."

Having pronounced the man dead, Pearson notified the office of the medical examiner and gave them the pertinent details. Someone in the medical examiner's office then informed the police, who came at once, photographed the body, established the fact that it was Axel Schmidt, and arranged to have the body removed. In order to do this, the hinges of the bedroom door had to be unscrewed, and the door torn off. The odor now filled the house, and Mrs. Copley was glad to be invited to stay for a few days with her daughter, just up the street.

It was Tim who first wondered about Millie's present whereabouts. His thoughts, in fact, were entirely of her: Where was she, and what would happen to her now?

After the body had been removed and the tide of people and confusion in the room had receded, the family, saddened and bewildered, lingered over the pathetic note written in Millie's tiny, unmistakable scrawl. It was actually addressed to Amanda, and certainly did not, upon closer scrutiny, project the anticipation of death but merely of departure.

Tim tried to explain it all to the little girl, who loved Millie more than any of them. "Something has happened to Axel," he said, "and he has died, and Millie is missing. We don't know where she is." Her face clouding around wide, uncomprehending eyes, Amanda replied, "Oh, poor Axel . . . I hope they find Millie."

All that was found belonging to Axel were a few clothes, and a copy of *Les Liaisons Dangereuses*.

The press had, in this instance, got on to the story even before the police, and it was an alert and industrious reporter who informed the police department that Millie had taken a plane to Rio the previous day. A detective was immediately assigned to follow her there and bring her back. The police believed that, even though the United States and Brazil had no formal extradition agreement under which Millie's return could be demanded, the Brazilian government could easily be persuaded to deport her as an undesirable alien. In the meantime, all the airports and the house on Chestnut Hill Avenue were being watched around the clock, in case she should return.

Millie never told anyone—ever—why she went to Rio. With Axel dead and his parents in Zurich, there did not seem to be any logical reason for going, apart from the desire to fulfill a cherished dream, a dream which had once included Axel but which retained a fixed position in her mind. There were those, of course, who leaned toward the theory that she had fled in order to avoid prosecution, but, as the police later indicated, she couldn't have left a clearer trail if she had tried.

All speculation soon came to an end, however, for much to everyone's astonishment, Millie was back even before the detective appointed to follow her had climbed aboard his flight to Rio from New York. She had checked into the Copacabana Plaza and, having spent twelve disturbed and inconclusive hours there, went back to the airport on Friday evening and took the night flight back to New York.

By now Millie's picture was on the front page of every major newspaper in the East.

In Rio, she had seriously considered the possibility of jumping out of the hotel window, and dying there in Axel's favorite spot. Evidently restored to a more rational frame of mind, she realized that there was no escaping what she had done or, for that matter, who and what she was—and the fact that she very much wanted Axel's baby.

Her unexpected and almost immediate return threw everyone off balance, and as a warrant for her arrest had not yet been obtained, the police at this point could only watch her every move. The flight clerk in New York reported that she had left the plane in a great state of excitement, and when asked in the cargo area what she wanted done with all the luggage she had left there, she replied, "You can't reach me," and fled. So rapid were her movements in departing from the airport that the detectives lost their quarry amidst the bustling and weaving people and taxicabs. They alerted their colleagues at La Guardia, should she decide to fly home, but she fooled them all once again by taking the train, which no one was watching. Actually, she had probably run out of money.

Around 9:30 on Saturday evening, Millie arrived at the North Philadelphia Station, where she hailed a cab. Millie did not seem to know where she wanted to go or what she wanted to do, and the driver was baffled. Finally Millie instructed him just to drive around the city for a while until she made up her mind. She was crying now, and the driver, a compassionate and sensitive man, realized he had a serious problem on his hands and kindly agreed to do what she asked. So long as the meter was running, what was the difference anyway?

After nearly forty-five minutes, Millie said she was ready to go home. Relieved, the driver took her to 437 Chestnut Hill Avenue, but when they arrived, Millie spotted an unfamiliar car standing alongside the house. "No," she said, "don't leave me here. Leave me down by the Bellevue Stratford." Getting out at the main entrance to the hotel, Millie handed the driver four dollars and told him to keep the change. It was $1.20 in excess of the fare, and the cabbie was pleased. In the next moment she dashed across the street, where she immediately jumped into another cab. The driver called the police.

At 10:15 Millie walked in the front door of the University of Pennsylvania hospital and said she needed help. She asked to see her former psychiatrist but was told that he was no longer there. The nurses scrutinized Millie carefully, trying to decide what should be done about her. She was still wearing the dowdy blue-satin dress, her gold beads, and two sweaters, one on top of the other. Tears had eroded the stale makeup on her face, and her hair hung loose now around stooped shoulders. Only the blue eyes, emphasized as they were by unexpected dark brows, contained the remnants of defiance; all else bespoke defeat and resignation.

She sat there alone in the hallway for a long time, waiting for a doctor to have a look at her. It was peaceful there, and sitting with her head bowed, the morbid silence of the hospital enclosing her, she had an opportunity to collect herself a bit. From time to time she drew out from under her sweater a print depicting a medieval stone figure, which she gazed at fondly and from which she seemed to derive comfort.

At last a doctor with white hair and heavy glasses appeared and sat down beside her.

"You have been here a long time," he said. "What is the matter?"

"I have to see a psychiatrist," Millie replied. "I'm not well."

"There are no psychiatrists on duty at this hour, I'm afraid. Who are you? What is your name?"

"My name is Millicent Adams." The doctor's back straightened. He had been listening to the radio and had seen Millie's picture in the paper, and suddenly recognized her as the girl for whom an international manhunt had been initiated the day before.

"Have you done anything, Millicent, that somebody might want to talk to you about?"

"Yes," she replied almost inaudibly. "I have killed Axel, and I need help." She began to cry.

"Wait here a moment, will you?"

Millie nodded her head.

The doctor dashed to a phone and called Detective Madden at the police department, asking him to come to the hospital immediately. At 12:22 the police arrived and arrested Millie. By 12:30, when her mother arrived, the hospital, deathly quiet twenty minutes earlier, had been transformed into a maelstrom of frantic activity and confusion. Mrs. McLeland, wearing sunglasses and accompanied by Tim, was obliged to fight her way through scores of pushing, chattering, bulb-flashing press photographers. The shouting was kept to a minimum by what remained of the hospital staff, but the atmosphere was urgent and intense; everybody wanted this story. It was a humdinger.

As the commotion increased, Millie appeared to withdraw into a sort of catatonic, emotionless state from which no response of any sort could be elicited. She had done with tears, it seemed, and behaved as though she were alone, and there was no one at all around her. She spoke only to Tim, who told her when to get up and go with the police.

At the station, Millie surprised her interrogators with her composure and the shrewdness with which she answered their questions. They were kind to her and endeavored to create an atmosphere of sympathy, but Millie was characteristically wary.

"Millicent, this is Mr. Martin Taplinger, our stenographer. What is your name, the name you were born with?"

"Millicent Adams."

"Are you known as Millie, as a nickname?"

"Yes."

"I will address you from now on—what name do you want me to address you by?"

"Millicent."

"Where do you live?"

"Four thirty-seven Chestnut Hill Avenue."

"How long have you lived there?"

"Since I was five."

"Whom do you live with there?"

"My grandmother."

"What is her name?"

"Mrs. Alice Copley."

"Who else lives there with you?"

"No one."

"Millicent, did you know Axel Schmidt?"

"Yes."

"How long have you known him?"

"Since June, 1961."

"How long have you been lovers?"

"Since the same time."

"Have you devoted yourself since then [to] going out with him exclusively?"

"Yes."

"During the past summer, where did your grandmother go for the summer?"

"Bay Head."

"Has she a summer home down there?"

"Yes."

"What did you do?"

"I spent the summer in Philadelphia."

"During this period of time, did Axel Schmidt stay with you?"

"I stayed with him."

"Where did you stay with him?"

"Forty-two Spruce Street."

"How often did you stay with him?"

"I lived with him."

"Did you ever travel as his wife?"

"Yes."

"Where did you travel as his wife?"

"Washington, D.C., New York, Maine . . ."

"Coming down to last week, Millicent, were you with him Friday night?"

"I said I lived with him continuously."

"Was he at your home on Chestnut Hill Avenue the next several days?"

"Yes."

"Was he at Chestnut Hill Avenue Tuesday?"

"Yes, he has been there approximately a week and a half."

"Do you know Frederick Purvis?"

"Yes."

"Who is he?"

"The brother of a friend of mine."

"And what is that friend's name?"

"Mary Purvis."

"Did you receive a gun from Frederick Purvis?"

"No."

"Did he have a gun?"

"Yes."

"Do you know the make of the gun it was?"

"Smith and Wesson."

"Was it a revolver or an automatic?"

"I don't know the difference."

"How did you obtain the gun that belonged to Frederick Purvis?"

"I just took it."

"Where did you take it from?"

"Where it was."

"Where was that?"

"Philadelphia, Pennsylvania."

"When was this you took it?"

"Some time during the summer."

"The summer of 1962?"

"Yes."

"What did you do with the gun?"

"I just took it."

"Did you bring it back home with you?"

"Yes."

"Did you sometimes use this gun, fire this gun?"

"Yes."

"When did you fire this gun?"

"I fired it in Bay Head."

"Have you fired this gun during the last week?"

"Yes."

"Where did you fire this gun during the last week?"

"Four thirty-seven Chestnut Hill Avenue."

"Who did you fire this gun at?"

"Axel."

"You fired it at Axel Schmidt?"

"Yes."

A considerable tension had built up, in spite of the prevailing semblance of calm, and the detective sergeant took this opportunity to send out for coffee and rolls. For a moment, the deadly quiet of the room was broken by a relieved bustle. So far, so good. It remained to be seen, however, how the sergeant would do with the more sensitive questions. Coffee break over, he continued, Millie remaining detached and impassive:

"What part of the house were you in when you fired the gun?"

"My room."

"Is that the rear bedroom?"

"Yes."

"At the time you fired the gun, was Axel dressed or undressed?"

"He was undressed."

"Completely undressed?"

"Yes."

"What part of his body did you fire the gun at?"

"The bullet hit his head."

"What did you do after the bullet hit his head?"

"I don't care to answer that question."

"What did you do with the gun?"

"I haven't the faintest idea."

"How long, if you know, did Axel remain conscious?"

"I wouldn't be able to judge. I think he died instantaneously."

"What did you do afterward?"

"As I say, I would prefer to remain silent."

"What night did this happen?"

"It was Tuesday night, five minutes past midnight."

"Would you care to tell the reason why you shot him?"

"No."

"Had you thought this over for a long period of time?"

"I do not choose to answer the question."

"Was there any particular purpose that you took the gun for when you took it?"

"I thought of killing myself."

"When did you first entertain the thought of killing Axel?"

"I choose to remain silent to the question."

"Do you remember hiding the gun?"

"What do you mean?"

"After you shot Axel."

"No, I didn't hide it."

"What did you do with it?"

"I don't remember. I didn't hide it."

"Have you bought any additional bullets for the gun since you acquired it?"

"It didn't have any then."

"Who purchased the bullets for you?"

"I don't want to answer that question."

"Did anybody know you had the gun?"

"This individual."

"Would you care to give us his name?"

"No."

"Is it a he?"

"I don't care to answer that question."

"Millicent, prior to your shooting Axel had you been out anywhere?"

"We spent the afternoon in the country."

"What time did you come back to the house?"

"I don't know exactly."

"Was it in the daytime or evening?"

"Early evening."

"Did you have any trouble at the house, any argument?"

"I don't choose to answer that question."

"At the time you shot him, what was your condition? Were you in a state of dress or undress?"

"I don't choose to answer that question."

"Were you with him Saturday?"

"Yes."

"Were you with him Saturday night?"

"As I told you, every night."

"Did you sleep with him Saturday night?"

"Every night."

"Every night for how long—all summer?"

"Since June, 1961."

"Do you know where the bullets were bought for the gun?"

"No."

"Did your brother buy the bullets?"

"No."

"Have you been having any arguments with Axel?"

"I don't choose to answer that question."

"What did you do with Axel's clothes?"

"Most of them were packed, because he was going to Europe."

"Did you pack the rest?"

"Yes. I put them in a box with things of my own."

"Did you know the gun was loaded at the time you pulled the trigger?"

"I don't choose to answer that question."

"Millicent, are those Axel's clothes?"—showing her a box of a man's clothes. "Is that one of the boxes you had the cab driver take to keep in storage?"

"Yes."

"Did you load the gun yourself?"

"I don't choose to answer that question."

"Are there any more spare bullets back at the house?"

"Yes."

"Where are they?"

"I don't know where they are now. They were in the kitchen."

"At what time did you load the gun?"

"I don't choose to answer that question."

"Do you know where Axel's pants are?"

"What do you mean, pants?"

"Did he have suit pants?"

"In the suitcase, I guess."

"Where are those suitcases? Are those the suitcases you took down on your trip?"

"No. I only had a few boxes."

"What did you do with them?"

"They are at the Beekman Hotel in New York at the moment."

"In your name? The name of Millicent Adams?"

"Yes."

"Have you been in communication with anyone since you came back?"

"I have not."

"When you came back to Philadelphia, what did you do?"

"I decided to go to the hospital and speak to a psychiatrist—Change that to, I went to the hospital to see a psychiatrist, with the expectation of seeing the police eventually that night."

"Why did you flee to South America?"

"I choose not to answer the question."

"Did you know that Axel was preparing to go to Europe?"

"Yes."

"Did you have an argument with him over his going to Europe?"

"I choose not to answer the question."

"Were you mad at him because he was going to Europe?"

"I will not answer the question."

"How long have you known that he was going to Europe?"

"His plans had varied for quite a long time as to exactly when he would leave for Europe."

"Did you have any argument with Axel over another girl that he had met on a trip?"

"No."

"Did you know he was going with a Portuguese girl?"

"He didn't go out with her."

"How do you know he didn't go out with her?"

"I was with him every night. I think he took her home once, perhaps from the airport."

"Did you have any fight with him over the girl?"

"No."

"Did you shoot Axel in a fit of jealousy?"

"I do not choose to answer the question."

"Did you know that Axel had gone to the German consulate on Saturday to have his passport renewed?"

"I knew he intended to go, but I thought he was going Monday. I didn't know he went Saturday."

"Did you want him to go to Europe on this trip?"

"I do not choose to answer the question."

"Did you fear, if he went to Europe, you would lose him?"

"I do not choose to answer the question. I would like to add that I do know at no time did he go out with a Portuguese girl."

"Did Axel know you had a gun?"

"I do not choose to answer the question."

"Did you ever show him the gun?"

"I think the same answer would apply there."

"Did you ever threaten him with the gun prior to shooting him?"

"I do not choose to answer the question."

"I know I have asked you this before: Would you care to tell me the reason you shot him?"

"No."

"Was it because you are pregnant?"

"I do not choose to answer the question."

"Are you pregnant?"

"Dr. Robbins thinks I am, but he has not made an examination. He only gave me a checkup."

"What made you think you were pregnant?"

"I didn't menstruate."

"For how many months?"

"I missed it only once."

"Did you have an argument with him [Axel] over your pregnancy?"

"I do not choose to answer the question."

"Did you feel he was running out on you?"

"I do not choose to answer the question. I should like to know if I can have a transcript of what I said."

"I will tell you, any promises I will make to you I will keep. I told you that before."

"You could add to that. I have asked to be able to read the answers I have given. I also want to be able to read the questions that I have been asked."

"I have told you that, if I make a promise to you, I will keep it, but I haven't made any promise to you yet, have I?"

"No."

"Millicent, have I threatened you in any way, shape, or form?"

"No."

"Did I promise you any inducements or rewards for making this statement to me?"

"Of course not."

"Have you made this statement voluntarily?"

"I have made this statement under duress of fatigue, emotional exhaustion, which I stated before giving the answers to the questions."

"Is it a truthful statement?"

"Yes."

"Millicent, I am showing you this gun here"—showing .22-caliber Magnum Smith & Wesson, Serial 52,7509, Model 53 revolver. "Do you recognize it?"

"Yes."

"How can you tell it?"

"It simply looks like the same gun."

"Do you recognize it?"

"It has the same features."

"Do you recognize the case?"

"Yes, I do."

"Thank you, Millicent."

Thus ended Millie's initial interrogation, much to the relief of all concerned. The police had duly noted that, although the girl was fey as a leprechaun, she was not so daft that she didn't know not to answer any question which might have shown motive or premeditation.

Throughout the questioning, Millie clasped the art print to her chest, to the mild annoyance of the police who were dying of curiosity. Only once did she relax her hold, so that one officer standing behind her got a quick look at what was pictured there, but it was of no particular significance to him.

At 2:50 A.M. Detective Madden announced to the press that Millicent Adams had admitted to the shooting and would be taken to the House of Detention for Women in Philadelphia and held without bail.

Millie was charged with first-degree murder, in which case bail is rarely granted. This meant that she would have to remain in prison until she was tried, and either acquitted and freed, or found guilty and sentenced. She was placed in a cell with a middle-aged narcotics addict, of whom she was absolutely terrified. Tim was very much upset by this and made quite a scene back at the police station, where he stood with his head against the wall, rocking back and forth, mumbling how bad it all was.

The police had no idea what to do with this curiously weedy youth, with his long, disheveled hair, faded levis, and baggy, unmended sweater. "Looks like a beatnik to me," someone commented. "And them with all that dough." Assuring him that they would do their best to get Millie moved into a private cell, they were able finally to send poor Tim on his way, but they knew they had not seen the last of him.

In the days that followed, one of Philadelphia's most eminent lawyers, an old friend of the Copley family, was hired to prepare Millie's defense. He already knew everything about the case, except the part about the unfortunate St. Bernard, which curiously never came to light.

One day, in the week after the murder, Detective Madden received a call from the handyman at Mrs. Copley's house. He said that there was still a terrible odor in the place and that he did not know what to do about it. Madden told him that it might be the mattress, and therefore to throw it out, but several days later the man called back to say that the odor persisted. This time the police went to the house, searched it, and eventually discovered the large, decaying canine corpse in the maid's room. All concerned were warned to keep quiet about the incident and apparently did so.

Publicity about the case grew by leaps and bounds, and having got the family through the preliminary phases, the lawyer who had originally been hired to undertake Millie's defense withdrew his services. He was afraid that his closeness to the family would somehow jeopardize his efficiency as counsel, and in any case, he was nearing eighty years of age and getting too old to sustain a long court battle in a controversial case such as this was turning out to be.

Another distinguished lawyer was called upon, and he in turn appointed a young attorney from another firm to assist him. The defense team ultimately consisted of William B. Kane and John Demmings, who for three solid months would do nothing but concentrate on how to save Millie.

Millie's arraignment on October 8 was a difficult and shocking moment for her. Having waited nearly an hour while a motley assortment of drunks and traffic offenders was disposed of, Millie stood before the judge at last, mute and tense, her red-rimmed eyes clouded with tears. The court simply stated the charges against her, while Mrs. McLeland, Tim, and a pair of sympathetic clergymen, friendly to the family, looked on, occasionally flashing reassuring smiles toward the stunned, pathetic figure at the bar.

The venerable old attorney, who was still formally on the case, had waived examination of his client by the court, asking that she first be examined by a psychiatrist. Emphasizing the fact that Millie had been under psychiatric care for over a year, the lawyer had clearly and deliberately set the stage for a defense which would revolve around Millie's mental condition.

In the meantime, Tim visited her almost daily in jail, bringing cosmetics, candy, and various delicacies to supplement the dreary, institutional diet to which she fell heir. Tim was extremely worried about Millie in prison. He told reporters that, even though she had been moved into a private cell, jail was obviously no place for a girl like her, and that she remained terrified of the other twenty-seven inmates awaiting trial. Often she refused to eat dinner with them in the prison mess-hall, preferring to remain alone in her cell, dining on a sandwich supplied by Tim and reading the various books that he brought her—an incongruous list which included *Platero I*, the poetry of Juan Jiminiz, and *The Hobbitt* by Tolkien. The rest of the family were good about visiting her as well, and Demmings was there everyday. The lawyer was puzzled because, in spite of the fact that she was miserable and frightened in jail, Millie maintained an icy calm in the presence of all visitors, and never, since the day of her arraignment, was observed to weep.

Around November 5, two days before the grand-jury hearing was scheduled to take place, Millie asked to have a pregnancy test. Inasmuch as she had been well aware of her condition for at least a month, this move was undoubtedly initiated by her lawyers, who most probably were anxious to create the impression that Millie had not been certain about her pregnancy at the time of the murder. Should this impression be successfully sustained in court, one strong element of the probable motive would be weakened, if not totally eliminated. On November 7,

William Kane formally disclosed that Millie was indeed pregnant, a scrap of news for which the press had been waiting ever since Millie's arrest. The next day, no citizen from New York to San Francisco who bought a newspaper was left in any doubt about it.

On November 17, Millie was indicted by the grand jury for first-degree murder and violation of the weapons law. On November 30, however, she was ordered committed to a confinement of no more than thirty-five days of mental observation at a small state mental-health center, a merciful liberation from the prison won by hard work and persuasion on the part of her attorneys. Again Millie remained absolutely mute throughout the fifteen-minute hearing. Sitting with her blonde hair neatly but severely drawn back from her face, hands folded in the lap of a flowered maternity dress, she refused to answer any questions or respond in any manner to directions given her. Her plea of Not Guilty had to be entered by the judge himself, after four psychiatrists, testifying in her behalf, stated that she should be examined further to determine the nature and seriousness of her condition. Kane then moved that she be committed, and the judge gave counsel thirty days to file special pleas.

There was no question that Millie would be happier at the mental-health center, which though state-run was as good as any private hospital, than in jail among the addicts, derelicts, and prostitutes, and that the ends of justice were equally well served by incarcerating her in a place where she would obtain the needed psychiatric attention. But the institution, being an "open," progressive, and liberally run place, presented certain security problems, which came under discussion at this hearing.

Basically it came down to a question of who was to pay the guards who would be required to see that Millie did not attempt to leave. It was finally decided that, inasmuch as the judge was committing Millie and not she herself, that the county should supply the guard, but that Millie would have to reimburse the county. Demmings had, of course, rejected any suggestion that she should go to the larger state institution. And so, like a queen going into exile, Millie departed for the smaller hospital silently and with considerable dignity, accompanied by her own special protectors.

Demmings and Kane now had slightly more than a month to tie up the loose ends of information relating to the case and to solve some of the minor mysteries. They had to find out much more about Millie's family, about Schmidt, and about her movements subsequent to the murder.

Questioning those who had gone to Axel's funeral on October 13, they discovered that, as with most funerals, the general tone was eulogic; everyone had come to praise the dead man, not to bury him. Many people came, not only from among Axel's colleagues and professors, but from Millie's family as well. Millie's grandaunt, a venerable old Boston lady whose courageous appearance in this circumstance surprised everybody, brought a bouquet of yellow roses which she laid on the casket. Later, she approached the lawyer engaged by the German consulate to represent Axel's family, and, speaking for the family as a whole, she told him of their sincere collective grief, and withdrew in her stately and dignified manner.

The German representative placed white chrysanthemums on the bier, having tried, he said, to choose a manly flower with which to honor the deceased. This sentiment was sympathetically received, although there was doubtless some unspoken conjecturing to the effect that if the deceased had not perhaps been quite so "manly," he might not be in his present predicament.

A friend of Axel's, who had lived in the same building and who had passed some time in the company of the two lovers, told Kane about the last dinner he had shared with them three weeks before Axel's death.

"They seemed to be enjoying each other's company as usual, though toward the end there did seem to be a bit of unhappiness between them. Axel was Millie's life. She just couldn't face up to the fact that he was leaving her. He was a great guy."

Richard Brewer, Axel's landlord, said that he liked them both: "I assumed they were engaged. I remember once how Miss Adams took a bouquet of fresh flowers to an elderly widow who lives in my building too. She was really sweet, that girl. A lovely couple, they were. I feel just awful about this."

One of the professors of applied physics at the university said: "Axel Schmidt was a brilliant student, brilliant. This is a great waste of human talent."

There also came many men from Minneapolis Honeywell, for whom Axel had worked, who, with their wives, attested to the brilliance of Axel's mind and to the fact that he was a "great guy" who could have done anything he wanted in his chosen field.

There was, of course, a dark side to Axel's character, which was also of interest to the counsel for the defense. They learned that Axel had been born in Dresden twenty-six years earlier of German parents, who were attached to the German diplomatic corps in São Paolo, Brazil, where they had lived for at least five years. There was little doubt that the family had been fascistically oriented. Axel had gone to Fascist schools in his early youth, and his father had worked for the Germans throughout the war. He was known to be autocratic and self-centered, qualities which were mitigated to some extent by the beautiful manners and fundamental social graces which had so charmed the McLelands. The prosecutor at Millie's trial was later to describe Axel as an egocentric character with a Don Juan complex who "fluttered like a butterfly from one petal to another," unmindful of the pain he caused; and it is not customary for the prosecutor to stress the failings of the victim.

One day shortly after Millie's departure for the mental-health center, a young man came into John Demmings' office, and said he wanted to talk to Demmings about Axel. He had long disapproved of Axel's attitude in regard to Millie and proceeded to explain why: "Axel told me once that he knew Millie was kind of nuts, but that she was the perfect type to have around. He could have her any time he wanted to, and she made no demands on him. She was utterly passive." He looked out the window for a moment, remembering. "You know, he kept her a virtual prisoner in that room of his, but she'd put up with just about anything so long as she could be with him. She was a masochist, I guess. She often told him she wanted to commit suicide, but he was tough, you know, or maybe just stupid. Anyway, he never took her very seriously."

This came as a bolt out of the blue to Demmings, who thus far had heard nothing but paeans to the young man's character, and his curiosity was increasingly piqued. His daily visits to Millie in jail had been unrevealing in this respect. Throughout her stay, she had maintained the stoic demeanor which she had assumed from the beginning, sharing none of her thoughts with anyone. She trusted no one and would say only that she loved Axel and that she did not know why or under what circumstances she had shot him, for she did not remember. This impassivity and apparent lack of feeling worried Demmings a great deal, for he knew that it was not indicative of what was really going on inside the girl, but rather represented an artificial, subconscious withdrawal from a reality which she found too painful.

One day, while still in jail, Millie had a disturbing dream just before awaking in the morning, and she had told Demmings about it when he came that day. They had been speaking about some of the things which had happened to Millie as a child, which had drawn some response from her, but when she spoke of the dream, she wept. Demmings was so elated that the girl was finally showing some feeling, even though that feeling involved her agony, that he rushed straight over to William Kane's office and told him about it. It meant that she was returning to this world and that she could now help them.

Demmings soon realized, however, that Millie's true feelings about Axel would most probably have been more candidly revealed before his death and to a person completely removed from her personal environment, such as her psychiatrist.

Dr. Riesman, one of the first to be consulted in the case, made himself available when the quest for information began, and his views, though not particularly sympathetic, were nonetheless illuminating. It was his belief that Millie had a most exaggerated capacity for self-loathing and that she regarded her relationship with Axel not as a love tie but as "an unnatural attachment to a cold and unfeeling individual who connived with her unhealthy wishes for suffering. The bond had become obligatory for her and developed a compulsive quality. Oddly enough," he continued, "she never said anything to me or to anyone else about wanting to do him harm, but he was obviously a very cold-blooded character, who, although he associated with her, often degraded her too." Later on, Riesman was to remark specifically about Millie's unnatural inability to feel anger toward Axel, her illness apparently preempting normal reactions.

Since Riesman had never had an opportunity to meet Axel, these judgments as to his character, and the strange, loveless bond which existed between him and Millie could only have been based on information elicited from Millie herself in the course of treatment. The portrait that emerged, therefore, was that drawn by a masochistic and self-deprecating girl whose reasons for loving a man were almost directly related to his ability to make her suffer. The contradiction, furthermore, between her image of Axel and the view sustained by nearly everyone else may be explained solely in the light of her abnormal condition.

Still, certain facts did emerge clearly: that Axel did not love her at all and, though always polite, did not behave lovingly toward her at any time; that he told her he would never marry her and that if she ever became pregnant, she would have to be aborted. He was clearly a very different person with Millie than he was with anyone else of his acquaintance, and his appearance was very deceiving. George McLeland had said: "She and Axel were always together during the last year and went up to Bay Head a lot. There wasn't a hint of a rift." And then, in one of the classic understatements of all time, he added, "But of course a girl doesn't always confide in her parents when she has trouble with a boyfriend."

One week in early December, Millie's attorneys went to New York and spent five days tracing her movements during the four hours she had been there prior to her flight to Rio. It was anything but easy, for she had covered a great deal of ground and in some places given a false name. They passed considerable time at the shop of C. P. Chen on West 57th Street, where Millie had spent $350 on size-eight dresses which she obviously couldn't wear. Chen had noticed that she was very heavy in the body and did not believe that she was actually buying the clothes "for a friend," but she had been wearing an obtrusive seven-carat diamond on her wedding finger—a gift from Grandmother Copley—and the salesgirls had been very impressed. Demmings had to explain to the crestfallen Chinese that this was $350 he would never see, that Millie was not well, and that she had meant them no harm. They said they were sorry.

On December 23, Demmings and Kane asked for the exact details of the charges against Millie. They wanted the exact day, hour, and minute that she was supposed to have shot Axel, and asked to be given copies of all documents, papers, diaries, letters, books, and other writings of the defendant, including her poetry, together with any confessions, admissions, or denials made by her to the police, and the results of the autopsy. They had decided to fight for a change of plea to a reduced charge. Millie's story about not remembering anything about the period prior to, during, or after the shooting had remained consistent, whether she spoke to counsel, psychiatrists, or police. Furthermore, since there had never been any mention of doing Axel harm (while talk of doing away with herself had been abundant), premeditation would be difficult to prove. And by all accounts, she was a very sick girl.

By this time it had become patently obvious to the District Attorney that, should Millie stand trial, no jury on earth was going to convict this pitiful, sick young mother-to-be, who had been so shamefully treated by the apparently hard-hearted and diabolical foreigner into whose clutches she had haplessly fallen.

The defense was equally anxious that Millie not stand trial. If she were to be acquitted, it could be only by reason of insanity. In that event she would be committed for life to a state mental hospital and could only be released under the statute law by the Governor with the consent of the Governor's Council or, in accordance with the then recent case interpreting the statute, by a successful petition for a writ of habeas corpus based upon a showing that she had recovered her mental health and was harmless to society. In at least some hospitals to which she might be committed, she would probably receive inferior care. The lawyers were concerned that the oppressive, psychologically and aesthetically impoverished environment in such a hospital might further damage her. They did not themselves want her to go "free," for she needed psychiatric care, and must have it one way or another if they were to be able to believe, in good conscience, that the public would thenceforth have nothing to fear from Millicent Adams.

Many conferences took place between defense counsel, the District Attorney, and his compassionate prosecutor, and together they tried to discover the best way to appeal to the judge to permit them a change of plea. The judge, a conscientious and utterly scrupulous old-timer, was finding this case, with all its highly unorthodox manifestations, one of the most "troublesome" of his long career.

Demmings, in the meantime, visited Millie periodically at the mental-health center, to keep her abreast of the various legal developments, and saw that she was making great progress. There was a small garden containing flowers, fir trees, and some rustic tables and chairs where Millie preferred to meet her visitors, and it was there that she always saw her lawyers, weather permitting. Demmings never failed to be impressed by the fact that she received as would a monarch, her manner distinguished by courtly, graceful gestures and speech, although now the icy stoicism had modulated to a gentle reserve when in the company of trusted friends. The constant presence of her special guard contributed to the regal aura Millie evoked, and this was added to by the fact that her brother, Tim, had managed to get a job at the institution as a kind of super handyman and served as Millie's loving protector. A great commiserator with suffering humanity, Tim felt that in addition to allowing him proximity to his sister, the job gave him a cherished opportunity to help people generally, and he was happy and useful there.

It was explained to Millie that they all hoped that the judge would permit her to plead Guilty to manslaughter and put her on probation, but that she would have to go through a pretrial hearing in February. She nodded, asked several typically searching questions, and indicated that she was sure she would be up to it by then.

It was believed that Millie's notable psychological improvement was due as much as anything to her anticipation of the arrival of her baby, which had been forecast for June. The quickening in her womb had evidently restored her will to live and her interest in the world outside her fantasies. The doctors had confided to William Kane their fear that, if anything was said about taking the baby away from her, she would perhaps try to kill it, herself, or both, at the time of delivery. The importance of this baby to Millie was twofold: First, it was all that remained of Axel, with whom she was still in love, and second, it constituted the ultimate desired "possession"; here was one thing that was incontestably hers to love and to care for, for the rest of her life, and in it too lay the potential of being loved in return for perhaps the first time. In fact, the baby might prove to be the key to her salvation, and everyone around her felt the importance of not jeopardizing her chances for it. But June was still half a year off, and there was the hearing to be got through.

The only member of Millie's family permitted inside the chamber during the hearing was Tim; the others were asked to remain upstairs in another room. The reason behind this was

that testimony to be given by the various psychiatrists, whether
for the defense or for the prosecution, was certain to be un-
complimentary and therefore embarrassing to the other members of the family. It was felt that they were suffering enough
as it was without being submitted to a semipublic denunciation.

Through it all Millie sat, plump and stoic, without makeup, her hair drawn back in the familiar bun, barely, it seemed,
aware of what was going on around her or what was at stake.
When called to the stand, her speech was alien, anglicized, as it
had evidently been during many of her sessions with Dr.
Riesman.

"The accent," he testified, "is artificial and is an expression of her wish to disown her very eastern accent. She used
to get annoyed that people thought that she was a foreigner or
came from England or somewhere like that." The court asked
if she had not perhaps acquired it from Dr. Riesman and
whether the accent was not native to England.

"No, it isn't," Riesman replied. "It is entirely artificial.
On one occasion for a few minutes she was able to give it up
and talk in her ordinary family way of talking. The degree of
misery in this girl, all through her life, is attested to by the fact
that she couldn't even accept her identity as a member of her
family by talking the way they talked. She had even to try to
break away from this."

Dr. Henry Kazin, another of the defense's psychiatrists,
who had examined Millie dozens of times in jail as well as at
the mental-health center, was to shed some added light on the
subject:

"Millie's dearest friend on earth, the girl to whom she
planned to leave all her belongings after her death—and she
indicated so in many letters and documents—was the person to
whom Millie felt closest. She had said that this was because
'she's more like me than anyone.' This little girl [Hanya] had
a Scottish mother and speaks with an accent which is identical
to Millie's; Millie, in identifying herself with this girl, talks
like her."

The hearing, which began with a reading of Millie's
statement to the police, was characterized by the fact that
everybody, including the prosecution, appeared to be on Millie's
side. Both prosecution and defense produced psychiatric evidence
showing that Millie's family life, right up to the present time,

had been utterly catastrophic, that she was suffering from a severe personality disorder—a schizoid condition—and that at the time of the shooting she had been completely disoriented and quite unaware of what she was doing. There had never been any variation in her story concerning the shooting itself. She had no recollection of the moment or exactly what she did immediately afterward.

Dr. Kazin testified that once, when he had gone to see her in jail, she had spoken about the dream of which she had already told Demmings. In her dream she had seen a searing white sheet of flame, accompanied by a loud report, as a result of which her own face and the front of her body were torn away. She had thought she was dead, but she woke up, most probably realizing that she had subconsciously recalled the crucial events of the night of October 2.

The Assistant District Attorney, who had collaborated so compassionately with Millie's attorneys in the effort to win a change of plea, testified that the state's evidence showed no premeditation or malice, that a single shot fired from a gun does not constitute extreme atrocity or cruelty, and that Millie was not engaged at the time in a crime punishable by life imprisonment. That eliminated murder in the first degree.

He agreed, furthermore, that there had been insufficient evidence to show malice or ill-will at the moment the crime was committed. That eliminated murder in the second degree. The prosecutor indicated that the self-identification of the victim with Don Juan had put the ultimate stress on the girl's disordered psychological condition, and that she could not be held fully responsible for her acts at the time. Her conduct in allowing the illegally possessed gun to go off, he said, was grossly negligent and reckless, and may have constituted involuntary manslaughter.

William Kane, Millie's chief counsel, argued that Millie's multiple suicide attempts and the wealth of self-deprecating testimony given at various times to psychiatrists, police, and friends alike indicated that she had definitely stolen the gun from the Purvis household with the intention of destroying herself. She herself testified that in the summer of 1962 she had tried to obtain sleeping pills from four or five different sources, and failed. He argued further that the frenetic organization of diverse transatlantic flights represented an alternative "escape" to suicide—an escape from the self, however, rather than from the law. Kane cited the fact that Millie had invited Axel's cousins from New York down to Philadelphia the weekend just prior to the tragedy; they had cancelled out at the last minute, but one could at least be certain that a week prior to September 30, Millie had no intention of shooting herself or anyone else.

Axel Schmidt, he maintained, was the worst sort of person with whom a girl in her mental condition could possibly become involved. A good friend of Axel's, who upon hearing of the tragedy had written sympathetically to Millie, had told both Kane and Demmings in a taped interview that he thought Axel's years in a Fascist school in Brazil had definitely shaped his character and colored his activities thereafter. He had spoken too of Axel's brutally cold, exploitative attitude toward Millie —an attitude which had clearly contributed the final blow to the girl's self-respect and already battered affections. Yet she had never expressed anger toward Axel or any desire to hurt him in return.

Moreover, the two state psychiatrists who had examined Millie when she entered prison, concurred with all the others in the opinion that the girl needed intensive additional treatment. Kane then implored the judge to accept a plea of Guilty to manslaughter and requested probation for a period of ten years on condition that Millie commit herself to the same mental-health center which had sheltered her up to this time.

This was, for the judge, a most difficult and delicate case. Were he to accept all the conditions recommended by the defense, he would be making a disposition for which there was no precedent; where insanity was involved, the usual thing was for the defendant to be found innocent of the original charge and be committed by the state to a mental institution. Who had ever heard of a defendant being trusted to commit himself? There were other troublesome factors: The girl was to be considered sufficiently "insane" at the time of the shooting as not to be held legally responsible, but sane enough now, a few months later, either to stand trial or be permitted to change her plea; a defendant must be judged thoroughly competent to change his plea, for technically this can only be done by the defendant himself, not his attorneys, and he must clearly understand the nature of the charges against him and the consequences thereof.

There had obviously been a big improvement in Millie's condition during her three-month stay at the mental-health center, strongly supplemented by her anticipation of the child. When Kane had questioned her, there could be little doubt that she had a palpable understanding of what was at issue:

"Millie, do you know what you are indicted for?"

"First-degree murder."

"What is first-degree murder?"

"It's deliberately premeditated murder."

"What is second-degree murder?"

"Any other murder."

"And what is manslaughter?"

"It can either be a voluntary killing, in a fit or rage, or involuntary killing as a result of gross negligence."

"Do you know what the penalties are for manslaughter?"

"Twenty years in state prison; up to twenty years in state prison, or up to two and a half years in a jail, with a thousand-dollar fine."

"Do you know what the penalty is for second-degree murder?"

"Life sentence."

"And do you know what the consequence is of first-degree murder, if you are convicted?"

"Yes."

"What is it?"

"Unless the jury recommends life sentence, it would be —death."

Throughout the hearing, the court had periodically to ask Millie to try to keep her voice up, for, although her speech had been clipped and precise, her voice was all but inaudible. Now it hung softly on the silent court, as she pronounced the final words. Tim shivered in his seat and closed his eyes.

There was no cause for alarm, however, for the judge had made his difficult decision and accepted the manslaughter plea, with ominous warnings of what would occur should there be any violation of the conditions set forth by counsel.

The hearing ended, Millie smiled for the first time that any one could remember during the long weeks preceding. Pulling out the pins in her hair, she allowed it to flow free again down her back and, with considerable gusto, applied a light lipstick to her mouth. The press was enthusiastic in the reporting of this sudden expression of relief, the atmosphere heretofore having been anything but lighthearted.

The reaction of the public to the disposition of the case demonstrated more than anything that the law is as much an expression of society's desire for vengeance as a manifestation of its quest for justice. The sentiment was rife that Millicent Adams, Brahmin child of a privileged segment of East Coast society, had "got away with murder," aided by "connections" and the shrewd placement of large sums of money. A promising young man had been wantonly killed under the most familiar circumstances, and the perpetrator of the crime was apparently to escape punishment. Maybe the girl was sick, but is not anyone who takes the life of another human being "sick"?

The press, while dutifully reporting any information relating to Millie's mental illness, were equally conscientious in the definition of her social status. Such headlines appeared as: THE DEB WHO KILLED, and were followed by stories about the "posh" schools which Millie had attended, her gala debut, and the house in which she lived on "exclusive Chestnut Hill Avenue." The women incarcerated in the women's reformatory outside Philadelphia very nearly staged a riot the day they learned that Millie was to escape prison; they had been sent there on far less serious charges, for which they were to serve long prison terms.

While it is true that a penniless lower-class girl in similar circumstances often fares quite differently, it does not necessarily follow that the disposition of Millie's case reflected an excessive leniency. However, it does imply that, were the funds necessary to secure the valuable time of lawyers and psychiatrists made available to the less-affluent members of society, the interests of humanity and justice might be served far better.

Millie stayed at the mental-health center for nearly three years, during which time she recovered her psychological equilibrium and watched, delighted, as her tiny daughter, born in the first week of June, grew and blossomed into a chubby pink-and-white toddler. The child was dark haired and black eyed, like her father, but had Millie's clear white skin, and was a constant joy to her mother as well as to most of the other patients at the institution, who spoiled and pampered her as they would their own. Millie was often permitted visits home, and the McLeland children were especially thrilled at the frequent opportunities to see Millie and to play with the baby. Mrs. McLeland had been separated from her husband, having once again grown weary of her spouse, and Tim spent a good deal more time at home now, in the company of his mother. Now that the competition had departed, he felt that he had a valid role in her house at last, and both he and Millie had come to feel considerably more sympathetic toward their mother; though she appeared to have the secret of eternal youth, she had yet to discover the secret of creating the conditions of happiness, either for herself or for other people.

When Lisa Adams was born, one of Millie's aunts— her father's sister, who lived out West and was deeply sympathetic to her niece—graciously sent Millie the thousand dollars necessary to cover the cost of doctor and hospital. What was even more beneficent was that this kind lady invited Millie to come and live with her and become part of her family. This was the happiest sort of thing that could have developed, for Millie could certainly not remain in Philadelphia, where she had become notorious. She would have been unhappy living with her mother in any case. She decided instead to continue her education, and just prior to setting off with Lisa for the city which would be her new home, she enrolled in the university there.

Millie usually goes home to Philadelphia at Christmastime, mostly to show Lisa off, but evidently feels no nostalgia for the place. William Kane received a post card from her early in 1967, which depicted a snowy woodland scene and contained a bubbly, girlish message:

> Tim and I have just come back from a lovely skiing trip, which we took up here just after New Year's. It was divinely relaxing and great fun. I'm sorry you didn't have a chance to see Lisa when I was up there at Christmas—she is really wonderful—maybe next time. So far I have an A in English, B+ in history and political science, and a B in math. The math grade really pleases me—I've always been so hopeless. Couldn't have done that back in 1962, could I? Say "hello" to John Demmings for me if you see him. With very best regards,
>
> MILLIE

Chapter V

Flora

BLACK Joey Adderson and his lawyer were just concluding their business, at least for the present. Joey said, "So how much do I owe you this time Mr. Lawyer Man?" and his face broke out in a huge grin as he withdrew an enormous roll of bills from his well-stocked pocket. This was not the first time Laurence Hammill had extricated Joey from the jaws of justice, and it would doubtless not be the last.

Joey had been pushing junk ever since bootlegging went out and now, ten years later, had incalculable arrests to his credit—but, due largely to Hammill's efforts, relatively few convictions. And Joey was not about to get out of this racket. Pushing booze, he had mostly been poor, grubby, and apologetic, and his creditors had been thick as flies in a meat market. Now he was rich, and not just by Negro standards but by any standards, which was not all that common in Chicago within the Negro community.

"Same as last time, Joey," the lawyer replied, smiling as he saw the bankroll spring into view.

163

"Well, I'll say one thing," Joey mused. "You're about the only basic expense I got that don't seem to inflate."

"You're one of my most dependable clients. You deserve some consideration for loyalty." Joey laughed his raucous, minstrel laugh, and peeled three thousand-dollar bills from the roll. "Well, dere you is, Mr. Lawyer Man, as we would say in Mississippi, an' don't spend it all on broads." More loud guffaws followed, then, taking as serious a tone as he could muster, Joey said, "Say, you know my daughter Flora, the one I told you about once?"

"Yeah, what about her?"

"Well, it seems that she's in a bit of hot water. It seems she pushed her boyfriend, some piano player, down the stairs, and as a result, it seems he died, and she's due to swing some time next month."

"You mean she was convicted of first-degree murder?"

"That is what I mean. An' if you don't do somethin', Mr. Lawyer Man, my li'l gal is gonna get killed next month, an' if you ask me, she's too good a piece to go out so young like that."

The lawyer decided that Black Joey must really love his daughter, for he had just paid her the only, and the highest, compliment he was capable of delivering to any woman. And furthermore, it was not his custom to trouble himself over anyone else's fortunes, relatives included.

"Where did this happen?"

"Clinton, Tennessee, an' that's where she's locked up."

"Yeah, well, I'll go down there and see her, Joey. You going to pay for it?"

"Yes, sir. Nothin's too good for my li'l girl. This ought to take care of your train fare and such." And he peeled off another two thousand, presenting it with a graceful flourish to his friend.

"Business must be good these days, Joey. You don't seem to be too hard up for folding stuff." Another great laugh pierced the inner sanctum of Hammill's office.

"Business is just great, my friend, an' it's gettin' better all the time!"

"You on the stuff, Joey?"

"What? Are you crazy?"

"Just wondering. How do I get to Clinton?"

The following day, Hammill climbed aboard a train

headed south, and he thought about Flora. It frustrated him that, inasmuch as Black Joey knew blessed little about the details of Flora's case, it was impossible for him to plan how best to broach an appeal in her behalf. The girl was only twenty-four, and good-looking by all accounts, so even in a state like Tennessee he might be able to create some sympathy for her.

After two days, and what seemed like half a dozen train changes, Hammill arrived in the drowsy rural town of Clinton. As he gazed around at the formless brick and wood buildings, strung together by telephone wire, the decaying bandstand in the square, the mongrel dogs snuffling in the dusty yards, and the sad, painted white sign, listing in gold the names of all those young men from Clinton who had thus far died in the war, Hammill thought how glad he was to live in Chicago. It was no Garden of Eden, but at least it wasn't dead from the neck up; there was ugliness, but life and action. He wondered, too, what the hell Flora had been doing here.

Presently, a portly Negro, wearing black pants, shiny from too much cleaning, and a rather limp officer's cap, appeared and announced that he was the taxi service. Hammill climbed into the rear of an ancient black Buick, along with several other people, and requested to be taken to the best hotel.

The other passengers looked with some amusement at their slick comrade, and, taking in his natty, dark suit, briefcase, and smoothed hair, wondered if he was a gangster or something, come to open up some den of sin in Clinton. The driver chuckled.

"Well, sir," he said, "De best hotel is de only hotel, so that is where you are goin'."

"Thank you very much."

"Don't thank me till you been dere." The amusement then became general, and Hammill was glad he was the first to be let off. Having paid his share of the cab, he stepped out into the road, steaming in the summer heat, and found that he was standing in a patch of melting tar. He looked up at the hotel in wonderment.

A vast, tottering, ante-bellum structure confronted him, its stately pillars testifying to grander times now happily covered with dusty wisteria, which masked the peeling paint and termite holes.

The porch swayed gently as he mounted the steps, and

he noticed that some of the floor boards were totally rotten. A couple of old-timers sat rocking peacefully, their eyes brightening with interest as Hammill approached. It was the best part of their day; something new was happening. He was thinking how he rather liked the place and was not a bit sorry that it wasn't the Drake when the front door swung open with a great creaky whoosh and out popped Theda Bara. At least that was the general demeanor of the lady who now assaulted Hammill with greetings, counsel, and mild remonstrance. "Welcome to Clinton, suh, I sure am glad to see yuh. I'm Mrs. Thackeray, an' I run the hotel. Lordy! Whatever have you got on your shoes there? Better wipe 'em good on the door mat, if you please. And mind the rotten planks on the porch. We used to have *three* old folks rockin' here, till one of 'em fell through over there an' broke her leg. In the hospital now. I've been tryin' for months to get a nigger over here to replace the bad ones, but, my God, they do hate to work, and when they do, they move like molasses, an' that's the truth. What brings you to Clinton?" she gurgled, ushering her guest into the hall.

"I'm here to see if I can get one of those niggers out of the death house."

"Oh?" Theda crooned, her suspicions aroused. "Are you an attorney?"

"Yes, ma'am. And I'd like to go up to my room and make some calls, as soon as possible. Could you give me the number of the sheriff's office?"

"Well, I sure can give you Jim's number, but you'll have to use the phone up in the hall. I'm afraid we don't have phones in the rooms." She smiled her most winning, southern-belle smile and assayed a look of wide-eyed innocence, which is not easily managed with eyebrows painted on in an oriental slant to the temple.

"Yes, of course. That'll be fine."

Mrs. Thackeray could not imagine why anyone would trouble himself to get a nigger out of anything, apart from the table or the house next door, but that was *his* business.

They trudged up the worn stair carpet, Hammill lugging his own bag rather than entrusting it to the decidedly lethargic porter below. As they entered the large, sunny but shabby room, with its crocheted bedspread, faded curtains, Gideon Bible, and overstuffed furniture, Hammill thanked the lady kindly and turned her gently out. He wanted to get to work and get out of this incredible place at the earliest opportunity. He knew, of course, that old Theda down there would be listening in to any and all of his telephone conversations and that there was nothing much he could do about it.

He quickly found the ancient telephone hanging in the hall and, getting Mrs. Thackeray on the switchboard, asked for the county jail.

"I'd like to talk to the sheriff, please."

"What about?"

"About Flora Adderson."

"Who?"

"Flora Adderson—a colored girl you have there from Chicago, convicted of murder, supposed to hang in a couple of weeks."

"Oh, yeah. We got a nigger gal in here, but her name's Flora Black." Hammill sighed.

"Well, I'm sure it's the same person, aren't you?"

"Yeah, maybe. You better talk to the boss."

After making certain hostile inquiries, the sheriff, realizing there was not a great deal he could do to stop it, agreed to allow Hammill in to see Flora. As it was already four o'clock in the afternoon, he would not be permitted to stay long, but it would be enough. Tomorrow he would have to see the judge and make his appeal, and he still had no precise knowledge as to the crime or the original charges.

When Hammill first saw Flora, his reaction was to straighten his tie, smooth his hair, and examine his fingernails to see if they were clean. He was startled, for although he had been expecting to find a handsome woman on the other side of the visitor's counter, he had not been prepared for Flora. Even in the faded gray inmate's gown she was obliged to wear, she was alluring, dignified, and monstrously attractive. As she walked along the wire partition which separated the cells from the visiting area, Hammill thought that she moved like a wild animal of exceptional grace—quiet, coordinated, cool, and utterly confident of her effect. He remembered that Black Joey had said she was a dancer.

Apart from the light brown skin, there was little of the "typical" American Negro in Flora's face; her nose was thin and straight, as were her firm lips, and her hair was very nearly straight—qualifying as what Negroes refer to as "good hair." The eyes slanted very slightly at the outer corners, imposing a perpetually shrewd expression. Whether she was actually shrewd or not remained to be seen. Bitter she certainly was, and self-contained. Here was a woman, Hammill mused, who was scheduled to die in less than two weeks' time, and she was coming on like Queen Victoria. She waited for him to speak first.

"I'm Laurence Hammill. I'm a lawyer. Your father sent me to see if I could do anything for you."

"He don't give a shit about me," she replied, shrugging and turning her head aside. "What the hell can anybody do now anyway?"

"Well, he cared enough to give me two thousand dollars and send me all the way down here from Chicago. If you tell me exactly what happened with this character you killed and what took place at the trial, I might be able to figure a way to get you out of here." He gave Flora what information he had from Black Joey, asking her to fill in where it was necessary. As he spoke, Flora gradually dropped her facade of ironic indifference and began to come alive. Her interest in living had been momentarily rekindled, and Hammill hoped that he was going to be able to justify it.

"Now, Flora, as I understand it, you did not *intend* to kill this man, is that right?"

"Of course not," she replied. "I was crazy about him. I just don't like being called a nigger, that's all, not even by a black man."

"This man was white?"

"Yeah. Didn't anybody tell you that? That's the part that made all those good white folks on the jury so mad at me —that I was livin' with a white man."

"Now wait." Hammill drew himself up on the edge of his chair, moving his face closer to Flora. The guard who was in charge of watching them—and eavesdropping—moved closer as well. "Were all the people on the jury white?"

"You were expecting maybe the Harlem Globetrotters? Of course, they were white."

"What about the grand jury—the first group you went before, when you were charged with the crime?"

"The same."

Hammill rose from his chair, zipping up his leather case, and said, "Good. I'll be back tomorrow, Flora, or the day after. I have to see the judge."

"Well, give the fat creep my regards and tell him I sure do appreciate all he did for me." The sculptured upper lip curled with contempt. "And next time," she added, playing with her hair, "come in the morning. I look better in the morning."

"Okay, Flora." As he turned to go, he suddenly thought of something. "Say, Joey doesn't know you changed your name. Why do you call yourself Black now?"

"'Cause that's what I am, baby—black."

A grand jury is required to represent a cross-section of the community in which a defendant lives, and in a town where at least one third of the population is black, there should be a representative number of Negroes on a jury. In the end it was not a very difficult appeal, for, although in the South such technicalities are all too frequently ignored, in this case it was enough to get Flora out of jail.

Flora did not look like the Negroes around Clinton, and essentially there had been some doubt as to her race. This may account for the oversight of having failed to place a Negro on the jury. The fact emerged during the hearing, as Flora explained how the tragedy had occurred and why, and from that moment on, there had been little question in the minds of the jurors as to what should be done with her.

Hammill held, on appeal, that the grand jury which indicted Flora had been improperly impaneled and that there had been a conspicuous lack of evidence showing premeditation and intent—so great a lack, in fact, that when Hammill threatened publicity and the creation of a cause célèbre, the judge decided to set Flora free.

Having settled his accounts with Mrs. Thackeray and bid a grateful adieu to her ramshackle establishment, Hammill headed for the prison to pick up Flora. Roughly a week had elapsed since he had arrived, and he was anxious to get back to Chicago and break the good news to Black Joey. He had been expecting to find a jubilant Flora waiting for him at the jail and was surprised by her despondent air; she sat in a plain, form-fitting black dress, holding a shapeless black handbag on her lap. In it was what remained of her worldly goods, and she stared at it with expressionless eyes.

"Well, Flora," Hammill opened, "you don't look like you'd just been given back your life."

"Have I?"

"This is no time to wax philosophical. We have a train to catch, so come on."

"Back to Chicago, eh?"

"Where did you have in mind?"

"Nowhere."

Although he had simply reserved a berth for Flora, and an upper at that, Hammill had a compartment for himself, and as they sat in it now, enjoying a drink—Flora's first in five months—she became more expansive. She began to talk about Black Joey, her mother, growing up, and her life as a cabaret dancer in Chicago and points east. As she spoke, Hammill thought that if any part of this sordid, predictable, but rather fascinating tale were recorded, it could be worked into an absolutely spectacular pornographic novel, on which somebody or other, perhaps even Flora herself, could make a fortune.

Several hours later, when Flora, catharsized and flushed with revelation, had finished, Hammill threw her a look that was mock-serious and said, "You know, Flora, you owe me a fee."

"What? After my ol' man gave you two G's?"

"That was only to cover my traveling and living expenses, which he clearly overestimated. It doesn't cover my time or my valuable professional services," he added facetiously. Flora eyed him, turning her head sideways.

"Well, since I've got no money, which you know damn well, I guess you'll have to get a free sample of *my* professional services." Before Hammill could stop her, Flora had unzipped and was halfway out of her clothes.

"No, no, Flora dear," he said. "I never bang my clients. It's bad business."

Flora, who had been wondering why he had not yet made a pass, regarded Hammill in bewilderment. "You don't want to screw me?"

"No, not particularly."

"Well, what the hell *do* you want then?" she asked, exasperated and not a little insulted.

"Put your clothes on, Flora. You look ridiculous sitting

there with your hands on your hips, half a dress on, and your bra showing. I want your diary." Flora stared at him.

"My what?"

"Your diary—the story of your life, your most intimate thoughts."

"Well, I don't keep no goddam diary, so what are you going to do about that?"

"Write one. I mean, *you* write one."

"Oh, for crissake, I got to get a job when I get back to Chicago. I can't be sittin' around writin' no goddam diary."

"You can do it in the daytime, when you're not working. Think of it, Flora—a whole book, all about yourself." The idea was becoming more appealing.

"Nobody'd read it but you?"

"Nobody but me—at least for a long time."

"Okay. It sounds screwy to me, but if that's what you want, I'll do it." They had a drink to confirm the agreement, and then another, falling into their respective bunks late.

Once back in Chicago, Flora availed herself of some of her father's connections to get a job dancing in a new club. The club was syndicate owned and operated, but that didn't seem to make much difference—weren't they all? The money was good, and people left her pretty much alone. During the day, she got more and more involved in the "diary," and it was beginning to take form.

Flora's literary style, a kind of crass blend of *True Romance* and *Little Orphan Annie* with a dash of de Sade, left a good deal to be desired, but the story, in any case, was told. At least *a* story was told; whether it was a faithful recapitulation of Flora's life is another question.

The story begins dramatically enough with Flora, aged six, being chased by a policeman from a crowd of spectators at a white folks' wedding with the admonition, "Beat it, you little black bastard." Right away we are presented with an example of the approach which is to characterize the entire account. At six, it was brought home to Flora that she was different in a way that did not please the majority of people and that the line of least resistance lay in staying out of their way as much as possible.

Flora's mother, father, and older sister lived on Chicago's

South Side, just across the street from a Catholic school, which contained only white children even though it was located in the heart of the Negro district. Flora found this rather strange, but she never thought to ask about it. Each morning, on her way to the public school, she met some of the girls who were going to the parochial school. They were incredibly neat in their blue uniforms and tan stockings, and had wonderful long ringlets or braids, which their mothers must have spent hours arranging, or so Flora imagined. She always hoped that they would take no notice of her as she passed by, for she was so terribly self-conscious about her worn skirt and shabby blouse, hand-me-downs from her sister, which contrasted so unfavorably with the other girls' pristine attire.

She wished that the one button left on her blouse was at the top, where it showed, instead of tucked away down at the bottom inside her skirt. Her white stockings generally had holes in them or huge darned patches, at which the Catholic girls would snicker—the darning had not always been done with the same colored thread. The only things of which Flora could be relatively proud were her white tennis shoes, which she washed every night before going to bed, then rubbed with chalk brought from school, and her smooth hair, which hung in a long braid down her back.

Curiously, Flora reports that the girls used to snub her because "I was neither light nor particularly 'good haired,'" which, together with the many other physical allusions, seems to indicate that when she was among colored people she felt "light" and pretty, but when among whites she felt "black." Flora's mercurial psychological posture had everything to do with the way she regarded herself and the world, and depending on her mood, she was either Venus or the lowest form of animal life; there was evidently no median. Hammill was known to comment frequently on Flora's ability to pass for white, yet her autobiography is studded with bitter references to her darkness.

While the little white girls snubbed Flora, now nearly nine years old, the white boys in the neighborhood did not, and she soon discovered the reason. They liked to play a game they called "hide-and-go-get-it," and though many of the white girls flatly refused to join them, Flora was cooperative—primarily because it gave her a feeling of "belonging" and being a legitimate member of the group. The game consisted of the girls running and hiding wherever they could—in bushes, cellars, or deserted outbuildings—and the boys would look for them. If discovered, the girl was expected to submit to sexual experimentation quite sophisticated for children of ten and eleven; some girls liked it, others did not, but Flora rather suspected that it was because they particularly liked doing it with her that the boys deigned to include her in their game. She resented the rough, selfish manner in which they went about amusing themselves when she was caught, and she tried her best each time to avoid detection, hopefully anticipating the squeals of some other girl—her assurance of having been temporarily spared this particular humiliation.

One day, while searching frantically for a place to hide, Flora came upon what was apparently a deserted shop and scurried down into the basement, feeling certain of avoiding discovery. Much to her surprise, there was another fugitive from prepubertal lust concealed in the debris—a colored girl like herself from the same neighborhood, though at least a couple of years older. Flora was startled at first, but as soon as the girl spoke and flashed a hospitable smile, Flora's initial apprehensions disappeared, and the mutuality of their present aims prevailed.

"Hey," the girl exclaimed, "I thought you was one of them fellas comin' down here after me."

"No. I'm hiding too. My name's Flora, what's yours?"

"Bertha."

"I've seen you before, but I didn't know you was in the game."

"Most of the time, I ain't. I live right near you over the delicatessen. I always wondered who you was, 'cause you're prettier than most."

"Thanks. We better keep our voices low, or it won't be no use hidin'."

"Yeah, that's right. Come on over with me so's I don't have to talk so loud." Flora scrambled over the broken boards, discarded concrete blocks, and other miscellaneous trash to the dark corner in which Bertha was ensconced. Comforted by the presence of her new friend, Flora hoped with all her heart that they would not be discovered and their privacy invaded.

"You know you're real pretty," Bertha said. "No wonder them boys like to get with you." Flora smiled, flattered by the compliment, though disturbed by the implications.

"I don't like it, though, bein' with them. They're so rough, as if you didn't have no feelin's or nothin'."

"That's right!" Bertha cried, exultant as people are when they find a comrade in thought at a moment when it is important for them to do so. "I can't stand 'em, an' I hope I never have to git married an' live with one of 'em for the rest of my life."

Both girls laughed till the tears came, and the older girl put her arm around Flora, stroking her shoulder. Flora relaxed completely, soothed by Bertha's touch, and soon let her head fall on the proffered shoulder. When Bertha spoke again, her voice was somehow changed. "I bet I know something you'd like," she said, placing her mouth close to Flora's ear.

"What?"

"Stand up. I'll show you. The janitor in my building gives me fifty cents every time I let him do it; I like it anyway. He's white—married, with kids an' everything, but he says that after a while, it's no fun with your wife anymore. And anyhow it doesn't hurt."

Flora rose slowly, looking expectantly into Bertha's round, friendly countenance. "Lord!" she thought. "I would fall right from the fryin' pan into the lousy fire." In an instant Bertha had got one of her legs between Flora's thighs and was moving her hips rhythmically. At first Flora resisted to some extent, failing to participate, but soon she had to admit to herself that it felt quite pleasant, and with Bertha's soft arms around her she had nothing to fear.

When it was over, Flora was flushed and out of breath, feeling suddenly ashamed; once again her craving for affection and companionship had been exploited by someone with more power than she. Still, Bertha had cared at least if she liked it, which was more than could be said for the boys, who were still hunting high and low for their favorite little girl.

"I'm goin' now," Flora said. "I have to go home."

"They'll catch you. Better stay here a while more."

"No. I better go."

"Do it again sometime, Flora?"

"No . . . I never heard of two girls doin' it anyhow. It ain't right." Bertha's expression made the remark seem silly.

"Well," she said, "you liked it though, didn't you?"

Flora felt hot all over her face and scalp, and she fled from the basement.

The boys had by now found a satisfactory victim, and Flora managed to reach home unmolested. Her family lived in an unspeakably dingy three-room apartment over an equally dingy establishment that functioned as a combination lunch room, confectioner, dry goods, and notions store. The place was owned and run by a man called Sam Garfinkel, with the help of his wife, and they had two rooms for themselves in the rear of the store.

The Garfinkels had a small daughter, Naomi, to whom Flora was utterly devoted. Sometimes Mrs. Garfinkel would give Flora twenty-five cents to baby-sit for an hour or two, and sometimes she would simply take advantage of the fact that Flora happened to be there; in any case, Flora loved to be with the child and immensely enjoyed the efforts required to entertain her. As a result of this mutual affection, Flora spent more time with the Garfinkels than in her own home, and little Naomi, who responded warmly to Flora's gentleness, profited perhaps more than anybody.

The Addersons' was not much of a home. Black Joey was forever out concocting some deal, and Flora's mother, a tough, proud woman, went out every day to clean the apartments of white people so that she and her family would not know the degredation of welfare. With Black Joey, you never knew if or when he was going to bring home any money, and more often than not, he drank up the proceeds of his sundry illegal schemes long before they found their way into the family exchequer. By the time Flora was eleven or twelve, her older sister Daisy was already spending most of her time in the company of boys—or looking for them—and that left nobody at all to look after Flora. Fortunately, Mrs. Garfinkel had grown genuinely fond of her, apart from the convenience of having a built-in nursemaid, and mothered Flora as though she were her own child.

There were only two things about this arrangement which Flora found disturbing: One was that whenever she left the Garfinkels' apartment in the evening to go to bed, Mr. Garfinkel would wink and give her some jellybeans and a licorice stick, or if Mama wasn't watching, pinch her breast or her buttock; the other thing was the difference between the Garfinkels' house and hers. Theirs was so neat and clean, cheerful too, with curtains and slipcovers that matched and temperature control so that it was warm in the winter and cool in the summer. At Flora's, it was just the opposite. She often told Mrs. Garfinkel that she wished her home could be nicer, at which point husband and wife would exchange meaningful looks, and Mrs. Garfinkel would say, "Well Flora, your mother has to work so hard every day that she doesn't have much time left for fixin' up the place."

"Daisy could help some. She knows how to clean and sew too. She's always out chasin' around with boys, that's why she don't help none, and Pop don't bring home enough money."

"Don't let it get you down, Flora dear. You're always welcome here, you know that."

"Yeah," Mr. Garfinkel added. "An' you're gettin' real pretty too, Flora."

The living room, where Flora and her sister slept at opposite ends of a dilapidated couch, stood darkly between the room in which Joey slept with his wife and the kitchen which inadequately served the family. The chipped enamel sink had no drainboard, and there was only an ancient gas stove and a small wooden table with four chairs, two of which were missing backs and a few slats here and there, all painted a bilious, peeling green. Flora's parents had the only proper bed in the house, a creaking brass structure, obtained from some seedy thrift shop, and when Grandma or anybody else came to spend the night, Flora was obliged to share it with them.

She hated this, because it meant that, unless her father came home exhausted and nearly paralyzed with bootleg liquor, she would undoubtedly be witness to their swinish sexual acts, which took place regardless of her presence in the bed. Many was the night when Flora, struggling to get to sleep and thus divest herself of the consciousness which made her an unwilling participant in an action which she did not yet understand, heard her mother shake Black Joey and say, "Come on, baby. Let's get some." Her father would grunt, rolling his great frame toward his wife and, with eyes still closed, would go through the motions of a rutting bear. It would then appear to Flora that her father was hurting her mother, and she despised him for that and her for tolerating it. More than anything, she resented the crushing indifference to the presence of their little girl and their callous disregard for her feelings and sensibilities. She was sure that Mr. and Mrs. Garfinkel wouldn't do that to Naomi, but then Naomi never had to move out of her room. . . .

In spite of periodic efforts on the part of her father's clever white lawyer, Flora noted that Black Joey did sometimes get sent to jail for a year and a day as a result of his business activities. She did not mind these absences at all, because it meant that she could sleep with her mother in comfort and warmth, undisturbed by the isolating sexual activity, which she found so repulsive. The trouble was that they were even poorer than usual when Joey was away, and her mother had to work like a horse so that they might have enough to eat and shoes to wear to school. At least when Flora's father was out of jail, the possibility existed that he would hit it big again, as he had once done, and they would be able to move into a nice apartment, get a new radio, a car, and perhaps even a fur coat for her mother. Last time, the fur coat was hocked and the car repossessed when the money ran out, but none of them ever lost hope that something big was just around the corner.

Joey's clientele consisted of every form of human scum, whether it was booze or snow (cocaine) they were after. To these disparate residents of the human scrap heap, Black Joey sold decks of cocaine, if he could get them, and "pints" of whiskey in small teapots. The latter made up the greater portion of his trade, for drugs were not really "in" yet, and booze was cheaper anyway. Joey's concoctions ranged in color from pale yellow to deep amber, depending on how he felt the day he made it, and cost $1.50 per pint. The children were well primed as to what they should do if the cops appeared: They were to push the little jugs out the window, if there were any about the place, and tell the police that their father was out. This only happened when Joey had fallen a bit in arrears on his monthly payments to Chicago's finest; otherwise they simply came to the door and said they were looking for him. They frequently ogled Flora and Daisy, but rarely tried to jostle them; Joey was a big man, and they were correctly afraid of the manifestations of his wrath.

Immediately following a friendly visit by the police, at which time a certain amount of cash generally changed hands, the girls would go for Joey's BB gun and shoot out one of the street lamps outside their window. The police could then report to their chiefs that hoodlums had pitched a brick through one of the globes, thereby justifying their presence in the neighborhood. This ritual went on for years, with Black Joey staying out of trouble so long as he continued to make his payments.

As Flora passed through her twelfth and thirteenth years, she became increasingly disturbed by the development of her body, finding the swelling breasts and sprouting body hair repulsive. When she began to menstruate, she was ashamed and miserable, for she knew that it all brought her closer to a sexuality which she thought to be cruel and exploitative, and which generally treated girls as objects—especially black girls. Flora's sister Daisy was already something of a tart, receiving many "callers" at the apartment when her parents were out. Flora was revolted by Daisy's preening, which seemed to occupy most of her time, whether the audience was a man or her own mirror, for at fifteen Daisy was already unabashedly sexual. But then she had never been subjected to the spectacle of her own parents' concupiscence as a child, and had probably been introduced to sex more or less normally.

Flora who at thirteen was growing increasingly attractive, was visited daily by a delegation of boys from school, all of whom had hopes that she would eventually bestow her favors upon them. The only one Flora liked was a boy called Freddie, who appeared to be the leader of the group and who rather enjoyed protecting Flora from the others. Flora knew that he was only trying to keep her for himself, but she liked his confident, arrogant air, and as yet he had left her pretty much alone. Freddie was three years older than Flora, and going steady with him provided her with a shield against the abuses and molestations visited upon many of the unattached girls, and she was never without a companion. They went skating in the winter, on picnics in the spring, with movies and dancing to the jukebox the staple in their normal entertainment diet.

This continued for two years, at which point Flora, going on sixteen, was no longer a little girl, and Freddie decided it was time that she began to be "nice" to him. Freddie had always been kind to her and never pushed her further in their courting than she wished to go. What Freddie did not realize was that it was fear rather than virtue which held Flora back; at the same time he knew that Flora frequently became exceedingly "hot in the britches" when he caressed her, and as he often pointed out, everybody else was "doing it."

On New Year's Eve, Flora's parents had gone out to celebrate, as had Daisy, leaving Flora and Freddie alone in the apartment. Flora, frolicking about the place like a child, had got herself dressed up in some of Daisy's sexy black-lace underwear, adding a filmy nylon peignoir to the costume, just for fun. Arranging herself on the couch in what she believed to be her best "Harlow" pose, she invited Freddie to have a look at her. To Freddie, this was not a game but a serious provocation, and he abandoned his habitual restraint. This time, the hot britches came off, and Flora was faced with the problem of how to stop Freddie from "raping" her.

At first she giggled a great deal, as she warded off his advances, but as Freddie grew more convinced that this time she meant for him to have her, his lust gained control of him, and he became rougher than he had ever been with a girl. Flora was frightened, and when the moment came for which Freddie had long been waiting and Flora had even longer been dreading, it was extremely painful, and she began to cry, begging him to stop. But Freddie did not even seem aware of her presence. Craning her neck to look at his sweating face and glazed eyes, Flora was filled with disgust. When it was over, looking at Flora's bitter, tear-streaked face and the mess he had made of her, Freddie said he was sorry. "It always hurts the first time, honey. Ain't nothin' to be done 'bout that."

"Get out of here," Flora snarled, "and don't come back."

"Flora, for crissake, why are you so damn special? It'll be better next time, you'll see."

"There ain't goin' to be no next time; now get out of here!" she shouted, at the top of her lungs. "An' leave me alone," she added quietly, turning her head away. Seeing that there was nothing to be done, Freddie left, as shouts of "Happy New Year" pierced the frigid midnight air. Inside, a distraught Flora washed and lay down on her couch, where she wept most of the night.

Three months later, Black Joey was back in jail. The furniture, such as it was, had been sold, and Flora, reading by candlelight, was obliged to sprawl out on the floor in front of the stove, in order to keep warm while doing her homework. Electricity, gas, and water had all been turned off, because they had not been able to pay the bills. The three women were obliged to use candles and kerosene lamps for light, and to get water in buckets from a fireplug outside the building. All three slept together in the big bed in order to stay warm through the night, for during that winter they often awoke in the morning to find the water frozen in the buckets, so that they had to break through the ice to perform their morning ablutions. (Flora swears that it is due to this Spartan ritual that her complexion remains radiant to this day.)

A salvaged coal stove, brought into the living room, was all that stood between them and the petrifying cold, and even the Garfinkels seemed to have lost sympathy with the family. Flora had not been by as much lately to baby-sit, although Naomi still asked after her wistfully.

One day in March, Mrs. Adderson, noticing Flora's thickened waist and drawn furtive demeanor, inquired as to whether she had been having her monthly periods regularly. Flora shook her head, her eyes averted from her mother's relentless gaze, and waited for the precipitation of abuse to begin. "Was it Freddie?" her mother asked firmly but without rancor. Flora looked up and nodded, a welcome feeling of relief flowing through her tense frame.

"Oh, Mama," she said, the tears starting to flow, "I'm so miserable."

"I know, I can see that," her mother replied. "These things happen, but it's not the end of the world."

"What am I goin' to do with this kid?"

"Oh, Lord, that's a long way off. We'll think about that when it happens. Might know," Mrs. Adderson mused, "it'd be you an' not that other tramp of mine. I'll say one thing: Daisy knows how to take care of herself."

"You seem to know how to take care of yourself too."

"An' just what does that mean?"

"You an' the ol' man."

"What me an' your Pa do is none of your damn business!"

"Well if it ain't none of my business, then why did I have to see it every time Grandma came to spend the night?" Flora's eyes blazed, her voice choking in tears of rage and self-pity.

"An' just where did you expect us to go, little Miss Knock-up? Down to the Plaza Hotel? You just shut your mouth, an' don't go givin' me no hard time! Ain't nobody but me goin' to see you through the mess *you're* in, an' that's for sure." In truth, there was less anger than desolation in the woman's polemic, for she knew what Flora faced.

Unfortunately, the principal of Flora's school, an officious and condescending white man, had also noticed the change in her appearance and behavior—a change still subtle enough as to be barely evident, but the man was forewarned by experience. One morning he invited Flora into his office, and observing her contours as she passed in front of the window, he was able to confirm his suspicions. Then, in a decision characteristic of his petty approach to the job, he refused to allow Flora to finish the school term, even though her condition could be easily concealed until June when school would be over. Mrs. Adderson immediately lodged a strong protest against the principal's action, but to no avail. If Flora came back to school the following autumn, she would have to repeat the entire grade.

That summer was a real scorcher, and the time seemed to drag by with all the sluggishness of life in the equatorial jungles. The days and weeks followed heavily one upon the other, presenting but one problem to the gradually inflating Flora: to survive the heat with a modicum of comfort. To escape the suffocating swelter of the apartment, which was now as hot as it had been cold in January, Flora frequently wandered off alone to the breezier banks of Lake Michigan. Sometimes she would sit on a bench overlooking the breakwater, remaining there for hours, watching the water lap at the rocks and thinking bitter thoughts about the wretched Freddie, who, though unwelcome, appeared each week to find out how Flora was.

When Flora's time came, almost two months early, she was totally unprepared, both psychologically and materially. With Joey out of jail now and the old dodge going well, there would have been money for a layette and most of the other things a new baby needs. But since it was still early in the eighth month, no provision had yet been made for the child's arrival.

One steaming day toward the beginning of August, while Flora and Daisy were cheerfully engaged in killing roaches, Flora felt her first pains. Assuming that she was suffering an attack of indigestion, she lay down on the couch and listened to the radio. It soon became apparent, at least to Daisy and her mother, that she was actually in labor, but Flora, unwilling to face the situation at this early date, dismissed any suggestion of getting herself to the hospital.

After a few hours, Flora began to feel the pains more acutely, and she finally agreed to move. No one had enough money on hand for a taxi, so Daisy was obliged to call the nearest public hospital for an ambulance. It was almost two hours before anyone arrived, and by this time Flora was suffering in earnest. Much to her dismay, moreover, she discovered that two policemen had been dispatched to collect her, rather than the white-robed medical attendant she had hoped for.

The latter were evidently too busy filling out their report to offer any assistance to the groaning Flora, and so, with the help of Daisy and her mother, she lifted herself painfully from the couch, and made her way slowly down the four flights of stairs to the street. There, instead of an ambulance, stood a patrol wagon.

The two cops had preceded Flora, passing her on the landing and pausing only briefly to tell her to be quick. As the three women emerged from the gloom of the entrance hall into the brilliant sunlight, they found themselves surrounded by curious neighbors, anxious to see what was going on. The appearance of a patrol wagon always caused a certain amount of excitement, as it usually meant that there had been a murder, or that a raid on a gin mill or policy wheel was in progress.

Flora, wearing her mother's "hoover" apron and a tatty pair of bedroom slippers, was not an imposing figure. Her hair had been braided into innumerable pigtails, "a practice," by Flora's own account, "diligently adhered to by many colored people when their women are in labor," and as she struggled to get to the wagon and remove herself from the curious stares which seemed to consume her, she felt like an offending freak.

Daisy was permitted to accompany her, for it looked as though they might not make it to the hospital in time. One of the policemen spoke to Daisy as though Flora did not exist: "If she has to let it out before we get there, let 'er lay down there on the floor." Daisy did not reply, but tried to comfort Flora, who was now crying out at regular intervals.

Upon arriving at the hospital, Flora "fell into the hands of a woman doctor," a circumstance which, judging by her account, Flora considered the culminating humiliation. To add to her feeling of degradation, everyone standing around her during the birth made remarks concerning the "typical" physical characteristics of the Negro female, taking special notice of her extraordinary "development" for the age of sixteen. No one was particularly moved or disturbed by Flora's suffering, although medication was given her to ease the pain. What Flora could not know is that the apparent indifference and detachment exhibited by doctors and nurses in maternity wards is felt also by white women, and bitterly denounced, but Flora would doubtless go to her grave thinking that the indelicacy of her treatment was related solely to the color of her skin.

When it was over, Flora was wheeled into a ward filled with other semiconscious and sleeping women—some of whom, much to Flora's amazement, were white. She had always thought that all white people went to private hospitals or had private rooms, it having never occurred to her that many of them were poor too.

Flora had dozed off almost immediately on entering the ward and was eventually awakened by the touch of a firm hand on her shoulder. It was the doctor who now, without her mask and shapeless working clothes, looked a bit more sympathetic. She told Flora that the baby, being almost two months premature, had been too small and had died. The doctor was surprised that Flora did not react to this news, but Flora's feelings were so equally balanced between sadness and relief as to have resulted in a kind of emotional stalemate, the outward manifestation of which produced no observable response at all. The doctor smiled and, placing a maternal hand on Flora's arm, said without sarcasm or condescension, "It's all right, you'll probably be back next year with a fine, healthy one."

Flora's problems did not end with the death of the baby, for while still at the hospital, she developed serious complications relating to her painfully swollen breasts. Generally, the postpartum care she had been receiving was inadequate, and among the things she failed to receive was medication that would reduce the soreness in her bosom and help dry up the useless milk. The breasts had become dangerously hard, and the pressure was so great that Flora could sleep only under heavy sedation. Nor would the milk drain off normally, the ducts having been choked off, and it was ultimately decided that Flora would have to undergo an operation.

When she was sent home at last, she was not only obliged to reappear among her family empty-handed but still very much ailing, and with her chest bound up and hurting enough to make her thoroughly miserable. Her mother had gone to fetch her, remarking that she looked terrible and that it was only because Joey was home that she could afford to lose a day's work. Daisy, who had had the couch to herself during Flora's absence, was not particularly overjoyed to see her either, but they all helped in taking care of her, and if they were piqued by the slowness of her recovery, they tried not to show it. All that remained of the entire experience were the scars on her breasts and an abiding fear and loathing of men, including her father.

Freddie turned up once or twice during Flora's convalescence, and each time she found that it was all she could do to speak civilly to him. One visit took place on her birthday, and Freddie appeared with a bunch of wilting flowers, asking for her hand in marriage. Flora was incredulous and later, laughing humorlessly, told her mother and Daisy, who merely exchanged solemn looks. As Flora scrutinized their faces, she realized that they must have known about it all along, that her mother and father had probably put Freddie up to it.

"Well, why not marry him?" her mother ventured. "He's stuck on you for sure. Been goin' around with a face like a dyin' dog ever since you been in trouble."

"Yeah, well, that's just what he looks like to me, a dyin' dog. An' besides, I want to finish school. You think it's right for a girl sixteen to get married?"

"When a girl finds a guy that wants to marry her, that's the right time to get married, believe me."

"An' what's that supposed to do for her?"

"Well, somebody besides us has got to feed you for the rest of your life."

"Like the ol' man feeds you? Is that why you got to go out an' clean houses, so *he* can feed *you*?"

"You shut your mouth! Freddy's a lot smarter than your Pa. He ain't goin' to be no bootlegger or dope pusher. . . ."

"An' what's he goin' to be, Ma, President of the United States?"

"All right! So what are you goin' to do? Stay in this dump for the rest of your life an' live off us?" Flora was very calm now, as she replied, "No. I'm goin' to finish school an' get a good job so I don't have to depend on any of those bums to feed me."

"You do what you want," Mrs. Adderson said, hastily putting on her coat. She had a job to go to. "If you're goin' to be stupid like that, I don't give a damn what you do. I'm goin' now. I'm late."

In September Flora went back to school to gather up the threads of her interrupted education. It was not easy to face her friends again, all of whom had by now been informed one way or another about the drift of Flora's fortunes during the past year, and Flora had been left with an enormous chip on her shoulder because of it. In general the boys who, ever attracted by Flora, were willing to overlook any indiscretion or shame were extremely good in dealing with Flora's "calamity"; in fact they never mentioned it head-on. The girls, however, seemed to take a special delight in offering back-handed sympathy and double-edged "understanding," never letting Flora forget that her experience had fundamentally isolated her from their intimate midst. Apart from Daisy, she had one good friend who stood by her, and that was enough.

Having got this far in her narrative, Flora suddenly begins to exhibit a noticeable increase in superficial self-esteem, which seems to grow in direct proportion to the intensification in feelings of persecution. Statements of fact suddenly appear curiously ambivalent, arbitrary, or simply invalid, and the essential story begins to meander in and out of Flora's social fantasies. To rescue the truth from wishful thinking or from a self-serving taste for the melodramatic becomes increasingly difficult. But in a sense the truth is not essential, for fantasy is part of Flora's reality, and often seems to reveal more of the person than would an unadulterated history.

Flora soon became accustomed to the omnipresent whispering and abrupt shifts in conversation which generally accompanied her appearance in a group, and after several months, it no longer disturbed her. She felt, in fact, that being shut out from the group inspired her to participate in everything that she could at school and to excel in all things she endeavored to do. She became a member in good standing of the Girl's Athletic Association, the Girl's Reserves, the Glee Club, the Latin Club, the Rifle Club, and the Drama Club. She made every effort that her manner of dress and general appearance should demonstrate refinement, restraint, and good taste, insofar as that was possible, and in her senior year she captured the lead in the school play. During this time Flora must have avoided all potentially compromising contacts with the opposite sex, for they play no part whatever in her narrative. She informs us only that the girls appeared to be enormously irritated by her sexual indifference, because it caused the boys to cluster around her to a greater extent than previously; she led them on to a point, and then just moved off. The only unpleasantness evolving from Flora's attitude was that she had no sooner established the fact that she had no interest in men than the assistant principal, who was a woman, began to make what Flora describes as "quasi-Lesbian passes" at her. What begins to emerge in Flora here is a strong feeling of being hunted as sexual prey. It seemed as though no one—man or woman—was able to regard her in any other way.

From the first moment she entered high school, Flora had aspired to a career in nursing and pursued studies in general science which were recommended as preparation for nursing school. At some stage after the "calamity," however, she was bitten by the show-biz bug and abandoned general science for dramatics. This had come about one year when Flora was persuaded to join a musical group known as "Hi-Jinks" as a result of which her talent for dancing was brought to the surface.

Dancing was made for Flora, for in it she found not only something in which she was vastly superior to other people, but in which to display herself as a desired but unattainable sexual object. She was very good at describing what it was that made her love to dance: "I don't know why, but when I begin to dance, everything goes out of my head but the rhythm. I don't even hear the music; I just start to move and go into another world. I can learn any routine in no time flat, but I don't really even need one. I could dance by myself, making it up as I go along and doing something different and exciting each time. The only thing I notice is the way people look at me, especially the men who can't take their eyes off my body, as if they'd like to eat me up, but they can't get at me. With the lights all warm on me and everyone watching and enjoying, I could go on dancing for hours without stopping."

By her senior year in high school, Flora was able to get jobs dancing in some of the smaller nightclubs around the Negro community, and thus she divided her life: dancing at night and going to school by day. In some clubs the last show was at midnight, and it was often painful to have to rise early the following morning and get to her first class on time. Had the school authorities become aware of Flora's extramural activities, she would doubtless have been expelled, and special efforts were required to conceal her fatigue, which, if noticed, could lead to exposure. Her family certainly did nothing to discourage this duplicity, as they were glad enough to have another infusion of "clean" money coming in, other than that which Mrs. Adderson earned by her sweat. By now Daisy was a proper prostitute and had moved out; they would none of them ever see any of that money. And although, since Repeal, Joey had concentrated his business efforts in the profitable area of narcotics, he had a tendency to dissipate his earnings in transient pleasures, larding away nothing to sustain his family during those infrequent periods when he was in jail and the flow of income was abruptly arrested. Flora had always described her father as a salesman, and luckily, in all the years during which she was in school, nobody had demonstrated the slightest interest in knowing what it was that he sold.

The day finally came in June when Flora was graduated and had done with school forever. Apart from anything else, this meant that she could sleep each day until noon, which she did with relish. She danced in a number of small cabarets, catering to both white and black customers, but got her first big break when she answered a call, posted in all the clubs, for chorus girls needed in the largest club in Chicago featuring Negro performers. Although exceedingly nervous about the audition, Flora reports that she danced marvelously, as usual, setting the club owners on their collective ear, and easily came away with one of the available jobs.

Reporting to work on the first evening, Flora was annoyed to discover that she would be sharing a dressing room with fifteen other girls, most of whom were in the habit of sitting around between numbers stark naked. It did not take long for Flora to become alienated from this collection of women. Unlike them, she refused to sit around in the nude, primarily because one of her breasts had been left scarred by her postpartum surgery, and as they did not understand her apparent aloofness toward men, they resented it and thought her insupportably square. One or two of the girls were kind to her, but she made few friends among them.

Flora continued to lead this strange, disoriented sort of life for two years, during which time girls came and went from the chorus line, replacements were made in the band, but Flora, doggedly chaste, remained dancing and minding her own business.

Then one day a young, light-skinned Negro came in as a replacement for the tenor saxophone in the band. His name was Alvin, but everybody called him Al, and unlike so many of the others, he had good manners and a curious kind of courtliness about him, which attracted Flora from the start. He clearly liked Flora as well and loved to watch her dance, the knowledge of which, in turn, inspired Flora to dance better and with more verve than ever. He was the perfect foil for her, for he was awed by her and reserved in his approach, and she derived enormous satisfaction from watching him trying to steal looks at her as he played, his eyes rolling up at her whenever he could remove them from the page of music in front of him. Always happy dancing, Flora was happiest dancing for Al.

It was predictable that he and Flora should start going out together after the show. Performers, generally keyed up after a night's work, can seldom fall directly into bed and sleep, and these two enjoyed going somewhere after the club had closed to have a drink and relax. Flora, delighted by the fact that Al evidently enjoyed conversing as well as looking at her, would drink Virginia Dare wine and listen to him speak of his life and his hopes. Sometimes they would drive out to the suburbs in Al's tiny Ford, where they would consume an early breakfast, and buy apples, grapes, oranges, and melons from a country fruit stand, and eat them at home later.

Ultimately Flora permitted Al to make love to her, and she found in him a lover who was gentle and kind, and of whom she need not be afraid. She was happy in his little apartment, stuffed with secondhand furniture, records, and as much recording equipment as he could afford; they would lie in bed listening to music produced by the greatest jazz artists in the world, and looking at the beautiful, distant places depicted in the travel posters that covered the walls, wondering about the people who went there. Undoubtedly, Flora would remember this as the happiest period in her life.

But prolonged contentment was not to characterize her lot, and restlessness conspired with vanity in Flora to thrust her into the next spiral of her convoluted life. Flora was happy, but she wanted good shoes, clothes to show off her body, enough money to have her hair straightened *every* month, and perhaps even her own apartment. She was tired of living with other people and being beholden to them; she wanted independence and mobility.

Flora had noticed that one of the girls in the chorus line, a lovely, slim, light-skinned girl like herself, turned up each evening in the most fabulous clothes and costume jewelry Flora had ever seen. She befriended the girl, whose name was Josi, and discovered that she was actually a very high-class hustler, with an intensely realistic philosophy of life.

"Face it, the job here at the club is just a way of meeting the Johns. They watch me and I watch them, and if I like one of 'em, I meet him after the show."

"I didn't think you got those clothes on the crummy pay we get here," Flora admitted.

"That's for sure, honey. That's for damn sure."

"But most of the guys who come in here are white," Flora said naïvely. Josi's smile was patronizing.

"That's the best kind. Don't you know that? They're loaded with scratch and wild ideas about what we can do for 'em, an' they leave you alone if you don't want 'em."

"Yeah, but what if you don't come across with all the wild action they expect? What happens then?"

"Honey, if you're black, they think they've had it great, no matter what you do, believe me. You can just lie there and think about what you're goin' to have for breakfast. They don't care. They're still goin' to tell their buddies that it was the hottest thing since Jane Russell's busted brassiere." Josi took a long drag on her cigarette, scanning Flora's frame from top to bottom. "You know," she said, "you're selling yourself cheap in this place. They're gettin' somethin' for nothin'. Don't ever sell yourself cheap, that's the biggest mistake you can make. If the price is high, they think they're really gettin' somethin', an' that goes for guys who run clubs. What d'you see in that horn-playin' spade anyhow?"

"He's nice to me," Flora replied simply.

"Yeah, but he ain't rich, honey, and he's never goin' to be, so if you like nice clothes, you better stick with whitey, 'cause that's where you get the folding stuff to buy 'em. An' get 'em to give you *things*, not money. That makes 'em feel cleaner somehow."

"But how much does it cost you to live?"

"Honey, I don't spend a dime."

Flora spent the night at home, instead of with Al, and as she lay there on the sagging couch, she pondered her encounter with Josi. She didn't like Josi's attitude about other Negroes; after all, she was black herself. But still, there was something in what she said.

Although the greater part of the club's clientele was white, many prosperous blacks came in, and Flora was always proud of them, because they were generally well-behaved and sophisticated.

The owner of the club, who was white, did not like the girls to sit with a Negro customer, unless he was a rich policy king, a racketeer, or somebody like Joe Louis, who came there often. The others tended to be the embarrassing, inelegant variety, who had saved up all year to have a big evening, and who usually ended by making fools of themselves, which was bad for business. Flora understood the anxiety and discomfiture, which made them this way, but despised them nevertheless with all her heart, for they served as an uncomfortable reminder of the world Flora hoped one day to leave forever. And it was obvious that she never would leave it if she failed to capitalize on her attractiveness to men other than Al.

Flora's interest had been considerably aroused by the attention focused upon her by one particular white man, who came to the club often, never taking his eyes off Flora while the show was in progress. Al was not unaware of this and watched the situation intently. Inevitably, a note was handed to Flora one night by one of the waiters, inviting her to join the man for a drink when she was through working. Flattered and sorely tempted, she considered the invitation, but she was worried about Al's possible reaction; he was jealous and possessive, a man in love. Besides, she knew that he had a low opinion of colored girls who consorted with white men, and she feared the

consequences of making him angry. So she refused. The man
was impressed but not discouraged.

Eventually, the band prepared to go on the road, and Al
was to go with it for a few weeks. A new show was being mounted
to coincide with the arrival of a fresh band, and Flora was obliged
to rehearse all day as well as work the old routine at night.
Exhausted most of the time during this period, she quarrelled
with Al frequently, and by the time he left, Flora was almost
glad to see him go.

Up to this point in Flora's personal account, the facts
relating to her life appear generally to coincide with what other
people know about her, and the narrative, though unsophisticated, flows with a minimum of contrivance. It is difficult to say
how it is that an unfamiliar narrative, which purports to be
factual, suddenly loses the ring of truth, or what precisely it is in
the depiction of events, impressions, causes, and effects which
informs the intellectual ear of the loss. Perhaps it is simply that
Flora, warming to the task assigned her and not a little dis-
mayed at the drabness of her life in retrospect, succumbed to
the temptation of making facts conform to the events which
animated her dreams, rather than the realities which burdened
her life.

Subsequent to Al's departure from the story, one is as-
sailed with serious doubts as to the veracity of the events re-
counted; from here on, one gets the feeling that Flora, enthusi-
astically creating a work of fiction of which she is the heroine,
basks in the vicarious glow of experiences she wishes she had had,
while at the same time exaggerating for dramatic effect, the
horror of experiences she wishes she had not had.

She relates, for example, that with the opening of the
new show at the club, her admirer from the white world returned, sitting at the same table he had occupied previously.
Again it is apparent that he came only to see Flora, and one
night, as she leaves the club to go home, she finds him waiting
for her outside in a white convertible. She gets into the car and
is informed that the man's name is Ted. Flora never describes
him physically, other than to say that he is white and attractive.
Ted asks her if she would like to go aboard his yacht (which is
presumably parked on the banks of Lake Michigan) and join
him in a nightcap. She accepts with pleasure.

The boat which Flora proceeds to describe would do justice to the most extravagant dreams of Walter Mitty. Climbing aboard, she and Ted pass through "doors," descend a ladder into the "galley, where the crew slept" and where there was a huge stove on which somebody was cooking bacon and eggs. They proceed from there through an enormous bar, paneled in mahogany, which runs the length of a similarly adorned "living room." All the while Ted has been unable to restrain himself from showering Flora with compliments related to her ladylike comportment, proud, erect carriage, and refined bearing and proportions, with the emphasis on how individual, how different she is compared with the other girls in the show. Just as Ted is about to introduce her to his friends, who are lounging about in the "living room," a very curious thing occurs: the Flora of the story becomes "Elsie," and the "I" is replaced by "she."

Elsie is clearly an exhibitionist. No sooner has she been presented to Ted's companions, than she peels off her clothes, spurred by their eager entreaties, and, dressed in nothing other than two men's mufflers, dances for them all to the strains of "Song of India." Her dance is voluptuous and brilliant, and the men, ignoring their white mates, are incapable of tearing their eyes from Elsie's magnificent body. What follows, predictably, is a good old-fashioned orgy, of which Elsie is the star and prime object of desire. All the men in the group are bent on having her, but Ted, who has been removing his clothes feverishly, gets to her first, leaving the others with no choice but to make love to the girls they brought with them for that purpose.

Flora's prose waxes fairly lurid at this stage, as she describes in true movie-mag style "the thrill in Ted's kiss," and the "power that was drawing us together like a magnet"; she frequently appears to forget in the throes of describing her own sexual fervor, that all this is supposed to be happening to "Elsie." Ultimately they retire to one of the many "bedrooms" in this extraordinary vessel, which Flora tells us has buff-colored walls and pale-lavender furniture, not to mention an elegant mirrored vanity heaped with expensive and delectable feminine toilet articles. Here, removed from the hungry stares of their fellow revelers, they engage in a series of superfornications which last for what is left of the night. "Elsie" is surprised at the degree of pleasure she derives from Ted's frantic lovemaking, as she had always been led to believe that white men were not very adept in this department. The dialogue here is fairly limited but neatly summed up as they finally fall asleep in one another's arms:

> Ted: "Oh, Elsie, I want you so badly—I'll give you anything you want!"
> Elsie: "Sweet music to my ears!"

Clearly, Flora had succeeded in overcoming her previous distaste for men, which did not, however, increase her self-esteem; formerly she could look down upon men as sex-obsessed animals, but now that she had become as keen a copulator as they, she was denied that bolstering sense of superiority and had to seek new forms of pride. As a result, there develops a trend toward depicting herself as "a normal"—someone who only lusts for love—whereas her partners in sex tend to be slightly depraved or so much in love that she cannot find it in her warm heart to deny them the comfort they so avidly seek. (In this latter context, and from the strictly "literary" point of view, Flora seems to be the natural precursor of Terry Southern's *Candy*.)

In the postorgy period, following the evening on Ted's yacht, Flora temporarily resumes her own identity and continues to enjoy an exciting sex life with Ted. We also discover that Ted has "connections" in the nightclub business and is soon able to get Flora an audition in the Sunset Club, a far better place than the one in which she has been working.

This turns out to be an unexpectedly humiliating experience, for although both the director and the producer of the show are impressed by Flora's dancing and general appearance, the two discuss at length the fact that Flora has a slightly darker complexion than some of the other girls in the line and how this might affect the situation. Flora stands and listens, her face flushed, as the owner argues that white patrons prefer light-skinned Negroes in the show; the producer, a black, insists that it is the black patrons—who are in the minority—who crave the lighter skins. In the end, Flora, unsure now that she really wants to work for these people, gets the job and is grateful for the raise in salary that comes with it.

Flora goes on to tell us that Ferris, the producer, was extremely kind to her, being particularly impressed with the speed with which she mastered the new routines. There was

something sinister about the man, though, which seemed to be
felt by all the girls, but which none of them could quite define.
They all carefully avoided him, except Flora, who allowed him to
chat and buy her coffee from time to time, just to be civil. Still,
she always suffered a certain discomfort in his presence, because
of the way in which Ferris would continue to stare at her intently, even though neither of them was speaking. Basically
Flora felt that her job was secure so long as she remained in his
favor, and so far he had done her no harm.

Then the day arrived when Ferris, seeing that Flora had
built up sufficient trust in him, perpetrated the act toward
which he had been moving ever since she came into the club.
The prelude to this was an invitation to share a sandwich and
coffee at an all-night drugstore after the last show, on a hot
Saturday in June. So unwillingly does Flora recall the events of
this night that we suddenly find that it is all actually happening to a girl called Angie, who told Flora about it later.

In this scene, Angie and Ferris are sitting on stools at a
counter, finishing their coffee, and Angie has thanked Ferris for
being so kind to her. Ferris replies that he could get her a
featured spot in the show if she would only be a little bit "nice"
to a certain man of Ferris' aquaintance, who wants to meet her.
The man, Ferris explains, has an interest in the club and has
seen Angie there. Angie now realizes that Ferris is a pimp for
some white man with a preference for colored girls and decides
finally to go with Ferris to meet him, for a featured part in the
show is what she has been longing for since the beginning.

"All right, Mr. Ferris. When will I see him?" Angie asks.

"Right now."

"At this hour?" Angie begins to wonder a bit about
this mystery man.

"Oh, sure. This guy stays up all night. He won't mind."

Leaving the drugstore, Ferris hails a cab, which Angie
thinks is rather peculiar for a man not making a great deal of
money, and comments on it.

"I'm in a hurry," Ferris explains, causing the girl to be
more uneasy than ever. "He's paying anyway."

Eventually they arrive at a brick edifice, which, unlike the
darkened apartment houses on either side of it, displays several
lighted windows. Flora does not know exactly where they are, but

thinks it must be somewhere near Clark Street. With mounting apprehension she climbs the front steps of the house. The door swings open even before Ferris reaches for the bell, and they enter.

They are greeted by a paunchy florid man with snow-white hair, wearing an ill-fitting dressing gown and chewed leather slippers.

"What the hell took you so long?" he demands of Ferris, before he had met or even looked at Angie. "The mutt's going crazy. I gave him the stuff hours ago." Angie looks at Ferris, hoping to receive some explanation of this strange remark. The man sweeps them up one flight of stairs into a kind of library, decorated mostly in brown velour, with a thick carpet on the floor and a few pieces of heavy furniture lined up unimaginatively against the walls. "This is Angie," Ferris says somewhat extraneously. "She's a great little dancer."

"Yeah, I know," the man breathes, eyeing Angie's slim body. "I've seen her."

"Who are you?" Angie ventures, looking into the rheumy blue eyes.

"Doesn't matter, does it, honey? You know why you're here."

"Yeah, I guess I do," Angie replies wearily, wondering how she is going to make it with this white slob. As she begins to undress, she notices that Ferris has gone from the room. "Where's Ferris gone?" she inquires.

"Getting the dog."

"The dog! What dog? Hey, what the hell is this?" The question is answered by the appearance of Ferris, who clings to a heavy chain, at the end of which strains an enormous black-and-white male mastiff. The animal, tense in every muscle, stands quivering in the doorway, and rolling its dilated eyes from one side to the other, while sweat pours from Ferris' black face. Angie is terrified and in a curious gesture of modesty plucks up her dress and holds it in front of her, as though hoping it would protect her from this beast.

"Get the rest of those clothes off, honey," the man says in an ugly voice. "I've been waiting a long time."

"Now wait just a minute," Angie interjects, her voice cracking in fear despite an effort to remain calm. "What's that

mutt got to do with this?" The man shoots a wicked glance at
Ferris, who has been avoiding Angie's look, concerning himself
with the dog. "Didn't you tell her?"

"She wouldn't have come," the distraught Ferris replies.
"I just wanted to get her here." The man utters an obscenity
under his breath, fixing his eyes once more on Angie's naked
body.

"Well," he says, "it's just that the dog has developed a
taste for nigra gals, an' I hate to deprive him. Now you just
get down on all fours; he won't hurt you none. Who knows, you
might even get to like it, eh, Ferris? Some of 'em do, you know."
Ferris joins him in a laugh. "Never can tell, Mr. Glazer," he
replies. Glazer. She knew that name; he was a part owner of
the club.

Angie's jaw sags as she begins to comprehend what these
two want her to do, and suddenly she begins snatching at her
clothes, which lie on the couch. "I'll be goddamned if I'm goin'
to get laid by some filthy mutt!" she screams. "I'm gettin' out
of here!"

Glazer by now, however, has produced a pistol from
somewhere, and aims it firmly at Angie's belly. The dog had been
fed some sort of powerful aphrodisiac and was obviously suffering considerably. "Get on your hands and knees, you nigger
bitch!" growls the dog's master, and Angie, cowed by the sight
of the weapon, obeys. The two men then sit down at an appropriate angle, watching intently, and as the dog approaches
her, reach for their zippers. Angie is afraid that she may be
sick: "Black scum or white scum," she thinks, her stomach
reeling. "What a thing to have in common."

Flora did not remain at the club after this, but decided
to withdraw her savings and try her luck in New York, a move
which she viewed both as an opportunity to shift into the big-
time and to get as far away as possible from the loathesome
Ferris. Flora was excited about going, for up till now she had
never ventured out of Chicago. No mention is made of the
godlike Ted, who presumably found himself summarily abandoned.

When she arrived in New York, Flora moved into a
rooming house in Harlem, which apparently catered to people in
show business. Across the hall from her resided Son and Sonny,
a pair who constituted possibly the littlest known dance team

in America. They were very black, smoked pot, were almost perpetually intoxicated, and Son was trying to learn how to play the
guitar, which drove Flora nearly mad. But they made no passes
at her, nor did they cause her trouble of any kind; Son, in fact,
became a true friend, one of the few Flora ever had.

Living in the same rooming house was a piano player
called Alec, who is described by Flora as a Negro who "passed"
for white and who was a paragon of refinement, cultivation, and
intelligence. But what Flora evidently admired most about him
was his "Venezuelan" accent and his admirable sexual restraint.
Also, he played in the band at the Cotton Club, one of the most
renowned emporia of its type in Harlem, if not the country, and
thought he might be able to help Flora get into the show there.
Flora ultimately acceded to his desire to sleep with her and was
soon enjoying a sex life which would have been the envy of a
Levantine prince. Her telling of it, however, reveals a dogged
determination to let her reader know that it was the quality of
the man, his superior style and charm—that attracted her, not
his sexual prowess or his serviceable connection with the Cotton Club.

In spite of the fact that Flora carried off the audition
with her usual easy brilliance, she ran into unexpected opposition
there. The show's star performer, an ebony-hued Negro called
Clarence, patronizingly explained to Flora that she was a shade
too dark to be in his show, and that he couldn't use her. It
was Chicago all over again. This made Flora boil, for, although
one had only to look around to see that Clarence had a strong
prejudice in favor of very light-skinned girls, Flora was infinitely closer to their color than to his. "You black bastard," she
thought, glaring at the cocky face, supercilious eyebrows, puck-
ered upward beneath a crown of oily marcel waves, "for two
cents I'd hang your balls on my Christmas tree!" Alec, who had
come to cheer Flora on, could see murder in her eyes and
thought it best to get her out of the place with all possible
speed.

It took all Alec's powers of persuasion and tact to work
Flora out of her homicidal mood, and the conversation which
she reports as having taken place at this juncture is one in which
Flora paints herself wistfully, yearningly as a model of virtue
and innocence—an innocence lost long ago in the basement of
an abandoned building.

"Look, Flora," Alec had purportedly said, "I'm not really sorry you didn't get that job. I know how your heart was set on it, but you're lucky to be out of Clarence's way. He goes after every girl in that line, and to stay in the show you have to—well, do a lot of things you might not like so much."

"Oh," responded Flora, surprised. "But I thought he was married and in love with his wife."

"Hey, come on, Flora. Listen, baby, you don't belong in this business. You're not cold and hard enough. You're just a sweet innocent kid, who dances because she loves it." And therein was contained the summation of Flora's longings and dreams.

Were it not for the fact that Flora frequently gave herself away by admitting how much she enjoyed her haphazard and exploitive sex life, even under relatively sordid conditions, we might almost believe in the fundamental innocence of Flora Black. But while it is apparently true that nearly every man she meets views her as an attractive animal to be enjoyed, it is also clear that each one of them serves some useful purposes in her life, with certain notable exceptions. There can be little question, that Flora's desire to sustain the innocent, little-girl image was doing constant battle with her conditioned tendency to see her personal value only in terms of a desired sexual object or as a provocative performer. It was ultimately impossible for Flora to despise her exploiters, for inasmuch as she liked what they did to her, she would have been obliged to despise herself as well.

The fiasco at the Cotton Club seems not only to have greatly disappointed Flora, but also to have caused her to forsake any attempt to adhere to fact. From this point on in Flora's narrative, events become confused in time, and characters are amalgamated, interchanged, and increasingly furnished with personalities born of Flora's fertile imagination. But the tale is always revealing.

The understanding that girls had to "do things" in order to enjoy continued employment at the Cotton Club—things which in Alec's judgment, Flora was much "too decent" to do —evidently prompts her to abandon the notion of working there and to seek a job on Broadway. She meets two brothers, Negroes, who function as theatrical agents and one of whom has spent many years abroad, the prime consequence of which, according to Flora, is that he speaks "faultless English." This man, whose name is Bill, becomes her lover, even though Alec is allegedly supporting her at the rooming house. Flora justifies this infidelity by informing us that Alec has a wife and two children somewhere, of whom he would rid himself, if his wife would give him a divorce.

At any rate, Bill introduces her into the intellectual Greenwich Village crowd and takes her frequently to spend cultivated little evenings in a racially integrated setting. Flora speaks at some length of visiting one interracial couple, who have as many white friends as black and who are both extremely cultivated. The men are all, of course, absolutely bowled over by Flora, regardless of their color, and fall all over themselves during the cocktail hour in their efforts to light cigarettes and simply have the pleasure of talking to her. "Later," she reports, "while we were playing bridge, the conversation turned to music."

In the dissertation which follows this piece of intelligence, Flora goes to considerable pains to inform us as to how dull and "washed out" the white guests appeared in relation to herself, Bill, and "Rosamond and Rosalie." This latter pair, Harlem's answer to the Quiz Kids, are described as "short, dark, muscular, kinky-haired Southern stereotypes," who nevertheless "toss around five- and six-syllable words and discuss Tschiakowsky [sic], Mozart, Handel, Bach, and Beethoven"—a pastime compatible with their status as students at the Juliard [sic] School of Music. "We played bridge," Flora concludes, "listened to the symphonic hour, and discussed Roosevelt." There is no mention of Bill having found her a job or even searching for one; in fact, there is no further mention of Flora's employment whatsoever.

Subsequently, Bill takes Flora to the home of another Village friend, a man identified as Skip. Here she meets Max, a "pure white man, with thick glasses, who works as a proofreader." He has had many older women as his mistresses, but he finds that Flora "provokes thought and deliberation" and does not merely appeal to him as a "good piece." Max inevitably wants to marry her, or at least he wants to marry the composite Self, which Flora has put together through Max's propositional eulogy of her qualities. In response, Flora comes up with an unlikely tale of denial based on society's attitude toward interracial marriages.

Max's reaction to this rebuff conforms to the best *True Romances* tradition: "Max stood silently for a long time, his head bowed. Finally, he looked up, and taking me in his arms, he looked at me, and he looked so kind and sweet and sort of sad all at once that I almost loved him and wanted to cry."

Occasionally the real Flora shines through, honest and brash, to lighten the reader's burden: "Had he been a wealthy man, I would have gone ahead and married him, and conventions be damned. But that's how it goes."

More parties in the Village follow the melodrama of Max, the lovable proofreader, during which time "Bill," the agent, metamorphoses into "Mel," and is built up to even greater heights of perfection. "Skip," the Village host of yesteryear, becomes "Tom," who has now taken to running a Sunday evening salon. Flora meets a colored man, married to a white girl, and endeavors to describe the excruciating "complex" he has about the situation, which is clearly driving him insane.

Here the narrative takes a truly surrealistic turn, and there no longer remains even the flimsiest patch of plot to stand on. The durable Alec, who has become Alex for this part of the tale, finds himself playing the cuckold, when one night he surprises Flora in her room with Mel: "While Mel gave himself up to the rapture of kissing his beloved (me), I listened anxiously for footsteps in the hallway." Mel had evidently paid Flora an unexpected visit, and she was anticipating the arrival of Alex at any moment. Ultimately the latter appears, catching Flora and Mel *in flagrante delicto*. Flora, ever the perfect hostess, jumps out of bed and introduces them in true Emily Post fashion: "Mr. Henry, Mr. Barber." This sanguine approach does not cut much mustard with the boys, who immediately break into a fight and eventually storm out of the premises in high dudgeon, vowing to see that Flora gets her comeuppance.

As this fractured fiction proceeds, we find Max (now sometimes called "Henry") back in the picture again, madly in love with, and wanting to marry, a beautiful colored girl called Lucy. A low-hitting vamp known as Margie does her darnedest to seduce Max, who nonetheless remains faithful and declares that he will continue to hold out for Lucy. Margie is thereby fit to be tied, and ultimately the two girls have a splendid hair-pulling, eyeball-gouging, back-scraping fight. Nobody wins, but at some later time Lucy, having become insanely jealous, starts a terrific row with Max, during which they both fall through a bannister onto a landing, and Max is killed as a result of hitting his head on a cornice.

Here, at last, we have emerged from the looking glass and are returned to the real world. Flora did indeed kill her lover, but it was not Max.

Late in the spring of 1944, toward the end of the war (about which Flora never speaks, in spite of her interest in "current affairs"), Flora turned up in Clinton, Tennessee, with a man, who was perhaps an amalgam of Max and Alex—an intellectual, white piano player with a wife and kids. The man's name in this part of the story is Paul, and Flora explains that, as they were very much in love, she had decided to join him on a tour his band was making of the South.

They were happy to be together, even in a miserable boardinghouse—the only one that would take them—where they lived in one small, dreary room, bathroom down the hall. Flora would stay up till Paul came home from Knoxville after the show, brewing coffee on a contraband electric burner they kept in the room. Before retiring to their squeaky double bed, they would sip the dark brew and discuss the various inconsequential happenings of the day.

One night Paul came home, and Flora failed to greet him with her usual enthusiasm. She lay instead in bed, looking out the streaked and dusty window, forgetting even to turn her head as the door opened. "Hey, how come all the cheer?" Paul's irony provoked only the slightest reaction, and he realized that something was seriously wrong. "I think I'm pregnant," Flora said in a dull, disinterested voice. "Do you want the baby?"

"Now hold on a minute. How can you be sure? Have you seen a doctor?"

"No."

"No," Paul repeated, relieved. "You haven't seen a doctor yet, and you're already a parent. You don't know for sure, do you?"

"It's happened to me before, and I know, don't worry."

"Well, Flora, we're not having any baby, honey. That I can tell you." Flora turned her head and looked at him as if at a stranger. "Why?" she asked simply.

"Flora, I have a wife, remember? We can't go around having babies, for God's sake!"

"I don't care. I want to have it. I know we're more in love than people like us should be, but if you'd leave your wife —you said you wanted to—everything could start working out for us."

"Flora, we've been through all this before. My wife *will not* divorce me, and I have no grounds to divorce her. Why can't you understand? You're so intelligent, but when the facts don't suit your will, you refuse to acknowledge their existence! What more can I say to you?"

"But you actually *live* with me. Doesn't that make any difference? Isn't that a fact?"

"Look." Paul's patience was wearing thin. "You don't have babies with people you're not married to, and that's that!" Flora thought of all the women in Chicago's South Side and in Harlem; they had babies with people they weren't married to and didn't even want them. She knew, too, that white people often got married and had children because it was expected of them, but they didn't necessarily want them either. Wanting them was the important thing, not some phony religious ceremony. She was going to have this baby, even if it meant leaving Paul.

"Well, we'll see," she said quietly, wondering in the deeper recesses of her mind if Paul, in spite of everything, was afraid of having a dark child with kinky hair—if he was, after all, like everybody else.

Paul was playing a three-week stint, and toward the end of it, Flora began to feel quite miserable, the burden of her psychological isolation weighing upon her as heavily as the morning nausea and other physical discomforts. She became diffident and melancholy, though Paul was kind to her as always. By this time it had been confirmed that Flora was pregnant, and Paul was making arrangements to get rid of the baby when they got back to New York. Flora did not tell him that she had no intention of going through with it; thus, relations between them were altered, but not strained or unhappy, and life proceeded roughly as before.

By the time June 5 rolled around, the trees were in full bloom, and insects buzzed in the moist, warm air. The roads were not yet swirling with dust, as there had been plenty of rain during the heavy spring nights.

It was Paul's birthday—he would be thirty-two—and Flora decided to venture out into the sun, have a stroll, and pick up a present for Paul while he was still asleep; working till all hours of the morning, he rarely got up before lunch.

Browsing through the local five-and-ten, she found a birthday card bearing the ageless caricature of a man sitting at a spangled piano, which emitted waves of musical symbols and notes; it bore the usual saccharine message, and Flora found it thoroughly appropriate. She then proceeded to wander about in the general store, hoping to be inspired as to what to get in the way of a gift. Inwardly lamenting her own lack of imagination, she ultimately settled on a claret red tie with a high, silky gloss; it would look fine, she thought, with Paul's dark blue suit. It was part silk, and she had to pay a bit more than she had originally intended, but it was worth it. The tie was carefully wrapped under Flora's watchful eye, and she bore it proudly home. Once there, she rummaged about till she found the mangled pen which she used to write letters home to Son and Sonny, and carefully inscribed the card: "Love forever, Flora."

When Flora returned, she discovered that Paul had got up, had lunch, and gone out. The woman who ran the boarding-house, ever hostile toward Flora, was not very informative:

"How should I know where he went? If he don't tell you, why would he tell me? Now don't be hangin' 'round here in the hall—folks don't like it. Wouldn't have you at all if I didn't need to fill the room."

"Jesus," Flora thought. "It'll be good to get back to New York, where at least the insults are more subtle."

Flora placed her gift with the card on Paul's pillow, and sat down to wait for him. She had picked up a newspaper during her outing and turned eagerly to the sports page to read about the latest events in the world of baseball. When not lost in the pages of a book of nineteenth-century poetry, which she carried everywhere with her, Flora passed her time memorizing baseball scores and batting averages, so she would have something to talk to the men in the band about when they were all together. Paul found it quite remarkable that Flora was able to tuck that amount of information away in her brain, when she had a mind to, and joked about it frequently to her continuing delight.

"Well, will you look at old egghead, soaking up the info?" he commented, finding Flora huddled over her paper late that afternoon. "How do you feel, honey?"

"Not bad. Where'd you go?"

"Oh, I stopped by the post office, and then had a game of pool with some of the guys. Got a letter from Marilyn. She worries too damn much when I'm away, I mean about the kids and all. I suppose it's hard for her to handle everything, though, and you know they ask for me all the time."

"Oh, come off it!" Flora exploded. "She just says that so you'll feel guilty and come back. Miss you? Are you kidding?"

"Well, why the hell shouldn't they miss me? I'm their dad, aren't I?"

"You've hardly been with 'em at all in the past year. . . ."

"Well, I wish I had!" He was angry now and shouting, as people do when touched by unwelcome guilt.

"So why don't you go on home then, and let me be?"

"Don't be stupid. I would just like to see my kids before they grow up and get married, do you mind? Hey, what's this?" he asked, glancing at the bed.

"Oh, nothing," Flora mumbled, moving toward the box. The anniversary spirit had been seriously impaired in the course of this exchange, and there were things Flora felt more like doing at the moment than wishing Paul a happy birthday.

"Wait a minute, my name's written on there. Let me see."

"Happy birthday," Flora said cheerlessly, handing over the box, "and many happy returns."

"Hey, I forgot all about it. That was real nice of you, Flora, it really was." Chagrined, he opened the card, smiled, and placed it on the bureau. Then he opened the slim box and fetched out the tie, amidst the rustle of tissue paper. As he surveyed it enigmatically, Flora said, "I thought it would look good with your blue suit. Why don't you try it on?" Paul smiled and walked to the mirror, unmaking his own tie without enthusiasm. It was perfectly clear that he did not like the new one, but Flora was too irritated about all this concern over the abandoned wife to care, and hardly noticed that he made no comment about it;

at least she remembered his damn birthday, which is more than anybody could say about hers.

Having constructed a large Windsor knot in the shiny red birthday necktie, Paul turned to Flora, hands on hips, and said:

"Let's face it, honey, that is a real nigger tie."

He was grinning—malignantly, Flora thought—and under the circumstances, it was hard to know how much malice, if any, was inherent in the remark.

Flora sat on the edge of the bed staring at him, her face devoid of expression. It seemed to her that she could not move. Suddenly, all the specters of the past formed ranks and marched against her: the callous, white, twelve-year-old sex fiends of her school days sought her once more; Mr. Garfinkel tweaked her young nipple for the last time; Ted breathed against her ear that she was hotter than any white girl he had ever had; and presiding over them all was the mastiff's white owner, sitting red-faced, perspiring, staring, masturbating, in company with the world's most repulsive black man, who had sold her down the river. She dropped her gaze slightly, glaring at the offending tie; she felt ill again and was reminded of the baby—the nigger-white baby that Paul would not have with her. She rose slowly and walked over to Paul, who had been speaking about being sorry and not meaning it "that way," but Flora had heard nothing. "Let me fix it right," she said and reached for the knot. Taking hold of the slim end of the tie, she began to tighten the knot. In an instant she had pressed it with all her strength against Paul's Adam's apple, while he, hardly believing, realized that she was trying to strangle him.

Curiously enough, he never touched Flora's face, where a few blows could easily have put an end to the attack; panicky, he fastened his grasp instead around her wrists in an effort to wrest the choking hands from his throat. The tie, with its thick knot, made an excellent noose, however, and Flora had hold of it in such a way that she was able to exert maximum pressure. Rage, hysteria, and determination increased her strength, and she did not seem to feel the kicks and wrenchings of her struggling victim. Neither spoke—Paul because he could not, Flora because an angered monologue was going on in her fevered and momentarily disoriented mind—and the only sounds were those of shod feet, scraping and beating the floor.

It was hot, and Paul had left the door open when he came in, in order to lure some air into their stuffy room. As they struggled, locked together like warring beasts, they moved toward the doorway and eventually through it. Paul's face was now purple, and his eyes bulged; Flora, never removing her gaze from his throat or her hands from the tie, was bathed in sweat from scalp to toe and seemed to have been imbued with the tenacity of a bulldog. They wrestled now on the landing, and their scuffling brought Mrs. Prill, the landlady, out of her room on the ground floor. She thrust her gray head, spikey with hair pins, out the door, and turned her pale-eyed gaze upward, just in time to see two bodies crash through the worm-rotten balustrade and fall to the stairs below the landing. Mrs. Prill's jaw fell open, and one hand shot up to fill the gap; Paul and Flora, still clutching one another, had crashed to the stairs, and now descended one upon the other, sometimes rolling, sometimes sliding, till they reached the bottom and lay at Mrs. Prill's feet.

For a moment Mrs. Prill did nothing. They both lay very still, and the terrified woman was utterly confused as to what she should do. Paul's head rested against a cornice at the base of a post, which marked the terminal point of the bannister, and he was bleeding profusely; Flora sprawled on the floor in front of the stair. When she saw the blood, Mrs. Prill decided to move.

Within five minutes the police were there, and they found Flora, now revived and apparently uninjured but for bruises, kneeling over Paul's inert body, sobbing tearlessly; he was dead, his tie flung back across one shoulder, soaked in the crimson of his own blood. "She killed him!" Mrs. Prill exclaimed. "I saw it. I knew there'd be trouble if I let one of 'em in here!"

Flora's trial, as described in her memoirs, was rather a dramatic affair, with Flora, elegantly dressed in "a little basic black in the three-figure price range." Her hair was smoothly drawn back from her face, and a jeweled clip twinkled at her throat, as she sat gracefully poised at a long mahogany table, listening to the comments which filled the room with an unrelieved buzzing: "Kinda elegant for a nigger, ain't she?" "I seen that gal in Chicago—you should see her dance!" "Just look at that dress, will you? The lines, everything." "Little black bitch. . . ."

Always the center, in her fantasies, of an admiring attention, Flora had painted a portrait of her trial which could not have corresponded less with the actual events. Dressed in the same undistinguished cotton dress she was wearing the day she was arrested, Flora was escorted roughly into the courtroom by two guards and deposited at a long wooden table. Huge, slow-moving metal fans hung from the ceiling, slightly disturbing the flies but hardly mitigating the stifling heat which filled the room. The crowd was generally sullen and hostile, and the remarks were anything but admiring. Flora may not have looked very much like a southern Negro, but as far as they were concerned, she was black, and she had killed a white man, which did not bode well for her. She had lost the baby two days after the fall, and, feeling ill and miserable, she had no fight and little pride left in her. Every face she saw was white and unsympathetic. Even the judge looked very much to Flora like all those leering, insensitive men who came nightly to see her dance, and though she had demanded counsel, the lawyer, by her own admission, didn't much care about defending her.

Had Flora been tried impartially and been able to obtain good counsel, there is little doubt that it could have been proved that premeditation was not a factor in the death of her lover; none but a woman whose senses had completely eluded her would seriously believe that she could strangle a man half again her size and twice her weight. Even though the man died at the climax of a quarrel, it would have been made evident that the actual circumstances of his death were accidental, for Paul had died as the result of hitting his head on the cornice, not as a result of strangulation.

In small southern American towns, however, when the defendant in a trial is a Negro, the administration of justice tends to be rather uncomplex; nobody worries about sudden impulse, temporary insanity, provocation, mitigating circumstances, or other nuances. Nobody worried about it in Clinton. Flora, who might elsewhere have managed a manslaughter charge, was convicted of first-degree murder, and sentenced to death by hanging.

In any decent prison, female inmates awaiting execution are guarded by female guards; in Clinton it was different. Flora, who had been placed in death row, alone and completely removed from any other of the prison population, was "guarded" by men, whose interests were anything but proprietary. On evening visits, one or more of them would take turns defiling her insensate body, leaving her to hope passionately that death would come soon.

Flora's own account of events in the death house sends her on a religious bender, in which people do occasionally indulge, when faced with imminent death, and contains a stirring account of rape and other violence, worthy of Ian Fleming.

One evening after supper, which was served at 5:30, Flora sat in her cell and wondered if the Almighty was going to be able to see His way to forgiving her various sins. She found that, although it couldn't possibly be worse than life, she was terrified of death and of what might happen to her if she were to be judged for eternity. Her reverie was abruptly interrupted by the appearance of one of the guards (whom Flora refers to as "turnkey"); leaning on one of the bars, he drawled, "You'd love to git outta here, wouldn't ya, honey?"

Flora did not look at him, remaining silent and apparently lost in thought. "What would be the point in getting out?" she thought. "The whole goddam world is a prison anyway. It's bigger out there, that's all, and you have to earn your daily bread."

"What's the matter? Yer not very friendly tonight, and I don't like that." Flora looked up at him now, her eyes narrow and full of hatred. This was the one she loathed the most. Thick, hairy, with the bloated flush of an habitual drinker, his pale eyes sunk into a fleshy brow, he represented the worst of what the poor white world had to offer—the quintessential "redneck."

"Why don't you get your ass out of here?" Flora snapped. "You're not supposed to be in here, and you know it. What's the matter—you so ugly you can't get any on the outside?" With that the thick neck modulated from pink to scarlet, and the guard lumbered toward her menacingly. "Listen, ya nigger bitch, who the hell d'ya think y'are? I'm gonna have me a piece o' that ass whenever I feel like it, see? You ain't goin' to be usin' it no more where you're goin' nohow!" At this he laughed hideously, revealing large tobacco-stained teeth, and moved in on Flora. As there was only one of them this time, she fought like a cornered rat, with tooth, nail, knee, and elbow. He hit her several times, and it hurt. Suddenly in the scuffle, lying under him on the cement floor, the breath nearly forced out of her, she found her hand on the gun which was strapped to his side. Unsnapping the holster flap, she drew it out, thrust the barrel into his heaving, fat side and fired. The huge body seemed to leap, and in an instant it was off her and lying on its back, a twisted grimace of pain on the face. Blood poured from the guard's torn flank, as he gripped the hole with his stubby hands, as if to close it and stay the flow. Within moments he died, and Flora felt jubilant. Glancing briefly down the corridor as far as she could see, she unclipped the bunch of keys from the guard's belt and opened the door of her cell. As she started to run down the hall, two or three more guards appeared in the lighted hole, which glowed at the end of the dark corridor, and opened fire on her.

Had it all really happened in this way, Flora would not be around to tell the tale, but it makes better reading than a more honest account, which finds Flora simply removing her shoe and slashing at the man's head with her spiked heel. One of the frenzied blows found its way to the temple, nearly puncturing what turned out to be a rather thin skull, and killing the man on the spot. Rather than standing triumphantly over the fat body, gloating like a forecast of Pussy Galore, Flora was appalled by what she had done; terrified of what the others would do to her when they found their comrade lying dead in her cell, she was found crumpled and shaking in the corner furthest from the body, staring with empty eyes at nothing.

Much to Flora's immense relief, however, when two other guards showed up for the nightly security check at about 9:00, they exhibited more fear than anger. Glancing only briefly at Flora, they converged on their friend's inert body and then withdrew immediately to a spot down the hall, out of earshot, where they spoke in excited whispers for several minutes. Returning to the cell, they dragged the body away and clanged the door shut behind them, still without speaking to, or looking at, the bewildered prisoner.

As Flora was later to understand, the guards' security had been jeopardized by this unexpected turn of events. They had originally been obliged to lie and connive in order to postpone the arrival of the female officers, who should have been guarding Flora from the beginning, and a report on this murder would have initiated an investigation into the entire ugly situation—a tender morsel for the liberal publicists. Furthermore, as Flora was already condemned to die, there seemed little to be gained by revealing the facts so that she might be prosecuted. The body was encased in chains and dumped into a lake thirty miles outside of Clinton. The man was reported mysteriously missing.

Flora had been in jail, awaiting the day of her execution, for nearly four months when she had her first visitor. It was late on a sultry afternoon in early fall when the matron came to Flora's cell and announced that there was someone waiting to see her in the visiting room. Flora couldn't imagine who on earth cared enough to come all the way to Tennessee to see her. She tidied up her hair, arranged the shapeless gray uniform as well as could be expected, and walked out into the hall. Moving with an accustomed grace still remembered from the dancing days, she entered the prisoner's enclosure and sat down, as Laurence Hammill introduced himself.

"I'm a lawyer," he said, "from Chicago. Your father sent me."

Chapter VI

How Goes the Life?

THE year 1931, like every other year in the late twenties and early thirties, produced a bumper crop in the fields of crime for the city of Chicago. The depression had left its mark on rich and poor alike, leaving an ethical void which was filled only by the despair of millions and the gruesome machinations of Al Capone and his ilk.

It was virtually impossible to find an honest public official in those violent and perverted times, and the vicious intergang wars which had started in 1929, threatened judge, policeman, and hoodlum alike. Social welfare was in its infancy, leaving the dispossessed to find solace in bread lines, soup kitchens, and the Salvation Army. Others turned to crime, generally without much success, for bums, derelicts, and paupers are no better equipped to succeed in crime than in anything else. People were discovering that a good crook was obliged to be as smart as the head of a corporation.

Among the endless accounts of Capone's diverse activities, there appeared on May 25 a story describing the shooting

211

of Steve Bimbo, King of the Gypsies, by one Paolo Nickolas; it seems that Bimbo had accused Nickolas of using Caponesque methods in an effort to usurp his kingdom, which included some 300,000 subjects in the United States at the time. In acting out his denial of the accusation, Nickolas confirmed its truth.

In July of the same year, forty-six lawyers, all members of the Canal Board, were recommended for disbarment, it having been discovered that all of them, appointed to various questionable jobs by friends or family, had been receiving rather large sums of money for doing nothing. In November, Timothy Lynch, a Teamsters chief in western Chicago for over thirty years, was gunned down while stepping out of a very expensive car in front of his equally expensive house; this inaugurated an era of fresh intramural hostilities, led by Red Barker, kin of the notorious Ma Barker, whose object was control of the entire Chicago area. On December 4, Frank McErlane, one of the cruelest of Chicago's gang killers and the inventor of the one-way ride, distinguished himself by being the first major hoodlum to die peacefully in his bed for as long as anyone could remember.

Two days later, a white slavers' establishment was raided, while the fourth estate's cup ran over in the telling of stories about the poor girls lured off the farms and into the big city by promises of good jobs, gay times, and prepaid bus or train fares. That the ads inducing them to come frequently appeared in the same papers which decried the practice appeared somehow irrelevant. The white-slave trade had, of course, been thriving long before anyone had ever heard of Al Capone or "Legs" Diamond, and the recruiting methods had not changed appreciably for half a century.

One summer evening, on a farm in Indiana, a lovely, milk-skinned girl sat in her room, a head of copper curls bent over the Chicago newspaper. Newspapers rarely came into her hands from Chicago or anywhere else, but her brother, who had been to the city to buy some farm implements, had brought one back so that she could read about society and the fashions. What she saw this evening, however, interested her more than dresses and parties.

She had been up since five in the morning, as usual, and having had supper with the family, was growing sleepy; it was already nine o'clock. As she read along drowsily, violet eyes diffidently scanning the pages, her heavy lids blinked wide: "Sales-girls Wanted," sang the ad. "No experience needed. $30 per week; room and board. Transportation paid. Call WAB-7335, or write Mr. Durfee, 117 Wabash Avenue, Chicago." Granted, it didn't say what was being sold or where, but for that kind of pay, what difference could it make? The girl's name was Margaret O'Brien, and as she climbed into her tarnished brass bed that night, pulling the homemade patchwork quilt around her chin, she felt that finally, this autumn after the harvest, her life might undergo a change.

Mrs. O'Brien had been pregnant with her fourth child when she and her husband had come over from Ireland during those terrible, hungry years to settle in the Midwest. Many of their friends and relatives had remained in the mill towns of the East, but Pa O'Brien was a good and dedicated farmer, and could not have lived away from the land. He loved the earth. It was one of the few things in the world that he understood, and he knew how to make it produce. Furthermore he had no use for city folk and the life they led; he knew that if a man stayed close to God and the land, he'd be all right.

In 1899 the O'Briens settled near South Bend. With the help of his three sons, two of whom were already half-grown, Pa knew that he could build up a prosperous farm. The more sons he had the better.

One wintry night, arriving almost simultaneously with the new century, Margaret O'Brien was born. Ma was ecstatic over her little girl; at last there would be someone close to her alone—someone, too, to help around the house. Pa, bitterly disappointed, announced that the baby looked like a boiled turnip and went off to sulk in the barn. By God, if she thought being a girl was going to keep her from hard work, she had another think coming.

And it never did. Pampered at first by her adoring mother, Maggie grew from a chubby, ruddy-white baby, her head a mass of unruly auburn curls, to a spirited and athletic tomboy of seven, at which point Pa decided that she could damn well do some work. Up at five each morning, Maggie helped with the cows—getting them fed, milked, and out of the barn—and collected the eggs. While the boys attended to the heavier chores, she would then return to the house and help her mother with the breakfast. No sooner was that over and the dishes cleaned up, than it was time to turn to the baking and washing, before starting the lunch. If it was haying or planting time, Maggie would take soup and sandwiches out to the men in the field, arriving as a rule astride Bob, a huge white gelding—the O'Briens' horse of all work.

Although she rarely elicited more than a grunt of acknowledgment from her father, Maggie thrived on the rough affection of her brothers, who would turn eagerly from their work at noontime, in anticipation of the sight of her copper head bobbing up and down in rhythm with old Bob's uneven gait. Shading their crinkled eyes against the strong summer sun, they would grin and shout their favorite nicknames at the little girl:

"Hey, what's a peanut doing on a horse?"
"Here comes frecklepuss with the feed bag!"
"So who ever saw a peanut with freckles?"
"It's little Mag on her saggy nag!"

Maggie laughed each day as though hearing their taunts for the first time, and giggled uncontrollably as the boys dragged her off her shaggy mount and struggled for possession of the lunch bag. They tickled her ribs and rolled her in the sweet grass, until she was weak from laughing. Pa, looking on only half amused, ate his lunch in silence; he had no time for this sort of nonsense.

"Maggie," he would say gruffly, "we got work to do. Get back to the house and help your mother."

These were happy years, and Maggie, thriving on hard productive labor, fresh air, and the pervasive love of her mother and brothers, bloomed into a ripe and healthy adolescent. Within twenty years, South Bend would become part of the new industrial society of the twentieth century, by way of the arrival of the Studebaker Corporation as well as other industrial concerns, which would sweep the fresh-eyed youths off the land and into the factories. But in the year 1919, it was still in the agricultural heartland of the country, where girls and boys like Maggie and her brothers might grow strong and unspoiled, innocent of the mores of the more socially interdependent multitudes gathering in the burgeoning cities.

Maggie was not entirely ignorant as to what city dwellers looked like, for on their infrequent visits to Chicago, the boys collected magazines and newspapers for Maggie and her mother. In subsequent weeks, the two women—one primitive, old-fashioned, aging, and skeptical, the other enthusiastic, optimistic, and credulous—pored over the glossy pages, marveling at the political and sartorial wonders and corruptions of the modern, urban world.

While Ma O'Brien, now in middle age, her face, hands, and body showing signs of a life of hard times and harder work, retained the mien of an Irish peasant, Maggie appeared to be plucked from a different tree. Whereas Ma's hair had the look of crinkled rust, Maggie's was massive, smooth, and shining; where Ma's kind, round face was marked and dry, Maggie's pale and lightly freckled skin was clear and fresh as the proverbial peach; and by contrast to the coarseness of Ma's features, Maggie's were simultaneously delicate and strong, the face dominated by the amazing wide violet eyes.

Maggie had never before brooded over the discrepancy between her meager wardrobe and the fashionable clothes she saw in the magazines. But on that summer evening, in the privacy of her sparsely furnished and unfeminine bedroom, she regarded herself critically in the mottled glass over her bureau and decided that her body deserved better than rough cotton and wool for the rest of its life. Her figure was full, but difficult work in all kinds of weather had prevented the appearance of any excess flesh on the strong frame, and her skin was certainly as good as that of the chic ladies whose pictures she had studied. Even her brothers had to admit that she had "class," and said that she ought to get off the farm while there was still a chance for her to marry somebody other than one of the other local farmers' sons, with whom she would spend the rest of her life in the pea patch.

Maggie's father surely wouldn't be sorry to see her go, but her mother posed a problem. In a family dominated by relatively crude demanding men, Maggie and her mother had clung together for warmth and understanding, and depended on one another for the gentle indulgences with which each was able to provide the other. But Ma was not an unintelligent woman and felt in the deepest recess of her heart that Maggie must go one day. Her two eldest sons had already left, having married local girls, and settled on farms nearby. Happily, they were able to visit often, for they continued to work for their father, and so it did not seem a true separation. Maggie, however, had been circling for the past three years around the question of going to Chicago and getting a job in a shop or restaurant; at first it had been easy to say she was too young, for there was nobody in the big town they knew with whom she could live and by whom she might be looked after. Now it was difficult to know what to say, except that Chicago seemed a long way from home, even for a girl of nearly twenty.

There was no telephone at the farm, so Maggie wrote to Mr. Durfee at 117 Wabash Avenue in Chicago to apply for the job she had seen advertised in the newspaper. She received a prompt reply, which was merely signed, "Durfee," saying that she was to notify him by return mail as to when she would be arriving in Chicago and that, if she would obtain a receipt for her train fare from South Bend and bring it with her to 117 Wabash Avenue, she would be reimbursed by Mr. Durfee, who would be there to meet her.

Ma had been reasonably calm in the face of Maggie's decision to respond to the ad. They had all scrutinized it together and concluded that it was an opportunity not to be missed. Only Pa harbored dark thoughts on the subject, but as he was unable to articulate the nature of his fears or the assumptions on which they were based, no one paid much attention to him. Ma knew that, notwithstanding Pa's apparent indifference to his only daughter, he had grown to love her, responding in spite of himself to her clean blossoming prettiness and the cheerfulness of her ever-useful presence. He would miss her as much as the rest of them.

Maggie was to leave on the first Monday in October, having been assured by Mr. Durfee that there was no hurry at all as to when she started work. She was leaving before the harvest, but that was mostly men's work, and she had labored twice as hard as usual during the summer in recompense.

Sunday morning the O'Brien family went to church as usual, dressed in the set of good clothes that each one possessed. Ma, Pa, the boys and their wives all lighted special candles for Maggie, who sat pale and still in the pew, her long auburn hair gathered at the nape of her neck by a huge bow and flowing down her back.

Lunch at the farm that morning was exceptionally gay, and for once Maggie had been allowed to remain idle, while her mother and sisters-in-law prepared and served the meal. The boys teased their sister as they had never done before, and Maggie, laughing and radiant, accepted their jibes with customary grace, knowing she was adored.

But at the railroad station the following afternoon, a sad, uneasy quiet prevailed over the little group, as they prepared to say good-bye to their young relative. One would have thought she was off to chart the Arctic wastes; everyone wept, including Pa, and advanced one by one to bid her farewell: "Hate to see you go, Mag. Who's goin' to bring us lunch?"

"So long, Frank."

"Hey, Mag, don't write, just send money, all right?"

"You bet I will, Pat, you old sod!"

"Don't do anything I wouldn't do."

"Yeah, take it easy. Not that we'll miss ye none!"

"I'll be so lonely without ye, darlin'—promise ye'll write every day."

"I surely will, Ma, I promise. You're not to worry none now, ye hear?"

Finally, Pa approached his daughter, and awkwardly, his eyes swimming, he said, "Fear God, Margaret, and be a good girl—as ye have always been. Good-bye, then."

"G'bye Pa. I'll remember."

They all stood staring down the line of rusting tracks long after Maggie's primly gloved hand, waving from the window, had dissolved with the train into the horizon. Ma was thinking that it would be a good while before they all sat together again in church on a Sunday morning; the others merely mourned.

The journey from South Bend to Chicago was long in those days, and as the train rattled across the flat squared fields of lush farmland, newly stripped of their fruits, Maggie had time to ponder her future. She was confident that Mr. Durfee would be nice to her, for he was an Irishman, and she would not be faced with an entirely unknown quantity. They would probably have a great deal in common. Looking down at her hands, she thought how nice it would be to do clean work in a shop and enjoy the opportunity to rehabilitate those ruddy rough claws, which spoke so eloquently of her customary way of life. She rather wished it would turn out to be a flower shop; she loved flowers, and surrounded by the smell of earth and blooming green things, she would perhaps feel somewhat less homesick. She hoped too that she would be able to sleep on Sundays, a thing which was never possible on the farm.

It was almost seven o'clock before the train arrived in Chicago, and Maggie, accustomed to eating her supper at six o'clock, had begun to feel hungry. She hoped they would save some dinner for her at the place she was to stay, for she only had eighteen dollars left after paying the train fare, and apart from the expense, she dreaded the thought of eating alone in a public place; she had never had a meal in a restaurant in her life—rarely ever, in fact, away from the family table.

Somehow or other, she managed to drag her suitcase down from the rack and to reach the street, where a porter put Maggie and her bag into a taxi. "And where might you be goin', Miss?" he inquired in a familiar brogue.

"One Seventeen Wabash Avenue," Maggie replied, smiling. The porter looked a little surprised, but transmitted the information to the cab driver and, doffing his cap, disappeared into the station.

"Don't you believe in tipping, lady?" the driver said as soon as they were under way.

"Excuse me?"

"You're supposed to tip guys who carry your bag."

"Oh, I didn't know. He was gone so fast. . . ."

"Where you from?"

"South Bend. We have a farm there."

"Fresh off the farm, eh?"

"Pardon me?"

"Nothin'. Just thinkin' out loud."

Peering out from the cab window, Maggie looked at Chicago for the first time. By contrast to South Bend, it was crowded and dirty, but what impressed her most was the noise. The noise of the big city was something for which Maggie had been totally unprepared; she had heard about the big buildings, the lights, the litter, and the bustle of people, but no one had ever mentioned the sounds: people laughing and shouting to one another, motors roaring, brakes screaming amidst the intermittent scrapings and squeaks of the trolley on its ubiquitous track, and music pouring forth from windows and doorways, even in broad daylight. Maggie found it all perfectly extraordinary and wondered how anyone could get any rest—how, indeed, she would be able to sleep amidst this cacophony. Still, it seemed to create an atmosphere of excitement and vivacity, which was apparently very stimulating, judging by the behavior of some of the local citizens.

The cab had stopped in front of a brightly lighted doorway over which was written the word TAVERN and through which a man appeared to be flying at great speed.

"Why are we stopping here?" Maggie inquired, alarmed.

"Because this is where you asked me to take you, lady."

"Is this One Seventeen Wabash Avenue?" Maggie's throat tightened.

"Yes, lady, this is One Seventeen Wabash Avenue, and you owe me eighty-five cents."

"Eighty-five cents!"

"Yeah, eighty-five cents." The cabbie had turned in his seat to face his trembling passenger. "The fare is seventy-five cents and the tip is ten cents. You're not goin' to forget to tip me like you did that porter back there."

"But this is a saloon," Maggie said quietly, delving into her purse. "I don't think this is where I'm supposed to go at all."

Seeing that she was close to tears, the cabbie softened.

"Well, what were you expecting, a square dance? Look, don't be bothered by the drunk they just threw out. This ain't a bad place. Just go in there an' ask 'em to help you out. Maybe you got the wrong address. You got a number of someone to call?"

"Yes. Mr. Durfee."

"Well, you go in there an' call him, all right?"

"I don't want to go in there."

"Well, lady, I can't drive you around Chicago all night while you decide where you're supposed to be. Can I?"

"No."

"Okay. Now go on, and good luck to you."

Maggie got out of the cab, her stomach fluttering. As she watched the taxi disappear around the corner, she felt that she was losing her last bond with all that was familiar and secure. If only she could fight off the imminent flow of tears . . . Weeping was not apt to impress anybody or solve her problem.

The tavern was fairly bursting with people, mostly men, and ablaze with light. Momentarily distracted by laughter and the rattle and clink of glasses, which competed successfully with the efforts of a shirt-sleeved piano player, Maggie recouped her loss of composure and began to look around the place with interest.

Essentially, she liked it, much to her own surprise. A long polished mahogany bar ran down one side of the room, at which many men stood, their feet propped jauntily on the brass rail at the bottom. A huge mirror, framed in swirling designs of multihued glass, formed the wall behind the bar, and reflected the bottles and their varicolored contents, which stood on its shelves. On the opposite wall were private booths, in which sat groups of four or six, and tables filled the space between. A dark wooden staircase rose to a second level at the back, though where it led was not apparent. What women there were appeared either to be waiting on the tables or sitting with their men friends in the booths; it occurred to Maggie that they did not seem to be the same kind of women that, say, her mother was or even that were pictured in the magazines, although they were smartly dressed and generally very pretty.

Suddenly a rough voice interjected itself into her reverie, restoring her self-consciousness, and asked her what she was gaping at. She turned and beheld one of the largest human beings she had ever seen, including her brother Patrick. She said she was looking for Mr. Durfee. At first he said suspiciously that he had never heard of anyone called Durfee, and Maggie's heart yawned; then he raised back his huge head, as though having miraculously arrived at a new insight, and said, "Oh, yeah, that's Pat. I'll get 'im. Just wait here." Maggie was so relieved that she felt like dancing, and for the first time since she boarded the train, her sunny face lost the expression of anxiety which had marred it throughout the long day.

People had now begun to stare at her, and she was happy to see the giant return in the company of a slim, wiry man of uncertain age, with crisp black curls and remarkable electric-blue eyes.

"And would you be Margaret O'Brien?" he asked, his voice reflecting the musical lilt of their common linguistic heritage.

"I am," Maggie replied, her eyes smiling. "And I'm surely happy to be seein' you, Mr. Durfee."

"Now," he said, looking up at his hulking companion, "what would ye be doin' leavin' this charmin' lady standin' here in the door like a hat rack?" Maggie laughed merrily, covering her mouth with her hands like a little girl.

"You know, Billy," he continued, "yer brain is solid muscle, like the rest of ye." The giant, reacting not at all to this mild chastisement, returned to his post at the door, fixing his vacant gaze onto the small portion of the street he could see from the heavily curtained window.

"Margaret," Pat said, softly now, taking her arm, "let's go an' sit down in one of those booths and have a chat, all right?"

"All right, but call me Maggie, please."

"Well, I don't know. Ye look such a lady . . . *I'm* goin' to call ye Margaret!" he said triumphantly, pleased at the effect this approach was having on Maggie, who never stopped smiling and laughing.

As they slid into one of the smaller booths, Maggie said, "You know, my big brother's name is Pat too. Isn't yer name Pat?"

"Now how did ye know me name was Pat?"

"Well I heard your friend—you know, the big one . . ."

"Billy. He's the bouncer. Dumb as Mrs. Murphy's ox."

"Oh . . . the what?" Maggie asked, giggling about the ox.

"The bouncer—Billy the Bouncer, we call 'im. Throws drunks out o' here when they start to give us trouble."

"Yes, I see. I think one was just on his way out as I was on my way in!" They laughed together at the joke, each looking hard at the other, each increasingly charmed by the other.

"Would ye be wantin' somethin' to drink, Margaret? A drop o' beer maybe, to put some curl in yer hair?"

"Well, you certainly don't need to put any in yours, but I'll join you anyway. I've had beer before—at the fair," Maggie concluded.

"Have ye now?" Pat said in mock admiration, as he signaled a waiter. "Two beers, Larry, while yer standin'."

"Yes, Mr. Boylan," the man replied.

Maggie, who had been searching in her bag for a hankie, raised her eyes quickly to the man sitting opposite her.

"Why did he call you Mr. Boylan? I thought yer name was Durfee." The blue eyes flickered a moment, and then, leaning forward on his elbows so that Maggie would feel the full intensity of their concentration, Pat said, "They call me Pat the

Gent, or Patty, or Patrick, just like yer big brother! Ye know, there must be a million blokes in Ireland called Pat."

"Yes, I suppose you're right. I can see why they call you the gent. My brothers—well, they're not quick like you."

Much to Pat's relief, the beers arrived at this moment, giving him an opportunity to change the subject again. Pat told Maggie about Ireland, which she had never seen, and Maggie told him about the farm and her family, and how they had to shoot old Bob last year, because he was too old and too sick to move anymore.

"But here," Maggie said suddenly, "ye haven't told me a thing yet about the job!"

"Oh, well," Pat began, draining his glass, "ye must be ready to drop by now, an' ye haven't even had yer supper. Let me take ye to the place yer stayin' an' get ye fixed up. We can talk about yer job in the mornin'."

"Is it in a flower shop?" Maggie's eyes were wide and eager. Pat thought he had probably never seen eyes that color before in his life—or hair, for that matter. The body wasn't half bad either.

"No," he said. "It's not in a flower shop."

Having collected Maggie's bag from big Billy, they left the bar—without, Maggie observed, paying for the beer. Pat hailed a cab, and a few minutes later they arrived at a shabby building on South Halsted curtained in heavy lace.

They were greeted by a lady of Wagnerian proportions, who wore what appeared to be a bathrobe trying to pass as an evening dress of brown crushed velvet. Her blonde hair had been overly crimped and piled in a disorganized mess on top of her head, while her dark red mouth shone like lacquer in the dim lamplight. The mouth broadened and opened as they entered, revealing a set of very fine teeth, and said, "Come on in, Patty. What the hell kept you? And this is Maggie?"

"Yes, ma'am. Margaret O'Brien. I hope I won't be any bother." The woman glanced quickly at Pat, her small black eyes seeking some explanation of this curious remark.

"I hope you won't either, darlin'," she said, chucking Maggie under the chin.

"Look, Maureen, the kid hasn't had anything to eat since lunch. Bring her up something to the room, will ye, like a good girl?"

"To the room! Why, may I ask, can she not eat down here with the other girls?"

"Just do it, Maureen," Pat snapped. "Do what I tell ye."

As they ascended the stairs, Maggie turned, full of questions:

"Is that the lady who runs the rooming house? From what she said, I guess there only girls living here. Are they all working for you, Mr. Durfee? I mean, Mr. Boylan. You know, you never explained why that waiter called you Mr. Boylan."

Pat said not a word as they walked quickly down the hall. Stopping in front of number four, he took the key from his pocket and opened the door. He placed the bag on the floor in front of the double bed and, moving quickly toward the window, drew the faded curtains. A simple armoire, a straight chair, a sink with pitcher and basin were all the furniture in the room, apart from the bed. It was larger than Maggie's room at home, and she thought it nice, in spite of its dingy bareness. Everything in the room looked as though it had once been touched with a stronger color; the walls were a cream which might once have been yellow, the curtains a pallid rose, faded perhaps from a bright pink, with etiolated greens and beiges making up the balance of the haphazard arrangement of colors.

"I have a brass bed at home, too, but it's not as big as this one," Maggie said, taking a positive line. It wouldn't be hard to cheer the place up a bit, if Mrs. . . .

"Now listen to me," Pat broke in. Maggie looked at him, where he stood, arms folded and leaning against the armoire. His face bore an expression she had not seen before—almost of anger and decidedly unpleasant. She sat down on the bed suddenly, as though pushed by an invisible hand. The fluttering returned to her stomach, as she prepared herself once again to withstand something frightening and yet unknown.

"You are not goin' to work in any flower shop, lady, and this is no boardinghouse. My name is not Mr. Durfee, an' you are not goin' to be workin' for me, but fer Mrs. Maureen-Joan Bailey downstairs, who is a madam."

"A what?" Maggie whispered, uncomprehending.

"A madam, darlin'. A lady who runs a brothel, as they call it in genteel circles."

"What's that? I don't understand anything," Maggie whimpered, the tears welling up.

"A whorehouse!" Pat shouted, staring straight at his miserable prey. Maggie's hands flew to her mouth, dilated eyes fixed on Boylan. "Well, if yer goin' to be sick," he said, "do it there in the bowl."

In an instant Maggie was herself again. Her back straightened, color rushed to her cheeks, and the violet eyes narrowed, becoming quite terrifying, Boylan thought. Sick indeed, she said to herself. Was she sick when she shot poor old Bob in the head, because no one else could face it, even Pa? And she had loved him the most.

"Look 'ere, Mr. Boylan, fer I presume that is yer real name," she began, the brogue thickening with rage, rough little fists clenched to her side. "I am not workin' as an 'ore fer you, Mrs. Bailey, or anybody else, so ye can just give me back the money fer my train fare, and I'll be gettin' on back to South Bend, where I belong. I never heard of anythin' so revoltin' in all my life. You are a disgrace!"

Boylan had expected the usual tears and pleas for deliverance and was rather pleasantly surprised by this spirited response.

"Is that so?" Boylan said ironically. "An' what if I don't let you go?"

"It's a free country. I'll go where I like! An' may our Blessed Lord take pity on ye an' forgive yer terrible sin." This evidently struck a hidden but sensitive nerve in Boylan, for he suddenly grew very angry. Uncoiling himself now from his casual stance against the armoire, he stood square, one fist on his waist, the other finger pointing accusingly at Maggie.

"Well ye know," he shouted, "stupidity is a sin too, an' if it ain't, it should be, an' that's fer sure! Here you are, Miss Hayseed, readin' an ad in the paper that doesn't tell ye a goddam thing—Mum an' Dad lookin' over yer shoulder, no doubt—an' sayin', 'Well, isn't that just fine, I'm goin' to work in a bleedin' flower shop for thirty dollars a week!' An' ye shove yer little backside onto a train an' come sashayin' into the pub shoutin' fer a bloke who's a total stranger an' expect to be treated like the bleedin' queen!"

"I don't expect to be treated like the bl . . . like the queen. I only expect to be treated like a human bein'."

"Well, there's lots o' folk about who got only one idea about what female human bein's is for, an' I agree with 'em! You think I can just let you skip out o' here, so that ye can go home an' spill it all to yer big brothers? How long d'ye think it'd be before they told the coppers about what happened to their dear little sister in the great wicked town? There's a law against this sort o' thing ye know."

"I wouldn't have to tell anyone. I'd just say the job didn't work out. . . ." Maggie began to panic now and hoped she could maintain her composure.

"Oh, that's great," Boylan blurted, laughing between the words. "Jesus, if I was as stupid as you, I'd surely be starin' out from behind bars right now, an' that's fer sure!"

"I am *not* stupid." Maggie spat the words out in the face of her tormentor. Boylan sat down on the bed, spent, and looked at her for a long moment.

"No," he said gently, "you're not stupid, Margaret. That is why I cannot understand how ye did such a dumb thing."

"Those who are not themselves evil don't expect to find evil in others."

"Oh, that's very nice. Would ye be learnin' that in Sunday school now?"

"There's no need t'be so snide! Why shouldn't a girl believe an ad that offers a job?"

Boylan sighed. "Because of the salary, Margaret. Didn't it occur to any of you good folks out there on the farm that the pay might be a touch high for a girl to peddle bloody weeds?"

Maggie was silent and, dropping her head and shoulders in a noncombative attitude, lowered herself onto the chair next to the window. It had begun to rain gently, and as though reminded of an oversight, Maggie started to cry noiselessly. Boylan appeared not to notice and continued to talk.

"Ye know, most o' these girls comin' in from the sticks are real pigs—thick both in body an' in mind—an' dumb as an ox. A lot of 'em don't have much family to speak about, at least that care about 'em none, an' ye can bet they been banged plenty by Harry the Hick by the time they're fifteen." Maggie was staring unseeing into the rain—and unheeding as well, or so it seemed.

"But yer different, Margaret. I mean ye don't miss a trick, an' ye look like a real lady—right out o' the magazines. I almost popped me eyeballs when ye walked into the place tonight. I mean t' say, even I can see ye don't belong in a dump like this."

A knock on the door brought Maggie's head around, and momentarily suspending his monologue, Boylan opened the door to admit Mrs. Bailey, who entered bearing a tray.

"Here's a bite o' supper for the princess," she said, smiling her lacquer smile.

"Knock it off, Maureen dear, an' get lost if ye would be so kind." Maggie couldn't help grinning a bit at Mrs. Bailey's indignant face, and as the woman departed, slamming the door behind her, she noticed that Pat was smiling too. "The old bag," he muttered. "There's no tart like an old tart, Margaret my dear, which brings us back to our little problem. But before we discuss it any further, you better eat something."

"What is it?" Maggie asked, uninterested.

"Well, I wouldn't bet my life on it, but it has the look of chicken pot pie. Eat it anyhow, before ye fall down in a faint."

"What do you care what happens to me?" Maggie said mournfully.

"Oh, now what? Are we feelin' a bit sorry for ourselves? Listen, this place is filled with girls who haven't got half o' what you got, an' feel lucky to be here!"

"I bet!" Maggie exclaimed, her mouth full of pie.

"Don't talk with yer mouth full, girl. It's not ladylike."

Maggie realized by now that the real danger had passed —that Pat had taken a liking to her and would probably try to help her somehow to avoid serving as a captive prostitute for Mrs. Bailey. What lay ahead, however, was still uncertain.

"Mr. Boylan . . ."

"Call me Pat, fer the love o' God."

"Pat, why can't I just work for you somehow? I mean I could be yer secretary or something. I know I could do something useful."

"Pimps don't have secretaries, darlin'. An' what are ye goin' to do? Help me fetch the girls in off the farm?"

"No. You could get me a job in the tavern—waiting on table."

"I don't really have anything to do with the tavern. That's only the place where we get the mail. Besides, I work for Maureen, an' her boss has houses like this all over the Midwest. I'm hardly in any position to be givin' you jobs."

"You could help me. You must know people."

"Yeah, but they're all involved in The Life."

"What life?"

"That's what they call the hustlin' racket," Boylan said absentmindedly. "Come to think of it," he mused, looking at Maggie, "can you dance?"

"I never tried."

"You think you could learn?"

"Yes."

"Well, I think ye could too. Ye got a lot o' class, ye know that?"

"That's what my brothers all used to say. That's why I wanted to come here, to get off the farm, so that I could get some decent clothes, get my hands soft like a lady, an' maybe learn about somethin' besides cows and vegetables. I thought with thirty dollars a week I could do some o' that. It did seem like a lot for a salesgirl."

"Oh, you'd be a salesgirl, all right, only ye wouldn't be sellin' petunias. Ye see, Margaret, it's yer own vanity that brought ye here—yer own pride."

"I know that," Maggie said solemnly, "an' pride is a sin."

"Now cut that out about the sin an' all, will ye please? It's the bloody end!" Boylan paused for a moment, looking out the window. It had stopped raining, and he was wondering what he would say to Maureen. Her employers would take a dim view of losing a plum like Maggie as a result of mere sentiment; he would have to make it appear otherwise.

"Well, you get some sleep now. I'll tell Maureen to let you alone, an' tomorrow we'll see what we can do about the other."

"But I won't stay here!"

"Ye have very little choice, darlin', an' don't start in with what ye'll do an' what ye won't do!"

"Yes, Pat. I'm sorry. I'm just afraid."

"Well, don't be, 'cause they wouldn't send ye any customers the first night anyhow." Maggie made a face and bid him good night.

Maureen Bailey could plainly see that Maggie was not cut out to be a garden-variety whore, and Boylan had little trouble persuading her that the girl would be more valuable to them working in a different environment, where she would come to the attention of a better class of men—richer men.

Through his contacts in the tavern at 117 Wabash,

Boylan managed to find a spot for Maggie in the chorus line of the Green Mill Gardens, a club owned by a friend of Maureen's called Mike Fritzel. Fritzel was a fairly big-time operator in the Chicago nightclub world in those days and started many a now-famous performer, such as Joe E. Lewis, in either the Green Mill Gardens or a later acquisition, the Chez Paree. One of the first to befriend Maggie when she began her brief career as a dancer at the Green Mill was a girl called Lucille Le Sueur, known to the world now as Joan Crawford.

Under the watchful eye of Patty Boylan, Maggie became a fair dancer. She did not have the greatest legs in the world, but neither were they the worst, and the face and torso, enshrined in sequins and feathers as they ultimately were, were something to behold. Pat did not absolutely have to come to each and every rehearsal, nor was he required to attend every performance, but he found much to his own chagrin that he had become rather fond of Maggie and had from the beginning developed a desire to protect her. Actually, when he thought about it hard—which he rarely did about anything—he had to admit that he just damn well wanted her for himself.

Maggie certainly had reason to be grateful. It was Pat who had saved her from the clutches of Mrs. Bailey, who had settled her in a proper boardinghouse, and who had found her a job. Granted, it was not the kind of work she had originally had in mind—she wondered what her mother, not to mention her father, would think if she could see her parading around in pink feathers—but it was work nevertheless, and thus far she had done nothing terribly wrong. She was not required to remove her clothes during the act, nor did she drink or smoke or consort with men other than Pat. She had become terribly dependent upon his constant presence and rarely saw or spoke to anyone else.

This latter circumstance troubled Maggie more than a little, for everything in her character and background would ordinarily have caused her to reject a type such as Boylan vigorously. She was astonished at her ability to allow his personal charm and specific kindness toward her to militate against the essential fact that he was a procurer, a blackmailer, and a cheat, which rendered him by almost any standards one of the vilest of men. His treatment of her, however, was no more crude than that, say, of her father, which produced in her the habit of responding without question or resistance to a voice of authority and to make the best of a hard situation.

She was disturbed too by the knowledge that many of her fellow Terpsichores at the club were prostitutes, a fact which she deduced from their cheerfully candid and ribald dressing-room conversation. Indeed, this was an exceedingly inappropriate situation for a good, God-fearing Irish girl to find herself in, but strangely Maggie was not as unhappy as she ought to have been. She had been cast upon the shores of a great city, among people whom she had been taught deserved to exist only in Hell, and had found them to be merely human.

One night, when Maggie had been at the club just under two weeks and had survived her first full performances, Pat took her back to the tavern. He bought her a beer, pigs' knuckles, and a sandwich, and told her how good she was in the show. Maggie was thrilled. Then he introduced her to a friend of his whose name was Thomas Hannon and whom Pat addressed as "Mr. Hannon." A well-dressed, graying man in his early forties, Hannon was extremely nice to Maggie and paid her many extravagant compliments, which made her blush. As he made ready to leave, he suggested that they might dine together sometime in the near future. Maggie smiled and looked to Pat for guidance but had no indication from his expression as to what she should say or do. She thanked Mr. Hannon and asked him to come to the club and see the show.

On the way home Pat put his arm around Maggie, rather absently, and noted with smug satisfaction that she did nothing to discourage it. Arriving at the boardinghouse, Pat did not, as usual, bid Maggie a cursory good night and return to the tavern, where he generally drank beer and played pinochle until all hours of the morning.

"I'm comin' up to yer room fer a minute, Margaret," he said. "There's somethin' I got to talk to ye about."

"Mrs. Allen won't like it, ye know."

"What d'ye mean? She's always sleepin' like a log by this time o' night."

The room was minute, and there was no place for either one of them to sit except the bed. Maggie took off her shoes and sat up by the head, against the pillows, yawning deeply.

"So am I borin' ye already, Margaret, an' me not even started?"

"No, Pat. I'm just tired. Ye know, I'll never get used to these hours, if I live to be a hundred. What is it ye want to tell me?"

"Well," Pat began, pulling one knee up with folded hands, "it's not so much what I want to tell ye as what I want to ask ye. I'm wonderin' . . . I mean, are ye very unhappy?"

Maggie couldn't have been more surprised. "Why d'ye ask?" she replied.

"Well, it's just that Mrs. Allen says ye spend all yer spare time up here writin' letters, an' she's heard ye cryin' . . ."

"Oh, I see," Maggie said, glad that she had not permitted herself to be too touched by this apparent display of concern. "You'll be wonderin' if I told my parents about you an' Mrs. Bailey an' the whole rotten thing, is that it?"

"That's not the whole of it, no!" Pat flared. "But ye can't blame me for thinkin' about it, now can ye? Well, have ye told 'em?"

"No, I haven't," Maggie snapped. "I'd be too ashamed . . . if they knew what I was doin'. I miss 'em, that's all. I never been away from home." The tears had now begun to flow, and, greatly relieved about the outcome of his inquiries, Pat was all benevolence.

"Well, now," he crooned, placing his arm around Maggie's shoulders, "maybe we can work something out. Maybe the next time one o' them big brothers comes to town, ye can have a little visit and get all the news."

"Oh, no. I couldn't do that. They think I'm working in a flower shop."

"Well, we'll plant ye in a flower shop fer the day, an' nobody need be the wiser. How's that fer an idea?" Maggie couldn't help smiling, though she knew the idea represented an effort to cheer her up rather than a sincere desire to reconcile her to her kin.

"Sure," she said. "That would be a good one, Pat. Ye know," she continued, "I couldn't go back to the farm now anyway, really. I know that. I mean, back to all that drudgery, day after day, an' just gettin' older, an'—well, not livin' at all." Her look was distant now and her mind back on the farm. She hardly noticed that Pat had placed his other arm around her, while instinctively she leaned her head against his chest.

"Didn't ye have no boyfriend or anything out there?"

"No. No one."

"Well, I can't believe that . . . I mean a beauty like you."

"I used to see some o' the boys at the square dances, but there was no one I particularly fancied. There was a Polish boy I liked all right, an' I used to let him kiss me sometimes, but my folks didn't like him because he wasn't Irish." They had a good laugh over that one, and Pat tightened his hold on her. Maggie shut her eyes, thinking sleepily that it was nice to be held like that. It was warming, and it even felt safe.

"Anyway," she mused, "I've made my bed, and I guess I have to lie in it."

"That's it," Pat whispered, "that's not at all a bad idea, come to think of it. Let's lie down here an' talk some more." The old reliable combination of mild spirits and a gentle fatigue were working their dubious magic on Maggie, to the extent that she was quite prepared to accept almost any suggestion that her companion had to offer.

"Did ye like it, Margaret, when the Polak kissed ye?"

"Yes, I did. It was nice," Maggie mumbled, eyes closed.

"And didn't ye never have no desire beyond that?"

"Oh, yes, I did. I mean it's normal, but I know it's wicked."

"Well," Pat said very softly, his hand resting gently on Maggie's leg, "God made it, right along with everything else, so how can it be wicked? I mean, if He made it, it must be good, isn't that right?" Maggie only smiled a little, her breathing a trifle heavier.

"Jesus," Pat thought, "what's she done now, gone to sleep? Here y'are, Patty boy, ready to pop a virgin, an' not one o' them coarse pigs either, an' she bloody well nods off. God, an' I'm ready to die fer it . . . if I can only get them damn panties off of 'er."

"Margaret," he whispered, sliding his hand up the length of her leg.

"Don't call me Margaret now," Maggie said, her eyes still closed, "an' don't take off all my clothes."

"Well, how about that?" Pat thought to himself. "Playin' possum an' just waitin' fer it all the time."

"Anything ye say, Maggie luv . . . help me a little darlin' . . ."

Hard experience had taught Patty Boylan that the morning after could be very tricky indeed with these young green ones, and a man had to move deftly to get through it all safe and sound. He had not been able to stay the night this time, for the bed was far too small, and in any case Mrs. Allen was laboring under the illusion that she was operating a respectable boardinghouse and might not take kindly to being disabused. Besides, it was always a good idea to let the girl be for a bit afterward, so that she could get herself pulled together and decide how to handle the rest of it.

He had got himself up early this morning, in spite of the fact that he had played cards well into the night, and bought some flowers with his winnings to take to Maggie. She'd like that all right, and anyway they didn't call him Pat the Gent for nothing.

Putting on his most cheerful face and clutching a large bouquet, he once more climbed the stairs of Mrs. Allen's boardinghouse and knocked on Maggie's door. "First it'll be the blushing," he thought, "then the tears and the guilt, followed most likely by an uncharitable word or two . . . where the hell is she anyhow?" He had knocked several times now without result, and was growing impatient. He tried the door and, finding it open, went in. No one was there. The bed had been neatly made, the few toilet articles arranged, and the rumpled dress from the night before hung up in the armoire. At least she hadn't tried to fly the coop. He sat down on the bed to wait.

Roughly half an hour later, Maggie, her head shrouded in a brown shawl, returned to her room to find Pat crumpled against the headboard of her bed, asleep with his mouth open, a fading bouquet of wildflowers dropping from one hand. She smiled down on him and took the flowers, sweeping the shawl from her shining head at the same time. Having determined to put the flowers in the porcelain pitcher provided by the management for morning ablutions, she crossed in front of the window toward the basin. In so doing, she momentarily passed through the shaft of sunlight which fell across Pat's face, and he awoke.

Rubbing his eyes and looking at her for a moment, he said, "An' where, might I ask, have we been so bright and early this morning?"

"To Mass. Thank you for the flowers. They're very pretty, even though you've been lyin' on them."

"You're welcome. An' what on earth made ye go off to Mass on a Thursday?"

"I went to confess my sins to God."

"Oh, dear Lord. . ."

"Don't worry, I won't be goin' again or disturbin' you with a lot o' talk about it for that matter. I promised God I'd not be back until I could honestly say I'd never do it again, an' I don't see much chance o' that in the near future, do you? Just kindly do me a favor, an' don't be usin' Our Lord's name every other minute, as though He were yer pet mule." Pat stared at her, uncertain of what he was hearing.

"Well, now, I declare! I come in here expectin' t' find ye bathed in tears o' remorse, an' here y'are, all cool an' sassy, bustlin' around like a mother hen. . . ."

"I am full of remorse, Pat, and guilt. An' don't make no mistake. But what's the good of it? It's not goin' to change anything, is it?"

"No, it isn't. I'm not lettin' you go, Margaret, if that's what ye mean. I know what's botherin' ye. Ye liked it, didn't ye?"

"Yes, I did!" Maggie shouted, flushing. "And so what?"

"An' it come as a big surprise t' ye, didn't it, because yer dear Ma an' the priest an' the whole bunch told ye it was a disgustin' sin, didn't they now?"

"How do you know? I never told ye that."

"Oh, fer God's sake, it's the same old story. My Ma told me the same damn thing."

"Mine never told me nothing."

"Well, that's a blessing anyway. Ye had a chance to make up yer own mind." Pat's mood suddenly changed. "Oh, Mag," he said gleefully, "I couldn't believe it was the first time. . . ." Maggie glowered at him. "I didn't mean it like that. I meant it was so marvelous. Most girls—I mean—oh, fer chrissake, I'm tryin' t' pay ye a compliment, an' it's goin' all wrong. . . . Yer a luv, it's all I'm tryin' t' say." Maggie softened somewhat, relaxing her belligerent stance.

"It's all right, Pat, it really is."

"Well, if it was all right, ye should be happy, shouldn't ye?"

"I'm not unhappy, Pat."

"No? Well I've seen happier faces on a bloodhound than on you t'day." Maggie giggled inevitably, thinking how clever Pat was in knowing how and when to reach for her humor.

"Now that's better. Yer a woman today, Margaret—not just a kid. That's not so bad is it?"

"No, I suppose not." She looked into his gay blue eyes. "Ye could be a worse man, though I don't know how."

"I wouldn't let nothin' bad happen to ye, all right? Now give us a kiss."

"There's a rehearsal . . ."

"It'll wait one minute. I'll take ye over."

After that, Maggie moved in with Pat, living with him in his room over the tavern; at last she had discovered the secret of the dark brown staircase. She continued to dance at the Green Mill Club, turning her pay over to Pat as a contribution to the running of their simple ménage. Although she knew that at her urgent request Pat had stopped working as an agent for Maureen and her gang, she did not know that he had success-fully resisted doing work of any kind ever since she appeared on the scene, and that they were living entirely on her twenty-five dollars a week. Fortunately, Pat rarely ever lost at pinochle and was thus able to supplement their meager income through his efforts at the card table. Maggie strongly suspected that he cheated and wondered what would happen if, discovered, he started to lose or was no longer allowed in the game.

All things considered, they were quite happy. God knows, Maggie had never become accustomed to any kind of luxury on the farm, and in a curious sort of way, she had come to love this alien creature called Pat Boylan. He took care of her, kept undesirable men away from her with the ferocity of a bantam cock, made love to her skillfully, and taught her the various tricks, learned over the years from his business associates, re-lating to the avoidance of pregnancy. Infrequently, he would come home and find Maggie in tears, brooding over the loss of a cherished dream involving marriage and a family. Sometimes this would cause Pat to become impatient and ill-tempered, but more often, applying all his talent as a shill, he was able to persuade her that, while any fool could settle down and spawn a bunch of mewling brats, they had too much class for that and needed to be free to become rich and prosperous. Pat never specified exactly how this was to be accomplished, but his confidence in the matter more than made up for the missing elements of real results. Maggie never went to church anymore, but she prayed some and wrote to her mother, albeit less frequently, promising to come home for a visit at Christmas time, which was fast approaching. She had little or no assurance, however, that Pat would permit her to do so.

Having shed her costume after the show and got herself dressed, Maggie usually found Pat sitting out front at a small table each night, waiting for her with beer and sandwiches. One cold December night, as she came into the main room she noticed that there was another man sitting with Pat, a man, in fact, whom she thought she recognized. It was Mr. Hannon.

"You remember Mr. Hannon now, Margaret, don't ye?"

"Surely, I do. It was a few weeks ago at the tavern."

"That's right. That's my good girl."

"I was wondering," Mr. Hannon said, "if you'd like to take me up on that dinner invitation some time soon." Just as Maggie opened her mouth to reply, Pat intervened.

"She'd love to, I'm sure, Mr. Hannon. Right, Margaret? Just name the day." Maggie, utterly nonplussed, could think of nothing at all to say. She merely looked from Pat to Mr. Hannon—Pat, who leaned eagerly toward Hannon while the latter stared, flushed and perspiring, at Maggie—and wondered what to make of it all.

"Well, that's fine then," he said. "I'll arrange it with Pat and get in touch with you at the tavern. Good night." Maggie smiled as sweetly as she could until Hannon had left the room, then she turned to Pat for some explanation.

"Now don't go gettin' all excited," he said before Maggie could say anything. "Mr. Hannon is a good friend of mine, an' I want ye t' be nice to 'im."

"I'm perfectly willin' to be nice to 'im, Pat, but what in the world do ye want me to go out with 'im for?" Pat, busily tracing designs on the tablecloth with his fingernail, darted furtive glances at her as he spoke, unable to meet Maggie's honest, questioning gaze.

"Well, now, Hannon's not just yer run o' the mill bloke, ye know. He's in the city government—aye, an' he's rich too an' could do a lot fer us."

"I don't get yer meanin' at all Pat." Pat's fingers fidgeted increasingly.

"I want ye to be nice to 'im!" he said, placing his face within two inches of hers. Maggie stared, unwilling to understand.

Suddenly Pat jumped up, taking hold of her hand and dragging her onto the street and into a cab; he did not say another word until they got home to their little room. The place was in a terrible disorder, because Pat had not been feeling very well and had spent the day in bed, while Maggie rehearsed for the Christmas show.

"Oh, it looks a fright," Maggie complained and began straightening up automatically.

"Just never mind about that," Pat said irritably. "Ye got a bloody mania fer neatness, anyhow, I swear t' God. Sit down there on the bed, an' I'm goin' t' tell ye a thing or two."

"Well?"

"It's my impression," Pat began slowly, sarcastically, "that you don't understand what I mean about bein' nice to Mr. Hannon, is that right?" Maggie remained silent, her gall rising gently.

"Well, what I mean is that Mr. Hannon thinks yer a beautiful rosy girl, an' he wants t' go t' bed with ye! He's got a wife that's about as excitin' as a cold bowl o' porridge, an' he's willin' t' pay plenty fer the privilege of havin' a go or two at you!" Maggie sat silent, her eyes shut, fighting the fear and the nausea, which threatened to grip her. Pat stared at her, his eyes hard, his chin thrust aggressively into the air in front of her, waiting. Finally she spoke quietly and slowly:

"You told me, Pat, when I came with ye, that ye wouldn't let anything bad happen t' me. D'ye remember that?"

"This isn't anything bad, fer God's sake. . . ."

"Now just a minute!" Maggie's temper flared. "Ye also seem to have forgot that I've got fond o' ye, God only knows how or why, an' I'm not of a mind t' go sleepin' around with a bunch o' bloody strangers!"

"Margaret, that's the first time I ever heard ye swear," Pat chuckled. "I like yer spirit, girl, I surely do."

"Now don't go tryin' that out on me again, Pat." There were more tears now. "Ye make me sick with yer Mr. Hannon!"

"Listen t' me, Margaret. I am a pimp, a procurer. That's

my trade. That's the thing I do best. It's only because o' me that yer not sweatin' in Maureen Bailey's place with some bloody truckdriver, an' so far ye had it pretty easy. Now I'm tellin' ye that ye can make real money—never mind that lousy twenty-five dollars a week at the club. The club is only good fer meetin' the people in the first place—gettin' 'em interested. The real money is in the Johns. Yer good-lookin' and' ye got a lot o' style. Ye can get the rich ones, the fancy ones, an' fer that kind o' money ye can choose the ones ye want—take 'em or leave 'em." Maggie was weeping, sobbing uncontrollably.

"It's only yer own vanity and stupidity that got ye here in the first place, ye know. Ye wanted expensive dresses, didn't ye? An' soft hands, isn't that right? An' to eat good food? Well, yer not goin' to get that on the farm or in a flower shop neither, I can tell ye that much. Yer either born to it, or ye hustle fer it, darlin', an' that's a fact! So cut out yer damn snivelin' and look at facts." Pat ceased his tirade and, taking off his shoes, started to get ready for bed. Maggie, moving like a hypnotic, did the same.

"I knew ye didn't love me at all," she said, getting into bed, "but I never thought ye'd do this t' me. Never."

"It's not so bad, ye know, Margaret. I couldn't stand fer ye t' be with some slob. It's different when they're a better class —they take ye to nice places an' give ye nice clothes, an' ye'll still be with me. I'll still take care of ye, Mag." Pat was almost tender now, which drove Maggie even further into the abyss. She wept the night through as Pat snored beside her.

When Pat finally woke up the next morning, Maggie was not in bed beside him. Assuming she had gone down to the bathroom, he stretched and rubbed his eyes, hoping to work the sleep out of them and face the new day. But as he looked around the room, he sensed something wrong. Where was the dress Maggie had taken off the night before, her toilet things? Throwing off the covers in a great flurry, he shot up out of bed and rushed to the closet. Maggie's clothes were also gone from the drawers, and so was the battered suitcase with which she first arrived in Chicago.

Having assured himself that she had fled, Pat lighted a cigarette and sat quietly thinking about what he would do next. First, he'd better get over to the club and tell them that Maggie was sick and would be back in a few days. He'd have to put Mr.

Hannon off too. There wasn't much doubt in his mind where she'd gone; it was simply a question of how best to fetch her back.

Maggie had risen as early in the morning as she dared, packed up, retrieved half her pay from Pat's pants pocket, and gone down to the railroad station, where she waited for the first train to South Bend. By the time Pat got up, she was well on her way, tear-streaked face pressed against the window, gazing unseeing into the rushing prairie. Pat had told her hair-raising stories of what happened to girls who tried to run away from their "protectors" and squeal on them—how they were burned with cigarettes, beaten up, sometimes even killed—but she knew Pat now and knew his character. So long as he was no longer answering to anyone else in the mob, she felt reasonably safe. Besides, he had left her little choice.

Maggie's mother was overjoyed to see her, and so were her father and the boys, who came around with their wives and children to see her and to hear all about her life in Chicago. She had only been there three months, but now that she was home again, it seemed longer. Her youngest brother, Frank, who had got himself engaged but was still living at home, had been thrilled to see her and had jumped right in the wagon and gone over to tell his brothers almost as soon as Maggie set foot in the house.

Maggie had thought that it would be difficult for her to lie about her life in Chicago without leaving some damaging clues as to her true status, but she found that a good deal of Pat had rubbed off on her in a short time. With all of them gathered around her—honest eager faces turned to hear all about it—she found it remarkably easy to create for them a life of modest elegance in a large and beautifully fragrant flower shop, where she was privileged to serve all the smartest people in the town. She was amazed at her own capacity for deceit— she, who had never told a lie in her life. By the time she was through, she all but believed it herself and was in an extraordinarily cheerful state of mind. Everybody stayed for dinner, and later, having promised to take good care of her little nieces and nephews who were too sleepy to make the trip home with their parents, she went upstairs to her old room. It was good to be back, but as she lay in the dark, listening to the sounds of a cold country night, she thought about Pat and fell once again into a profound melancholy.

It snowed that night, and the children had awakened with cries of joy, rushing, as soon as they were allowed, into the white playground, which had created itself overnight for their amusement. Maggie donned a heavy winter coat, whose fur trim had definitely seen better days, and ran out to play with them. Battles were fought, snowmen built, and everybody had a marvelous time; Maggie realized that it was the first time since she was a very little girl that she had been allowed to play in her own backyard without having a single chore awaiting her. She had not yet broken the news to her parents that she was not planning to return to Chicago and had no idea how she was to justify her decision in the light of the glowing report she had given them the evening before. As far as they were concerned, she was there to spend Christmas with them, and that was all.

Two days later it was Christmas, and Maggie, having spent most of her time helping her mother and making some simple presents for the children, had no time to dwell on her dilemma. Tom and the boys had gone off into the woods, as they always did on Christmas Eve, to chop down a tree, and having dragged it home on a sled, the children decorated it with paper and candy.

Christmas morning found Maggie in a panic about having to go to Mass and receive communion. It was obvious that she could not refuse or feign illness, for her mother was looking forward to this more than anything else; she absolutely had to go. On the way to church, Maggie's mother commented on her pallor and her silence, but Maggie only smiled weakly and patted her mother's hand. All during the service she sat with her head bowed and her hands clenched together. At communion the wafer seemed to swell in her throat, and the blessing entered her ears as an indictment.

Maggie felt numb on the way home from church, but, she was nevertheless prepared to enjoy the rest of her Christmas.

Ma had baked a turkey and masses of pumpkin pie, which were consumed with great gusto at lunch, after which everybody indulged in a long winter nap. Later on, Maggie and her sisters-in-law bundled the children up in preparation for the ride home in the open sled, and it was with great misgivings that she waved them all off, just as long wistful shadows fell across the snow-blanketed yard. Happily, she had no idea that she would never see them again.

The following morning, they all rose as usual at five o'clock, Pa having asked Maggie to collect the eggs for breakfast as she had always done. It was nice in a way to blend once again into the routine of the farm, mostly because it was familiar and therefore safe. Thus it was with an air of contentment that Maggie took the basket down from its peg and, tying a woolen scarf around her face, headed for the barn.

The chicken coop was connected to the barn, and on winter days, whoever collected the eggs usually walked through the barn to the coop in order to avoid being out in the numbing, frosty air any longer than necessary. As Maggie approached in the dark, she did not see that the heavy doors, normally tight shut during the night, were slightly ajar; so anxious was she to get inside to the warmth that not even in the act of sliding them open did she notice anything strange. Closing the doors behind her, she raised her lamp higher in order to find her way to the low door which led to the chicken coop. As she made her way across the floor, stumbling occasionally on the uneven boards and catching straw in her shoes, she was aware of a rustling behind her, which somehow did not sound like one of the cows. She turned, half afraid, and saw a man in a city suit looking drowsily up at her from a pile of straw, on which he had obviously been sleeping. It was Pat.

Making every effort to control the onset of panic, Maggie slowly put the lamp down on a milking stool and, drawing her coat more closely about her, stood stock still. In a matter of seconds Pat was on his feet, brushing the straw from his hair and clothes. He stopped abruptly, fixing Maggie with a hard and quizzical look, which he held several moments before he spoke. Maggie said nothing, merely standing and staring.

"Well, Margaret, it's a hell of a way ye made me spend Christmas, an' that's fer sure."

"I didn't ask ye t' come. How did ye find it?"

"Oh, that wasn't too difficult. Most o' the folks around here seem t' know yer old man's farm. Not a bad spread at all."

"What are ye doin' here?"

"What the hell d'ye think I'm doin' here? I'm takin' ye back t' the city, that's what!"

"I'm not goin', Pat, t' be yer special whore! It's bad enough I've already been with you, but as fer the other—well, it makes me sick!" Pat's eyes narrowed and his face flushed; his temper flared suddenly. Moving closer to Maggie, he stuck his finger out before her face, stabbing at the air for emphasis.

"Just listen t' me! I been lyin' here in this stinkin' barn fer a day and a half just waitin' fer you t' come in here alone so's I could knock yer silly teeth out! I told ye before that ye couldn't go back, an' bein' with me fer a couple o' months don't change anything. I got an investment in you, and yer hardly in a position t' say yea or nay. Yer comin' back an' ye'll damn well do what I say, or I'll spill the whole thing t' yer dear old Ma, an' everybody else by means o' the U.S. mails, an' won't they be happy t' hear it?" Maggie's eyes flashed.

"I don't give a damn what ye do, they wouldn't believe it anyway. I'm not comin'." Pat smiled and looked at the floor, arranging strands of straw with one foot.

"Margaret, it would appear that ye forgot what I told ye about what happens to little girls who think they can just drop in and out o' the system whenever they bloody well feel like it. . . ."

"Ye can't scare me, Pat. I know you. Ye wouldn't—" Maggie was arrested in midsentence by a vicious blow to the side of her face, delivered by Pat with the back of his bony hand. Stunned, she rocked backward, coming to rest against a wooden beam. The blow had hurt her, but she managed to remain on her feet. Her eyes were wide now, and she was more frightened than she had ever been in her life.

"What d'ye take me for?" Pat went on. "One o' yer innocent little hayseeds, who lets ye play with 'im a little, an' then stands there sweatin' while ye trot home with yer virtue tucked up in yer little panties? Just because I went a bit soft on ye, fer chrissake, ye think ye can come an' go as ye damn please?"

"Don't use that language. . . ."

"An' don't be tellin' me what the hell bloody language t' be usin' either!" he shouted, hitting her on the other side with an open palm. This time Maggie fell, sobbing and holding her head. Pat loomed over her, threatening.

"I got a mind t' break yer bleedin' . . ." As he raised his hand again, the barn doors crashed open, and as Pat whirled and Maggie lifted her battered face from the floor, Frank entered and began walking slowly toward them.

Maggie had never thought how small Pat was compared to her muscular, corn-fed brothers, but as Francis Paul O'Brien, his face flushed, strode quietly toward Pat full of rage and hurt, he looked like a giant. Without speaking a word, he grasped the astonished pimp by the front of his coat, twisting it in his hand, and lifted his great calloused fist.

"Don't, Frank!" Maggie screamed. "You'll kill 'im! Don't do it, fer the love o' God!"

"Fer the love o' God, Mag, I *ought* to kill this serpent," Frank said, in a voice distorted by emotion. "After what I heard, how in God's name can ye defend 'im."

"I don't know. I can't explain it t' ye, but I just don't want ye t' hurt 'im . . . please!" Frank put the terrified man down and let his hands fall to his sides. His pain was apparent and oppressive. "All right then," he said. "Ye better go with 'im, for yer not t' be stayin' here and tellin' us no more lies. An' God forgive ye." He turned, Maggie hanging on his arm, pleading. Roughly, he shook her free and strode out toward the house.

"All right," Pat said. "That settles it. Let's get out o' this place. I got a car down by the road—if it's not snowed under by now." Tears streamed down Maggie's face.

"What about my things?"

"Ye can get more in town. Come on, before that gorilla that happens t' be related t' you comes back here an' murders us both." Sobbing and with Pat dragging her by the arm, Maggie stumbled toward the road through the last frosty dawn which they would ever again be awake at that hour to see. During the long drive back, neither one said a word.

Unbeknownst to her, Maggie had just entered The Life. By protecting Pat Boylan out of affection for him, understanding full well his intentions of exploiting her feeling for him as well as her body, she entered a world from which there is rarely any escape.

Maggie went to dinner with Mr. Hannon and with many more men, after her return to Chicago, and turned over whatever they gave her to Pat. Bitter of Frank's reaction to her situation and assuming that by now he had told the entire family, she more or less abandoned her moral inhibitions and tried to make the best of a bad thing. Guided by the same perverse and inappropriate affection which, combined with the moral qualms, had previously made the idea of sleeping with other men repellent to her, she now did so willingly for Pat's sake and for the enlargement of their mutual affluence and satisfaction. Having undergone this psychological transformation, she had thereby acquired the core of the prostitute's mentality, a phenomenon which she would have been the last person to understand.

They rarely had occasion to quarrel, except when Pat infrequently strayed with another woman, and during those brief moments of introspection which Maggie sometimes allowed herself, she had to admit that her life could be a great deal worse. The men whom Pat found for her, mostly smitten oglers of the Green Mill Gardens chorus line, were relatively substantial people, who took her to attractive places to eat and drink and bought her the kind of clothes she had always wanted to wear. These were the sort of men who became regular customers, which, happily for Maggie, obviated the necessity of having to have sexual intercourse with total strangers every day of her life.

Furthermore, Maggie's men taught her a great deal about how to be a lady, a role for which she had a natural aptitude in any case. From them she learned how to dress, how to speak, and how generally to comport herself in public and in the company of other people; she learned how to judge a good wine or a good soufflé and came to know the phonies from twenty-five yards off. She read a great deal in her spare time and became very well informed. There were not all that many gentlemen in Chicago in these days, but those there were soon found Maggie or were found by Pat. The latter was, of course, delighted with Maggie's progress, both cultural and professional, especially inasmuch as Maggie remained devoted only to him through it all; it was thanks to him, after all, that she was now a suitable companion for Pat the Gent.

Maggie continued to dance at the Green Mill, until one day a man came along who showed a serious interest in her; Pat had her out and in another job within the week. Fritzel had by now opened other clubs in different parts of town to which Maggie could go, and it was nice to have a change of scene from time to time. Maggie was never a stripper, but she developed to a point where she was frequently given solo parts as a straight dancer, and it was in this capacity that men really took notice of her. She attracted not only those looking for a mistress but those looking for love; in four years, Pat had to move her as many times.

As the years wore on, Maggie grew rich, and not from dancing in nightclubs. It was not long, in fact, before she stopped dancing altogether and concentrated on being a first-class courtesan, a job which she had grown to like. She and Pat had long since moved from the sleazy room at 117 Wabash Avenue, which had been closed during Prohibition, and now occupied more luxurious quarters in a better part of town, where Maggie could better entertain her clients. Many of the more posh restaurants had private rooms, which were elegantly appointed and which justified an infinitely higher standard of dress for the evening, which Maggie also enjoyed.

What Maggie liked best about the life is that she did not have to work hard—she had had enough of that on the farm to last a lifetime. She could sleep late in the morning and had plenty of time during the day to be with Pat or pursue her own activities. She also relished the idea of being the confidante of so many rich and important men, most of whom were in business or politics and many of whom, to Maggie's bafflement, had very attractive wives.

What she didn't learn about human nature and the nuances and conflicts of married life wasn't worth knowing. She discovered that a wife, regardless of how attractive she might be, is never as exciting to a man as a woman who is not his wife. She learned also that there were an extraordinary number of women for whom sex was a tool either to entrap a man initially or to obtain some desired object, be it a child or a diamond; after the object had been obtained, no further interest in the matter needed to be demonstrated. She discovered further that many men shared their wives' low opinion of sexuality and only found it appropriately expressed with suitably debased individuals, such as prostitutes. However, most of the latter category found that they were better satisfied over at Maureen Bailey's place than in Maggie's company, which offered more than a mere physical presence.

Supervising all these liaisons with an ever-vigilant eye was Pat, who never let any one man stay too long or get too close. Few bachelors were permitted to taste the coveted fruit, regardless of their wealth; there was always a chance that one of them might actually fall in love with Maggie and take her away from her dearest friend, protector, and chief beneficiary.

As Maggie approached the age of thirty, her blooming beauty began to fade. The long nights, lack of air and exercise, combined with far too many large, rich meals, had begun to leave their inevitable mark, and she and Pat decided that the time had come to diversify. Besides, she was getting a bit tired. She often wondered too, and sadly, what had become of her family, with whom she had no contact whatsoever since that blighted Christmas almost nine years ago.

Giving out the news that they were planning a two-week vacation, Maggie and Pat set out on a monumental house-hunting spree, during which they must have tramped and prodded their way through every available large house in Chicago's better neighborhoods.

At last one day they were shown a five-and-a-half-story house on Washington Street. The moment they walked into the ample and lavish entrance foyer, with its divided staircase curving gracefully to the floor, they knew it was what they had been looking for. Duly noting the elegance and propriety with which this handsome couple was dressed, and charmed by Maggie's soft and cultivated speech, the agent had no doubts whatsoever that he was dealing with one of Chicago's most respectable young families. Withdrawing nearly all their savings to make the first payment, Maggie and Pat bought the house within the week.

"You know that nice little sort of drawing room to the left as you come in, Pat," Maggie asked a few days later. "Don't you think that would make a nice waiting room?"

"Waiting room? What the hell do we need a waiting room for? Waiting for what? Why can't we just have the girls sittin' around in the great cavern of a vestibule on the first floor, an' let the gents go up there an' look around? Y' know, we could have a piano up there an' settees. . . ."

"Now listen, Patrick," Maggie remonstrated. "We are not running a cheap, two-bit place like Maureen-Joan Bailey, with people layin' about in the halls. This place is going to have a refined and conservative atmosphere, if I'm to have anything to do with it, with good-looking, nice girls and a peaceful feel to it."

"Well, haven't we got fancy these days? How the hell

can a whorehouse be refined and conservative, darlin'? Sounds more like a rest home t' me."

"Don't be a sod, Pat, and mind your tongue with that language. Don't you see that if it's the right sort of place, it will attract the best customers—the rich ones, like I used to have?"

"Yes, Margaret. Of course I see that. That's not the point. What I'm wonderin' is where we're goin' to find the beautiful, refined girls to fit into this gorgeous atmosphere? Those sorts o' girls don't always want t' be whores, y' know."

"Will you stop calling them whores! I know it's what they are, but—well, just call them . . . girls. Besides, they don't have to be refined, just so they're not crude and tough."

Placing his arm gently around her shoulder, Pat said, "You just want a houseful o' darlin' farm girls just like you, isn't that it?"

Maggie smiled. "That's it," she said. "And you're the bloke who can find 'em, eh, Pat?"

"Well, I'll certainly do my best fer you, Margaret, indeed I will."

And so, after a couple of months of redecorating, arranging, fuming, and hustling, Pat and Maggie were ready to open the smartest house in Chicago, which would come to be known simply as "Margaret's." Maggie had been an important factor in persuading the girls, unearthed by Pat, that they were not venturing into the jaws of hell; her charm and warmth made them feel that they would be at home in her house and that, should misery strike at them in the darkness of some terrible lonely night, Mrs. O'Brien, as she was known, would be there to provide a motherly shoulder upon which to weep. And thus it was that, with Maggie attending to the human element and Pat managing the business aspect, they were able to launch a highly successful operation.

They had no trouble finding clients. They had slightly more trouble finding girls, simply because Maggie's standards were so high. Pat finally managed to persuade her that they must have a few real pros in the place to keep the others in line and establish a properly professional atmosphere. There was a lot to learn, after all, as in any business, and Maggie, having led a somewhat sheltered existence as ladies of pleasure go, was not in a position to provide instruction in some of the cruder realities. Ultimately, she gave in on this issue, admonishing Pat that if there was trouble with any of the girls, he had her permission to give them a good bash. Maggie at this stage had toughened considerably, and beneath the benevolent exterior there had developed a woman with a hard sense of reality which stopped just this side of cynicism, and a shrewd sense of how to balance graciousness with self-interest. The Life had been relatively kind to her, and she knew it.

From the start, the greatest problems they had were with the girls. There were those who just didn't take to the work and wanted to go home to Mother if they had one; others tried to steal extra money on the side, either by rolling their Johns or by wheedling a fee in addition to the one paid downstairs upon entering; many were drug addicts, and they posed the greatest problem of all. Maggie didn't like losing her girls any more than any other operator did, but she didn't like the idea of having them beaten up either. Clearly something had to be done to regulate the situation; apart from anything else, her clients liked to think that, should they get used to a particular girl, they might have her again. The constant turnover, endemic to this occupation, was decidedly bad for business.

In the roaring twenties, the heroin addict was something relatively esoteric, the great majority of drug users being "sniffers"—that is, users of cocaine. "Snow," as it was known to the addict, was available for about four dollars a deck and came wrapped in much the same form as a stick of chewing gum. The user would pour some of the powder onto the back of his hand and sniff it up into his nostrils, and thus the total process came to be know as a "snow job."

The trouble really was that too many of Maggie's girls were sniffers, and they spent entirely too much time thinking about how to obtain their snow and not enough concentrating on how to please their clients. One night, as Maggie lay sleepless in bed, she prodded Pat awake and insisted on discussing it.

"Fer the love o' God, Margaret, what may be on yer mind at this unholy hour?"

"The girls. We've just got to get them sorted out, Pat."

"Oh, a good belt in the mouth'll set 'em straight. Now go to sleep, Mag. It's Monday—the only night we ever get any rest around this place."

"No, Pat. I can't sleep a wink. We've got to talk about it. A belt in the mouth does not solve the problem, and you know it."

"All right," he said as though issuing a statement. "We'll bloody well talk about it, if that's what's goin' to make ye go to sleep. Now what d'ye propose we do, chain 'em to the bleedin' beds?"

"Listen, Pat. It's the ones on the stuff. They're the worst. Why can't we just get rid of 'em the second we know they're on it?"

"That won't settle it fer the ones who are left stealin' an' weepin', darlin'. At least the sniffers are happy as long as they have enough stuff. Those others . . . Jesus!"

Maggie was silent a moment, staring at her knees shrouded by the dusty wool of the blanket. A thought was taking form. "Pat," she said in the throes of discovery. "I just had an idea."

"God help us."

"Stop your clownin' and listen. You said at least the others were happy as long as they had the stuff, right?"

"Right. Yer hearin' is first rate."

"Well, why can't we provide it for 'em—as much as they want or need. Right here, so they're not trampin' all over the town lookin' for it and sulky when they don't find it?" Now it was Pat's turn for silent reflection.

"You know somethin', Margaret? On top o' bein' a darlin', yer a bleedin' genius." He paused for maximum effect as Maggie sat up, proud as a mother hen. "The only trouble is, it's highly illegal."

"Well so's hustling and pimping, for all that. What's the difference?"

"No difference to me, Margaret, but there's a difference to the law. The law enjoys whorin' as much as anybody—maybe more. But drugs, that's a little different. They haven't all taken that up yet, ye see. Ye can't pay 'em off so easy where that's concerned."

"So what? We might as well be hung for a sheep as a lamb. I think we should try it."

"Good girl! I been thinkin' we should try it fer ages now, but I was afraid about yer scruples. I'll talk to Mike an' some o' the others tomorrow first thing." Maggie was always perfectly willing to allow Pat to accept credit for all good ideas, whether his or hers, as it seemed to be so important to him; of major importance to her was to get things working smoothly and keep them that way.

"I must say," she mused, "I really don't see why they bother with it."

"That's because you never worked in a house, thanks to me."

"I know, but I still don't see it. . . ."

"Nobody knows whether they take up sniffin' so they can stand the Johns, or whether they take up whorin' to be able to pay for the snow. An' nobody will ever know, either, so go to sleep now, darlin'. You're a brilliant girl, an' I love ye."

"That's the first time you ever told me that, Pat, in all these years. You know that?"

Mumbling, half asleep, Pat said, "Is that so? Well it must be because I'm so exhausted. Go to sleep now." Maggie smiled to herself, knowing he would never forgive himself this moment of weakness.

Actually, Pat had been acting as a contact between addicts and pushers for years, due to the fact that so many of the girls he dealt with became addicts sooner or later. In this way, he had always been able to count on a few extra dollars when he lost at pinochle. In those days, he had always made the girls meet their connections on the outside, removed from his presence and presumably his knowledge. Now he had good reason to move his rather small operation in this area onto home ground and expand it besides. No one could deny that Margaret had the perfect front for it, and Pat knew everybody in the business; it would certainly not be difficult for them to organize.

Before too long Maggie's personnel, apart from the people who took the coats and the money, were all sniffers, and peace reigned, as business boomed in the House of Margaret O'Brien. Thanks to Pat's diligent efforts, the girls had as much snow as they needed to keep them in that state of chemical euphoria necessary to preserve their peace of mind, and any girl who threatened to leave was faced with being cut off from every major connection in the city. Few left, and those who did regretted it.

As the word got around among the inhabitants of the underworld that there were large supplies of snow to be had over at Maggie's place, a new type of client began to turn up—the junkies. At first they were discouraged from coming, unless of course they wanted a girl. Generally they did not. An addict in need of his narcotic is interested in nothing else in the world but getting the stuff and taking it into his body.

Again Maggie and Pat found it necessary to conduct a series of long pillow talks, the net result of which was that they embarked on a new project, satisfying a clientele which lusted after a different product—cocaine. They decided at the outset that sex and drugs should be kept absolutely separate. Maggie didn't want the junkies messing around with the girls, and so far as she was concerned, there was no reason why the regular clients had to know anything at all about the availability of drugs in her house. What she provided for the junkie was the drug, at a slightly higher price than he found it on the street, and a place to enjoy it undisturbed among people afflicted with the same disease—a haven for the dreamers and the dispossessed.

There were few needles around among the junkies in the early 1930's, although it had started. Every now and then, a man would walk into Maggie's place with a needle taped to his under-arm, and he would be thrown out immediately. What little people knew then about heroin and the types who used it, they didn't like, and they avoided them both diligently.

Nobody could just walk into the place off the street in any case; a man had to come recommended by somebody else and thoroughly checked out by Pat before he was allowed inside. If he was there for sex, he was shown upstairs; if he came for a snow-job, he was shown into a spacious room in the back of the house on the first floor, where he would be served his deck, with a sandwich and coffee, then left alone with the radio playing soft music, to dream.

For the first few years the business ran as smoothly as the proverbial silk, and neither Maggie nor Pat had anything much to complain of or worry about. Once a week, the "bagman" for the local police and vice squad came around to collect the customary fee in their behalf, which he did generally after sampling the wares on sale upstairs. This man, a political hack of the sort which abounds in most large cities, always sported a black derby hat and a huge umbrella of the same somber hue, which he took with him wherever he went in fair weather or foul. As he made his rounds of the various bawdy houses, gin mills, and gambling establishments, people would casually drop bundles of bank-notes into the folds of his umbrella as he stopped to chat. No conversation on the subject was necessary; they all knew why he was there and what they were required to do, and generally they did it. If they did not, the little man would smile, tipping his hat to them politely, and they would be raided within two days and out of business within three.

The alderman in Maggie's district together with his co-alderman, was another of Maggie's "protectors." Maggie had discovered that the world was chockablock with men who would gladly protect a lady from anything whatsoever, provided that the price was right, and inasmuch as she was growing richer by the minute, she could feel safe as a bedbug in a mattress factory. She was slightly worried about the sniffers. As far as she knew, the authorities knew nothing about this aspect of her operation, but she could not be sure as to the reaction such knowledge would inspire. On bad days she visualized herself and Pat being carted unceremoniously off to some municipal dungeon; on good days she figured it simply meant that some day she might have to drop a bit more into the umbrella.

The day of judgment finally came in January, 1932. It was a snowy Friday evening, and business was booming.

"It's nice to get in out of the cold," Detective John Meyers said as he entered, shaking the snow from his hat and cape. Maggie had not known Meyers, who had never, like some of the others, stopped by the house to see if everything was all right, and she wondered what he was doing there. He had someone with him, whom he did not introduce right away; instead, he suggested that they go into Maggie's private office to talk. Maggie didn't like the smell of these two and grew increasingly nervous as the minutes dragged by. "Pat would have to be out tonight," she thought. "Nothing good ever happens to me when it snows."

Hiding her fear beneath the gracious smile, which had become her trademark, she ushered the two men into her office just under the staircase.

"You are Mrs. O'Brien, is that correct?" Meyers began.

"That's right. I am."

"Mrs. O'Brien, this is Sergeant Donald Mangun of the narcotics squad."

"Narcotics," Maggie breathed, barely audible. "Narcotics, is it? Well, you know, I've got girls here—I figure that's why you've come. What would you be wanting with me?"

"It has come to our attention," Mangun said, "that there is a room in this house reserved for the exclusive use of cocaine addicts who obtain the drug from you and Mr. Boylan. Isn't that right?" Maggie stared at her desk, silent. What was the use of lying? They seemed to know the whole setup; they had only to look around in back, and they'd see a bunch of them right in there now, sniffing and dreaming. Damn Pat! Where was he?

"Well, that's about right," she said at last. "And how, may I ask, did all this come to your attention, as you put it?"

"Through a man named Carrick."

"Carrick?"

"An addict."

"Ah, Carrick. We threw him out of here—him and his needle."

"Yes, so he said. Will you show us the room now?"

"Why should I?"

"We'll have to search the place."

"Do you have a warrant? Let me see the warrant, if you please."

"Certainly." Meyers produced a document which looked as though it might have been a search warrant, although Maggie wouldn't have known one if her life depended on it. If only Pat were here—he would know all right.

"Well," she said, "you can look to your heart's content. I have work to do."

The two policemen, seeing they were to get no help, poked around the place till they reached the darkly comfortable, well-furnished sitting room, where several men sat silently sipping coffee and listening to the radio. The telltale wrappers had been left on small tables and in ashtrays nearby, some still containing bits of the white powder which had become the addicts' life and their solace.

"What happens now?" Maggie inquired in a peremptory tone, as they returned from their tour.

"I'm afraid that I must place you under arrest."

"And what is the charge?"

"Possession."

Maggie suddenly panicked, and her temper flared. "If you are still in possession of your senses you will clear out of here," she retorted. "I have a great many friends in very high places in this town, who just might take a dim view of your busting into my place and making trouble for me."

"We did not 'bust' into your place, Mrs. O'Brien, and I have a warrant, which gives me the right to come in and search the entire house if I think that is necessary."

"And what did you find back there that incriminates me?"

"Six men sitting with open decks of cocaine in front of them."

"And what makes you think they got the stuff from me? How do you know they didn't bring it in here themselves? Any of our clients has the right to sit wherever he chooses in this place. I don't watch them every minute."

"Would you like us to conduct a thorough search of this house until we find your supply?" They had her in a tight corner, from which there was clearly no easy way out.

"No, I certainly do not want you tearing the place apart on a night like this. I do not."

"Then perhaps you would be so kind as to accompany us to the police station," Meyers said with the faintest touch of irony.

Leaving instructions for Pat with the cashier and the bouncer, Maggie fetched her coat and departed.

At the police station she was booked and charged with possession of narcotics but was released as soon as Pat was able to post the necessary bail, which was later that night. The next step was to find a sharp lawyer and get out of this mess as expeditiously as possible.

There was in Chicago at the time a renowned criminal attorney who had gained a considerable reputation for his work in the Federal courts. Business came to him from Al Capone and various other hoodlums, as well as from some of the more respectable lawbreakers, and it was to him that Maggie ultimately turned in her hour of need.

This attorney was an exceedingly busy man in the 1930's, and was often obliged to refer some of his clients to his assistant and chief acolyte, a young lawyer appropriately called Peter Justice. Thus it was that Maggie was greeted, on the day of her first visit to the lawyer's offices, not by the great man himself but by Justice.

"I've come to see your boss," she announced in her soft voice. She was very smartly dressed that day, with her copper hair piled up on top of her head in a mass of curls, and noting the sedate demure manner, cupid's-bow mouth, and violet eyes smiling at him, Justice thought he had never seen anyone so marvelous. "Well, he isn't here," he said, staring at Maggie. "He's in court on a murder case and asked me to try to do what I could for you. It is Mrs. O'Brien, isn't it?"

"That's right. I called earlier in the week." The cupid's bow parted and turned up at the corners as, placing her gloved hand on Justice's cheek, Maggie said, "But you're a baby! You've still got fuzz on your chin! How are you going to help me?"

Justice was paralyzed. "Well," he started, his voice cracking a bit, "I think I can. I wouldn't be trusted with the case if I couldn't handle it. I look a lot younger than I am."

Maggie sighed. "All right, baby," she said, "then let me tell you what you need to know, and we'll see."

It became apparent to Maggie after conferring with Justice awhile, that, although he was young and perhaps a trifle green, he was no fool and, what is more, under the circumstances would devote himself to her problem in a way that the more experienced lawyer might not. Justice had heard all about Maggie's House and was actually rather thrilled to meet her; it was hard to believe that this charming woman was what she was.

"What I don't understand," Maggie said, "is why they let me run a house for four years without making a peep, then all of a sudden come down on me like the avenging angel over a bit of snow."

"Narcotics is considerably more serious than the other," Justice suggested. "I mean, it can do people a lot more harm, especially if they graduate to heroin." Justice was pleased that he knew so much about the problem; he had done his homework.

"You mean sex doesn't do anybody any harm, Mr. Justice?" Maggie was kittenish, enjoying the effect she was having on this handsome young man.

"Not so far as I'm concerned," he replied. "In fact, in my opinion, prostitution shouldn't even be considered a crime."

"Well, you're a very sensible young man, I must say. That's just what I've always thought myself." They laughed heartily, enjoying the relaxed mood that had developed between them. "I think that before long you had better come over to my place and have a look around—get some idea of the setup. I was arrested purely on the basis of what they saw in that room, and as far as I can see, they can't prove anything by that."

"The tip, you say, came from a junkie who was angry because you threw him out of your place?"

"That's right."

"Not a very reliable source of information, but you said they did see the room where people were using cocaine?"

"Yes, they did."

"Did they show you a search warrant, Mrs. O'Brien?"

"Oh, please call me Maggie. I like it better. I did see it for a minute, yes, but they didn't give me time to read what it said or anything. I wouldn't have known what it was supposed to say. Pat would have known, but he was out."

"I see. Well, let's go over to your place Mrs.—Maggie, and you tell me exactly what they saw."

Justice did the best he could to appear nonchalant about the visit to Maggie's house, but if the truth were known, he had never been inside such an establishment in his life and was unmistakably excited about it. Looking at him, Maggie sensed this but would rather have died than let him see that she knew.

Justice was astonished by what he saw when he entered Maggie's club. He had been led to believe, by his parents among others, that houses of ill-repute were invariably run by brazen hoydens of indescribably evil character and that the girls, generally lodged in a vulgar, glittering, and lascivious ambience, were hideous ambulating disease-carriers, heavily painted to conceal the rot beneath. Instead, Justice was ushered into a tastefully furnished and dignified foyer, dominated by the curving staircase and a splendid crystal chandelier which hung from the center of the ceiling. To the left was a large room filled with books and papers, where men sat smoking and chatting; to the right there was a coat room for guests.

Arriving at Maggie's office behind the stairs, Justice was introduced to Pat who, groomed as he was like a proper businessman, seemed a very civilized sort of fellow. As Maggie had some domestic business to attend to, Pat accompanied the young lawyer on the rest of the tour.

"Up here," he explained as they reached the top of the stairs, "is where all the rooms are—here, and on the next two floors as well. As you can see, when the girls aren't too busy, they sit around in this part, playin' cards and what-not in their jockey suits, where they can relax a bit, an' let the Johns get a look at 'em at the same time. Maggie and I have the top o' the house."

"But the girls are really beautiful," Justice exclaimed, gazing at the many lovely calves, ankles, and thighs encased in net stockings, which seemed to grow out of the brief lacy costumes all the girls wore. Some faces were solemn, others were sweet, but all were pretty, and smiled charmingly at Justice as he passed. The landing on the second floor, where they congregated, was comfortably furnished with sofas, chairs, and tables, and provided a meeting ground for the girls and their clients; doors leading to three or four rooms were evenly spaced around the curving walls, their molded exteriors shining and clean.

"Why do you call those costumes jockey suits?" Justice inquired innocently. Pat's eyes twinkled.

"Surely you can figure that one out, Mr. Justice. What do jockeys do, after all?"

"They ride horses."

"Well, these ride men." Justice flushed as the girls nearest them began to giggle cheerfully. "I think you better stay here a while an' get a real education," he continued, enjoying Justice's discomfort. "These girls'll teach ye more in an hour than ye ever learned at law school in a year, that I can assure ye."

"I suppose we could all do with some educating of one sort or another," Justice parried, watching Pat's expression change.

"Yeah, well, I guess that's right too."

"Now I want to see that room downstairs in the back, and I want you to tell me exactly what the situation was when Maggie showed the cops around."

"She'll have to do that herself. I wasn't here at the time." Pat did not like Justice's use of Maggie's first name.

"Yes. So she said." Justice noted with some satisfaction that Pat had dropped his condescending paternalistic tone. "I can't get over how nice those girls look," he continued gaily. "I mean you could almost take one home to Mother." Pat was increasingly irritated by this young fellow and was becoming peevish. Hoping to regain the dominant position, he chose this moment to give Justice some of the harsher details.

"They're all cocaine addicts, Mr. Justice. That's how we keep 'em on the job. If they leave here, they're cut off."

"I see. They like cocaine more than men, I suppose."

"They hate men. Once they've worked in a house like this, no matter what kind, they have nothing but contempt for our sex, I can promise ye. They know the Johns are only here because their own women are too bleedin' clean to' soil with cheap lust."

"How do you handle the traffic?"

"We got anywhere from twelve to fourteen girls working in shifts for three dollars a job. If the John wants it a second time, the girl has a buzzer she pushes, and the bouncer comes an' shows the sod out. The big nights, of course, are Friday and Saturday—actually, they start comin' at noon then, and we go on until seven in the mornin'. Then it's clean up, change the sheets and the cold cream jars, fumigate the place—"

"Why the cold cream jars?"

"Well, y'see, most o' these guys come in here with a load on. Now the girl figures they don't know what the hell is goin' on anyhow, so she just covers the inside o' one hand with cold cream an' slips it under her backside. She grabs hold o' the guy, an' he thinks he's got it in 'er, an' that way she don't have t'be bothered with actually bangin' the sod."

"What happens when the John discovers he's been cheated?"

"Why's he been cheated? He comes off the same in any case. I'll tell you, the thing about hookers is that they're lazy an' vain, an' all they want in the world is for somebody to love 'em —man or woman, doesn't make any difference which—an' treat 'em like the ladies that they are not. . . . It's a fairly hopeless situation, when ye come t' think of it, but once they're hooked on it, it's hard fer 'em t' get out, especially if they're on junk, an' they need the money all the time. It's still the easiest way fer any dame to make a buck, though, an' that's a fact."

Pat felt better, having delivered himself of this enlightening speech, and slapping Justice on the back, he proceeded back down the stairs. "Well, ol' man," he said jovially, "I hope I didn't shatter all yer illusions about my lovely little girls."

Justice was looking a bit pale; he was as yet unaccustomed to hearing so much raw speech at one time. "Do you dis-

cuss these various things with Maggie—I mean, frankly like
that?" he ventured.

"Oh, God, no!" Boylan replied. "She doesn't even want
to know about all that. I take care of these things for her. Margaret has had a rather pampered existence, y' know. She'd never
sit still fer talk like that. She's quite a lady, after all."

"Yes, she is."

Justice was relieved to be placed once again in Maggie's
gentler care and concluded his rounds with a viewing of the
room which had produced all the trouble. Maggie explained just
where everyone had been sitting and how many wrappers there
were and exactly what was said. There were no sniffers there that
day, nor would there be for some time to come.

Justice's next visit was to the police.

It was not ultimately a difficult case; Justice got Maggie
off on a motion to quash, the charges being suppressed because
the document presented to Maggie as a search warrant turned
out to be a fake; no judge had signed it. Furthermore, there had
been no warrant for her arrest. In fact Maggie was never prosecuted—not this time or ever.

Margaret O'Brien and Peter Justice subsequently became
great friends, especially after he discovered that she loved to
cook. She would often call him on a slow night and say, "Hello,
baby. How about some dinner?" and he would run over after
work to the house on Washington Street, and sit chatting by
the hour with Pat, while Maggie prepared some rare gastronomic
delight, and then the conversation might run on into the small
hours of the morning.

Maggie was very refined in those days and became more
so, it seemed, each year. Eventually there was no trace of either
an Irish brogue or a midwestern twang left in her voice, and she
always dressed with exceptional good taste. She hated perfume,
habitually using bath oil instead, of which she said that the scent
became stronger with the passing of the day, being most potent
at night, when it was supposed to be. She became interested in
the arts, and often sent Justice paintings or bits of sculpture as
presents on his birthday or at Christmas. Justice, ever chagrined
about being designated as Maggie's "baby," grew a moustache in
an effort to appear older and more substantial, and he has not
abandoned it to this day.

In the winter of 1933, the year after Maggie's arrest, Pat developed pneumonia, and one snowy night, with Maggie sitting on the bed holding his hand to her mouth as though trying to breath new life into it, he died. "It's true," she had said trivially in her immense grief. "Nothing good can happen to me when it snows."

Maggie was thoroughly shattered by Pat's death, and for many months she would see no one but Peter Justice. She would talk distractedly about Pat, or they would just sit together and read, enjoying the quiet. Pat had been her shield, her lawyer, friend, and lover, and there would be no replacing him. At thirty-five, she felt that her life was over. She even lost interest in the house, for which she now had a new manager, and business had never been better. She depended increasingly on Justice to keep her from totally losing contact with the real world, and he worried about her a great deal.

One day, late in 1935, like a bolt from heaven and without any preamble, Maggie called her friend and said, "Baby, I'm getting married—going away. I want to say good-bye and I love you." She closed the house and just walked away from all that was past, presumably to become a housewife—and perhaps even a mother, who could tell? No one knew where the man had come from or who he was, and Maggie was never heard of again in Chicago.

The Life is not kind to the more "mature" woman, and most aging prostitutes just wilt painfully and die alone in some rooming house or public hospital. A surprising number, however, manage to marry as did Maggie, and there are those who say they make very good wives. These are the lucky ones.

Chapter VII

For Love and Money

IT was April 5, 1961, and a judge had solemnly passed sentence of life imprisonment on two people, both of whom now lowered their heads and wept. The man—tall, handsome, graying, and in his early forties—cried out, "Thank God!" for he had narrowly escaped death, and turning toward the girl, he shouted, "We'll fight it, darling. We're still alive."

The girl, a redhead, rounded in body and face, once possessed of enormous sex appeal, manifested a somewhat different reaction. "No, no," she moaned, "I'll be an old woman when I get out!" And the matrons led her away.

The setting for the climax of this unhappy drama was the Los Angeles County courthouse, where on April 6, 1961, the most sensational triangle murder case since the roaring twenties reached its ultimate conclusion, sending Carole Tregoff and Dr. Raymond Bernard Finch to prison for life.

In 1922, the Rev. Edward Wheeler Hall and his mistress, Eleanor Mills, were found shot to death beneath a crab-apple tree on the outskirts of New Brunswick, New Jersey. No one was ever convicted for this murder, although many suspected the cuckold, Mr. James Mills, and in 1926 Mrs. Hall and her two brothers were tried and subsequently acquitted. In 1928, Ruth Snyder and Henry Judd Gray were executed at Sing Sing for the slaying of Mrs. Snyder's husband Albert under similar circumstances.

Both these cases had been subject to a tremendous amount of play in the press, but nothing to compare with the orgy of eager reportage which accompanied the events leading up to the conviction of Tregoff and Finch. For months prior to April 6, the last day of the court proceedings, a line had formed as early as six o'clock in the morning outside the courthouse, consisting of people anxious to obtain the best seat in the house. Certain of these people, more interested in crude profit than in witnessing the agonized proceedings, arrived early, then sold their places in line to some latecomer for as much as ten dollars.

Life imprisonment in California, which still retains the death penalty, includes the possibility of parole after seven years; however, the average time spent behind bars prior to parole, for both men and women, is eleven years and four months. Under these circumstances, Carole Tregoff would be an "old woman" of thirty-five when she got out; Finch, fifty-five. Finch was grateful to be allowed to live even in prison; Carole was already regretting that portion of her life which was to be lost.

How on earth, the fascinated public wondered, does a good-looking young girl like Carole permit herself to become involved in something so serious? How can she be so stupid? So reckless? Part of the answer surely lies in her background, but part is to be found in that portion of the human mind which controls, or fails to control, people's emotions, and the secrets of which, subtly coloring their character, can only be guessed at by the frustrated sociologist or puzzled intellectual.

The press had described Carole variously as Finch's friend, paramour, receptionist, secretary, and also as model and cocktail waitress. They were not confused; she had been all these things within a remarkably short space of time.

Born in 1935 to Mr. and Mrs. James Tregoff, the descendents of Russian immigrants, Carole had an early childhood that was anything but idyllic. In spite of the fact that her father adored her, which partially compensated for her mother's unfathomable indifference, Carole was a lonely little girl, an only child who never overcame the crippling shyness which overpowers most children at some point in their lives. Her parents seemed to be constantly embattled, and when she was three years old, they divorced.

Her mother evidently did not want her, and inasmuch as her father had to appear early each morning at a restaurant in downtown Los Angeles, where he worked all day as a chef, he was obliged to impose upon a good friend and neighbor, Mrs. Belle Morris, who agreed to look after the child. Mrs. Morris, who had been married previously, had a son called Donald Williams who was close to Carole's age and served as a playmate for her. Mr. Tregoff visited his daughter often, maintaining a close tie with her, and all things considered, life could have been a good deal worse for her.

When Carole had been living with Mrs. Morris for just over three years, Mr. Tregoff fell in love with a pretty woman who worked as a waitress in the same café. They used to enjoy having a drink together after work and chatting about their respective problems, and eventually they were married. One of the reasons Jim Tregoff wanted to marry this woman, whose name was Gladys, was because she seemed more than willing to have little Carole come back to live with them, and promised that she would always love her and look after her as though she were her own. Joint custody had been awarded the Tregoffs at the time of their divorce, but, as Gladys Tregoff was to testify later, "Carole is her daddy's girl, and so she has always been with him more than her mother."

Gladys Tregoff was as good as her word, and insofar as her father's modest salary could provide it, Carole had everything that a little girl needs to grow into a healthy teen-ager. She traded cards, skipped rope, chewed gum, became a cheerleader, tried baton-twirling, wore bobby sox, put her hair up, talked on the telephone, and held hands in the movies. Living as she was in a relatively unsophisticated atmosphere, Carole's interests turned early to the more fundamental relationships, and by the time she was sixteen, she was going steady. At eighteen, upon graduating from high school, she married her childhood sweetheart and became Mrs. James Pappa.

Jimmy Pappa was proud of his young wife, she was outgoing, pretty, and very sexy, which was important to him. Jimmy had what amounted to a mania for all things which spoke of virility, whether it was large muscles or the manner in which a man combed his hair, and having a wife whose face, body, walk, and manner bespoke an uninhibited sexuality was very good for his "image."

A construction worker by vocation, Jimmy was also an avid physical culturist, what some would describe as a muscle man. Many specialized health foods found their way into his carefully monitored diet, and he performed strenuous daily exercises to keep his overdeveloped form from running to fat. Some of his clothes required special tailoring to accommodate his bulging arm, chest, and leg muscles, about which he was inordinately vain. Carole, too, admired his physique immensely.

Shortly after her marriage, Carole went to work as a commercial artists' model, posing for calendar art and various other nonfashion ads. This incipient career only bloomed for three weeks, however, for although Carole had not yet been obliged to pose in the nude, Jimmy did not like the idea of his wife spending most of her spare time in the company of artists and photographers under compromising circumstances. They had their first real quarrel over this; Carole liked the work, as it flattered her ego and provided her with some extra money in the bargain. Ultimately, Jimmy admitted that he really disapproved of married women working at all, but inasmuch as his salary failed to provide the small luxuries Carole demanded, he had little choice but to permit it.

Thus Carole abandoned her modeling career and began to look around for some other occupation. Since she did not possess any specialized skills, there was not a great deal she was equipped to do, but she finally came upon an ad announcing that someone was in need of a receptionist. The job turned out to be located in the impressive new West Covina Medical Center halfway between Los Angeles and Pomona, and having survived the interview, Carole was hired. The clinic was owned and operated by Dr. Raymond Bernard Finch, who was to be Carole's employer and boss.

Bernie Finch, the product of an urban professional background, had decided at an early age that he wanted to be a doctor like his father. He had been brilliant at medical school, although, as an only child he had evidently been spoiled and pampered, the results of which made him unpopular among some of his classmates. He had become egocentric, selfish, and intemperate, qualities which failed to moderate as he reached adulthood, but he was a fine surgeon and successful with women, suffering no apparent sense of inferiority. There was an inflexible peevish facet in his nature, which found him breaking his racket if he lost at tennis and working himself into a proper rage if given a wrong or misleading clue during a game of charades.

Bernie's father, Dr. Raymond R. Finch, was an optometrist, who had made a substantial fortune in California by subdividing his suburban property when the big real-estate boom began on the West Coast after the war. As a result he was able to send his son to the University of California and then to the College of Medical Evangelists, an institution run by the Seventh Day Adventists. Bernie divided his internship between the White Memorial Hospital in Los Angeles and another Adventist institution, and then opened a clinic with his brother-in-law. Catering to the fashionable matrons who lived in and around the rich suburban community of West Covina, they built a lucrative practice.

In the early 1940's Finch married a girl called Frances, whom he had known since they were both in high school, and they produced two children. Around 1948 the marriage started to go sour, due largely to the influence of one Barbara Dougherty, a very attractive, athletic brunette, whose own marriage was in the process of breaking up. The two couples had become friends and were often seen together on various social occasions. When the smoke of the ensuing battles cleared away, both couples were divorced and married to each other's spouses, Bernie having divorced Frances in 1949 to marry Barbara Dougherty, and Forrest Lyle Dougherty having married Frances Finch. Frances' two children went to live with their mother and stepfather, while Barbara brought her only offspring, a daughter, to share her new home with Finch. Bernie married Barbara in 1951, and two years later she gave birth to a son, named Raymond Finch, or Raymie, as they were to call him. From the time of Raymie's birth onward, this marriage also began to deteriorate.

Barbara had been upset, ill-tempered, and depressed after Raymie's birth, which irritated Bernie, and it was that year that he embarked on his first love affair since marrying for the second time. The woman involved was also married, a circumstance which presented many emotional as well as logistical problems, and by the end of 1954 it was over. In the meantime, it did not appear to Bernie that his wife's mood had improved very much, and in 1956 he began paying court to a lonely divorcée who was not unreceptive to his attentions. This also went on for approximately one year before it petered out, and toward the spring of 1957, a voluptuous little redhead called Carole Pappa came to work as a receptionist at the clinic, which event changed the entire course of several lives.

When Carole first turned up at the medical center, her marriage was going along very well. She would stop at the supermarket every day on the way home from work to buy the groceries needed for dinner, and go home to Jimmy who, having ceased his labors at 3:30 or 4:00, would already be there waiting for her. They made love happily every night, and sometimes went to a movie or watched television. Curiously, Carole never became pregnant in nearly four years, but this did not appear to disturb either one of them unduly. Carole sometimes felt that it was not an exciting or particularly inspired existence, but it represented no less than that to which either of them had previously been accustomed. "Mrs. Average American," Carole must have thought. "That's me."

Carole was seated at her desk outside the doctors' offices when Bernie first saw her, and she was quite a sight. Her hair, naturally a potent strawberry blonde worn short and curly, had been chemically altered to a deep copper tone, and on this Monday morning it shone in the matinal sun, which streamed through giant windows into every office and corridor. She wore a short-sleeved cashmere sweater of pale green, which clung to her full bosom like another skin and reflected the mossy hue of her eyes. Bernie could not see the rest of her, which was hidden behind the desk, but what he could see produced a strong impact upon him, stronger perhaps than would be usual, had he first come upon her later in the day and in some more public place. Seeing her like this in his most familiar environment, before he had fully adjusted to the new day, was startling, delightful, but strangely unbalancing.

As he entered, she looked up from her magazine and smiled; she had dimples like an overblown Shirley Temple, but the expression in her eyes was far from innocent.

"Good morning. I'm Dr. Finch."

"Oh, I'm happy to meet you. I'm Carole Pappa, the new receptionist."

"Has anyone shown you around the place?" Finch inquired genially.

"No, not yet."

"Come on. I'll take you for a guided tour. My secretary is here and can take over for a minute."

Bernie was delighted to have an opportunity to exhibit his domain to so attractive and impressionable a witness, and keenly savored every moment. Strolling down the various corridors that connected the different sections of the clinic, they had an opportunity to chat, and Bernie was delighted to see that he had succeeded in impressing his newest employee.

The tour ended, Carole returned to her desk, where someone was waiting to show her how to use the intercom system. Bernie strode briskly into his office and, finding himself confronted with a mass of paperwork, spent the better part of the morning thinking idly about Carole. The following morning he had to operate, however, and he thought he had better get himself pulled together.

Bernie had been busy in the weeks that followed, and he had not found as many opportunities as he would have liked to chat with Carole. He spoke to her each day briefly and thought about her a good deal, spinning amorous fantasies in his mind whenever he had a chance to relax. Shortly after 5:00 each day, he would watch Jimmy's ancient tan Ford as it weaved through the parking lot, turned, and headed back toward Los Angeles. He wondered about Jimmy Pappa; this girl should certainly have been able to do better than to get permanently stuck to a construction worker.

When the pressure eased a bit at the clinic, Bernie decided to ask Carole to have lunch with him. Having become a trifle bored with eating lunch each day with the secretaries and nurses in the clinic cafeteria, Carole was thrilled at the prospect of something more glamorous for a change. She took greater pains with her attire the day she was to lunch with Bernie and, eschewing the usual skirt and sweater, donned a dress which showed more of her bosom than usual as well as more leg. She was not, however, thinking in terms of seduction; with girls like Carole, it is instinctive to put themselves together as attractively as possible for any male companion, regardless of the circumstances. Basically, Carole still thought of Dr. Finch as one of those relatively unattainable people who inhabit another world, are almost generically removed from the majority of other people, and whose tastes, interests, and demands are unique to them.

Their lunch date was uneventful, both materially and conversationally. Bernie spoke mostly about himself, his achievements past and future, while Carole listened. In order to afford himself a brief space in which to eat, he eventually asked her about her family, in which he was not really terribly interested; his attention focused, however, when she came to the part about Jimmy. Could he detect the slightest note of apology or contempt, or was it his imagination? Unconsciously Carole had begun to make comparisons between Jimmy and Dr. Finch in the furthest recesses of her mind and, without being aware of it, rationalized the genesis and quality of her own involvement. As yet she could not quite think of Finch as compatible, but it was in the offing.

The roadhouse in which they had shared that first meal together was located conveniently near the clinic, and in subsequent weeks they met there frequently at the noon hour. Their conversation ultimately became more personal and eventually intimate. Finch confided in Carole about the problems which beset his marriage and which were growing daily more obtrusive. He and his wife had been talking about divorce, but thus far had been reluctant to do anything definite about it. Curiously, nothing much had changed in the Pappa household, apart from the fact that Carole occasionally appeared distracted and strangely thoughtful, where she had never been before.

Soon Bernie and Carole, always seated now in the darkest and most isolated booth in the restaurant at lunchtime, found themselves holding hands, kissing, and exchanging intimate secrets. Carole, fundamentally embued with standard middle-class values, had not given much serious thought to where all this might lead; in Bernie's mind, however, there was only one place it could lead, and that was to bed. His burgeoning desire for Carole was taxing him with sleepless nights, a reduced concentration span, and more trouble at home than he had experienced in a long time. Barbara had finally announced that she was initiating formal divorce proceedings.

Soon after this occurred, Carole informed Bernie that Jimmy was planning a brief trip, the purpose of which was to visit his mother, who lived up north near San Francisco. He was to get some time off over a bank holiday, a day which was not to be a holiday for the employees of the West Covina Medical Center. They made plans to have dinner together the night Jimmy left. Inasmuch as Barbara had reached the point where she no longer cared whether Bernie was actually working late, playing poker with the boys, or sleeping with another woman, her possible concern over his whereabouts on this occasion posed no problem. Carole, apart from anything else, was delighted that she did not have to go with Jimmy to see his mother, who she thought was very sweet but something of a bore. She never liked Jimmy when he was around his mother anyway, for reasons which were quite beyond her capacity to articulate.

On the appointed evening Carole fairly ransacked her closet, pulling every dress she owned out of it and ultimately discarding each one in disgust, cursed the circumstances which made it impossible for her to buy a new one for the occasion. She held up to her body an emerald-green satin number, which Jimmy had bought her the year before to attend a wedding; she wondered how she could ever have found it attractive with its inexpensive gloss shining crudely under the electric light. Remembering that Bernie had told her once that one of the chief characteristics of the "great unwashed" was that they were almost invariably overdressed for any given social occasion, Carole finally decided on a plain black crêpe with a straight skirt and deep V-neck. It was a relatively good dress and showed off her figure nicely, although she wished with all her heart that she had a really beautiful piece of jewelry to place at the nadir of that neckline plunge.

The Pappas lived in a small apartment house at the north end of Los Angeles, and it was there that Carole was collected at 8:00 by her eminent employer. This time Bernie had decided to take Carole to one of the better Japanese restaurants downtown—a fabulous sprawling place high on a hill overlooking the city. The surrounding area had been planted with oriental pine, the gnarled trunks and flat cloudlike shapes lending an authenticity unmatched by any of the other similar places, and lanterns lighted the entrance and adjacent gardens. Carole was charmed and genuinely excited, having never been to such a place in her life; few people of her immediate acquaintance could have afforded it.

They laughed a good deal during dinner and thoroughly enjoyed themselves, although a certain somberness engulfed Bernie's innermost thoughts from time to time, as he allowed his mind to drift back to the gathering storm of Barbara's divorce action.

Under California law, all property is held in common by husband and wife, which in Bernie's case included his interest in the clinic, their expensive house in the West Covina hills, three automobiles, a power boat, and whatever they had in various bank accounts. Notwithstanding these compelling material considerations, Bernie did not want the adverse publicity which would be incurred by divorce proceedings; the clinic was new and, though growing, still operated in the red. A divorce action coming at this time, with all the accompanying whispered conjectures and scuttlebutt, could easily jeopardize his chances of building it into a solidly successful operation quickly, as he had anticipated. If he were able, on the other hand, to persuade Barbara to get a Nevada divorce, the publicity would be less, and he could keep most of his money.

He was sorely tempted to share some of these troubling thoughts with Carole, principally to relieve his own mind; the pressures that were building there, as a result of the insalubrious massing of unwelcome and threatening concerns, corrupted his peace of mind and undermined his pleasure in being with her now in circumstances he relished. Ultimately he balked, afraid that total candor at this moment would spoil the evening, the outcome of which was still not absolutely certain.

When dinner was over, Bernie debated taking Carole for a stroll in the dark formal gardens which provided the setting for the restaurant, but decided instead to go to a Polynesian place for coffee and a dance. This was a great success, for it gave Bernie the opportunity he sought to get physically close to Carole and gauge her responses, which were unequivocally positive. There seemed little point in waiting any longer.

Once back in the red Chrysler convertible, of which Bernie was extremely proud, they did not dissipate their energies on further conversation but kissed each other frantically, as lovers do for the first time or following painful separations. When Bernie moved, however, toward those private and special parts of Carole's body which had occupied the greatest portion of his thoughts, she appeared to withdraw and manifest an uncharacteristic inhibition. It suddenly occurred to him what was wrong, and one can easily imagine the conversation which followed:

"I love you," he said, amidst extravagant pronouncements as to the perfections of her physique and their effect upon him. Abstracting this statement from the onrushing, passionate whole, Carole said, "Do you really? Are you sure?"

"About what, darling? That you have the most tempting body in the world?"

"No, silly. That you love me."

"If I wasn't sure, I wouldn't have said it. I want you more than anything on earth."

This evidently did the trick, for they spent the night, sleepless, in a motel, where Bernie's deepest longings and most luxurious, intemperate daydreams were generously transformed into reality.

The late Dorothy Kilgallen was later to refer uncharitably to all this as "the college freshman technique." She informed her readers, further, that Carole had, throughout her life, wanted to be noticed and to be loved within the context of the True Love ideal. She read bad poetry, sang sentimental songs, and "even dreamed in poetic terms." Somehow Miss Kilgallen had discovered that the boys with whom Carole had gone to school learned that, to make it with Carole, they had to play the game; she was not just another petting partner, but Venus, Eve, Isolde.

At a later and much less carefree moment in her life, Carole was to be characterized as a "latter-day Lady Macbeth," to which she responded by asking, "What's a Lady Macbeth?" It seems unlikely, therefore, that she would have had the slightest insight into the identities of the other three ladies, apart perhaps from Eve about whom she may have heard something in Sunday school. Certain members of the fourth estate, however, are rarely denied their amusements over something as trivial as exaggeration.

It had been a glowing night in October when Carole became Bernie's mistress, and throughout the autumn their romance burned—in restaurants, bars, automobiles, motels, Las Vegas casinos, and even hospital corridors. Before long, they established a permanent love nest in one of West Covina's more elegant motels. For months Jimmy Pappa remained ignorant and happy, while Barbara Finch grew more militant, inflexible, and vindictive.

One night, within earshot of the Finches' Swedish governess, Marie-Ann Lidholm, Bernie threatened during a quarrel to kill Barbara by forcing her into a car and pushing it over a cliff. By May, 1959, Marie-Ann was writing home to her mother in Gothenburg, Sweden, about some of the dark events which beclouded the lives of her employers: "Mrs. Finch told me everything in the morning. . . . He told her that if she didn't take everything back about the divorce, he had a man in Las Vegas to whom he would pay thousands of dollars to kill her."

Barbara Finch had evidently taken this threat seriously, for the following day, on May 15, she called in the West Covina police, who dismissed it as a domestic squabble. She had then consulted a private detective about acquiring a bodyguard, saying, "I probably won't be alive by Christmas."

The month of May was decisive in the sense that all the various elements, both psychological and practical, came to focus on the adulterous couple at once. Barbara Finch knew by now of the affair in progress between her husband and his "secretary," and had shattered the relative peace of the Pappa home by calling Jimmy one night and telling him all about it. Jimmy was astonished, wounded, and furious. In a matter of weeks, having had the whole thing out with Carole, he agreed that she should move out of the house and that they should be legally separated.

In the meantime, Barbara Finch had made manifest her threats against Bernie in regard to the divorce, claiming half of everything he had, plus a temporary alimony of $1,650 per month and $350 per month in child support, until such time as the divorce became final. Her attorney's fee was to be $15,000 and court costs $3,000, both of which she demanded that Bernie pay. In addition—and what infuriated Bernie to the extent that he had physically attacked his wife—Barbara had frozen their joint accounts, so that he could not even cash a check which was not also endorsed by her. She had obtained a restraining order, which utterly crippled Bernie's ability to spend money until the time of the hearing, scheduled for June 11, when the matter of division would be formally settled. Meanwhile, all Bernie's assets and income were channeled into the frozen joint account. On June 7, an affidavit was filed showing Bernie to be in contempt of the order to pay two thousand dollars in legal fees, five hundred dollars in court costs, and two hundred dollars per month in alimony. A hearing on the contempt charge was scheduled for July 23.

The initial action was not taken by Barbara Finch, however, until Bernie had seriously threatened her life the first time. At this point she began to be genuinely frightened and was even advised by an actor friend to obtain a gun with which to protect herself against possible future attacks. Actually, had Bernie been less violent and somewhat more diplomatic in his relations with his wife, he might have saved himself some grief as well as some money, but such was not his temper.

Needless to say, the Finches did not see a great deal of each other during this period, Bernie spending all his time either at the medical center or with Carole, and Barbara whiling away the tormented hours of her days playing tennis at the South Hills Country Club, which happened to be conveniently located at the foot of the hill on which the Finches lived. Barbara loved tennis, and during these frustrated and unhappy months, it had served as the only activity which could take her mind off the troubles which besieged her.

Barbara's plunge into divorce action and Carole's departure from Jimmy's house were coeval events, Carole having then immediately gone back to her former foster parents, who were living in Las Vegas. This turned out to be extremely convenient for Bernie as well, for not only did Bernie welcome the opportunity to get Carole into another state and out of reach of the California divorce courts, but it placed Carole at the heart of the rich Las Vegas night life for which they had both acquired an exceptional taste. Carole got a job as a waitress at the Sands Hotel, where by day she catered to the wishes of a rich and demanding clientele, while by night she was transformed into another spoiled and impatient customer on the arm of Dr. R. B. Finch.

Living again with Belle Morris, however, had its severe limitations. It was nice to renew her connections with the family, especially Don Williams, her childhood friend, but it meant that she and Bernie were continually faced with the problem of where to go to be alone and how to explain the whole situation to Mrs. Morris. Most of the time they were obliged to meet in the middle of the day, as it was only by night that Bernie could hope to solve some of the problems which had to be sorted out somehow between himself and Barbara. The knowledge that he was out with Carole only served as fuel for her fires in any case, as the litigation grew more abrasive.

In view of all this, the lovers decided that they had better rent an apartment of their own in Las Vegas, either in a rooming house or a motel, as they had done in West Covina, so that they would always have a place to meet and could do so any time they wished. This meant, however, that Bernie had to fly to Las Vegas each time he wanted to see Carole, which only contributed to the frantic quality of his complicated and emotionally taxing life.

In the period between the beginning of May and the third week in July, 1959, Bernie could only be described as a nervous wreck, a desperate and driven man, pursued by the amalgamated furies of love, lust, pride, greed, and the pressures of his work. His days during the last twenty months had consisted of a kind of marathon, with operations in the morning, a frantic dash by plane to Las Vegas at lunch time to see Carole, back to the clinic for more work in the late afternoon, then the apprehensive drive home, where he would spend the evening and most of the night locked in combat with Barbara over familiar and apparently irresolvable issues. He began going to a psychiatrist two or three times a week after work, and in late May, he grew so desperate about the financial straitjacket in which he found himself that he forged Barbara's name on a check for three thousand dollars. His only consolation was Carole—her body and her empathy.

By now Carole knew every detail of the terrible hot war which raged between Bernie and his wife, and which posed a serious threat to her as well. She and Bernie were in love and had even spoken of marriage, which Carole was sure would become a reality were Barbara Finch not so much in evidence. Carole occasionally permitted herself to daydream about living in the big ranch house on Larkhill Drive, whose rooms, views, and swimming pool she had heard so much about, picturing herself as the smartly dressed matron who would drink her Tom Collins and eat her lunch at the country club in the company of other women of leisure. Furthermore, in spite of her general lack of intellect, she had fully grasped the implications of the community-property laws, the disadvantages of which had become an obsession with Bernie.

Although it would be foolish to try to guess exactly what was said during the many intense discussions which Carole and Bernie had concerning their difficulties, it is safe to say that, whenever they weren't making love, they were hashing out "the problem." Certainly they had long since shifted from the general to the particular and had decided to take some sort of action, for there were indications to this effect in May, when Carole left Jimmy and went to stay with Belle Morris.

One night, when she was still at Belle's, Carole and Don Williams found themselves out on the porch after supper sipping Cokes, and Carole began to ask what Don thought were some very strange questions. As Don later testified, the dialogue had gone something like this:

"Listen, Don," she had said innocently, "do you know any people—I mean, criminal types and racketeers—around Vegas?"

Don was astonished. "Well, no. I don't know any myself. I know they're all around here and who some of 'em are, even. But I never had anything to do with them. Why?"

"Well, I have a problem that can only be solved by somebody like that. I mean they would know how to go about it."

"What's it all about?"

"I can't tell you that right now, 'cause there's somebody else involved who's quite well known, and it wouldn't be fair."

"Come to think of it," Don said, attracted by the mystery, "I do know someone who knows a person like that— a classmate of mine from college. I don't know why, but he seems to know a lot of these guys pretty well. I'll ask him if you want me to, but I don't know how it'll work out."

"Do that, will you?" Carole urged. "And let me know as soon as you've found out anything."

A short time later, after Carole had moved out of Belle's into her own little apartment, she received a call from Don saying that he had made contact with his friend, who had put him in touch with a certain John Patrick Cody.

"What sort of a guy is he?" she had inquired anxiously.

"I don't know. I haven't seen him yet. Just talked to him on the phone."

"Well, is he a murderer, a thief, or what?"

"I'm not sure. I know he's not involved in gambling, though. Dick said something about bum-check passing and blackmail, stuff like that, but I'm not really sure. You'll have to talk to him yourself and decide what you want to do."

"Okay. You set up an appointment with him some evening around six when I get off work, and we'll go and talk to him. You can come too, if you like."

"Okay, Carole. Will do. I hope you're not in any trouble. . . ."

"No. I'm not in trouble—not yet anyway," she added, laughing. "Do it soon."

The meeting was arranged a few days later, and on the evening in question, Don and Carole went off together to meet John Cody in Foxy's tavern. They recognized him instantly, standing at the bar, for, as they both remarked later, he looked exactly like those movie gangsters back in the thirties. With his hair slicked back from a pocked brow, his pointed shoes, dapper dark suit, and white-on-white tie, he might have come from Central Casting. Having introduced themselves, the three sat down together and ordered some beers. Carole was clearly nervous, hardly knowing how to begin. Bernie had told her to be extremely careful and to try to find out as much as she could about this character before putting any sort of proposition to him. She needn't have worried about getting the interview going, for Cody did most of the talking.

Cody was a cheap petty hoodlum about whom the most that could be said was that he possessed a certain vulgar good looks. Lean and slight, he was not a strong man, nor did he speak with any authority or charm, but his fingernails were clean and his clothes flashy and neat, and that was enough to persuade Carole that she had latched onto the real article. Carole asked many of the same questions that she had asked Don when Cody's name was first introduced, but Cody was elusive and unenlightening; he was content to let Carole believe anything she wanted as to what he was capable of doing. He admitted to nothing but at the same time failed to deny anything. He spoke mostly of his triumphs in relation to women and his exceptional attractiveness to them, hoping perhaps to interest Carole and enjoy some success with her. Williams stayed out of this conversation to a large extent, watching the other two as they tried to shake each other down. There was a certain fascination in observing the ladies' man and this sensuous woman work on each other, each eagerly looking for the signs of potential personal gain. The meeting ended, according to Williams, without mutual assumptions having been established or any specific deals having been made.

The next time, however, Carole and Cody met alone, and shortly after that, Dr. Finch joined them for a third rendezvous. In the months that followed there were a number of people who would have given a great deal to know precisely what went on at these meetings and what the doctor and his mistress actually said to Cody, let alone what was understood between themselves. These are things that no one will ever know, and which, had they been known, would have changed the course of subsequent events considerably. Established as a certainty—only because everyone involved admitted to it—was that there came a time when Cody was given $1,400 by Carole, money which came from the doctor, to deal somehow with Barbara Finch. Also validated as fact was that Cody, having been paid half this sum, failed to do whatever it was that he was supposed to do, slipping off instead to dissipate the money at the gaming tables. Intimidated by his furious employers, he then apparently collected the second half, promising that this time his mission would be accomplished. On this occasion, however, he simply disappeared with the cash, and neither Carole nor Bernie saw or spoke to him again until the following winter, when they confronted each other in court.

The summer of 1959 was unpleasant for everybody in the Los Angeles area. There were too many oppressively hot days, when an ill wind blew hot and dry across the parched hills, and the smog, gathered down under the clouds, was unable to roll out over them. People coughed and wheezed, their eyes smarting, their breath coming in painful gasps, and on the leaden, humid days, housewives could hardly drag themselves from the house to the supermarket, so hot and so weary were they after their eight hours' sleep. The suicide rate rose slightly as did the number of homicides, and only the cheerless unfreshening occasional rains came to cool the restless inhabitants.

By July, Finch's obsessive preoccupation with Carole and the accelerated machinations of his wife to obtain the divorce in California were seriously endangering his ability to

work, a condition which was causing his father grave concern.
The senior Finch, living just next door but a bit further down
the side of the hill, was able to observe his son's comings and
goings, and was not encouraged by what he saw.

Carole also had reached the end of her patience and was
anxious to have the thing resolved one way or the other. She
told Bernie that, however it was ultimately solved, they were
going to have to do it themselves, and on the night of July 18
they drove together from Las Vegas to West Covina to see
Barbara Finch and settle the issues once and for all.

They had an early dinner at a small restaurant in Las
Vegas, and, finishing around 8:00, climbed into Carole's 1957
de Soto and drove to West Covina. It was a relatively clear
night, which boasted a moon and some stars, with a subdued
breeze rustling through the spiked fronds of the palm trees.
They hardly spoke at all during the long drive, each lost in his
private thoughts, both sharing an isolating gloom, which
threatened to engulf them.

It was nearly midnight when they arrived in West
Covina, and having decided to leave the car in the parking lot
outside the country club, they walked up the steep hill off Larkhill Drive, which led to the Finches' house, Carole carrying
Bernie's brown attaché case. There were lights on in the house,
but no car in the garage, indicating that Barbara was still out.
They walked into the garage and sat down on some steps which
led into the house and prepared to wait. Holding hands, they
looked at each other from time to time, but did not speak.

The Finches' ranch-type house, situated at the top of a
hill so steep that it could not be seen from directly below, was
typical of California. Shaped essentially like a squared horse-
shoe, it was painted pale green, trimmed in a reddish brown,
and surrounded by thick box hedge, which led along the walk-
way to the front door. The endemic aquamarine swimming pool
sat in the center of the U, protected from view by the two-car
garage which thrust itself out into the wide parking area just
in front of it. Winding up the steep, curving drive, therefore,
one's first view of the house was really of the garage, the front
door being situated around to the side.

The house had a sweeping view of the barren Covina
Hills, whose rounded brown contours were often steeped in

sinister purple shadows or hot summer haze. The house itself, and the South Hills Country Club just below, were surrounded with plane trees, scrub pine, bougainvillea, small palms, poplars, and masses of yellow, white, and lavender wildflowers, which grew exuberantly among the rocks. A curious species of short sea-green cactus sprouted everywhere in lieu of grass, the individual blades of which stood stiffly, like coarse fingers of juicy ripe flesh which bled if torn from the ground. Inhospitable as it was, the cactus was more refreshing to look at than the dusty, treeless, reddish hills, contoured as though for cultivation and covered with inflammable scrub.

The country club, nestled at the foot of the residential section, squatted in the midst of a lush palm-lined golf course, dark green clay tennis courts, and a vast swimming pool, which was surrounded by tables, umbrellas, and various other furniture designed for lounging. The club itself, roughly fashioned in striated stucco, was trimmed in a sick green and sported a roof of terra-cotta, apparently covered in sand and small rocks. Yellow and orange zinnias lined the drive, and the ample parking lot held its share of large expensive cars. This is where Barbara Finch spent most of her time and where Bernie often relaxed in happier times on weekends.

They had been waiting for nearly forty-five minutes when they became aware of headlights sweeping over the roof of the senior Dr. Finch's house next door and illuminating the thriving shrubbery which lined the long drive. Carole and Bernie stood up tensely and moved to the far side of the garage. For an instant Bernie could not think why Barbara was in the Chrysler, for this was his own car; he had forgotten that he had switched cars with her a few days before, at her request. The car slid into the garage and came to an abrupt halt as Barbara spotted the two standing in the night shadows. The radio was playing the current popular hit, "Love Me Forever," and Carole remembered thinking how loud it was.

Eyes staring, mouth open, Barbara said not a word but suddenly bent over and reached under the seat of the car. As she got out, her two astonished visitors saw that she was holding a .38 revolver in her trembling right hand. Finch flew at her, grasping her arm and wrenching the gun free from the terrified woman. Lunging into the front seat of the car, he grabbed something and threw it at Carole. As startled as she was, Carole managed to catch it and saw that it was a shaving kit. It contained bullets for the gun.

Up to now, everyone had remained mute, Barbara from terror, Carole and Bernie from the shock of finding Barbara with a gun. As soon as Bernie had the gun in his possession, however, the two Finches erupted like festering volcanoes, screaming, rasping, babbling, struggling. This so startled Carole that, not being able to think of anything else to do, she ran outside into the drive and hid herself behind the thick, glossy bushes.

As she crouched there unable to see, she was aware that the terrible struggle going on between Bernie and his wife was becoming increasingly violent. Barbara screamed, as Bernie apparently struck her, and then another voice intruded itself into the mayhem, pleading, "Oh, please, Dr. Finch. Don't kill me! Don't!" It was Marie-Ann Lidholm who, disturbed by the noise and shouting she had heard from inside the house, had come to help her beleaguered employer. Soon afterward, confused, hysterical, and drenched in sweat, Carole heard Marie-Ann utter a muffled cry and then fall silent.

Passionately wishing that she had never come, never met Bernie, never been involved, she became aware of Barbara's voice again and Bernie's threatening to kill her if she and Marie-Ann did not get into the car immediately and be quiet. Then fuzzily, through the thick leaves, she saw Barbara Finch running down the drive, Bernie close behind, and then a shot.

When the police arrived, they found Marie-Ann wandering around the garage, sobbing. She led them to the place by the side of the hill where a lonely poplar tree guarded the crumpled, shoeless body of Barbara Jean Finch. Bernie was gone, and Carole, still huddled behind the shrubs, was too stunned and too much afraid to move so much as a muscle. There in the dark, eyes wide, ears primed to any sound, Carole did not even know who, if anyone, was dead. Her only visitor was Frosty, the family hound, who would periodically snuffle into the bushes to be petted, then run out to receive an enthusiastic welcome from the police, who scratched him and petted him also, as they milled around his dead mistress. Frosty was upset, and Carole was terrified that his interest in her bush would eventually give her away.

Such was not the case, however. What with having to photograph the body, get it to the morgue, hunt for evidence, pacify and question Marie-Ann, and try to restore some sort of order to the Finch household, the police were much too busy to notice Frosty's frequent forays into a particular bush. Marie-Ann's chief interest at this point was that the children should not be wakened or have to be told, in the midst of this chaos, that their mother was dead.

Barbara had been wearing a white crêpe dress, sleeveless and low-cut, which now was stained crimson with her blood, the bullet having entered her back high, just beneath the left shoulder blade, and progressed into the heart. Her purse was nowhere to be found, nor was her watch or her rings. Nor was the gun. There was blood everywhere in the garage and on the front seat of Barbara's car, from wounds inflicted on her by Bernie with the butt of the gun. There was also an indentation about two inches wide in the rough stucco of the garage wall on the left side, where Bernie had hit Marie-Ann's head against it in his rage and panic. They found Barbara's shoes and a torn rubber surgical glove on the floor of the car, and they found the shaving kit with the bullets, which Carole had dropped in her flight. Then they found the attaché case.

Opening the case, the police discovered a curious array of tools and other objects, among them an eight-inch butcher's knife, two ten-foot lengths of rope, several hypodermic needles, a flashlight, a hammer, half a box of .38 cartridges, and a bottle of Seconal tablets. The chief detective glanced meaningfully at the other police officers, who stared into the case, told one of them to put some tape around it and place it in the back of the patrol car. Several other policemen were still searching for the gun but, having had no success, announced that they should have better luck the following day, when they could continue the hunt by daylight. After several hours, they all departed, taking with them what evidence they had been able to uncover in the dark, including a statement from Marie-Ann Lidholm. Carole remained in the bushes, while Frosty whined around the poplar tree, sniffing the damp ground where his mistress had lain.

It was well after the break of dawn, around 6:00 in the morning, before Carole crept, stiff and exhausted, from the bushes and descended the drive leading away from the scene of all this horror. Stumbling along the road which led out onto the main highway, she realized that if Bernie had taken the car last night, she had no way at all of getting back to Las Vegas. As she passed the country club, she was surprised to see her little car still sitting there in the parking lot, where they had left it. Relieved, she flung open the door and collapsed on the front seat, closing her eyes for a moment and enjoying the feel of the cool plastic. The keys had been left in the car, and after a brief rest, Carole switched on the ignition and headed back to Las Vegas. She wondered where on earth Bernie was and how he had managed to get away. It also occurred to her now, with some bitterness, that she did not remember hearing Bernie call for her before he dashed away, and that he could not possibly have any idea of what had become of her.

When she finally arrived back in Las Vegas, she found Bernie, to her great relief, sound asleep on the bed in her apartment. He was fully clothed and sleeping like a dead man. Looking down at him for a moment, she contemplated waking him; there were a dozen questions she wanted to ask him, things she needed to know and assurances she required for her own peace of mind. She decided to have a cup of coffee and a shower first. She was tired and dirty, and needed to relax and maybe sleep a while herself before facing Bernie.

But Carole and Bernie never had an opportunity to discuss anything, for just as Carole stepped from the shower and slipped into her robe, the doorbell rang, shattering the morning silence and waking Bernie with a start. They looked at each other, wanting to speak but neither was able. Carole walked slowly to the door, opened it, and found the West Covina police in the corridor.

"Mrs. Carole Pappa?"

"My name is Carole Tregoff. I'm not with Mr. Pappa anymore."

"Yes. Well, you are Carole Tregoff Pappa?"

"Yes."

"We're looking for Dr. Bernard Finch. Is he here, Miss Tregoff?"

"How did you find my place?"

"Oh, that wasn't very difficult. Is Dr. Finch here? We would like to talk to him." Carole hesitated a moment, thinking that she might lie and put them off, but they were sure to look around the apartment. As she opened her mouth to answer, Bernie appeared in the doorway which led to the bedroom.

"I'm here," he said. "What can I do for you gentlemen?"

"Are you Dr. Raymond Bernard Finch of Twenty-seven fifty Larkhill Drive, West Covina?"

"Yes, I am."

"It's my unpleasant task to inform you that you are under arrest."

"What for?"

The officer cocked his head and said with a wry expression, "For the murder of your wife, Dr. Finch."

Carole and Bernie were questioned separately by the police, which was the beginning of most of their troubles. A good indication of Bernie's state of mind was that, in spite of the fact that Marie-Ann Lidholm had been witness to the events of the night before, he endeavored to convince the police that he had been with Carole in Las Vegas all night. He even went so far as to take them out to the airport to show them his Cadillac, which the parking attendant confirmed had not been moved since Friday, July 17. All this was to no avail, however, and Bernie was subsequently arraigned and held without bail.

In the meantime, Carole had recited a completely different tale to her interrogators, which solidly incriminated not only Bernie but, to a certain extent, herself. It had apparently not occurred to her that, inasmuch as the only two souls who could place her anywhere near the scene of the crime were Bernie and the dog, one of whom surely posed no threat, she could easily disclaim any knowledge of the tragedy or the circumstances surrounding it. She could be fairly sure that Bernie would not say anything to involve her, for the fact that she was with him on the night in question neither enhanced nor detracted from his own essentially dangerous position. Besides, he loved her and would surely do everything he could to help and protect her from any threatening situation.

But Carole's mind was clearly not functioning even as well as it normally did, and wallowing in confusion, bewilderment, and panic, she told the police exactly what had happened. Without Finch to guide her, she was utterly devoid of craft or stratagem, and she described in detail all their movements on the previous night, explaining that they intended to stage a decisive "showdown" with Barbara Finch. Later in the day, the police drove Carole to West Covina and had her reenact for them the events leading up to the shooting. It became perfectly apparent at this time that, from where Carole had been hidden, she could not have actually witnessed the fatal act; her reason for being there, however, remained unclear.

Carole was feeling considerably better at the conclusion of this phase of the investigation and had to some extent regained her confidence and composure. This being the case, her inner antennas failed to pick up any danger signals when the chief detective casually asked her about the attaché case. By way of response, Carole guilelessly told him how Bernie had asked her to take the case out of the car and how she had carried it into the garage, where they waited for Mrs. Finch. The detective wanted to know if Carole could explain the presence of some of the things in the case, which was not after all an ordinary doctor's bag, and Carole obliged by discussing certain items and rationalizing their presence in the case. The detective did not at this time ask Carole how she knew what was in the bag.

On the way back to Las Vegas, they chatted about Carole's apartment in the Fairview Arms. She said that it cost $150 per month and that she had rented it in order to remove herself from the heat generated by the love triangle, and especially by Barbara Finch, who she thought had behaved very unreasonably in regard to Bernie. They thanked her very much for her help and said that they would be calling her when they felt she could be of further assistance.

It turned out that, in order to get back to Las Vegas on the night of July 18, Bernie had stolen two cars, one of which had been abandoned in a restaurant parking lot, while the other was found near Carole's apartment. He told the police that he vaguely recalled running through some orange groves, over rough mounds of loose earth, and without making any admissions, indicated that he might have dropped the gun as he ran. (The police subsequently combed the area with mine detectors but found no weapon.) Having reached the home of a neighbor, he headed for the garage, where he found a car, the keys to which were stuck in the visor. A good many miles further on he switched to a temporarily abandoned police car, which got him back to Carole's apartment. Neither the neighbor nor the owner of the police car chose to press charges; to do so would in any case have been a merely gratuitous action, since Bernie was already to be placed under indictment for first-degree murder.

The preliminary hearing, preceding trial, took place on July 29, and Carole, who up until now had not been permitted to see Bernie or communicate with him in any way, was called upon to testify. Arriving in court at the appointed hour, her hair freshly done, and dressed as though for a ladies' luncheon, she was clearly not suffering from anxiety or apprehension. It soon became apparent that this day was to be as trying for her as it was for Bernie.

The prosecutor, who was assistant district attorney of Pomona, in whose jurisdiction the crime had been committed, hammered away at the intimacy of Carole's association with Bernie, stressing the illicit sexual aspect more than seemed absolutely necessary at the time. Ultimately Carole broke down under this barrage, insisting that they were in love and that their relationship was not the cheap, tawdry affair that it was being painted. What upset her more than anything, evidently, was that the world was not to be allowed to view her as the romantic heroine of a tender and poetic love story, nor Bernie as the gallant and sincere lover; if things continued in the present vein, they would emerge as common fornicators and adulterers, conspiring to murder for convenience and material gain. It was all too horrible to be real.

When Carole had pulled herself together to some degree, the prosecutor, assuring her that he was almost through, asked her about the brown attaché case. Still unable to see the possible danger in answering such a question, Carole said that Bernie had asked her to bring it with her up to the house. Once again she was asked whether the items in the case were things she thought doctors would normally carry, and still failing to sense the web which was being woven around her, she calmly proceeded to justify, as she had done for the police to a lesser degree, the presence of every article in the case, hardly ignoring a single one. The prosecutor never referred to specific items unless she had mentioned them first, and when she had finished, he asked her how she knew what was in the case. Her answer was predictably unsatisfactory, and as she stepped down from the witness stand, the prosecutor told her that she was under arrest for conspiracy and murder in the first degree.

During the latter part of the questioning, the room had been unnaturally silent, and the tension which had been slowly building suddenly erupted at the moment of Carole's dramatic and totally unanticipated arrest. As the judge banged his gavel for silence, the members of the press appeared to go berserk, climbing indiscriminately over each other and the rest of the audience to get to the phones. This was the biggest news break any of them had seen in months. Carole, stunned and weeping, was led away by a matron, while her parents clung to one another miserably and stared at Bernie, who sat with his head bowed in silence.

The basis for Carole's arrest was her testimony regarding the attaché case, which by now had been dubbed the murder kit by a determined prosecution and an equally zealous press. Whether or not she would be tried as codefendant with Bernie rested on the admissability of this testimony as evidence. No one, it seemed, had informed Carole that anything she said might be used against her; otherwise she might have testified differently.

The trial did not actually begin until the first week in January, for in the months that preceded it, trial dates were set and postponed several times, as separate appeals were made in Carole's behalf. Jerry Geisler had agreed early in August to represent her, although he was at the time a very sick man, soon to be bound for the hospital. His two principal assistants, who would actually conduct the defense, contended that, inasmuch as Carole had not been advised of her rights either at the time of her questioning by the West Covina police or at the time of the hearing, her testimony could not be used as evidence. The state had admitted that its entire case against her was contained in this testimony, and, ironically, had the present rules of evidence obtained—rules which have been firmly in effect since the historic decisions pertaining to Escobedo in 1964 and Miranda in 1966—Carole would be free today. Had she been a brighter girl, moreover, this protection would have been unnecessary; in life one also pays for stupidity.

On August 4, Carole, now languishing in jail, was interviewed by various members of the press, whom she told that she was no longer in love with Dr. Finch. Obviously in a flip and careless frame of mind that day, she laughed a great deal during the interview, the smile turning to a sneer when asked if she still loved Finch. She just wanted out, she said, complaining that she was always hungry in jail. "I just want to dye my hair, get lost, and eat for a week."

A couple of days before, a supermarket clerk had identified Finch as the man who had bought an eight-inch butcher knife and a flashlight a few days before the murder, both of which had been found in the murder kit and described precisely by Carole. A few days later, Judge William M. Martin ruled that Carole's self-incriminating testimony at Finch's hearing would be admitted as evidence.

On September 16, Carole left the prison, her parents having raised the $25,000 required in bail. The prosecutor expressed his annoyance, stating that he wanted her back in jail and the bail raised to $100,000. Furthermore, he said, he would ask for the death penalty for Carole as well as Dr. Finch, to whom bail had been denied.

The first trial was scheduled to take place in the Pomona Superior Court on November 24. A change of venue was granted, however—as a result, among other things, of pressure brought on the district attorney by the press to make the trial easier for them to cover. It was also determined that a more representative jury might be found in Los Angeles County, and that the defendants would be spared the tiring daily commute from Los Angeles, where they were in jail, to Pomona, fifty minutes away. They would also have time for light meals, rest, and conferences with their respective attorneys.

By December, several appeals were pending. Carole's attorneys had by now appealed to the Supreme Court regarding Judge Martin's decision as to her pretrial testimony and were awaiting a decision. In the meantime, Bernie's counsel, a distinguished West Coast attorney by the name of Grant Cooper, had become extremely concerned about the adverse pretrial publicity, which threatened to prejudice the defense's case seriously.

Hardly a day went by that the public failed to be treated to photos of Carole dating from her modeling days or of Jimmy —huge, muscular, and hairy, gleaming nakedly over captions saying he still loved her and wanted her back. Pictures of Carole, dressed in very short shorts, upside down, legs over the back of a chair, or kneeling coyly "en bikini," or stretching herself in an off-the-shoulder leotard, accompanied sensational editorial speculations in papers from coast to coast about the "do-it-yourself murder kit" and various other aspects of the case. Cooper introduced a public opinion poll, which purported to show that almost half of the persons questioned had formed an opinion as to the guilt or innocence of Carole and the doctor, and that it would therefore be impossible to obtain an impartial jury. Cooper sought to have the trial moved from Los Angeles County to some other jurisdiction, but the judge decided that he would reserve decision on change of venue until after the questioning of prospective jurors.

The diligent prosecutor's threats regarding Carole's bail had evidently not been idle, for by December, bail had been revoked and she was back in prison. December was generally a bad month for Carole and Bernie. Carole turned twenty-three on Christmas Day in jail, where she received fruit and candy like all the others but was not allowed any other presents, nor did she receive cards, because the prison censor had the day off.

The day before, Christmas Eve, she had word that Justice William O. Douglas of the Supreme Court had refused to halt the trial, now scheduled for December 28, in Los Angeles County Court. It was reported that "Miss Tregoff wanted the proceedings held up until she could file an appeal from rulings against her by the California state courts. She had asked the state courts to postpone the trial, but her petitions had been denied without opinion." Carole's birthday was not a very happy one, needless to say. A few days earlier, Bernie lost his appeal for a change of venue. It had taken a month, but a jury of six men and six women had finally been chosen, and the trial was ready to begin.

January 4, 1960, was the first day of the trial, which was to be one of the longest in legal history. It was to be complicated, difficult, and frustrating for all concerned—the defendants, their counsels, the prosecution, the jury, and perhaps most of all the judge. Essentially, the adversary positions taken were as follows: While Finch's defense was to contend that he killed his wife accidently during a struggle for the gun, Carole's attorneys would endeavor to persuade the jury that, although it was certainly to Carole's advantage to have Barbara Finch out of the way, she had had no part in either planning her murder or assisting the doctor in its expedition. Moreover, they insisted right up till the day of the trial that Carole had been indicted solely on the basis of incompetent evidence and that the Los Angeles

County grand jury which indicted her lacked jurisdiction in the case, because any conspiracy which may have been involved took place in Nevada, not in California.

The prosecution understandably held a somewhat less benign view. It was the state's contention that the combined evils of lust, hatred, and greed had caused Bernie and Carole first to conspire to kill Barbara Finch and then to drive to West Covina on the night of July 18 with the intention of injecting a dose of Seconal into her veins, placing her in her car, and pushing it off a cliff. The prosecution held further that Carole knew very well what was in the attaché case, because she had intended to assist Bernie in the use of its contents. The only thing that stopped her, they insisted, was the totally unexpected circumstance of Barbara Finch turning up with a gun, which had fouled the entire plan and brought Marie-Ann Lidholm into the scene as a witness.

So far as Carole was concerned, the question of intent was very important here, for implicit in the conspiracy charge was the contention that all during the drive from Las Vegas to West Covina, Carole had had it in her mind and in her heart to murder Barbara Finch. Unless the state could prove that the alleged conspiracy which took place in Nevada was acted upon in California, they were in a serious legal bind and would have difficulty in getting her convicted. It made no difference that she actually had no part in the shooting, for the maximum penalty in California for conspiracy to commit murder is the same as for first-degree murder—death in the gas chamber.

The prosecution, opening its case, had announced its intention of calling upon no fewer than fifty witnesses, the first of whom not surprisingly was Marie-Ann Lidholm. The courtroom, the largest in Los Angeles, held 265 seats and was jammed to capacity. All ears and eyes turned now from the defendants to focus on the wholesome, blonde young woman who walked uncertainly toward the witness stand. Glancing briefly at the jury, Marie-Ann wondered, somewhat irrelevantly, whether in America they always had juries which were evenly divided between the sexes. Having then been sworn in, she sat down.

At the instigation of the prosecutor, Marie-Ann told the court in a soft, halting English about the events of the night of July 18. She spoke of having heard shouts from the garage and Mrs. Finch crying for help, and of having burst in to find Mrs.

Finch on the floor, covered in blood, with Dr. Finch standing over her, his face contorted with rage. She told the court how, when he saw her, Finch had come over and, seizing her by the shoulders, had smashed her head against the garage wall, making a grapefruit-sized dent in the plaster, as she pleaded for her life. She told also of the threats and hideous verbal battles to which she had been privy in the months which preceded the killing. In conclusion, she told of picking herself up off the garage floor and running into the house to call the police, terrified that any moment Dr. Finch would return and try to kill her, as he had threatened to do earlier.

Under cross-examination Cooper asked her why, at the time she was first questioned, she had told the police about hearing shots during the scuffle in the garage. The prosecutor, coming to her rescue, suggested that Marie-Ann's imperfect pronunciation was to blame, that she had meant to say "shouts" rather than "shots."

On January 10, a famous movie star spent the day at the trial with her producer, taking notes voraciously, explaining that she was preparing for a new film in which she played the part of a girl awaiting execution for the killing of her lover. The producer opined that Dr. Finch didn't look like a murderer or Carole like a femme fatale. She looked more, he said, like the wife of a construction worker—a young matron, who would never stray. Later in the trial, Erle Stanley Gardner was to appear with his wife, presumably to cull some additional material for use in their TV series, featuring the fabled Perry Mason.

On January 13, a virus epidemic which had swept southern California put a temporary halt to the trial. The state was preparing to offer evidence regarding the apartment which Finch had provided for his mistress when a male juror and one of Carole's lawyers were both stricken. The judge called a three-day recess, but inasmuch as the juror had not yet recovered at the end of that time, an alternate had to be produced, leaving the jury with five men and seven women.

One of the next witnesses brought by the prosecution was Donald Williams. Nervous about having to testify, Williams glanced furtively at Carole several times as he spoke; he realized his testimony, regardless of how inconclusive it was, would be highly damaging to Carole, and the thought gave him pain. He described, simply and without drama, how Carole had asked him to help her to find some sort of hoodlum to assist her in solving a difficult problem, of which he had no specific knowledge. He insisted that he had at no time heard Carole make a direct proposition to anyone and that the conversation with Cody at Foxy's tavern had revolved strictly around Cody— what he did and how he operated with women. During the cross-examination, Williams denied that he had ever told the police that murder had been mentioned in his talks with Carole about hiring a thug; the police, he said, had grossly distorted his story.

Then they brought on John Patrick Cody, and there was a stiffening—a general leaning forward—throughout the packed courtroom. Cody, fetched out of a Minnesota prison where he was serving time on a bad-check rap, was now being held in custody by the Los Angeles authorities for the duration of the trial.

Cody's testimony electrified the spectators, exhilarated the press, and gave Carole one of her worst days in court. He told the court that Carole had hired him for the sole purpose of killing Barbara Finch. He said that he had received partial payment when the deal was made, on the understanding that he would get the rest after Mrs. Finch was dead. He said that Carole had given him maps of the Finches' house in West Covina, in addition to plans of the Hollywood Hills Hotel, where Mrs. Finch sometimes stayed with a woman friend at times when she was particularly apprehensive about Dr. Finch. He continued to explain how he had tried to talk the two out of going through with it and how Carole had insisted. He had also tried to appeal to Finch, telling him in private that Carole wasn't worth it, but he had not listened, explaining instead how Cody should use the shotgun in the Cadillac to kill his wife. Cody insisted that he did not like this, that it was too messy, but Bernie had merely responded by saying, "When you shoot her, tell her the bullet comes from Bernie." This appeared rather unlikely in view of the fact that shotguns do not fire bullets, but the police did find a shotgun in the Cadillac, which corroborated that much of the story.

Cody continued his macabre tale by saying that, when he returned from West Covina the first time and told Carole that Barbara Finch was dead, it was the only time he had ever seen her happy. However, an untimely call to Bernie from Barbara Finch revealed that Cody had not fulfilled his part of the bargain, and the lovers were enraged. Cody, it seemed, had got cold feet on the night he was to have carried out the execution and had simply disappeared into the nearest saloon to consume his ill-gotten gains in liquor and gambling.

Confronted by the infuriated doctor, Cody described how he had advised Finch simply to take Carole away and forget about the money, then see how long Carole would stick with him. Later, Carole told Cody in a temper, "If you don't do it, the doctor will do it, and if the doctor doesn't do it, *I* will do it!" Or so Cody testified. Convinced that the pair had no intention of changing their minds as to murdering Mrs. Finch, Cody somehow managed to collect the rest of his money and set out once more for West Covina, with instructions not to forget to make it look like a robbery. Again Cody reneged at the crucial moment and returned to Las Vegas with hands untainted by the blood of Mrs. Finch. This time he did not come back to his employers, being unwilling to face their wrath. He spoke to Bernie on the phone, however, and Bernie had said in a terrible rage, "Okay. This time we'll have to do it ourselves."

Having squeezed as much censure as possible from Cody, the prosecution turned him over to Mr. Cooper for cross-examination, during which Cody's credibility as a witness was seriously damaged. He admitted to having been a perjurer, a blackmailer, and a thief—a man who would lie for money but who lacked the guts to kill for it. His present status of convict did little to enhance his appeal.

Attacking first the main portion of Cody's story, Cooper asked the hoodlum if it was not in fact true that Carole had hired Cody to seduce Mrs. Finch in order to set the stage for a blackmail attempt. Was anyone to believe that a man of Dr. Finch's intelligence would expect that he could get someone killed for a mere $1,400? Had not the endless dialogue on the subject of Cody's sexual appeal and prowess been related to the role he was to play in the Finch drama? Had not Cody suggested during an earlier interrogation that, while she was not a prostitute, Carole had allowed Cody himself to sleep with her when Bernie was away?

Pervading the air around all these questions was the ugly, half-suggested possibility that the state had made a deal with this bum, which included lying for them, so that they might have the satisfaction of destroying this highly desirable young girl. This was unpleasant, and the jury was sure not to like it.

One thing became increasingly apparent, as this whining, vain, bloodless weakling attempted to answer the questions put to him, and this was that, if they were not downright stupid, Carole and Bernie had shown the most abysmal judgment imaginable in their choice of a paid partner, regardless of the reasons for which he was hired. If, however, Cody had received promises of immunity or release from prison for his help in convicting Carole along with Dr. Finch, it was to no avail, for held as he was in custody by the Los Angeles authorities, he ended by spending more time in jail than he would have simply serving out his time in Minnesota. But nobody knew, at the time, how long this trial was to drag on.

Although Cody ultimately denied having ever stated that he had made love to Carole, Dorothy Kilgallen—never one to turn down a juicy morsel—had rooted around and found this tasty scrap, which she reported happily, along with various other opinions and prognostications. Cody, she said, claimed that he made love to Carole because it enhanced his ego, "which is as big as his shoulder pads." Carole, it would seem, "made friends a little too easily with bums for someone who was trying to crash the country-club set."

In the light of this spirited journalism, one can well understand the anxiety concerning the press expressed the previous month by the counsel for the defense. Even prior to Cody's testimony, Miss Kilgallen had failed to contribute appreciably to the enhancement of Carole's public image: ". . . If Miss T. declines to explain to the jury some of the factors that appear to link her with the death of Mrs. Finch, she is a cooked goose, or the California equivalent thereof . . . [Carole] might have fed the authorities a couple of wrongos . . . No one taking a long thoughtful look at Carole would doubt that she was interested in men more than in sculpture, soccer, or Scrabble, and few fail to understand why a man might lose his head over her . . . with her milk-white skin, voluptuous figure, and sliding, red-brown eyes, that are more mysterious than candid. It is hard to imagine her spending an afternoon playing canasta with the girls if she could find anything better to do, and it looks as if she has always been able to find something to do and someone to do it with."

In a frantic "recap" for her avid fans, Miss Kilgallen had

described Carole's arrest as having taken place at "one of these preliminary razzmatazzes, familiar in Perry Mason mysteries, but foreign to New Yorkers . . ." The judge, gauging the source of the "razzmatazz," forbade members of the jury to read any newspapers or watch television for the duration of the trial.

As the trial stretched on, witnesses were produced who appeared to know a good deal about the things which Carole found to do and with whom she did it. Various landladies and motel keepers from West Covina and Las Vegas were produced, whose testimony concerning some of the temporary apartments which had housed Carole, dated the love affair back to at least April, 1957. One said that the couple would sometimes arrive as early as 9:00 A.M., sometimes around the lunch hour, spending two to three hours at a time there almost every day.

Another woman, keeper of the Monterey Park Apartments in West Covina, said that the couple had thanked her when they left, saying that they had enjoyed the apartment very much. The witness, a solemn unsophisticated woman who was taking her job at the moment very seriously, looked bewildered as the roar of mirth swept through the courtroom, over the admonishments of the judge, and she was left with a puzzled, uncertain expression on her face. The incident provided a rare moment of levity for Bernie, who roared with laughter, and for Carole who lowered her eyes and smiled a very broad smile to herself.

Various friends of Barbara Finch appeared as witnesses for the prosecution, giving testimony damaging only to Bernie. A Mr. Adair, one of Mrs. Finch's dapper young tennis-playing friends, said he had taken her out to dinner on the night of July 18, along with another couple. All three testified as to the fear in which Barbara Finch had lived during her last days—fear that her husband would appear at the house one night and murder her.

Barbara's divorce lawyer, in whose office Adair was employed as an investigator, showed the court pictures of Barbara Finch with her left eye bandaged as a result of one of Bernie's attacks. He also said that Bernie had owned a gun and a permit to use it for a long time, testimony which was backed up by the man who had sold Bernie the gun in 1950. A ballistics expert said that the gun would have had to have been fired at a maximum distance of four feet, in view of the wound that it made. The judge then told the jury that they were to regard this portion of the testimony as evidence as to the state of mind of the deceased, not as proof of Dr. Finch's guilt. It also spoke volumes about the state of mind of Dr. Finch, already attested to by his distraught father, who told the court about Bernie's visits to the psychiatrist. "He should have been committed," the elder Finch had concluded glumly. "He was not himself."

On February 2, nearly a month after the commencement of the trial, the state rested its case after the judge, apparently reversing the earlier decision, ruled that Carole's testimony at Bernie's preliminary hearing could *not* be used as evidence. Unfortunately, Carole had made statements to the police in West Covina and the detectives in Las Vegas, which corresponded exactly to what she had said at the hearing, and inasmuch as these statements were ruled admissable, very little was gained by the other more favorable ruling. Carole claimed that no one advised her of her rights at the time of her initial interrogation by the police, but there had been no other witnesses present to say so. The defense was later to call to the stand Mrs. Gladys Tregoff, Carole's stepmother, who had accompanied Carole to the hearing and was therefore able to attest to the fact that no one had advised Carole on that occasion of her right to remain silent.

In conclusion, having reiterated all the various damning facts brought out by the evidence presented thus far, the prosecution left the jury with this to ponder: If Carole and Bernie had really driven to West Covina on July 18 intending to reach some sort of extrajuridical agreement with Barbara Finch on the subject of the divorce, what ill-advised muse had prompted them to let Carole—the mistress and thorn in Barbara's side—go along? And what, moreover, could possibly have caused them to choose midnight as an appropriate hour in which to do this?

During the taxing months prior to Barbara's death, Bernie had been plagued not only by serious personal problems but by professional difficulties as well. At various times during their careers, many doctors must face lawsuits brought against them by dissatisfied patients, but since 1953, the malpractice and damage suits brought against Bernie, most of them still pending at the time of the trial, had reached a total of $750,000. One of these suits, involving a claim of $100,000, had been initiated by none other than Carole's husband, James Pappa.

Jimmy was a big man, with enormous shoulders, a wavy pomaded pompadour, and heavy eyebrows which turned up toward the center of his brow, giving him a worried, slightly quizzical expression. He approached the witness stand nervously, straightening his thickly knotted tie, which was already straight, and an air of renewed interest and expectancy pervaded the court.

Jimmy told the jury that, shortly after Carole had started to work at the clinic, he had gone to Dr. Finch himself with a knee ailment. The upshot, he said, was that, while supposedly removing a small growth under the kneecap, Finch had severed a nerve, leaving him with a permanent limp.

Carole's erstwhile spouse presented a rather different picture of her than had some of the other witnesses. He said that Carole was a "good kid" and that they would still be together if it weren't for Dr. Finch. "Carole seemed to fall completely under Finch's spell. . . . I didn't realize what was happening till Barbara Finch called to give me the bad news. . . . He made a mockery of my marriage. I guess I should have given him the beating he deserved when I found out he was going out with Carole, ten months before Mrs. Finch's death." Jimmy had been under the impression that, at the time of Carole's temporary release on bail, she had not been overly apprehensive about her future. He said that she had phoned him then and asked him to take her waterskiing, but that her lawyer had forbidden her to do it. "She said that all the fun seemed to be going out of her life. She was acting as if nothing was wrong, and there was Mrs. Finch dead and Carole involved, but it didn't seem to hit her at all. She's a great little actress."

Jimmy insisted, furthermore, that Carole had been a "perfect bed mate" the entire time she had been seeing Finch and that for this reason he had suspected nothing. "She was always eager at night, despite the fact she saw Finch at lunch hours. . . . He [Finch] tries to make people believe I was impotent."

A curious sideline in this long trial was the extent to which the sexual egos of the men involved with Carole would affect the impression of her, which was forming among the jury. Each one, in an effort to preserve his manly pride and promote his image of virile sexuality, boasted of his attractiveness to

Carole at one time or other, and not the least of these was Finch himself.

Bernie's appearance on the witness stand had been anticipated only slightly less eagerly than the moment at which Carole herself might follow, and it turned into quite a performance. Denying vehemently that Carole could have possibly continued having sexual relations with Pappa during the period in which she was seeing him nearly every day, Finch declared that he would marry her if he were free to do so, that he loved her and was confident that she still loved him. Having thus established his claim to her favors over that of his competitors, he launched into the principal themes of his defense.

It was Bernie's immutable contention that he had absolutely not intended to kill his wife and that he had not conspired with Carole, Jack Cody, or anyone else to do so. The shooting, he said, had been accidental, the gun having gone off as he attempted to throw it away, after he had wrested it from Mrs. Finch's grasp. Although he admitted to having had other affairs before Carole came on the scene, he insisted that it was only due to his wife's postpartum frigidity that he had entered into a relationship with Carole. He and his wife, he said, had even made a sort of "armistice agreement" in 1956, in which it was understood that each would go his own way without censure or reprimand from the other. He had gone to his home on July 18, he assured the court, to agree that he and Barbara should be divorced and that he should part with a sizable portion of his fortune.

The high point of Bernie's testimony was his moving version of the death scene. Barbara had started to make a run for his father's house, Bernie told a transfixed audience, and ran down the drive toward the dirt steps leading to it. Before setting out after her, he had tried to fling the gun away, and as he drew back his arm, it discharged, hitting Barbara in the back; she staggered a few more steps and went down. Seeing his wife fall, he ran to her side: "She opened her mouth a little bit and said, 'I'm sorry, I should have listened.' I started to cry, and she said, 'Take care of the kids,' and then she went." Finch now wept, as did three women jurors who broke down in tears at the conclusion of this tragic story. This was the first time that the jury had been visibly moved during the entire trial, and it seemed to represent a definitive triumph for the defense. With Finch unable to regain his composure, the trial was recessed till the following day.

The prosecutor was enraged, demanding of Finch on cross-examination whether he had not in fact invented this whole touching death scene in order to avoid the implication that he left a dying woman on the lawn. Finch denied this vociferously, swearing that every word of what he had said was true. He admitted having struck Mrs. Finch on the head, but only because she was wielding the gun, and he was afraid she would shoot him. He did not know why he had been so rough with Marie-Ann or fled in a panic from the scene in stolen cars. He was in a daze, he said, and had not been able to think or act rationally.

Cooper had been having a hard time with Finch, who thought he had all the answers and tried in a sense to conduct his own defense, frequently undermining Cooper's efforts. Finch's attorney was finding him inflexible and hard to control —an arrogant egomaniac, who had to win at any game and have everything his way, including this trial.

Cooper saw Finch as a man who had to be looked up to in order that his ego might not suffer; the trouble, he decided, was that his wife saw him as he was, whereas Carole put him on a pedestal, seeing him as a truly glamorous, admirable figure. Finch did not have to do what he did for the money, for his clinic and various real-estate projects were destined to pay off handsomely. But he couldn't bear to let anything get away from him, and he needed Carole's blind devotion.

Bernie had been on the witness stand for four days when they finally called Carole. It was Valentine's Day, and the crowd outside the courthouse, knowing that the star of the show was to appear in person, was denser than ever and in a more sentimental mood. Amidst the pushing and shoving bodies, various comments escaped into the February air:

"Finch looks like a nice man."

"Wait till you see Carole, she's lovely."

"I pray for her parents, poor things."

"I find it's like reading a book. You can't stop until you get to the end."

"You learn not to get mixed up in things like this. I feel so sorry for that girl. I can't understand how she got mixed up in such a thing. Her birthday is only three days from mine. We were born under the same sign, and people born under that sign usually stay out of trouble."

The trial relieved the boredom of some, and those who were lonely were afforded someplace to go where they would be with other people, sharing something. Others were drawn to it as to the gore of a shattering automobile accident, at which one is irresistibly compelled to look, in spite of inner warnings not to do so. All enjoyed it.

Much of the popular excitement generated by Carole's forthcoming occupation of the witness stand emanated from the fact that there had been some doubt as to whether her attorneys would allow her to testify. Fearful of what she might say under cross-examination, they had serious reservations about it, but now in a spirit of renewed confidence, they announced that Carole would take the stand.

At the time of this announcement, the prosecutors and various defense attorneys made some revealing statements to the press regarding the fearful toll the trial had been taking of them personally. One does not normally think of this aspect, wondering principally how the defendants are holding up, but now the public was reminded of the terrible tensions under which the others lived as well. The chief prosecutor, Fred Wichello, was taking three capsules of Sodium Seconal at night to sleep; Grant Cooper found that he had to go to bed at 8:30 in order to survive the next day; Donald Bringgold, one of Carole's attorneys, had been plagued by crackpot calls, while Robert Neeb stayed up half the night making notes and reading the transcript of the previous day's proceedings. Rexford Eagan, also on Carole's team, said, "We live, sleep, eat with it, and wake up a dozen times a night. This is a fight, Mister!"

When the trial began, Carole had been contained, attractive, neatly coiffed and groomed. Now she was bedraggled, in spite of a new pink sweater, knitted by her stepmother, to protect her from the drafts which abounded in the vast courtroom. Her face was puffy, her expression miserable, the dark roots of her hair clearly visible, as she bowed her head in chagrin and dejection.

Her early testimony had been absolutely essential to the prosecution in terms of placing the car in the country-club lot and attesting to the element of lying-in-wait, both of which reflected Bernie's intentions. She suffered in the knowledge that

she had hurt him, and did not know what she was to do now
to save herself.

Throughout the proceedings, the prosecution always referred to Carole as "Mrs. Pappa," lest the jury forget that she
had been another man's wife at the time of her affair with the
charming doctor, while the defense attorneys preferred to call
her "Miss Tregoff." It was to Miss Tregoff that the first group of
questions was directed, and Carole spoke without drama or emotion about the part she played on the night of July 18, 1959.
This phase of the questioning completed, the prosecutor who
had been waiting, motionless and attentive like a bird of prey,
sprang to his feet and, in a voice reeking of sarcasm, asked Mrs.
Pappa if she might not be so kind as to repeat some of the high-
lights of her version of the events. He had been curious to know,
for example, why, since they had come only for a friendly chat,
they had seen fit to arrive at midnight and park the car at the
country club rather than in the Finches' own driveway. Carole
balked; she didn't know.

Wounded by the initial volley, Carole burst into tears
but managed to go on speaking. She said that Barbara Finch had
pulled a gun on her. How long, she was asked, had it taken Mrs.
Finch to produce the pistol? "Just time for her to turn around,"
was the answer, "to take the gun out of the car and turn
around." Dabbing at her reddened eyes, Carole continued, "An
instant later she turned around and had the gun in her hand. He
[Finch] threw something at me. I grabbed it. It all seemed like
the same instant. I guess it was the shaving kit. I grabbed it and
ran into the bushes, and didn't see much else after that, except
Mrs. Finch running down the driveway holding the gun." The
prosecutor pointed out that everybody else, including Dr. Finch,
seemed to be of the opinion that Finch had the gun during
Barbara's futile flight. How was it that Carole saw so clearly,
from behind the bushes, that the gun was in Mrs. Finch's possession. Carole blubbered. She couldn't remember, but swore
that she had not plotted with anyone to kill Mrs. Finch. The
prosecutor pressed her on the subject of conversations which
were alleged to have taken place among Carole, Bernie, and
Cody in Los Angeles County, whereas her own counsel had concentrated primarily on those which had taken place, somewhat
more safely, in Nevada.

Then came the questions about the attaché case, and a

good deal of Carole Tregoff Pappa came to light through her answers.

Q. Did he [Finch] take anything with him when he left the car?
A. No sir.
Q. Did you?
A. Yes sir.
Q. What?
A. I took the brown attaché case.
Q. Has there ever been any doubt in your mind as to whether you took the case out of the car that night?
A. Since I have remembered it, no. However, there was a time that it wasn't important. I just never thought about the bag. It didn't seem to have any significance.
Q. But some ten days later, you had no difficulty in remembering every item in that bag, isn't that correct?
A. Not every item. I recalled some things about it.
Q. What can you recall that was in it?
A. I recalled the flashlight, rope, the carving knife, the shaving kit and the bottle of Seconal capsules.
Q. Hammer?
A. Yes, sir. I am sorry. I thought I said that.
Q. Who told you to say it was unimportant? Did anyone tell you to say that on the stand?
A. No! [Like a shot.] No one told me to say anything at all except the truth!

The spectators gasped, and the bailiffs had to call for order.

By this time, the jury would be wondering why, if the bag seemed so unimportant, Carole had remembered everything that was in it or why they had taken it at all. The questioning continued, centering now on the period following the arrival of the police.

Q. Were you scared of them [the police]?
A. I don't know what I was scared of. I was just completely panicked.
Q. Weren't you curious as to what had happened to the defendant Finch at that time?
A. I don't think I thought of Dr. Finch at that time.
Q. Didn't you wonder whether or not he had been shot?
A. I don't think so.

Q. You were madly in love with him at that time, weren't you?
A. I was in love with him . . . at that time, but after what I'd seen, I wasn't thinking whether I was in love with anyone.
Q. He was the most important thing in your life at that moment, wasn't he?
A. Apparently not, if I didn't think of him. . . .
Q. Why did you remain hidden five or six hours?
A. I don't know, I was scared.
Q. Weren't you waiting till you could leave without being observed?
A. I don't know what I was waiting for.
Q. Didn't you ever make that statement to anyone?
A. I believe, sir, something like that in the past.
Q. Why didn't you want to be observed?
A. Mr. Crail, when I have been frightened in the past about things I would rather not talk about, I have ran and hidden, and I think this went back to maybe childhood experiences.

The chief prosecutor, Fred Wichello, who had been sitting next to Finch, suddenly turned to the doctor and in a moment of compassion, sadness, or perhaps even remorse, said, "You know, if we'd met a year or so ago, we would probably be good friends."

And Finch replied oddly, "But we are."

On February 18, the defense rested its case, and the jury was locked up, even though the final arguments had not yet been heard. The judge explained that this was "because there has been a certain pressure in the air," referring undoubtedly to the editorial speculations which continued to fill the press throughout the world. Having become a genuine cause célèbre, the case could now be followed in every detail by a housewife in Tokyo as well as by the residents of southern California, Detroit, New York, and New Orleans.

The court was adjourned for several days, while the judge determined what instructions should be given the jury; as in every murder trial, it was absolutely essential that the jury understand the charge given it, in order to arrive at a just and proper verdict.

On February 24, the defense began its summation, starting with arguments on behalf of Carole. Breaking the solid front of innocence which had heretofore been maintained by the defense as a whole, Robert Neeb conceded that Dr. Finch might have murdered his wife but that there was insufficient evidence to incriminate Carole as well:

"In all the testimony and evidence there isn't one single proof that Carole, on the night of July 18, caused any injury, struck anyone, used any weapon, pushed anybody, or touched anyone—certainly not Mrs. Finch. Unless," he continued, "you believe in your mind and heart and soul that on the night of July 18, Carole Tregoff was going from Las Vegas to West Covina with the direct intent to kill, she is entitled to acquittal in this case. This is the thing you have to find: that this young girl was going mile by mile with the intent to kill. . . . If there is any blame that attaches to Carole, it is an age-old story of a young girl in love with a man. That is her only crime—if you, in your own good hearts, can call it a crime."

In conclusion, both Neeb and Bringgold, Carole's second attorney, urged the jury not to return a split verdict, reminding them that the penalty for conspiracy was the same as for first-degree murder. They were battling with all their combined power for total acquittal.

On February 25, one of the jurors developed a bad toothache, and the trial was delayed.

The following day, Grant Cooper began his arguments in favor of Dr. Finch, who sat with tears in his eyes as his counsel told the court that the surgeon's wife had named him in her will as guardian not only of their son but of her daughter by her first marriage. Cooper said that Mrs. Finch had exaggerated when she told friends about Bernie's attacks on her. "She wanted him over a barrel so that she could get a larger divorce settlement. . . ." He went on to say that Finch was much too intelligent to murder his wife in such a blundering manner. Using a gun furnished for this purpose, he then demonstrated for the jury how Finch accidentally shot his wife in the back, by executing a kind of "tennis backhand" throw, which culminated with a click, as the gun's hammer fell. The murder weapon itself had never been found.

As for the murder kit, Cooper denounced this highly prejudicial characterization of the attaché case and reminded the jury that under the rules of circumstantial evidence, if two reasonable uses of such evidence are presented, the one establishing the defendant's innocence must be accepted by the jury. In other words, Cooper hoped that the members of the jury would find it in their hearts to view the objects in Finch's attaché case as ordinary physician's tools.

Cooper's arguments lasted for three days, and on the last day, in a surprise move, he tried to introduce new testimony. But the judge ruled that the three potential witnesses mentioned by Mr. Cooper did not appear to him to be important enough to justify reopening the case.

Cooper's use of irony and dramatic emphasis was keenly observed by several Hollywood scriptwriters, who had been following the trial, and as he finished his plea, his client, as though on cue, threw his arms around the weary attorney, saying, "Thanks, Grant. You did a swell job."

By March 3, it was the state's turn to sum up. Beginning with a strong denunciation of Finch's "death scene," Fred Wichello, the indignant prosecutor, characterized it as a monstrous lie and castigated the doctor for his "second-rate soap opera." Pointing to Carole, he told the jury that there sat a "latter-day Lady Macbeth," who had goaded the surgeon into murder and was ready to stand by his side during the "operation," like a surgical assistant with scalpel and suture. She wanted Mrs. Finch dead and herself married to the doctor, because she did not want to be discarded as his previous sweethearts had been. Wichello also decried as "preposterous" Finch's tale of armistice, saying that it was "contrary to human experience," and thereby revealing, to some extent, his own naïveté.

Throughout the trial, Wichello had appeared not only naïve in certain areas but profoundly puritanical, an image which could have been contrived to appeal to the relatively unsophisticated jurors. Certainly his best hope lay in the fact that the jury would be offended by the idea of the lustful activities of these two married people and that they would come to view Finch as an irresponsible playboy and Carole as Jezebel. Dorothy Kilgallen was later to express this point of view in another of her series on the case:

"The possibility of becoming Mrs. Finch, with tennis-club memberships, weekends in Palm Springs, a $21,000 boat in Balboa, charge accounts, and a pink or white Cadillac, movie-star friendships, and headwaiters bowing, must have been dizzying."

Wichello concluded that it was a very hard-boiled girl

who bargained with Jack Cody, and a stupid, naïve girl who testified as she had at Finch's hearing and ran to hide herself in the bushes when the going got rough. Apparently convinced that Carole was the type who might even kill again, should anyone stand between her and what she wanted, Wichello demanded the death penalty.

On March 4, the jury began its deliberations; a week later, they were still at it, unable to reach a verdict, and on March 12, after they had deliberated 37½ hours, the foreman announced a hopeless deadlock. A mistrial was declared, as Carole wept uncontrollably, and Bernie fumed, angry and frustrated.

The foreman, who was an investigator for the treasury department, said that the jury had disagreed on both defendants as to the murder charge, splitting ten to two to convict Finch, and eight to four to acquit Carole, but that they had been split four to eight against a conspiracy conviction, indicating that most of them had not believed Jack Cody.

The two holdouts against Finch were a Negro and a Mexican, both of whom had manifested an almost total inability to understand the points of law as they were put to them in the charge, and who felt that they were treated with condescension and impatience by the white jurors who had tried to guide them. In the end, they voted for acquittal, refusing to follow the others, and insisting that "the law wasn't written right" and that either both defendants should go to the gas chamber, or both should be acquitted.

On March 18, Carole was released from the county jail on $25,000 bail, raised once more by her loyal and long-suffering parents, who greeted her as she emerged into the spring sunshine. They had spent the last twenty-four hours in efforts to scrape together the $2,625 needed in premiums, offering up the house as collateral for the rest. Exhausted if not beaten, the three of them formed a melancholy little group as they drove away from the jail on that cheerless day, with little to look forward to except an utterly unpredictable second trial, scheduled to begin on May 23.

They needn't have felt so despondent, however, for the feeling in the air was distinctly positive. Reflecting the mood of general optimism which prevailed, Miss Kilgallen wrote: "Judging from the attitudes of the jurors who were deadlocked, it seems likely that Carole will go free at the trial coming up, regardless of what happens to Dr. Finch." But she was impelled to continue on a more characteristic note: "If she does, she will probably revert to her childhood pattern and hide for a while, run to some other room to escape the nightmare. At twenty-three she is beautiful, alluring—and a failure."

As might be expected, the trial was temporarily postponed, while Carole's lawyers assayed certain legal maneuvers that would disqualify the new judge, Leroy Dawson, on grounds of prejudice. The judge, an abrasive, peppery man, had apparently made certain private statements relating to the case, indicating his belief that Dr. Finch and his mistress were guilty. Having appealed to the United States Supreme Court, Carole and her indefatigable team anxiously awaited a decision, though not in a spirit of abundant optimism; in the meantime, a new jury was picked from a group of 240 candidates.

The trial began on June 27, before a jury of eleven women and one man, although they had not yet received a decision on the appeal. On June 29, the answer came: Judge Hugo Black refused to stay the second trial, delivering his opinion without explanation.

As the proceedings got under way, Carole reflected a transformation in her attitude. Whereas during the first trial she had generally been cooperative and plucky, making an effort to keep herself attractive, now she was slovenly, sullen, and difficult to manage.

On July 19, she sent word that she had a serious case of hives and was too sick to come to court. Dawson immediately dispatched a doctor to investigate Carole's condition, which turned out to be quite normal, although she continued to complain of hives. Refusing to allow the doctor to examine her chest, she said she did not feel like dressing and going to court that day. It then became necessary for the doctor to call in two male deputies to get Carole out of bed and onto her feet, while Mrs. Tregoff endeavored, with the help of a policewoman, to get her dressed. Nearly ready, Carole said that she wanted to go to the bathroom alone, but the policewoman refused to permit her to do so. Humiliated and angered by this, Carole slapped the woman and punched her smartly in the stomach, as a result of which she was taken to court in handcuffs, where the outraged judge promptly revoked her bail and had her remanded to jail for the duration.

The trial dragged on for seventeen weeks into November, essentially a rehash of the same material. No new evidence was offered, apart from the fact that Bernie admitted pulling the trigger "accidentally," a minor adjustment on his previous testimony. Everyone showed the strain of waiting and the frustration of uncertainty, as the jury once again went into seclusion for their deliberations.

After they had deliberated for sixteen days and more than sixty hours, the judge, in a startling and unprecedented move, called the jury into the courtroom, announcing that the evidence clearly showed a "willful and deliberate taking of life," and urged them to reach a verdict of guilty without further delay. The various attorneys and employees of the court said that they could not remember when a judge had ever before made such a statement to a jury in a murder case.

Cooper was furious and lodged a strong protest, accusing Dawson of invading the jury's province. In a stormy session, the judge responded that Finch had obviously concocted the death scene, asserting that in his opinion, Cody, an admitted liar-for-pay, was more believable than Finch. He added further that he had duly informed the jury that they were not legally bound by his opinion, and that a 1934 amendment in the penal code gave him the right to discuss evidence and give such an opinion. The net result of Cooper's subsequent protestations was a citation for contempt and a five hundred dollar fine. Carole remained withdrawn and unmoved, as the jury returned to their chambers.

As was the case in the first trial, the jury had not only to decide whether Carole and Bernie were guilty or not guilty, but to what degree—the judge having provided them with a choice between first- and second-degree murder. A finding of guilt in the second degree for Finch would probably mean that Carole would go free, inasmuch as the absence of premeditation is implicit in the charge; if Bernie killed Barbara spontaneously and impulsively on that grim night, then it could not logically be assumed that Carole had "conspired" with him to do so.

These alternatives greatly complicated the task set before the jury, which, as the judge later indicated, was hardly a Blue

Ribbon group. Some wanted both convicted of first-degree murder and conspiracy. Others wanted Finch convicted but not Carole. Most wanted them both convicted of something, but were not happy with any of the alternatives available to them within the scope and framework of the law. Few really understood it all, nor could they cope with the nuances and ramifications of the complicated charge they had received.

As with the first jury, there had been disaffection among the members of this bunch right from the start. Most jurors wanted the only man among them to serve as foreman, presumably *because* he was a man. There were three, however, who wanted an outspoken lady, whose husband turned out to be a truck driver who habitually ate his supper at the café in which Carole's father served as chef. Indignant about the judge's remarks, this woman had told the bailiff that there wasn't any use in his spreading out exhibits on the jury-room table, that he was wasting his time because she had already made up her mind.

Another juror had responded to the judge's admonishments by exclaiming, "Did you hear that? He's got a lot of nerve!" This woman, seeing a photo of Mrs. Finch after one of Bernie's attacks, commented, "Why, look at that little bitty cut. My old man hit me with a plate one time and gave me a bigger cut than that!"

Another opined that Mrs. Finch got what she deserved; any woman who would hold her husband up for that much money, just so she could spend her time playing tennis, had it coming to her. These were the people who were to decide whether Carole Tregoff and Bernard Finch were to live, die, or spend the rest of their lives in prison.

Incredibly, after seventy hours of haggling, the foreman announced another deadlock; they had decided on Finch's guilt but could not reach an agreement on the degree, and again many had wanted to let Carole off altogether. Thus, after fifty-nine ballots, the ultimate fate of Carole and Bernie was yet unknown and unpredictable.

The judge, by now nearly apoplectic with rage, restated his earlier opinions, implying not only that this was a rotten jury but that some of its members may have had no business being on it. "I know of no way," he said, "to punish a person who deliberately lies to get on a jury." Not only had this jury apparently chosen to ignore the evidence but was evidently unmindful of the cost to the various participants in time, money, distress, and inconvenience. Thus far the two trials, which had lasted a total of 228 days, had cost the state of California over $200,000 and the defendants $400,000 in fees and bail. Nevertheless, Judge Dawson was obliged to order a third trial, conceding that "obviously the case should be retried. We cannot put a price tag on justice." This was on November 7. On November 9, the District Attorney from Pomona ordered an investigation of the jurors.

Hoping to gain some advantage by way of this second failure, the lawyers for the defense sought to gain the right to argue motions seeking freedom for their clients, on the grounds that a third trial would place them in double jeopardy. In spite of the fact that the jury had made the results of their deliberations known, the court had not formally received a verdict, so this effort also failed.

With another cheerless Christmas in the offing, Carole was not as discouraged as she might have been. Admittedly she would be a year older and still in prison, but having been informed as to the disposition of this second jury, she was able to feel for the first time that she might escape the strong arm of justice. She felt that she had already suffered enough, what with the tension, the uncertainty, and the humiliation of intermittent spells in prison, and that people, sensing this, would respond even more compassionately to her plight.

Swept by this mood of general optimism, she decided to accept an offer she had had to play an angel in the prison's annual Christmas play, to which the head matron reacted by exclaiming, "Carole, an angel? Great day in the morning!" The play was called *The First Christmas*, and judging by the interest it generated among the press, one might have thought it was a Broadway opening; prison officials, however, permitted no outsiders in the audience, and remained tight-lipped about Carole's performance.

The New Year, 1961, came into being on one of those cold gray days, which is entirely unsuited to California, and on January 3, the third trial began. This time the jury consisted of ten men and two women, Judge Coleman presiding.

Only one thing occurred to alter the circumstances which had obtained at the other two trials, and that was inspired by Jack Cody. Grant Cooper, having become physically, psychologically, and financially exhausted by this marathon legal process, had turned Dr. Finch's case over to another lawyer, Maxwell Keith. One day Jack Cody approached Keith in court during a recess, wanting to know what it was worth to Dr. Finch for him to change his testimony. Keith was appalled but decided to do or say nothing about it. On the fact of it, such an exposé of Cody could be sensational and might impress the jury. But on close scrutiny, it became apparent that, inasmuch as nobody had demonstrated much faith in Cody's dependability as a witness from the start, it was more likely that they would assume that he was lying now in order to speed up the proceedings and hasten his release from jail. With a man like Cody—a study in perfidy, amorality, avarice, and weakness, despite a corny romantic streak —how is truth to be distinguished from falsehood?

On March 27, just short of two years after it began, the saga ended. Carole and Bernie were both found guilty of conspiracy and murder, Bernie in the first degree and Carole in the second. Although in Carole's case the finding was self-defeating, because of the potential penalty accruing to the conspiracy charge, it did indicate the jury's lingering reluctance to impose the death penalty upon her. According to a new state law, the jury would now be obliged to choose between death and life imprisonment for the two in a separate proceeding, scheduled for April 3. It could be another week before Carole and Bernie would know whether they were to live or to die.

In the course of their deliberations on April 3, the jury asked if they could impose a life sentence *without* parole and were told that they could not. Nevertheless, they chose to be merciful, and on April 5, the erstwhile lovers were sentenced to life imprisonment, with the possibility of parole in seven years, subject to the approval of the state authority.

Even today, there is much controversy about Carole, not only as to the degree of her guilt but about the nature of her personality. Some say she is stupid, others that she is reasonably bright; some saw her as an avaricious, socially ambitious sexpot, others as a perfectly normal female, who, through an understandable weakness of character, fell under the spell of a man she loved and was led by him into an unaccustomed evil. All, however, agree that she was guilty and that at the time she behaved stupidly.

How then was it possible that two juries were unable to convict her? Or could it be that they were simply *unwilling* to convict her? We may assume from what evidence there is that the female jurors tended to identify and sympathize with her, while the male jurors, to some degree sexually influenced, seemed to want to protect her from any serious harm. Most responsible and knowledgeable people, involved and uninvolved directly with the case, expressed the belief that, had Carole been tried alone, she would have gone free.

Carole is serving out her term at Frontera, the California Institute for Women, located about an hour outside of Los Angeles in Corona. She spends most of her time, when not doing her regular job in the prison hospital, reading, knitting, and writing letters to her family, and has been described by her superiors as an ideal prisoner. She has been for many years a leader of her cellblock, a position which entitles her to her own small but extremely cheerful room.

There have been a few bad moments, which have caused her grief and frustration. When she had been at the prison a little over a year, the state authorities quite arbitrarily forbade further correspondence between herself and Bernie, who was in the Tehachapi Institute for Men in another part of the state. Even though their letters were strictly censored, it was some consolation to them both to be able to communicate and share one another's thoughts. Now this was ended, and who could tell when or if they would ever speak to each other again?

She also heard through her parents that Jimmy had remarried and had a baby. She suddenly felt, on hearing this news, the relentless passing of time and the unwelcome advancing of her own age. She had not had a baby; maybe now she would never have one. . . .

During her second or third year in prison, Carole embraced Catholicism, in hopes of finding a way to live gracefully with the frustration, solitude, and dullness of prison life. She is fatter now, rounded out by the starch of prison food, and has lost most of the glamour for which she was known during those dramatic courtroom days, but she has somehow learned to live with it all.

The prison is a good one, offering many opportunities to learn and to be useful, and the promise of parole shines steadily for its inmates from the uncertain future. Carole was eligible to be considered for parole in 1968, but was denied it. Her case will probably be reconsidered in 1970, at which time there should be a better chance for her. In the meantime, she can only hope.

Chapter VIII

Conclusion

For centuries, scholars and laymen alike have allowed themselves to become preoccupied with comparisons between men and women on a wide variety of subjects, crime being no exception. Many of the resulting conclusions turn out to be merely theoretical, and in no area is this more evident than in the analyses of criminal behavior.

That is not to say that there are no statistics, for there are; it is only a question of how to interpret them. Statistics for any particular criminal activity show women to be fewer than men, although they have been gaining, due either to an actual increase in female criminality or to an increase in the female population.

For example, in New York City, in 1965 (Saturday being the day most frequently chosen for murder) only fifteen husbands were killed by their wives, whereas eighteen wives died at the hands of their spouses. Only thirteen common-law husbands

were killed by their "wives," but twenty-four common-law wives
were killed by their "husbands." And, while sixteen females were
killed by male friends, only ten males met a similar fate. However, twenty-four children were killed by their mothers, while
fathers killed only six of their children.

So far as other crimes are concerned, 5,028 men were arrested for robbery in 1965 as compared to 339 women; for feloni-
ous assault the relative figures are 10,601 to 1,860; for burglary
they stand at 8,645 to 268, and for grand larceny 3,633 to 613.
Men and boys stole 5,901 cars, while women stole only 297; and
whereas 1,507 male forgers and counterfeiters were caught, only
329 female forgers fell into the hands of the law. In the possession of dangerous weapons, there was a tremendous difference:
1,290 men arrested as compared with 95 women.

In certain areas of crime, the gathering of statistics becomes extremely difficult. No figures appear, for example, specifically for the rackets or for shoplifting, although estimates are
made mounting into the millions. Shoplifting is included in
larceny, and rackets might include larceny, robbery, fraud, extortion, murder, and so forth. In 1966, the deputy police commissioner of New York wrote: "In regard to shoplifting, it should
be noted that not all these crimes come to the attention of the
police, since a great many of these are handled by the large stores
without resorting to arrest. The actual value of property stolen
in shoplifting is therefore unknown. Our figure, which amounts
to $354,553 in 1965, is based on those cases reported to the
police, and is not broken down according to the sex of the thief."
Rape is another crime, which often goes unreported, because
often the girl feels too humiliated to admit that it happened.

It is true that the majority of shoplifters caught, though
they may never be arrested, are women and that the failure to
prosecute is largely due to the success with which women employ their feminine wiles at the moment of discovery. This is
generally corroborated by department-store managers, who admit
to being infinitely more hostile to the male shoplifter (often a
narcotics addict) than to any female thief. In any case, the male
thief is easy enough to spot among the familiar hordes of milling
pawing women, each one armed with the inevitable shopping
bag or oversized handbag.

The value of property stolen in robberies in 1965 amounted to a staggering $4,657,144, of which $210,924 was gleaned from bank robberies. Interestingly, shoplifting accounted for some $40,000 more than did the more glamorous pursuit of bank robbery.

Unfortunately, these statistics do not reveal the true extent of criminality, either among men or women, because a great deal more crime is committed than is reflected in police reports, which only account for those crimes which have been reported or detected. If we may assume, on the basis of other available information, that women conceal their crimes more easily and somewhat more successfully than men, then we may also assume that there is more undetected crime among women than among men.

Possibly the only environment in which the criminal may be studied closely is in prison, and this is most unsatisfactory for two reasons: First, the prisoner behaves and thinks differently in jail than out of it, and second, prison populations consist generally of the least professional and therefore the least dangerous elements of the criminal population. As in the rest of the world, the criminal world is divided into two kinds of people—the winners and the losers; jails are populated by losers, for if they had been smarter, more powerful, and more in control, they would not be there.

Bruce Jackson, in an excellent article on caste and careerism in crime in the *Atlantic Monthly*, January, 1966, describes this phenomenon from a vantage point of two years' experience interviewing male prisoners and law-enforcement officials throughout the United States. "A state prison," he observes, "is largely populated by people who are not too bright—impulse criminals (whose offending act reflects, not a life pattern, but a set of extreme circumstances—most murderers are in this category); chronic convicts (a large group of men, who stay out for short periods only because they don't know how to get along anywhere but in prison . . .); some habitual offenders (those who can't manage to stay out of trouble, but who still base their value systems on the world outside); and a very small number of professionals, who had a run of bad luck or a moment of carelessness. . . .

"Some have got what they deserve; some are oversentenced; some belong in mental institutions; some shouldn't be in any institution. . . . Prison populations reflect only that part of the criminal world that isn't smart, rich, dishonest, or lucky enough to stay out of jail . . . unfortunately, the whole system is one in which the hydra heads are plucked and not the trunk."

While these remarks were made strictly in reference to male criminals, the same observations could be applied to the population of women's prisons, with some minor variations. In addition, the configuration of any prison group will reflect the ethnic and economic characteristics of that portion of the society which the prison serves. In the large cities the prisoners will be made up primarily of the poor: Negroes and Puerto Ricans in New York, Mexican-Americans on the West Coast, and so on. Those whites who find themselves in jail belong generally to the less affluent classes as well and are frequently subject to many of the same corrupting influences in their habitual environment as those of other ethnic groups.

Returning to Mr. Jackson's exposition, those "impulse criminals" of which he speaks are typified by the large numbers of women who commit assault and murder—generally, as we have seen, upon members of their families or among close friends. The typical inmate of such institutions as the Women's House of Detention in New York stays out only for short periods because she cannot get along on the outside; these are mostly Negro prostitute-addicts, whose view of life, men, and themselves is so distorted that they are considered a pariah anywhere but in prison. Among women, those people who might be considered habitual offenders are usually involved in prostitution or drugs. The others—the chronic shoplifters, forgers, extortionists, and so on—find it easier to escape detection.

What Mr. Jackson says about the "trunk" of the criminal body remaining largely untouched is directly related to what we know about the ways in which the public contributes to criminal activity through cooperation, carelessness, or apathy, and to the advantages of being rich. "While the rich and professional obtain competent and expensive legal aid," remarks Mr. Jackson, "the poor, despite recent Supreme Court decisions regarding procedure and representation [Gideon, Escobedo, Douglas, Pointer, etc.] are at an appalling disadvantage."

Nothing could more clearly illustrate this point than the contrasting situations of Flora Black and Millicent Adams, for while Millie was certainly no professional, she was comparatively rich—at least rich enough to hire two first-class lawyers. Nothing was to be gained by putting Millie in jail, where she would have grown more disoriented and ill than she was to begin with and would not have received the kind of help that finally cured her. As for the public, the chances of anyone being threatened again by Millie are miniscule. Similarly, had Flora been executed or imprisoned for life, no constructive purpose would have been served. Prior to the events in Tennessee, Flora had never committed an illegal act in her life, apart from her half-hearted stab at prostitution-with-friends, and was certainly unlikely to commit another murder.

Although Flora might have been helped very much by such Supreme Court decisions as Escobedo and Miranda, had they obtained back in the forties, the unhappy fact is that these decisions also frequently prove helpful to offenders deserving of prosecution. A case mentioned earlier among the opening remarks of this study, wherein a woman escaped prosecution for the murder of her four-year-old son, is a case in point.

The mother, a Mrs. Powe, had not been formally apprised of her right to remain silent and to obtain the advice of counsel before making any statement. Her subsequent signed confession was ruled invalid as evidence. In referring to the recent decision, the assistant district attorney for Kings County said, "Were it not for this decision, we would have been ready to proceed with this case and let this defendant be punished. Therefore, with great reluctance, I ask that the indictment be dismissed." The judge, irate and unhappy, was forced to quash the indictment, and Mrs. Powe thanked him with all her heart. "Don't thank me," said the judge. "Thank the Supreme Court. Don't thank me at all."

Margaret O'Brien never went to jail because she was a professional, protected by and allied to other professionals, and because the society in which she operated sanctioned her criminal activity. The politicians and police protected her, as did her satisfied customers, the fact that she was technically a criminal being academic and irrelevant then as it is now. Today as then, no one knows exactly how many public officials take graft, but surely many more than make the headlines. Graft and collusion continue to thrive among the many other underreported crimes, such as shoplifting, prostitution, gambling, bookmaking, loan sharking, drug pushing, and abortion, and it is in these areas— the criminal endeavors encouraged and supported by society— that the professional grows fat.

On the basis of what has been established as to the elusiveness of successful professional criminals and the resulting difficulty of studying them, it is obviously impossible to seek out the women in the group. Furthermore, the fact that the vast majority of organized crime appears to be conducted by Sicilian-Americans, operating on a regional basis, would preclude any possibility of finding women among its leadership.

Traditonally, the Sicilians' treatment and view of women most closely resembles the Muslim attitude, under which women become useful possessions rather than contributing partners. Under the Sicilian system the marriage of a young woman is arranged, and on her wedding day her husband and his friends stage a mock abduction of the bride, to emphasize the principle of male domination through force and violence. The woman spends the rest of her life in a totally subordinate role, preparing food and caring for the physical needs of her husband and children, and may not be expected to know anything of her husband's affairs. Consistent with the fundamental cultural pattern, women would rarely participate in an administrative sense in the activities of the underworld—that is, paid assassination, gambling, loan sharking, armed robbery, extortion, or high-level narcotics distribution. In fact, unless they came from outside the Sicilian subculture, they would never be relied upon even as passive collaborators in any undertaking other than prostitution.

The greater participation of women in aggressive forms of criminal activity in the Midwest during the 1930's may be partly due to the fact that they emanated largely from a lower-class Anglo-Saxon background, wherein few such cultural restrictions existed. The Sicilians have long since preëmpted the Irish, the St. Valentine's Day massacre having eliminated the last of the great Irish gangs.

That women play a small part, if any, in organized crime constitutes one of the few elements which sharply divide the worlds of male and female crime. The underworld doubtless has its female decoys, middlemen, and assorted hangers-on, but this is essentially a world in which everyone, from the most exalted boss to the lowest hired gun, is a man.

Not all those who qualify as professionals are members of the Cosa Nostra. The bulk of the American population is moving into an exploding middle class, and hence white-collar crime is on the rise—that is, offenses committed in the course of daily business or professional activity by persons in relatively high positions.

White-collar crimes tend to be repeated time and time again, rendering their perpetrators more criminalistic in a sense than the people of the slums, whose crimes are usually direct physical actions, often provoked by the victim. "Respectable" people make out fraudulent tax reports, misrepresent facts in a business transaction, bribe public officials. Dishonest lawyers obtain illegal acquittals for their clients; doctors perform unnecessary operations for which they charge excessive fees; secretaries, bookkeepers, and corporation executives alike embezzle immense sums of money. The victims of this sort of crime are not individuals, identifiable to the criminal, but a vague anonymous group. Similarly, the criminal cannot be identified by his victims, nor does he feel their resentment, so these practices continue and spread. Operating unsuspected within the secure atmosphere of their social and professional environment, these lawbreakers rarely go to prison, and if they do, they spend little time there.

The amateur is always the first to be arrested, for he almost invariably is closely associated with his victim and is easily traced. A professional like Valda Adams poses serious problems for law-enforcement agents, because she deals habitually with strangers who have no previous connection with her. In addition, her victims are frequently so chagrined when they realize that they have not only been "taken" but have collaborated in their own loss that they fail to report the crime. Mrs. Mayer waited nearly a full year before going to the police; others never go, taking their secret with them to the grave.

What with her money and her lawyers and connections, Valda manages to stay out of jail most of the time, serving short terms here and there between bails. It is unlikely in any case that going to prison would promote a serious change in her habits, formed over a lifetime within an esoteric, antisocial culture. For the public to be protected from her, Valda would have to be put away for the rest of her life, but the crimes she commits do not technically warrant so serious a punishment.

Much the same is true of the class of determined offender to which Annette Le Duc belongs—the kind who "can't manage to stay out of trouble, but who still base their value system on the world outside." It is extremely doubtful that the experience of being in prison has altered the frame of mind of this self-interested revolutionary, nor has it modified her belief in the justice of her cause. On the contrary, a short prison term every so often rather satisfies the craving that this sort of person is apt to have for a taste of martyrdom; a longer sentence in the company of other embittered antisocial women, affording time to brood and feed on her own malcontent, sends her back to society more hardened against it than previously. Again, this type would have to be incarcerated permanently to insure her impotence, and the law will not permit it. One may deal only with the consequences of her actions individually as they arise.

The urge to punish is strong in society as a whole and is based on clear and traceable psychological principles. In a recent article called "The Panacea of Punishment," Dr. Karl Menninger is quoted as having said that the need of the public to see criminals punished derives from an equal need to reinforce the control of its own antisocial impulses. This theory, shared by many psychologists and criminologists, is rooted in the assumption that all people are at certain times troubled by various illicit feelings, and that those generally referred to as criminals merely act out those feelings to a fuller extent, because they lack the restraining psychological agent that ultimately deters most of the rest of us. By punishing those who actually commit the acts which we are only tempted to commit, we purge ourselves of the resultant feelings of guilt.

The continuing debate between those who favor punishment as a way of disciplining lawbreakers and those who see more to be gained from efforts to rehabilitate them represents a battle between two basic philosophies. On the one hand there are those, fearful of the old adage, *"Tout comprendre, c'est tout pardonner,"* who take the traditional view that the courts must return to a "get tough" policy and stop mollycoddling criminals. The threat of punishment, they say, acts as a deterrent, whereas permissive treatment and "understanding" merely make the criminal bolder.

On the other hand, others take the view that the public is ultimately in greater danger from the prisoner who has been subjected to a totally negative prison experience. According to the Department of Correction in New York City, some 92 percent of all prisoners are returned to society, most within a very short time. It would, therefore, seem reasonable that efforts to modify rather than exacerbate the prisoner's hostility while he is incarcerated are more beneficial in the long run to the public as well as to the prisoner himself.

The fact is that the laws which deal with people who rape, murder, kidnap, assault, and steal too often reflect the highly charged emotionalism of the victim and his kin rather than the objective attitudes of those whose specific function it is to seek just solutions to the problems created by such criminals. To be absolutely fair, the law cannot reflect the vindictive bitterness of the mother of a raped and murdered eight-year-old girl, for there is virtually no punishment vicious enough to compensate for such a crime, and in seeking one, we risk a return to the Middle Ages. Regardless of what is done to the perpetrator of such an act, the little girl cannot be returned to her suffering parents alive and well; punishment only feeds their hunger for vengeance and retribution.

The turn-of-the-century discovery that man has a subconscious and is conditioned as much by his environment as by what he inherits from his parents produced the modern polemic regarding Free Will versus Determinism. The punitive attitude toward crime is an indication of a continuing belief in the notion that people are endowed at birth with some sort of God-given inner governing agent that tells them the difference between what is Right and what is Wrong in any given situation. The alternative approach implies an understanding that the concept of right and wrong are arbitrary and variable, and must be learned by a person when still very young.

Valda Adams lived in a society which taught her a system of ethics which is precisely opposite to that of the bourgeois world—that what is right is what serves the purposes of her people, and what is wrong is whatever contradicts those purposes. Ellen Riley was similarly taught her mother's morality before she learned, under rather traumatic circumstances, about that of the dominant portion of society. Ellen could hardly have been accused of having chosen "wrong" behavior over "right"; she never had that choice, for she had not been taught the difference. Deprived of conventional, parental moral instruction, what is right is that which insures survival.

So far as the current trend away from punishment and toward rehabilitation is concerned, women's prisons have generally been in the vanguard of reform. Those who favor the change are mindful of the fact that society's desire for vengeance against those who break its laws is emotionally rather than rationally oriented, and that much of this hostility can be muted by producing results within the prisons indicating that the public will be benefited as much as the prisoner. The belief is that a prisoner whose psychological problems have been treated in prison adjusts more easily to society, and a prisoner who has been taught a trade while in prison will perhaps manage to stay off the public welfare rolls. This is the kind of argument that gets through to the taxpayer and which has been used successfully by many a female superintendent.

As any sophisticated prison official knows, the worst aspect of life in any prison is the mere fact of being incarcerated, isolated from children, friends, normal sexual activity, and familiar haunts. In addition to this, the disciplinary routine in many prisons represents a cure that is decidedly worse than the disease.

When a lawbreaker, whose behavior has been largely conditioned by a corrupt and hostile environment, is incarcerated in a prison whose approach is punitive, there is little reason to expect any improvement whatsoever in the prisoner's attitude.

The so-called revolving-door phenomenon in so many city prisons, which house mostly prostitutes and narcotics addicts, is illustrative of this. Not only do the girls leave prison unchastened and unrepentent, but they are generally back on the street and enjoying their first "fix" since imprisonment within an hour of release; often they are picked up at the prison by their pimp or "connection." For the drug addict, a short prison term merely serves as a means to "get a cheap habit" through an enforced abstinence; that is, when she gets out, her addiction only costs her $10 per day rather than $100. When the cost gets back up to the point where she can no longer afford it, the chances are good that she will be arrested for prostitution or possession and return to jail for another short term.

It is apparent then that, for certain categories of prisoners, serving time in jail is an exercise in absolute futility—an exercise which, apart from anything else, adds another cost to the taxpayer's growing burden. One sometimes gets the feeling, listening to prison superintendents, law enforcers, psychiatrists, and so forth, that the only reason many "criminals" are sent to jail is to satisfy the public that "something is being done" about problems which offend their sensibilities. To leave this pathetic herd alone, to live out their grim and tawdry lives as best they can, would imply approval of their way of life.

Some states, Massachusetts among them, have come to rely increasingly on probation as a means of imposing discipline on criminals, especially young first offenders. In cases where it is obvious that a prison term would do more harm than good, the offender is often placed on probation for an extensive period of time, during which he or she is required to report at various intervals to a probation officer, who offers guidance and keeps a watchful eye on his charge.

Mrs. Jessie D. Hodder, superintendent of the Massachusetts Reformatory for Women in Framingham for more than two decades, was one of the first in her profession to understand the importance of separating prisoners according to categories. She found that they generally fell into the imbecilic, psychopathic, physically ill (that is, epileptic), alcoholic, or normal classes. To permit them to live all together created enormous problems.

In those days drugs had not taken on the importance
they have in recent years among the criminally inclined, and
even today alcoholism is a greater problem among female offenders in the Boston area than drugs. Drink, the "Irish disease,"
has always caused trouble in areas possessing a high concentration of lower-caste Irish, whereas the use of drugs has become
the preferred method of escape among Negroes and Puerto
Ricans of big cities such as New York. New York, moreover, is
a major center for the narcotics trade, and thus readily provides
the temptation of easily obtainable drugs.

Women like Mrs. Hodder and Florence Monahan, a
person equally experienced and sophisticated about the business
of correction, were among the first to endeavor to create a more
salubrious, positive physical atmosphere in the prisons. Mrs.
Monahan always made it quite clear that a sentimental permissive attitude toward punishment only elicited contempt from
the prisoners, who still craved some disciplined form for their
lives. In addition to initiating a practice of hiring doctors and
psychiatrists as permanent additions to prison staffs, many of the
more forward-thinking prison officials tried to encourage a new
approach to prison architecture.

Essentially, prisons are designed either on a high-rise
vertical form, or on a horizontally extended cottage principle.
The Women's Reformatory at Framingham represents a mixture
of old and new concepts. The central portion consists of a large,
five-storied brick building, designed along Victorian lines, while
the newer parts have been created as cottages, with a single
ground floor containing rows of rooms leading into receiving and
recreation areas. Westfield Farms, in Bedford, New York, has
also added many new cottage-style buildings to its forbidding
nineteenth-century complex, and early in 1967, Westchester
County produced a new ultra-modern women's facility in Eastview, New York.

The emphasis in this kind of prison is training rather
than punishment. The women's quarters are referred to as rooms
rather than cells, and the decor emphasizes the distinction. Superintendents of such prisons have found that, given more comfortable and attractive surroundings in which they may take
pride, prisoners become more tractable and more interested in

contributing toward the maintenance of their buildings, an attitude which also affects their personal appearance. In addition, work and learning are emphasized, eliminating idleness from the daily prison routine. At Framingham, the women make state and national flags in large open workrooms; they also learn how to make men's shirts and attractive clothes for babies and small children, which they enjoy. Much of the furniture at Framingham is made in a men's prison nearby, which stresses the same methods.

Ellen Riley served her time in the Massachusetts prison, living in an old building during her first imprisonment and in one of the new ones during the second. Prison officials noticed a distinct change in Ellen's attitude toward the prison when she lived in better quarters, although her positive relationship with the prison psychiatrist did much to contribute to her vastly improved general attitude.

The rate of recidivism is extremely high among all kinds of prisoners, apart from murderers who are generally any prison's best behaved group. (The psychopathic killer released unwisely or too soon from a mental home, may kill again, but the average person convicted of homicide never repeats his crime.) It is not inconceivable that Ellen, despite her earnest wish to change the direction of her life, will fall back upon her old habits. Habits developed and practiced over a long period of time are hard to change, even for the most strong-willed individual which poor Ellen is not. Her chances are good, however, and the prison's efforts will not have been in vain if it can count Ellen among the one in ten whose life it has helped to rebuild.

The success which liberal officials have had in bringing about reforms in women's prisons is, of course, largely due to the prevailing belief that women are naturally less violent and more responsive to sympathetic treatment than men. That they are less able to do serious physical damage is certainly true, but this is related directly to their inferior physical powers; were they genuinely less violent, the common prison practice of confiscating razors, scissors, steam irons, and such would be quite unnecessary. Women prisoners have been known to break every object in their rooms and inflict serious injuries upon other people in the course of a tantrum. It is the a priori assumption of violence and intractability in the male which leads to the oppressive regulations and atmosphere in men's prisons, but the possibility should be considered that it is precisely this atmosphere which contributes toward their hostility.

Carole Tregoff has paid dearly for her weakness and stupidity, for she has been at Frontera, the California Institution for Women in Corona, California, for seven years at this writing. Under California law, life sentences are automatically reviewed after seven years, and on March 6, 1968, the Women's Board of Terms and Parole met at Frontera to decide whether Carole should be paroled. It is unusual for those sentenced to life imprisonment to be granted parole on the first appeal, and Carole did not constitute an exception; she was denied parole, her case to be reconsidered in fourteen months. Prison officials, who described Carole's comportment as exemplary, told the press that she took the ruling calmly and conducted herself with composure and dignity. "She thanked the board," one spokesman said, "and I think she thought it was a fair decision."

Frontera is situated in flat open farmland, where birds twitter on the long rows of telephone wires and gaze down at the plowed fields, grazing cows, and meadows of alfalfa. The air smells of dung and earth, and it seems a strange place for a prison. Built in 1952, Frontera houses up to 985 women, 25 percent of whom are in for selling or possessing narcotics and 25 percent for forgery. The rest are serving terms for various forms of homicide, assault, and crude theft.

Designed as a series of connecting cottages and administrative buildings, Frontera looks more like a girls' boarding school than a prison, and a tour of the interior does little to alter that impression. The rooms are cheerful and neat, bright colors and modern furniture prevailing, and the facilities are extensive. The vast modern kitchen is equipped with the most efficient machinery available, operated by the prisoners, and the food is good. There is an attractive cafeteria for members of the prison staff and a fully equipped hospital wing, complete with maternity ward to accommodate prisoners who arrive pregnant.

This is where Carole worked for a good period of time as a nurse's aid, and while she may never have children of her own, she has certainly helped bring many into the world in this capacity. It was always sad for her to see the babies leave after six weeks or so for the inevitable foster homes, in which they stay till their mothers are freed.

There is also a sort of general store at Frontera, where prisoners may buy cigarettes, candy, cosmetics, and other odds and ends for their comfort and amusement. For those interested in improving themselves while in prison, there are secretarial courses, courses in hairdressing, a well-equipped science laboratory, and various classes offering academic subjects taught at the high-school level.

There is also a nurse's training course made available by the prison, which is very popular. No one is sure whether the popularity of the course is due to its intrinsic merit and appeal or to the fact that it is taught outside the prison in a hospital in the vicinity, affording the girls an opportunity to get a change of scene once a week. Many of the girls who sign up for this course have been drug addicts, and as prison officials are well aware, narcotics are more readily available in hospitals than anywhere else. Some girls like to plan ahead.

Apart from attending the nurse's training course, there are only four other circumstances in which a girl may leave the prison: to testify, to act as defendant, to perform an off-campus job, or to obtain special medical care not available at the prison.

Mrs. I. R. Carter, who is the superintendent at Frontera, is concerned that the cottages have become too large and that at her prison they employ a staff for sixty-five women equivalent in size to that employed at Framingham to look after thirty-five. It is not an easy task to find people who want to work in a prison and have had the required two years of college and one year of paid experience. All superintendents, in fact, agree that their most difficult problem by far is finding good people to staff the prison. Too often people who come academically well-equipped are neurotic in some way and have ulterior motives in wanting to work in a women's prison; just as often, people who have the right attitude are not well-enough trained. To find the right combination of training, compassion, firmness, and psychological health poses a constant challenge.

Mrs. Carter has found, as have many of her colleagues, that second-degree murder and manslaughter are on the rise among women, mostly, it would appear, because men seem to trust them more as accomplices. Some of these women, while not legally insane, are psychopathic and are isolated, as they are in other modern prisons, in special units. Among these are the child beaters and killers, often found to be near-morons who simply cannot cope with the daily tensions and details of ordinary family life.

Carole Tregoff is considered a model prisoner at Frontera —quiet, reasonably bright, and cooperative. She is very wary of publicity, because she knows that the parole board which must decide her future is sensitive to public opinion. She wonders whether, had the money not run out and had she been able to appeal the final decision, she might not be free, but such thoughts are not allowed to occupy much of her time. In addition to her usual work routine, she frequently makes use of the softball fields and tennis courts in order to keep her weight down, never an easy thing to do in prison.

One of Carole's fellow inmates expressed an interest in talking with a recent visitor to the prison and was permitted to do so as they made a short tour of the science lab together. The girl, Alice, was anxious to introduce her guest to a pet frog which lived in a glass container among carefully arranged rocks and herbs. "Nobody feeds him but me," she explained, "and he don't eat nothin' but live flies. See this container here full of flies? Well, that's breakfast, lunch, and dinner for old Froggie here, an' you should see him catch those little buggers! Y' see, his tongue is all stickylike at the end, and he just lays there watchin' the fly with his big eyes, an' when it comes by his face, he flashes his tongue out, an' that's the end of the fly. I could watch 'im fer hours, but of course they won't let me. I work in the kitchen most of the time. . . . You like the food here? I think it stinks. I could make better stuff 'n that with one arm tied behind my back. . . . Yeah, I know it's a good prison if you like prisons— there's plenty to do an' nobody treats you bad—but see, I'm here on a bum rap. This fellah I was goin' with, he was passin' a lot of rubber checks, an' they thought I was doin' it too. It was him got me in it in the first place. God knows where he is now. . . . I mean, who needs bein' put away, locked up in the middle o' nowhere, away from yer friends? Lemme tell you, there are some weirdos in here—I'd give anything just to talk to my girl friend from home for a while. I been here two years already, an' who knows where everybody'll be by the time I get out?"

Had a supervisor not put an end to this monologue, Alice would certainly have talked on for the rest of the day. Mrs. Carter explained that the girl was known for her compulsive chattiness, especially on those occasions when she had the ear of someone from the outside, to whom she could air her grievances.

Alice was very interested in the clothes worn by people who visited the prison, as indeed were all the prisoners. Wearing a uniform every day, the girls missed participating in the fads and fashions enjoyed by women on the outside. There were occasions on which they were allowed to dress up in their own clothes, but they naturally never had the opportunity to buy any new ones. Carole still clung to the pink sweater, knitted by her stepmother to keep her warm in court, though more for sentiment than utility; by now it was worn and moth-eaten, but it was a reminder—a link to the normal world outside the wired fences which enclosed Frontera.

Mrs. Carter explained that the attitude of the public toward her prison reflected the feelings of two distinct groups found everywhere, the one favoring good treatment without "coddling" and the other remaining incensed by the very idea of "making things good for the crooks." The latter group, she suggested, would appear to be composed primarily of members of the lower middle class—people who work hard for their money, live honestly, often with great effort, and resent having exconvicts coming out of prisons and competing with them for jobs.

When the new prison in Westchester was opened, prison authorities scheduled an "open house" at which visiting taxpayers would be able to view the results of several years of effort on the part of various state agencies and social-welfare groups, who had designed and organized the new facility. Those who went, by and large, approved these efforts, but others who merely read about it were dubious as to the wisdom of creating an environment which, in many cases, would represent a more comfortable and attractive way of life than that from which the prisoners came.

Sheriff John E. Hay of Eastview had announced that "our women prisoners are not 'bad girls.' They are human beings and they deserve to be treated as such. We want a bright cheery jail that will bring out the best in the women." And cheery it is, with walls and plumbing fixtures in pastel shades, doors painted red, green, yellow, and purple, music and news broadcasts piped into the rooms at the flick of a knob, jalousied windows boasting a view of nearby fields, silos, and woodlands, and wardrobe hooks, which automatically lower under pressure to prevent suicides. In addition, there are several large recreation rooms equipped with easy chairs, libraries, and TV sets, and areas set aside for weaving, knitting, painting, home economics, and studies in gardening, typing, and telephone techniques.

Prison critics as disparate as Arthur Koestler and Florence Monahan have often suggested that it might help the cause of jurisprudence if, before meting out sentences, judges would visit the prisons to which they condemn the offenders. Certainly the superintendents of the prisons described here would have nothing to fear from such a visit.

Regardless of the efforts made to make them more comfortable and productive, prisoners like Alice still complain about prison life. As with girls in boarding school who would fundamentally rather be somewhere else, there is always more to be found wrong than right about the institution containing them and those who run it, "griping" being the most prevalent pastime.

There are rules and regulations in any institution, a condition which is especially irritating to prison inmates who are more than usually antisocial and hostile to authority. In most prisons, the girls are not permitted to have scissors, nail files, razors to shave their legs and underarms, or steam irons, which they feel they need to press their good clothes. In some prisons even certain types of makeup, such as eyebrow pencils, are not permitted, for all these things may be used as weapons during one of the small skirmishes which break out periodically among high-strung prisoners.

Many of these deprivations are considered nothing less than brutal by the girls, but they often find ways to make up for them, using burnt matches to darken their eyebrows and employing various typically feminine ruses and tricks to achieve their ends.

Lillian Fish of Westfield Farms tells of a certain period during which virtually dozens of her girls were complaining of bad backs and insisting on being furnished with boards to be placed between the springs and mattresses of their beds. Upon investigation, it turned out to be a highly successful method of pressing clothes: The girls had discovered that by placing a pleated skirt between the mattress and the board, the job of ironing was beautifully accomplished overnight, and in the absence of steam irons this system had become quite the rage.

The habitual vaginal examinations administered to female prisoners each time they leave or enter prison, for whatever reason, have also been a source of constant irritation and humiliation. Experience, however, has shown that when it comes to concealment, no part of the body is more ideally suited than that which is most peculiar to the female. Tightly packed, folded, or stuffed into a rubber "finger" (used by bank tellers when counting money), narcotics, cash, and small weapons have frequently found their way into prisons in this manner. Still, it is natural to resent such an unsavory ritual.

Essentially the prisons where girls serve longer sentences are infinitely better than those where they are merely in detention, being held for trial or sentencing, or serving short terms. City prisons are relatively bad, because everyone who is apprehended by the police and cannot afford bail is dumped upon them, regardless of whether or not there is room at the time or whether detention is really necessary. Moreover, court schedules are overly crowded, and in places like the Women's House of Detention in New York, women wait months to be tried and sometimes weeks to be sentenced before they are sent to another prison.

Anna Kross, New York City's former Commissioner of Correction, had been battling since 1963 to get the new institution for women built on Riker's Island, but it will not be finished until 1969 or 1970. In the meantime, the women must remain in the "fortress of despair" in Greenwich Village amidst the roaches and general deterioration.

The larger prisons, on the other hand, which house

women coming from all over the various states to serve longer
terms, are most often situated out in the country where there is
elbow room and space to expand if necessary. The Woman's
Reformatory in Clinton, New Jersey, was built, like Frontera, in
open farmland, on which much of the food eaten in the prison
is grown. Up to four hundred inmates are housed there, 60 percent of whom are Negroes and 25 percent of whom were, in
1966, serving time on narcotics charges, usually combined with
prostitution. Forty were serving life sentences for murder, and
the rest were there for assault, shoplifting, and forgery.

Edna Mahon, superintendent at Clinton and one of the
most respected figures in the business of correction, spoke, as
had Mrs. Fish at Westfield, of the importance of recreation out
of doors. At Clinton the women may take long walks around the
prison grounds and participate in a variety of outdoor games
made available to them. In a crowded cramped city prison there
is barely enough room to walk the corridors, much less get any
fresh air or real exercise.

Miss Mahon also spoke of the manner in which patterns
of crime shift and vary, not only according to the social makeup
of any given area's population, but according to what misdeeds
the lawmakers of a particular state are most concerned about at
any given time. One cannot help but be reminded of the situation in Massachusetts, where "crimes" involving various forms
of sexual promiscuity are still harshly punished, and of Ellen
Riley, whose unorthodox courtship and marriage was so sternly
judged by the community authorities.

It has been often observed that the fewer the laws the
fewer crimes there are and criminals to commit them; it is also
true that the fewer people the courts send to prison, the less
damage the prison can do to prisoners generally. Such organizations as the Vera Foundation in New York seek to minimize the
amount of time an indigent offender must spend in jail while
awaiting trial, either by putting up the money for his bail or by
having the person released on his own recognizance. The question posed by Vera is simply: "How do you compensate a person
for time spent in jail, due to his or her inability to make bail,
when he is subsequently acquitted?" It might be pondered
further why an individual should be exposed to the potentially

corruptive influence of prison life if he is not even ultimately to be adjudged a criminal?

As mentioned earlier, a greater use of probation would tend to minimize these effects; the time may come, in fact, when prisons will be rendered obsolete, except for the psychopathic and criminally insane. The National Swedish Correctional Administration has been experimenting with a concept known as family prison. Under this system, convicts are permitted to live in small frame houses, situated in special compounds provided by the state, and to work at their ordinary jobs, under the careful scrutiny and supervision of the correctional authorities.

The most similar program operating in the United States on a large scale is the work-release plan in effect in nearly half the states. Under this program prisoners hold regular jobs in the community during the day, for which they receive their usual salaries. But they must return to the prisons at night, and they may see their families only during normal visiting hours. The Mississippi State Penitentiary at Parchman permits conjugal visits two Sundays each month, but the practice is opposed by the United States Bureau of Prisons, and thus has little chance of being adopted elsewhere in the U.S.

One of the principal objectives of these liberalizations is to shield the convict from the most common corruptor in any prison—homosexuality. In all men's prisons, some effort is made to separate the known homosexuals from the others, but in women's prisons homosexuality is so prevalent—either because the girls tend to lesbianism before they come in, or because they fall into it so easily upon arrival—that the authorities have generally given up trying to sort them out.

Homosexuality is bound to develop in situations where men and women are forcibly segregated from one another for long periods of time, and there is very little that anybody can do about it. It happens in prisons, and it happens in the army. (It even happens in boarding schools, although far less often since sexuality among this age group is so comparatively little developed and the inhibitions regarding it so strong.) The best any prison can do is to create a general atmosphere of disapproval, discourage it, and minimize the opportunities for practicing it. Most important, however, is to try to prevent anybody from being drawn involuntarily into a homosexual experience and to punish aggressors severely, so as to discourage further efforts. There are extremely good reasons for doing this:

1. Homosexual intercourse, even between consenting adults, is illegal in many states. Correctional-institution staff members are obligated to carry out the law whether or not they think the law is a reasonable one.

2. If these controls are not exercised, it is possible for nonhomosexual offenders who have conflicts about their sexual role to respond to exposure by engaging in homosexual acts. It must be recognized that sexual conflicts are exacerbated by the emotional deprivation that results from confinement.

3. Close controls are necessary to prevent the possibility of physical sexual assault and seduction through bribery.

4. Homosexuality in prison represents a very serious threat to the security of the institution. The sado-masochistic nature of many of these relationships can lead to disregard of rules and regulations, extreme exploitiveness, dependency, assaults, and suicide attempts. It is not rare in prisons to have an inmate lacerate her arms with a broken light bulb or to break windows in a state of extreme agitation. It is often found that the motivating force behind this behavior was a desire to be transferred to psychiatric prison ward where her girl friend was housed.

While many heterosexual women will fall into homosexuality while in prison, this does not necessarily mean that they will be permanently "converted." It is simply a question of substitution, the longing for human warmth and having someone who will serve as a constant companion and intimate confidante. In prison this natural psychological drive cannot find its expression in the normal way, due to the absence of the opposite sex, so it releases itself on a member of the same sex, much as a young summer camper might develop a "crush" on a popular counselor.

In a special study made by three New York City psychiatrists on homosexuals in prison (Harvey Bluestone, M.D.; Edward O'Malley, M.D., Ph.D.; Sydney Connell, A.S.C.W.), the observation is made that in many cases the physical aspect of a homosexual relationship is not as important as the psychological aspect. In other words, situations develop where one of two women is decidedly the "male," not only in her appearance and manner but in the protective dominant position she assumes vis à vis her more submissive and dependent "female" partner.

This psychiatric team also learned in the course of its research that there are marked social differences between the homosexual male prison population and the equivalent group in a women's prison. Among the men there is generally less drug addiction, higher educational levels, and better work histories, whereas almost all the women manifest the triad of homosexuality, drug addiction, and no work history other than prostitution. In the New York Women's House of Detention the percentage of such women, largely Negro, runs as high as 80 to 90 percent; that is to say, 80 or 90 percent had histories of homosexuality before they entered a prison.

The exact reasons for the differences between homosexual male prisoners and their female counterparts are elusive, but may be traced to the essentially different relation which men and women have to the sex act itself: Woman is the "object," Man is the aggressor; women can be forced, men cannot. The fact is that the female homosexual inmate of a city prison is more apt than not to be a true man-hater, and specific case histories reveal some of the reasons behind this attitude.

The above-mentioned study, made among the inmates of New York City prisons, was based on several hundred cases taken mostly from the Women's House of Detention. Each case revealed an extremely pathological family background, which differs qualitatively from the kind of family pathology frequently found in middle-class life. A large number of these girls were illegitimate and never knew their fathers. Many were brought up haphazardly and indifferently by relatives. A large number were in and out of children's institutions during their developmental years and were first tempted to experiment with homosexuality there. Those who were brought up by their parents frequently had mothers who were alcoholic and/or openly sexually promiscuous, and fathers or substitute fathers who were sadistically brutal and who abused them sexually.

For many of these girls, the first heterosexual experience consisted in being raped at an early age—often before puberty—

by a group of boys or by one of these substitute fathers, by whom they frequently bore children. Very few of them report having ever enjoyed the heterosexual act, and most deny having ever engaged voluntarily in sex other than as a prostitute. The normal pubescent sexual fantasies were for the most part homosexual in nature, and many girls continue to derive pleasure only through giving pleasure, even within the homosexual context.

Within these childhood conditions, there are no models of heterosexual life and no opportunity for positive identifying with another female figure. For people in prison, individual family disabilities are accentuated by all the manifestations of cultural deprivation, which characterize the poor in our society. An unsuccessful lifelong search for a good mother—loving, nourishing, protective, and dependable—has dominated the unconscious drives of this type of woman. For many of them, prison offers the only type of society in which they can feel really comfortable and secure, for they have removed themselves from the heterosexual world which they find intolerable, into a one-sex milieu which they may well have been unconsciously seeking. And this is true in spite of the fact that the opportunities for specific homosexual acts are fewer in prison than outside of it.

It is therefore evident that, although living in prisons and in other kinds of monosexual institutions may contribute to the development of homosexuality in an individual, the initial inclination toward it is usually very pronounced among the people who are destined for prison. To accuse prisons of serving as "breeding grounds" for homosexuals is therefore inaccurate, especially in regard to women who, regardless of previous history, move so willingly toward it with a minimum of encouragement from the hardened members of the homosexual group.

In former times, those whose views were liberal in regard to the question of penology were primarily interested in making punishment just and humane—their only concern being with individuals already convicted of a crime. The influence of Determinism, however, has produced a new emphasis—away from punishment—whose principal aim is prevention through curing the social conditions which breed crime. Rather than undertake the rehabilitation of the convict, the new social order would in a sense seek to "rehabilitate" the incipient criminal, thereby obviating the need for his incarceration.

What is the solution? As Arthur Koestler and various others have pointed out in their investigations into the problem, those committing the most serious crimes, such as murder, are those who are least apt as amateurs to repeat their crime, whereas the minor crimes—ranging from petty larceny to illegal parking—are the ones most frequently repeated. Therefore, in order to follow the punishment-as-deterrent thesis to its logical end, the law would have to deal most harshly with those committing the most oft-repeated crimes and allow the others to remain under a beneficent supervision. As of today this is an impracticable theory. Hence one is faced with the inevitable question: How valid is the concept of punishment per se? Does it do any good at all, apart from satisfying the public's outraged and sometimes self-righteous craving for vengeance? On the other hand, if abandoned, what is to stop the emboldened criminal from running amok? Is there, in fact, any way of arresting the development of criminals, male or female?

Among insects the female of certain species is more deadly than the male; among human beings, her poison is of but equal potency, but when she chooses to use it, the victim is often caught unaware, for her sting is well concealed.

Suggested Further Reading

Books

FREEMAN, LUCY. *The Abortionist*. New York: Grove Press, 1963.

GLUECK, SHELDON AND ELEANOR. *500 Delinquent Women*. New York: Knopf, 1934.

HENRY, JOAN. *Women in Prison*. Garden City, N.Y.: Doubleday, 1952.

HORWITZ, JULIUS. *The Inhabitants*. Cleveland: World Publishing Co., 1960.

KOESTLER, ARTHUR. *Reflections on Hanging*. New York: Macmillan, 1957.

LEWIS, ANTHONY. *Gideon's Trumpet*. New York: Random House, 1964.

LOMBROSO, CESARE. *The Female Offender*. New York: Philosophical Library, 1958.

McMANUS, VIRGINIA. *Not For Love*. New York: Putnam & Co., 1960.

MONAHAN, FLORENCE. *Women in Crime*. New York: Ives, Washburn, Inc., 1941.

MURTAGH AND HARRIS. *Cast the First Stone*. New York: Cardinal, 1958.

POLLAK, OTTO. *The Criminality of Women*. Philadelphia: University of Pennsylvania Press, 1950.

ROCHE, PHILLIP, M.D. *The Criminal Mind*. New York: Farrar, Straus & Cudahy, 1957.

SMITH, ANN D. *Girls on Parole.* Boston: Houghton Mifflin, 1956.

SULLIVAN, KATHERINE. *Women in Prison.* London: Stevens & Sons, 1962.

SYMONS, JULIAN. *A Pictorial History of Crime.* New York: Crown, 1966.

WARD AND KASSEBAUM. *Women's Prison.* Chicago: Aldine Publishing Co., 1965.

WEIHOFEN, HENRY. *The Urge to Punish.* New York: Farrar, Straus & Cudahy, 1956.

YOORS, JAN. *The Gypsies.* New York: Simon & Schuster, 1967.

Articles

BLUESTONE, HARVEY, M.D., O'MALLEY, EDWARD, M.D., Ph.D., AND CONNELL, SYDNEY, A.S.C.W. "Homosexuals in Prison," N.Y. City, Department of Correction, 1965.

BOWERS, JOHN. "Big City Thieves," *Harper's,* February, 1967.

JACKSON, BRUCE. "Who Goes to Prison," *Atlantic Monthly,* January, 1966.

SMITH, SYDNEY, Ph.D. "Delinquency and the Panacea of Punishment," *Federal Probation,* September, 1965.

"Symposium on Morality," *American Scholar,* Summer, 1965.

"Women in Trouble," *This Week,* August 1, 1965.